917. 94
K
2016

BTT 6/2016

P9-BYL-422

lonely planet

Yosemite, Sequoia & Kings Canyon

NATIONAL PARKS

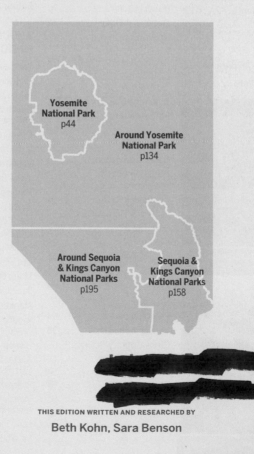

Yosemite
National Park
p44

Around Yosemite
National Park
p134

Around Sequoia
& Kings Canyon
National Parks
p195

Sequoia &
Kings Canyon
National Parks
p158

THIS EDITION WRITTEN AND RESEARCHED BY

Beth Kohn, Sara Benson

Contents

YOSEMITE FALLS P103

KINGS CANYON NATIONAL
PARK P158

JOHN ALVES / GETTY IMAGES ©

SIERRALARA / GETTY IMAGES ©

Contents

MICHAEL LAWENKO DELA PAZ / GETTY IMAGES ©

BRIDALVEIL FALL P104

Welcome to Yosemite, Sequoia & Kings Canyon

With wild rock formations, astonishing waterfalls, unimaginably vast swaths of granite, humbling peaks and a four-season dance card, the Sierra Nevada is no less than perfect.

Backcountry Bonanza

Spanning 400 miles across Central California, the Sierra Nevada encompasses dazzling mountain canyons and some of the highest peaks in the country. Trails lure you to verdant valleys of wildflowers and desolate lightning-prone pinnacles. Bears tear open logs, marmots whistle in warning, and crickets and frogs harmonize to a nightly fever pitch. Something about spending time in the wilderness resets your brain. You step back, assess the situation with fresh eyes and put things into perspective. Maybe it has something to do with the timelessness of the landscape – the ancient glaciers or the glow of the lakes at dusk and dawn.

Peak Season

Punctuated with fairy-tale spires, knobby domes and talus-encrusted mountaintops, admiring all the Sierra Nevada scenery might just put a crick in your neck. A jaunt through Yosemite Valley is a ticker tape parade of granite skyscrapers, with Half Dome taking a deep bow. Tempestuous Mt Whitney lords over the south, and the formations visible from Tuolumne Meadows – the jagged apex of Cathedral Peak, the pale wedge of Lembert Dome and the spiky crest of Unicorn Peak, to name but a few – are certain to fuel your dreams.

Time Warps

This region has a past both wide and deep. Glaciers, although receding, gnaw at granite shoulders as they have for millennia. Prehistoric forests loom and the volcanic forces that moved these mountains to life still rumble underfoot and in simmering hot springs. Trails show the routes taken by indigenous Californians – the Sierra Miwok, the Paiute and the Shoshone – who traded between the western foothills and the Eastern Sierra; grinding stones and ancient petroglyphs have endured. Pioneers discarded mining camps to the elements, creating desolate ghost towns and the remains of forgotten railway lines.

Winter Wonderland

For solitude and serenity, winter rules. Summer may be high season, but you might well question why. The peaks are some of the highest in the US, regularly rising above 11,000ft, occasionally reaching 14,000ft, and blanketed by snow for much of the year. Snow paints the trees and splatters the mountains. There's full-moon snowshoeing and cross-country adventures, plus the chance to camp under a giant sequoia. Go swooshing across the hushed backcountry, barreling down some powdery slopes, or just stay inside and warm your toes by a roaring wood fire.

Why I Love Yosemite, Sequoia & Kings Canyon

By Beth Kohn, Writer

Anytime I have a few spare days, I pull out my road atlas and hiking maps and start scheming up a new Sierra Nevada adventure. Snow camping under the giant sequoias? Hiking a creek canyon blazing with fall aspens? Searching for (and swimming in) *the* bluest lake in the High Sierra? I could spend a lifetime exploring this area and I'd never tire of its hidden waterfalls, starry nights, bear cubs, natural hot springs, coyote cries, ski slopes and 10,000ft mountain passes, and the amazing people I always meet along the way.

For more about our writers, see page 256

Above: Cathedral Peak (p67), Yosemite National Park

Yosemite, Sequoia & Kings Canyon

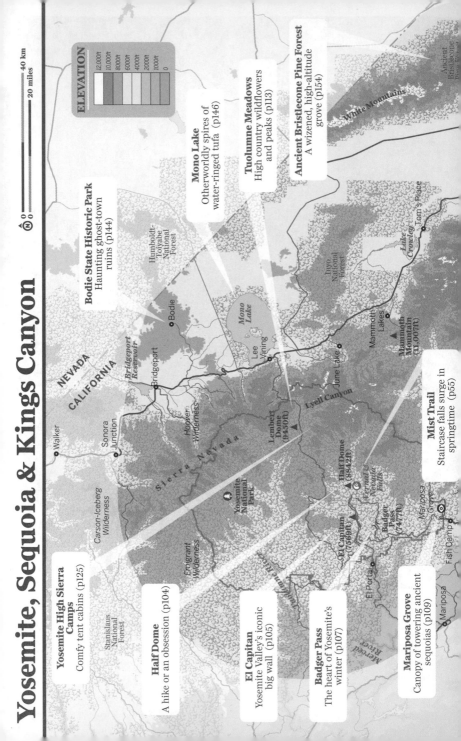

ELEVATION

| 12,000ft |
| 10,000ft |
| 8000ft |
| 6000ft |
| 4000ft |
| 2000ft |
| 1000ft |
| 0 |

20 miles — 40 km

Yosemite High Sierra Camps
Comfy tent cabins (p125)

Half Dome
A hike or an obsession (p104)

El Capitan
Yosemite Valley's iconic big wall (p105)

Badger Pass
The heart of Yosemite's winter (p107)

Mariposa Grove
Canopy of towering ancient sequoias (p109)

Bodie State Historic Park
Haunting ghost-town ruins (p144)

Mono Lake
Otherworldly spires of water-ringed tufa (p146)

Tuolumne Meadows
High country wildflowers and peaks (p113)

Ancient Bristlecone Pine Forest
A wizened, high-altitude grove (p154)

Mist Trail
Staircase falls surge in springtime (p55)

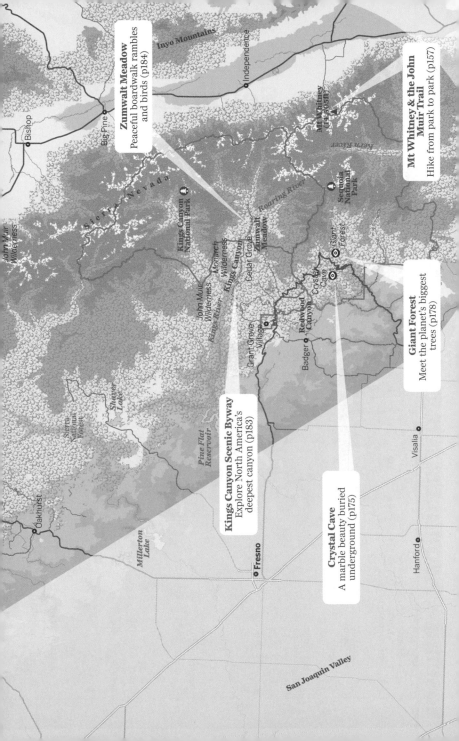

Zumwalt Meadow
Peaceful boardwalk rambles and birds (p184)

Mt Whitney & the John Muir Trail
Hike from park to park (p157)

Kings Canyon Scenic Byway
Explore North America's deepest canyon (p183)

Giant Forest
Meet the planet's biggest trees (p178)

Crystal Cave
A marble beauty buried underground (p175)

Yosemite, Sequoia & Kings Canyon's
Top 16

1

Spring Waterfalls

1 Nothing can strike you speechless like water plunging off a cliff. Standing at the base of a massive waterfall, hearing its roar and reveling in its drenching mist is simultaneously invigorating and humbling. Yosemite holds some of the world's greatest collections of waterfalls and, in springtime, Yosemite Valley is spray central. In addition to the seasonal creeks tumbling over the Valley's walls, the iconic cataracts of Yosemite Falls (pictured; p103) and Bridalveil Fall (p104) will satisfy any falls fanatic.

Giant Forest

2 When it's time to pay your respects to the most massive trees on the planet, there's nowhere better than in Sequoia National Park. Giant sequoias *(Sequoiadendron giganteum)* can live for almost 3000 years, and some of those ancient ones standing in the Giant Forest have been around since the fall of the Roman Empire. The the world's largest living specimen, the General Sherman Tree (p178), is taller than a 27-story building and measures over 100ft around its massive trunk – crane your neck up in awe at its leafy crown.

JFPPIX.COM / GETTY IMAGES ©

DRIENDL GROUP / GETTY IMAGES ©

Climbing Half Dome

3 Just hold on, don't forget to breathe and – whatever you do – don't look down. A pinnacle so popular that hikers need a permit to scale it, Half Dome (p104) lives on as Yosemite Valley's coveted cocked-top jewel and a must-reach-it obsession for millions. It's a day hike longer than an average work day, an elevation gain equivalent to almost 480 flights of stairs, and a final stretch of near-vertical steps that melts even the strongest legs and arms to masses of quivering jelly.

Hiking the Mist Trail

4 This hike (p55) was made for springtime, when the thundering waters of the Merced River form the 'Giant Staircase,' ricocheting 594ft from Nevada Fall and then 317ft down from Vernal Fall (pictured) on the way to meet Yosemite Valley. Pack your lunch, and maybe a rain jacket for the trail's namesake mist. With water gushing all around you, the panoramic views are certain to boggle your brain.

Kings Canyon Scenic Byway

5 Marvel at soaring granite walls and river-carved clefts deeper than the Grand Canyon on this scenic drive (p177), which connects Grant Grove and Cedar Grove in Kings Canyon National Park. Pull into Junction View just before sunset or dawn to truly appreciate this glacier-smoothed canyon, which John Muir called 'a rival to the Yosemite.' Twisting hairpin turns, sheer drop-offs and mile-high cliffs are all part of the thrill as you wind down to the bottom of the canyon alongside the rushing Kings River.

El Capitan

6 A pale fortress rising abruptly from the Yosemite Valley floor, the glow of dusk on El Capitan (p105) is a majestic spectacle. A formation most formidable, summiting the sheer granite and splintering cracks of this monolith is the vertigo-conquering achievement of a lifetime. Now the world standard for big-wall climbs, it was once deemed impossible to ascend. Strain your eyes to find the glowing moth-like bivvies dangling from its face at night, and bite your nails tracking the climbers' progress by day.

DAVID CLAPP / GETTY IMAGES ©

Crystal Cave

7 Step through the creepy Spider Gate to explore the subterranean tunnels and cool passageways of this rare marble cave (p175). Among hundreds of caves that have been discovered in Sequoia and Kings Canyon National Parks, only this one is open to the public. A hotspot for biodiversity, this marble karst cave is full of stalagmites and stalactites that appear frozen in time, as well as even more impressive hanging curtains and flowstone formations. Guided tours are given daily during summer – don't forget to dodge those bats!

Yosemite High Sierra Camps

8 Who said you had to bust your back to trek overnight in the mountains? In the tradition of European hut-to-hut hikes, each of Yosemite's five tent cabin camps (p125) sits in the spectacular high country, spaced one day's walk from each other in a splendid alpine loop. Spend each day bouncing almost weightlessly down the trail, and then end it with a hot meal – prepared by someone else – and the possibility of a hot shower. Warning: this may be addictive. Top right: Merced Lake High Sierra Camp

Mariposa Grove

9 Pace the needle-carpeted trails in a cathedral of ancient trees (p109), where almost 500 hardy specimens rocket to the sky. In the early evening, after the crowds have gone, you can explore in solitude and contemplate the thousands of years they've witnessed. Fire scars blaze the trunks, and you can walk through the heart of the still-living California Tunnel Tree and wonder at the girth of the Grizzly Giant. Snowshoe or ski here after the road closes for winter to see its yearly hibernation, and snow camp beneath a giant. The grove was closed for restoration works and due to reopen in spring 2017.

Zumwalt Meadow

10 There's something magical about Zumwalt Meadow (p184), secreted deep inside Kings Canyon and hedged against soaring granite walls. Here abundant bird life peacefully flits between trees, and you'll have an excellent chance of spotting mule deer or even a black bear and her cubs munching on sweet grasses and berries. Zumwalt Meadow is a living geology lesson, wildlife primer and Zen meditation all wrapped into one. Traipse across the footbridge and out onto the wooden boardwalks for wide-angle views of its lushness.

Tuolumne Meadows & Tioga Road

11 Winter makes you wait to take in Tuolumne's beauty, but it's so worth it. In summer, make a beeline for Yosemite's high country (p113) for carpets of wildflowers and a cornucopia of alpine lakes. Climbers clip in to tackle the park's high peaks, backpackers eagerly lace their boots and mules plod the trails to stock the High Sierra Camps. Explore the granite eye candy at one of the Cathedral Lakes (pictured) or roam Tuolumne's creek-laced main meadow.

PLAN YOUR TRIP YOSEMITE, SEQUOIA & KINGS CANYON'S TOP 16

10

11

Bodie State Historic Park

12 Hopscotch back in time to the era of the lawless Wild West, and imagine the quick-draw bar-room brawls and frenzied gold strikes of this former boom town (p144). One of the West's most authentic and best-preserved ghost towns, it's accessed via a long road that bumps toward a desolate high valley. Now a serene landscape dotted with weather-battered wooden buildings, in its heyday it was renowned for its opium dens and more than five dozen saloons.

Mono Lake

13 Brought back from the brink of extinction by local conservationists battling the might of Los Angeles, this enormous basin (p146) – the second-oldest lake in North America – is truly a sight to ponder. Salty tufa castles rise from subterranean springs, standing watch where mountains meet the desert. Migrating birds feast on clouds of lake flies once relished by local Native American tribes, and bubbly volcanic craters and deep rock fissures buffer this vast blue bowl.

THOMAS RAMSAUER / SHUTTERSTOCK ©

PAIGEFALK / GETTY IMAGES ©

Mt Whitney & the John Muir Trail

14 In for the long haul? Load up that pack and connect the dots from the heart of Yosemite to the pinnacle of Mt Whitney, the highest peak in the contiguous USA. A true adventure, this 200-mile-plus trek (p157) goes step-by-step up and over six Sierra passes topping 11,000ft. Cross chilly rivers and streams between bumper-to-bumper Yosemite Valley, the roadless backcountry of Kings Canyon and Sequoia, and the oxygen-scarce summit of Mt Whitney.

Ancient Bristlecone Pine Forest

15 Respect your elders and pay homage to some of the oldest living things on earth (p154). With some estimated to be about 4000 years old, these gnarled and wind-battered stalwarts have certainly stood the test of time. From Independence, wind your way up the high-altitude road to the White Mountains, stopping midway to admire the distant spiked ridge of the Sierra Nevada and the valley below. At the solar-powered Schulman Grove Visitor Center, get your bearings and catch your breath before admiring these wizened survivors.

Badger Pass

16 Play like a puppy dog at California's oldest ski resort (p96) where fun is paramount and the hills are gentle. It's the center of winter activity in Yosemite, so bring the kids to get them started on skis, or send them tubing down an easy slope. With a convenient shuttle from the Valley, it's also an easy-to-reach terminus for ranger-led snowshoe walks to Dewey Point (pictured) and overnight cross-country trips to Glacier Point Ski Hut. At the end of the day, don't forget to treat everyone to hot chocolate piled high with whipped cream.

Need to Know

For more information, see Survival Guide (p223)

Entrance Fees

Yosemite: $30 per car ($25 November to March), $20 per motorcycle, $15 per person on foot or bicycle.
Sequoia & Kings Canyon: $20 per car or $10 per person; admits to both parks

Money

Yosemite: ATMs in Yosemite Valley and Wawona; credit/debit everywhere.
Sequoia & Kings Canyon: ATMs at Lodgepole, Grant Grove, Cedar Grove and Stony Creek; credit/debit everywhere.

Cell Phones

Yosemite: Reception sketchy; AT&T, Verizon and Sprint have best coverage.
Sequoia & Kings Canyon: Coverage nonexistent; some limited reception at Grant Grove.

Driving/ Transport

Ample parking and year-round frequent free shuttle service in Yosemite Valley. Free summer shuttles in Sequoia and Kings Canyon's Grant Grove.

When to Go

Hetch Hetchy •
GO Apr-Jun

• Tuolumne Meadows
GO Jul-Sep

•
Yosemite Valley
GO Any time

Kings Canyon
National Park
GO May-Sep
•

Desert, Dry Climate
Dry Climate
Hot Summers, Cold Winters

Sequoia
National Park
GO Any time
•

High Season
(Jun–Aug)

➡ Temperatures in Yosemite Valley and lower areas of Sequoia and Kings Canyon soar above 90°F (32°C), but higher altitudes are sublime.

➡ Yosemite waterfalls can dry up entirely.

➡ All park trails and facilities are open.

Shoulder
(Apr–May & Sep–Oct)

➡ Spring is Yosemite's waterfall season, with crowds usually at weekends only. High country and Sierra passes are inaccessible.

➡ Autumn is splendid, with fall foliage. Temperatures drop in late October.

Low Season
(Nov–Mar)

➡ Winter snows close the high-elevation roads. Most facilities shut down in and around the parks and crowds disappear.

Useful Websites

Yosemite National Park
(www.nps.gov/yose) Official
park website.

Yosemite National Park
(www.facebook.com/Yose
miteNPS) The park's official
Facebook page.

**Sequoia & Kings Canyon
National Parks** (www.nps.gov/
seki) Official park website.

High Sierra Topix
(www.highsierratopix.com)
Excellent Sierra Nevada forums.

yosemitenews.info
(www.yosemitenews.info)
Forums with deep Yosemite
knowledge.

Lonely Planet (www.lonely
planet.com/usa/california)
Travel summaries and advice
forum.

Important Numbers

Yosemite National Park	209-372-0200
Sequoia & Kings Canyon National Parks	559-565-3341
Recreation. gov (camping reservations, all parks)	877-444-6777
California road conditions	800-427-7623

Exchange Rates

Australia	A$1	US$0.71
Canada	C$1	US$0.75
Europe	€1	US$1.06
Japan	¥100	US$0.81
New Zealand	NZ$1	US$0.64
UK	£1	US$1.52

**For current exchange rates
see www.xe.com**

Daily Costs

**Budget:
Less than $100**

➡ Park entrance fee: $10–30
➡ Campsite: $15–30
➡ Daily shower in park: $5
➡ Dine at inexpensive restaurant outside park or fast-food option inside park: $10
➡ Buy food to cook from markets in or outside parks: $20

**Midrange:
$100–250**

➡ In-park lodging, midrange hotel or B&B: $80–200
➡ Non-fast-food meal in a park restaurant: $20
➡ Yosemite bicycle or rafting rental: $31–35
➡ Sequoia Crystal Cave tour: $16

**Top end:
More than $250**

➡ Room in a top park hotel: $200–450
➡ Meal in a park hotel restaurant: $40–60
➡ Yosemite rock climbing instruction: $150

Opening Dates

Yosemite

Park open year-round, 24 hours a day. Tioga Rd closes approximately mid-October until summer. Glacier Point Rd beyond Badger Pass is closed November to May. Road to Mariposa Grove is closed November to April.

Sequoia & Kings Canyon

Parks open year-round, 24 hours a day. Scenic Byway closes mid-November through mid-April. Mineral King Rd closes late October through late May. Crystal Cave closes December through April.

Park Policies & Regulations

Wilderness permits Required year-round for overnight backcountry trips.

Campsite reservations Yosemite campsites can be reserved up to five months in advance.

Pets In national parks, pets must be leashed and are restricted to certain areas.

Food storage To protect wildlife, food and scented items must always be stored properly.

Half Dome Permit required to summit.

Fishing Anglers must possess a California fishing license.

Getting There & Around

YARTS buses connect Yosemite to Merced and Fresno year-round and to Mammoth Lakes in summer. Amtrak trains run to Merced and Fresno, which also has an airport.

In Yosemite, free and frequent shuttle buses ply Yosemite Valley year-round, making car travel unnecessary; free seasonal shuttles also travel within the Mariposa Grove and Tuolumne Meadows areas. There are Valley connections to Tuolumne Meadows and Glacier Point.

The summer Sequoia Shuttle connects Visalia to the Giant Forest area of Sequoia National Park. Amtrak service runs to the park gateway of Visalia (via Hanford). Big Trees Transit buses connect Fresno with Kings Canyon's Grant Grove in summer.

Sequoia and Kings Canyon run free shuttle bus routes in summer. There is no park transportation to Cedar Grove, Crystal Cave or Mineral King.

For much more on **getting around**, see p239

What's New

Mariposa Grove

Agreed: sequoias and asphalt aren't an optimal combination. Expect a more natural experience as Yosemite tears out most of the parking lot at this iconic and well-loved grove and institutes a peak season shuttle from a new South Entrance hub. After a two-year closure, look for new accessible paths and the conversion of roads to hiking trails when the grove reopens in spring 2017. (p108)

Park Anniversaries

Wish the National Park System (NPS) many happy returns as it reaches its 100th year in 2016. In 2015 all three parks celebrated auspicious milestones: the 125th anniversary for both Yosemite and Sequoia and 75 years for Kings Canyon.

Reintroduction of Sierra Nevada Bighorn Sheep

Outfitted with GPS and spiffy radio collars, these federally endangered mammals were released in Yosemite and Sequoia in 2015.

'Wild' Effect

Inspired by Cheryl Strayed's bestselling book, the parks have experienced an increase in long-distance backpackers. Donohue Pass exit quotas now limit the number of hikers leaving Yosemite on the John Muir Trail.

Yosemite Concession

Aramark/Yosemite Hospitality has taken the reins from DNC at Yosemite's lodgings, eateries and commercial tours and activities. Still no word on any changes in the works, so time will tell.

In-park Shuttles

Public transportation is improving at the parks, with Sequoia visitors benefiting from a free shuttle service expansion to the Foothills area. Hopefully Yosemite will keep the free Valley–Tuolumne Meadows service and the traffic-calming Badger Pass–Glacier Point route.

Tuolumne River Plan

Look for changes in Yosemite's Tuolumne Meadows area, as the implementation of a new environmental plan will reconfigure parking, trails and some services. The gas station will close, so fill up in Lee Vining.

California Drought

In addition to dismal river levels in Kings Canyon and a shorter waterfall season in Yosemite, the multi-year drought has stressed forests, increasing wildfire danger and susceptibility to threats like the western pine bark beetle.

Public Transportation from Fresno

Go car-free! From Fresno's airport and Amtrak station, YARTS Hwy 41 buses service the Yosemite Valley year-round, and Big Trees Transit runs a summer shuttle to Kings Canyon. (www.yarts.com; www.bigtreestransit.com)

Rush Creek Lodge

Brought to you by the fabulous folks at the Evergreen Lodge, this much-anticipated family resort will open its doors right outside Yosemite's Big Oak Flat Entrance. (p125)

For more recommendations and reviews, see lonelyplanet.com/yosemite

If You Like...

Views

Lift your eyes and adjust your road-weary pupils to stark mountains, ethereal lakes and vertiginous canyon cliffs. You could gaze for a lifetime – it never gets old.

➡ **Glacier Point** A dizzying overlook onto Half Dome, with falls pouring from all sides. (p106)

➡ **Mono Lake** Canoe through this beautiful blue bowl and discover why locals refused to let it die. (p146)

➡ **Alabama Hills** Movie set famous, its blazing orange hills give way to soaring snow-tipped peaks of granite. (p156)

➡ **Buck Rock Fire Lookout** Summit this remote fire lookout atop a rocky mountain perch looking out over the Great Western Divide. (p182)

➡ **Mt Dana** A grueling ascent pays off with an exquisite panorama of the High Sierra and Mono Lake. (p69)

➡ **Kings Canyon Scenic Byway** This jaw-dropping scenic drive plunges into one of North America's deepest canyons. (p177)

➡ **Minaret Vista** Eye-popping views of the Ritter Range, the serrated Minarets and the remote reaches of Yosemite. (p152)

Waterfalls

Mesmerized by springtime flow? Grab your rain jacket and let the never-ending spray work its magic.

➡ **Yosemite Falls** The thundering cascades draw stares from across Yosemite Valley. (p103)

➡ **Waterwheel Falls** Turning like a turbine – traipse the high country to reach these unusual cascades. (p84)

➡ **Mist Falls** Kings Canyon has a trick or two up its sleeve, and this is one of its largest. (p168)

➡ **Bridalveil Fall** After thundering in spring, its wispy summer trickle shows you how it got its name. (p104)

➡ **Vernal & Nevada Falls** Hike here to see the steps of the 'Great Staircase' leap and plunge. (p55)

➡ **Rainbow Falls** Be wowed by the prism that jets off its waters near Devils Postpile. (p152)

➡ **Lundy Canyon** A plethora of cascades surrounded by beavers' dams and shimmying aspen. (p145)

➡ **Tokopah Falls** Sequoia's 1200ft beauty bounces off the canyon cliffs. (p164)

Hiking

Though the sights may look lovely from the car, you need to stop, smell and touch to really experience the landscape.

➡ **Panorama Trail** With falls aplenty, this picturesque trek descends from Glacier Point to Yosemite Valley. (p58)

➡ **Shadow Lake** Day hike to one of the most accessible backcountry lakes in the Ansel Adams Wilderness. (p149)

➡ **Mt Hoffman** Share the sights with marmots at Yosemite's midpoint, a stark high peak that's easy to summit. (p63)

➡ **Zumwalt Meadow** Mosey around the wildflowers between river and canyon, listening for birds and looking for wildlife. (p184)

➡ **Mirror Lake** An easy hike with a renowned reflection of Half Dome. (p53)

➡ **Little Lakes Valley** Azure high-altitude lakes with vistas of enormous peaks. (p152)

➡ **Moro Rock** Climb the steps to this iconic dome with views of peaks above and foothills below. (p179)

Winter Activities

Revel in the hushed pine forests or scream down a powdery mountain chute. The bears may be slumbering, but you don't have to!

➡ **Mammoth Mountain** Steel yourself for a gondola ride to 11,053ft and a season that practically lasts until summer. (p148)

➡ **Badger Pass** Beginners will love the gentle hill at California's oldest ski resort. (p96)

➡ **Winter ski huts** Strap on the skins or snowshoes and set out to rustic stone cabins. (p95)

➡ **Ice-skating** Practise those rusty pirouettes under the gaze of Glacier Point. (p35)

➡ **Snow play** Go tubing and sledding at dedicated areas inside and outside the parks. (p35)

Giant Sequoias

The biggest trees you'll ever see, thankfully preserved, and the original reason why these parks were created. They're living lightning rods and habitats for incredible ecosystems.

➡ **Mariposa Grove** Over 500 giants live on, including a walk-through tunnel tree. (p109)

➡ **Giant Forest** Don't miss a gander at the hefty General Sherman Tree, by volume the largest living tree on earth. (p178)

➡ **General Grant Grove** A sequoia playground of hollow specimens, and the site of the country's first ranger station. (p183)

➡ **Redwood Canyon** In a land full of superlatives, this out-of-the-way grove earns another: the largest sequoia grove in the world. (p183)

Top: A team of climbers on El Capitan (p105)
Bottom: Hiking, Yosemite National Park (p44)

➡ **Tuolumne Grove** Kids can tromp through a hollowed-out tunnel and cross-country skiers make tracks here in winter. (p61)

➡ **Merced Grove** Yosemite's smallest and most tranquil grove harbors two dozen specimens. (p61)

Swimming

Chock-full of deep lakes, careening rivers and veins of gentle streams, there are endless water adventures to choose from. You can swan dive into pools, simmer in boiling liquid or plunge into an icy pond.

➡ **Merced River** Suit up and wander down to Yosemite's best summer splashing or sit on boulders and soak up some sun. (p92)

➡ **Hume Lake** Sandy coves and beaches lure families to this pleasant lake and campground. (p184)

➡ **Eastern Sierra Hot Springs** Find a solitary soaking spot with a mountain view, then strip down to your birthday suit. (p150)

➡ **Muir Rock** Cannonball off John Muir's lecture site and do laps from shore to shore in the lazy summer sunshine. (p185)

➡ **Tenaya Lake** Build sand castles on the beach and coax those toes into the chilly water. (p112)

➡ **Kaweah River** Beat the heat in Sequoia with a dip in the river's Middle and Marble Forks. (p176)

Backpacking

Break out that bag and put some distance between you and everyday life. With a wilderness permit, you're ready to roam.

➡ **Rae Lakes Loop** Get acquainted with the Kings Canyon backcountry on a jaunt between a chain of sparkling lakes. (p169)

➡ **High Sierra Camps** Feel a spring in your step while trekking without the weight of a tent or food. (p125)

➡ **Rancheria Falls** Dodge bear scat along the Hetch Hetchy Reservoir during a spring hike past raging Wapama Falls. (p85)

➡ **Whitney Back Door Route** Sneak up on Mt Whitney from Sequoia and forgo the permit lottery for this popular peak. (p157)

➡ **Ansel Adams Wilderness** Some of the Sierra's most dramatic scenery abuts Yosemite in the Inyo National Forest. (p149)

➡ **Hoover Wilderness** Escape the summer crowds here or use its trails to access Yosemite's northern backcountry. (p143)

History

Take a few steps back in time to see who and what have come before.

➡ **Bodie State Historic Park** Journey down a back road to this beautifully preserved ghost town, among the best in California. (p144)

➡ **Laws Railroad Museum** A slice of life from late-1880s Eastern Sierra, with period buildings and a historical railway station. (p153)

➡ **Ancient Bristlecone Pine Forest** The world's most mature trees, some of these specimens have been standing for over 4000 years. (p154)

➡ **Eastern California Museum** Highlights the work of Paiute and Shoshone basket makers, pioneer alpinists and Manzanar artists. (p155)

➡ **Yosemite Museum** Rotating exhibits complement a recreated Native American village and excellent docent interpreters. (p100)

Extreme Adventures

Not one to seek out creature comforts or follow the pack? Up your adrenaline level with a few local favorites, but feel free to invent your own.

➡ **Ice Climbing** Steady your ice axe and strike a pose in a frozen waterfall along Lee Vining Canyon or the June Lake Loop. (p145)

➡ **Rafting the Merced River Canyon** Bounce over the spring runoff that ends up here as Class III to VI rapids. (p92)

➡ **Hang Gliding** If you're certified, leap off a cliff at Glacier Point and float down to the Valley. (p94)

➡ **El Capitan** Summit the big wall of a lifetime. (p105)

➡ **Badwater 135 Ultramarathon** Push your mortal limits with a little jaunt between Death Valley and Mt Whitney. (p23)

➡ **Mammoth Mountain Bike Park** Scream down the mountain on two wheels as you flirt with the perils of gravity (p148) .

Month by Month

January

Short days and freezing temperatures mostly empty out the parks, and ice-quiet solitude has never looked so stunning. Skiing and other snow sports reign supreme.

✨ Chefs' Holidays

At Ahwahnee Hotel, meet top chefs from around the country as they lead cooking demonstrations and offer behind-the-scenes kitchen tours in January and February.

February

Daytime temperatures gradually begin to inch up as days get longer. The ski and snowboarding season hits its stride and the long Presidents' Day weekend brings out the snowhounds.

👁 Horsetail Fall

For two weeks at the end of the month, this thin, seasonal cascade becomes Yosemite's most-photographed attraction. When the sun sets on clear evenings, the flow lights up like a river of fire.

March

When it's sunny, Yosemite Valley can top out at almost 60°F (15°C), though ice forms in the evenings. Spring feels like it's creeping closer at lower elevations.

✨ Yosemite Spring Fest

Badger Pass Ski Area (www.badgerpass.com) hosts this winter carnival on the last weekend of each ski season, usually in late March or early April. Events include slalom racing, costume contests, obstacle courses, a barbecue and snow-sculpting.

April

Don't forget tire chains – there's still the possibility of snowstorms during winter's last gasp. But by the end of the month, the dogwoods start to bloom and the waterfalls a▓▓▓▓▓▓▓▓▓

🏃 Fishing Season Begins

Anglers froth at the mouth counting the days until the last Saturday of the month. Why? It's the kickoff date of the fishing season, and the trout are just waiting to bite (www.wildlife.ca.gov).

May

On Memorial Day weekend flocks of vacationers flood the area and the spring snowmelt courses through park waterfalls. Chilly nights punctuate the occasional 70°F (21°C) day.

✨ Waterfall Season

The warmer weather means cascades gushing off the hook. Yosemite's most famous attractions demonstrate their vigor, and seasonal flows like Hetch Hetchy's Tueeulala Fall and Silver Strand Falls, plus Sentinel Fall in the Valley come to life.

June

The high country has begun to thaw, and the summer visitor influx begins. It's the best time to explore trails below 8000ft, though you'll want snow gear to hike m▓▓▓ ▓▓▓▓▓.

🏃 Tioga Road Opens

Though it varies year-to-year, by now this crucial trans-Sierra highway is usually plowed and open. The Eastern Sierra suddenly feels a little closer, and hikers feel that itch to strike the trail.

July

Snow has usually receded from the higher elevations, though mosquitoes often wait to greet you there. At exposed lower ground, summer heat may leave you wilting at midday.

🎊 Badwater 135 Ultramarathon

About 30 years ago someone came up with a preposterous idea: why not run a race (www.badwater.com) between the highest and lowest points in the continental US? Over 60 hours, runners attempt a nonstop course from Death Valley to Whitney Portal.

August

Temperatures in Yosemite Valley and the lower areas of Sequoia and Kings Canyon keep rising, making an escape to the higher altitudes a refreshing relief.

🎊 Tuolumne Meadows Poetry Festival

A poetry festival on the grass in Tuolumne Meadows. How can you beat that? Wildflowers and words take center stage during a weekend of workshops and readings.

🎊 Perseid Meteor Shower

The debris from Comet Swift-Tuttle puts on a glittering display as the Perseid meteor shower hits its peak. Away from city lights, stargazers revel in a fiery cavalcade of shooting stars.

September

The summer heat begins to fizzle as the month progresses, giving way to brisk days and frigid evenings. The crowds recede and waterfalls are at a trickle.

🎊 Yosemite Facelift

The biggest volunteer event of the year – in Yosemite or any other national park – sees climbers and other grateful souls descend for a major clean up (www.yosemiteclimbing.org) at the end of the season. The result? Over 100,000 pounds of garbage removed each year.

October

The weather's hit-and-miss, with either Sierra Nevada sunshine or bucketfuls of chilling rain. Mountain businesses wind up their season and diehards take one last hike before the first snowflakes appear.

👁 Autumn Foliage

Fall colors light up the Sierra Nevada and leaf-peeping photographers joyride looking for the best shot. Black oaks blaze dramatically in the undulating foothills, but it's the stands of aspen that steal the show as they flame gold under blue high-elevation sky.

November

Deep snow shuts Tioga Rd and – ta-da! – it's the unofficial start of winter. The Thanksgiving holiday reels in families, and backcountry campers tune up their cross-country skis.

🎊 Vintners' Holidays

Toast the close of the year's harvest with prominent winemakers and fruits of their labor. Wine-lovers descend upon the Ahwahnee Hotel each November and December for this annual wine- and food-tasting extravaganza, with seminars and wine tastings galore.

December

Vacationers inundate the resorts during the week between Christmas and New Year's Day, though otherwise the parks remain frosted and solitary. Think snowshoe hikes and hot chocolate.

🎊 Bracebridge Dinner

Held at the Ahwahnee Hotel, this traditional Christmas pageant (www.bracebridgedinners.com) is part feast and part Renaissance fair. Guests indulge in a multicourse meal while being entertained by more than 100 actors in 17th-century costume.

Itineraries

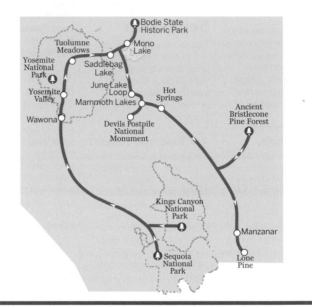

14 DAYS Grand Tour – Sequoia to Alabama Hills

Hikes, hot springs and spectacular geology show off the best of the Eastern Sierra and the national parks.

Kick off the trip with three to four days in the **Sequoia** and **Kings Canyon National Parks**, touring the ancient trees, ethereal caves and show-stopping river canyon. Heading north, camp at **Wawona** and budget a day for the southern reaches of **Yosemite National Park**. Spend *at least* three days exploring the miraculous falls and granite monoliths of **Yosemite Valley**, then hike the trails of Yosemite's high country while camped at **Tuolumne Meadows**.

East of the park, take a full day to explore the surreal countryside around **Saddlebag Lake**, then journey over to **Mono Lake**. Detour north to the ghost-town ruins of **Bodie State Historic Park**, and then south for the mountain vistas buffering the **June Lake Loop**. From **Mammoth Lakes**, hike to the bizarre formation of the **Devils Postpile National Monument** before heading to **hot springs** at sunset. Next, wind up the road to the **Ancient Bristlecone Pine Forest** to breathe the thin air and marvel at the gnarled time-capsule trees. On your final day tour the solemn remains of **Manzanar**, and catch a film-worthy sunset at the Alabama Hills in **Lone Pine**.

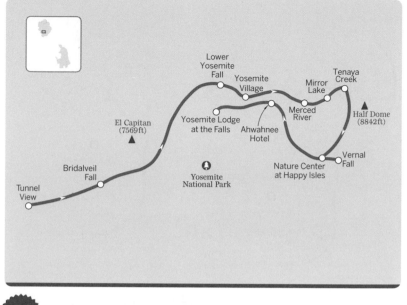

1 DAY Yosemite Valley in a Day

If you really, really only have one day to see Yosemite, this whirlwind tour ticks off all the must-sees.

On your way in, stop at **Tunnel View** to drink in views of the entire Valley, with the iconic Half Dome front and center and Bridalveil Fall plunging in the distance. Drive over to see heavenly **Bridalveil Fall** up close; put on some flip-flops or galoshes and pack rain gear if it's spring, because the spray turns the sidewalk into a flowing creek. Aim your camera at its misty rainbows and yell over the thundering water. Afterward, pull over just east along Southside Dr and try to spot the microscopic-sized climbers working their way up the sheer granite of El Capitan. Keep your eyes peeled for wildlife wandering about the meadows, and then park in one of the Valley's day-use parking lots. Rent a bicycle from Yosemite Lodge or Curry Village and ride to the viewing area at the base of **Lower Yosemite Fall**. Follow the bike path to **Yosemite Village**, and hitch up at Degnan's Deli for a lunch of fresh sandwiches and soup.

Saunter over to the Yosemite Valley Visitor Center, explore the center's exhibits of park geology and wildlife, and peruse the Yosemite Conservancy Bookstore. Saddle up again and ride east on the dedicated bike path, crossing the **Merced River** and eluding four-wheeled traffic. Continue on to **Mirror Lake** and snap a photo of Half Dome's dignified reflection in its shallow waters, and stroll along **Tenaya Creek** to find quiet nooks to sit along its shore. Pedal south to **Nature Center at Happy Isles** to hear what sounds the park animals make, and consider a longer hike up the short but steep trail to **Vernal Fall**. If you don't have time for the 2.4-mile round-trip, you could stop at the footbridge below the fall. Zip over to the historic **Ahwahnee Hotel** for a well-deserved cocktail or coffee, and then return the bike before indulging in the excellent food and views at the Mountain Room Restaurant at **Yosemite Lodge at the Falls**.

⑧ DAYS Yosemite Complete

Pack in all of Yosemite's major sights on a greatest hits tour of waterfalls, sequoias and high-country vistas.

Spend your first day strolling the crowd-free **Yosemite Valley** loop trails. Next day, experience mind-altering views hiking the drenched **Mist Trail** to **Vernal and Nevada Falls**. Be a lazy toad the following day, floating the **Merced River** – the best rafting views you'll ever have. Reserve day four to huff and puff the Four Mile Trail to **Glacier Point**, the park's most famous viewpoint, or take a climbing class with the Yosemite Mountaineering School.

Drive out to Hetch Hetchy for a day trip and hike to **Tueeulala and Wapama Falls**. Next morning gobble down breakfast at the historic **Wawona Hotel**, park at the **South Entrance**, and explore the ancient **Mariposa Grove**. Pack a lunch and hike to thundering **Chilnualna Falls**, near Wawona. The following day marvel at **Olmsted Point** from the Tioga Rd viewpoint, and take in the dazzling views from the sandy shores of **Tenaya Lake**. Wind up your trip with a wander around the Sierra Nevada's biggest alpine meadow while camped at **Tuolumne Meadows**.

② DAYS A Weekend in Yosemite

Feast on a multi-course banquet of Valley attractions, scenic overlooks and giant sequoias.

On Saturday, pack a lunch and head out pronto to conquer the long upward climb of either the **Mist Trail** or the **Yosemite Falls** trail, giving yourself oodles of time and lots of scenic breather stops along the way. Quench your thirst post-hike with a celebratory drink at the festive Mountain Room Bar in **Yosemite Lodge at the Falls**, and in the evening, hear the rangers spin tales around the flames at a convivial Campfire Program.

On your final day, pack up and proceed to **Glacier Point**, stopping en route for a leisurely stroll to vertigo-inducing **Taft Point and the Fissures**. Save lunch for when you get to road's end, in full view of Half Dome and Vernal and Nevada Falls. Continue past Wawona to the **South Entrance**, ditching the car for the shuttle to take a gander at the giant sequoias of **Mariposa Grove**. Return to the historic **Wawona Hotel** for a dinner in its classy dining room. On your way home, catch the remains of the day at the magnificent **Tunnel View** lookout, taking in one last Valley eyeful before leaving.

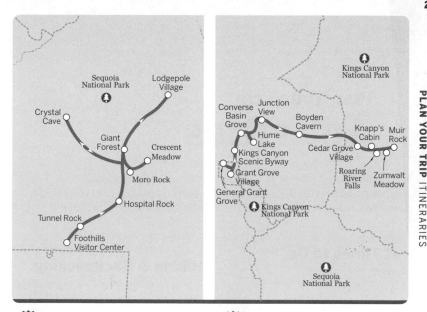

1 DAY Sequoia National Park

Big trees, deep caves and high granite domes are all on the agenda for this day-long tour of Sequoia National Park's biggest highlights.

Start your day at the **Foothills Visitor Center** to get oriented and grab late-afternoon tour tickets for Crystal Cave. Head north on the Generals Hwy, stopping at **Tunnel Rock** – visualize squeezing through in a Tin Lizzie – and to see Native American pictographs and grinding holes at **Hospital Rock**, near riverside swimming holes.

Arriving in **Giant Forest**, let yourself be dwarfed by the majestic General Sherman Tree, the world's largest. Learn more about giant sequoias at the kid-friendly Giant Forest Museum. Snap a photo of your car driving through the Tunnel Log, or hop on the park shuttle for a wildflower walk around **Crescent Meadow** and to climb the puff-and-pant stairway up **Moro Rock** for bird's-eye canyon and peak views.

Picnic by the river at **Lodgepole Village**, then visit the chilly underground wonderland of **Crystal Cave**, where you can marvel at delicate marble formations while easing through eerie passageways.

1 DAY Kings Canyon National Park

From giant sequoia crowns to the depths of the Kings River canyon, this twisting scenic drive is an eye-popping revelation.

Start in **Grant Grove Village** at the northern end of the Generals Hwy. Take a walk in **General Grant Grove**, encompassing the world's third-largest living tree and the gigantic Fallen Monarch. Drive down the **Kings Canyon Scenic Byway** (Hwy 180). It passes through the Giant Sequoia National Monument, where you can bump over a dirt road to **Converse Basin Grove** and hike to the lonely Boole Tree. Cool down with a dip at **Hume Lake**. Back on the scenic byway, which starts descending precipitously, pull over to survey the canyon depths and distant peaks from lofty **Junction View** and take a tour of **Boyden Cavern**.

Cruise past **Cedar Grove Village**. Feel waves of spray from roadside **Roaring River Falls** and admire striking canyon views in verdant **Zumwalt Meadow**, a bird-watching spot with a boardwalk nature trail. At truthfully named Roads End, cool off at the beach by **Muir Rock** before turning around and driving back to catch a canyon sunset from historic **Knapp's Cabin**.

Plan Your Trip
Activities

Every time you get home from a Sierra Nevada vacation, all you can think about for weeks is your next trip. Maybe it's the granite. Or the big, big trees. Whatever it is, hikers, climbers, horseback riders, river runners and skiers all have that same eager look here.

Best Times to Go

Backpacking June to September

Cycling May to October

Hiking May to October

Horseback riding June to August

Mountain biking June to September

Rock climbing April to October

Swimming July to August

White-water rafting April to July

Winter sports December to March

Top Outdoor Experiences

Backpacking John Muir Trail and summiting Mt Whitney

Cycling Yosemite Valley's paved trails

Hiking Half Dome, high above Yosemite Valley

Mountain biking Mammoth Mountain

Rock climbing El Capitan in Yosemite Valley

Swimming, tubing & kayaking Merced River in Yosemite Valley

Skiing Downhill or cross-country from Badger Pass

Snowshoeing In Sequoia's Giant Forest

Stargazing From Yosemite's Glacier Point

White-water rafting Cherry Creek

Hiking & Backpacking

Whether strolling leisurely along the floor of Yosemite Valley or schlepping a 60lb pack over a high pass, hiking is the way most visitors experience the Sierra Nevada. And it's no wonder: over 1600 miles of trails traverse a diverse and spectacular landscape, ranking the region's national parks among the world's most incredible hiking and backpacking destinations.

Some of the parks' most spectacular sights can be visited via short, easy trails, a few of which are wheelchair-accessible. Many of the most famous hikes are day hikes, but they often involve steep ascents and descents. Avoid the crowds and blistering afternoon heat by starting early if you're tackling those trails in summer. Depending on last winter's snowpack, some trails may be closed until late spring or even midsummer, especially in the high country.

Permits are not required for day hikes into the backcountry, with the exception of Yosemite's Half Dome and Mt Whitney. All overnight backcountry trips in the parks require permits. If you're planning on hiking the most popular trails in summer, apply for permits many months in advance.

Maps, Books & Online Resources

Bulletin boards posted with trail maps and safety information are found at major trailheads. For short, well-established hikes, free maps handed out at park entrance stations and visitor centers are usually sufficient. Occasionally a more detailed topographical map may be necessary, depending on the length and difficulty of your hike. These are usually sold at park bookstores, visitor centers and wilderness permit-issuing stations.

US Geological Survey (USGS; www.store. usgs.gov) offers topographic maps as free downloadable PDFs, or you can order print copies online. In-depth hiking and backpacking guides include Wilderness Press' excellent *A Complete Hiker's Guide* series, with titles for Yosemite, Sequoia and Kings Canyon. The Sequoia Natural History Association (www.sequoiahistory.org) sells fold-out trail map brochures with descriptions of several day hikes in each of the most-visited areas of Sequoia and Kings Canyon National Parks.

Group Hikes & Backpacking Trips

All national parks offer free ranger-guided walks and day hikes, most frequently in summer. Ask at visitor centers or check seasonal park newspapers for current programs and schedules. Paid guided hikes and outdoors classes are offered by the following:

➡ **Yosemite Conservancy** (p231) Guided natural history, wildflower and photography hikes, plus overnight backpacking trips, including to Half Dome.

➡ **Sequoia Natural History Association** (☏559-565-3759; www.sequoiahistory.org) Private naturalist-guided hikes.

➡ **Sierra Club** (☏415-977-5522; www. sierraclub.org) Day hikes, backpacking trips and volunteer vacations in the Sierra Nevada.

➡ **Road Scholar** (☏800-454-5768; www. roadscholar.org) Outdoors-oriented 'learning adventures' and hiking trips for those aged 50 and over.

➡ **Yosemite National Park Concessionaire** (www.yosemitepark.com) Private and group guided hikes and overnight backpacking trips, including trips for beginners.

➡ **Southern Yosemite Mountain Guides** (☏559-642-2817; www.symg.com) Long-established outfitter offering expensive guided hiking, backpacking and packhorse-supported trips.

Long-Distance Trails

Several long-distance trails pass through Yosemite, Sequoia and Kings Canyon National Parks, most famously the 211-mile John Muir Trail, which starts in Yosemite Valley and follows the Sierra Crest all the way to Mt Whitney (14,505ft). The daunting 2650-mile Pacific Crest National Scenic Trail extends from Canada to Mexico, passing through the High Sierra. The province of experts, these trails can be a lifetime achievement for those who manage to thru-hike the entire distance, but many people choose to hike them in smaller, more manageable sections. For more information on both trails, consult the Pacific Crest Trail Association (www.pcta.org); for trail conditions, call ☏888-728-7245.

HOW HARD IS THAT TRAIL?

We've rated Sierra Nevada hikes by three levels of difficulty to help you choose the trail that's right for you.

➡ **Easy** Manageable for nearly all walkers, an easy hike is under 4 miles, with fairly even terrain and no significant elevation gain or loss.

➡ **Moderate** Fine for fit hikers and active, older children, moderate hikes have a modest elevation gain in the range of 500ft to 1000ft and are usually less than 7 miles long.

➡ **Difficult** Hikes have elevation gains of over 1000ft, are mostly steep, may have tricky footing and are often over 8 miles long. Being physically fit is paramount.

All hikes, from day hikes to backcountry treks, follow marked, established trails and unless otherwise noted, the distance listed in each hike description is for a *round-trip* journey. The actual time spent hiking will vary with your ability. When in doubt, assume trails will be harder and take longer than you think.

Cycling & Mountain Biking

Bicycles are an excellent way to explore Yosemite Valley, where rentals are available. Twelve miles of mostly flat, paved trails pass nearly all of the Valley's most famous sights. Wear a helmet and ride defensively – the path isn't always clearly marked, and many visitors pay more attention to gawking than steering.

For serious road cyclists, Yosemite's Glacier Point Rd ascends more than 1200ft over 16 miles. Tioga Rd/Hwy 120 is a more grueling route, climbing almost 6000ft from Yosemite Valley to lung-busting Tioga Pass, then dropping dramatically – make that *frighteningly* – down Lee Vining Canyon to finish at Hwy 395 near Mono Lake, a 45-mile total trip.

From Lee Vining, you can ride south on Hwy 395 and pick up Hwy 120 east again to knock out a spectacular Eastern Sierra loop by taking Benton Crossing Rd back west to Hwy 395. This is the route of the annual, open-registration **Mammoth Grand Fondo** (www.fallcentury.org). The 16-mile June Lake Loop offers outstanding cycling, too, as does the road to Twin Lakes.

Sequoia and Kings Canyon don't have many places for cycling, although some paved roads in Sequoia's Giant Forest and from Cedar Grove to Roads End in Kings Canyon make for easy, mostly level rides –

just watch for traffic. Hard-core cyclists could ride the Kings Canyon Scenic Byway/Hwy 180, which drops almost 2000ft in 35 miles as it nerve-wrackingly winds its way down to the Kings River. Of course, you have to turn around and climb back up in order to get out – whew!

Note that all trails within the national parks are off-limits to mountain bikes. You'll need to head to Mammoth Mountain for that, with over 80 miles of single track, from downhill runs to free rides, plus shuttles, gondolas and chairlifts.

Rock Climbing & Bouldering

With 3000ft granite monoliths, sheer spires, near-vertical walls and a temperate climate, Yosemite is no less than the world's holy grail of rock. Camp 4, Yosemite Valley's cheap, no-reservations walk-in campground, has for decades been the hangout for some of climbing's legendary stars. Yosemite's granite, mostly deemed impossible to climb until the 1940s, necessitated entirely new techniques, equipment and climbing styles. In 1947, using hand-forged steel pitons, Swiss climber John Salathé and Anton 'Ax' Nelson became the first to climb the Lost Arrow Chimney, regarded as the most difficult climb of its day. Next came a team of illustrious climbers who changed the sport forever, including Yvon Chouinard, founder of the company Patagonia, and Royal Robbins, a pioneer of clean-climbing techniques.

Attacking the world's greatest single slab of granite in stages between July 1957 and November 1958, big-wall pioneer Warren Harding took 45 days to climb El Capitan's now world-famous Nose route. In 1994 Lynn Hill free-climbed the route in less than 24 hours. In 2010 Dean Potter and Sean Leary speed-climbed the Nose in just over 2½ hours. Needless to say, climbing has come a long way.

Today the climbing spirit soars as high as ever. During spring and fall, climbers flock to Yosemite Valley, and boulder-strewn Camp 4 remains ground zero. Need a climbing partner? Check the Camp 4 bulletin board. Looking for used climbing equipment? Camp 4. Want route information from fellow climbers? You guessed it.

LEAVES OF THREE, LET IT BE!

Watch out for western poison oak on the western slopes of the Sierra Nevada below 5000ft elevation. This poisonous shrub is most easily identified by its shiny, reddish-green tripartite leaves, which turn crimson in the fall, and its clusters of green or white berries. In winter, when the plant has no leaves, it looks brown and twiggy, but can still cause a serious allergic reaction if it touches your skin. If you accidentally brush against poison oak, scrub the area immediately with soap and water or an over-the-counter remedy such as Tecnu, a soap specially formulated to remove the plant's itchy urushiol oils.

LEAVE NO TRACE

Before you hit the trail, learn how to minimize your impact on the environment by talking with park rangers and visiting the Leave No Trace Center for Outdoor Ethics website (www.lnt.org).

Food

➡ Store food in a bear-resistant canister.

➡ Never feed wildlife and avoid leaving any food scraps behind. Wild animals can become dependent on handouts, causing disease, starvation and aggressive behavior toward people.

Hiking & Camping

➡ Stay on the trail – making and taking shortcuts contributes to erosion.

➡ Camp at least 100ft from water and, if possible, the trail.

➡ Always yield to stock animals.

➡ Camp in existing sites or on durable surfaces. Keep campsites small.

Fires

➡ Don't start any campfires over 9600ft or above the tree line; additional restrictions may apply during the summer wildfire season.

➡ Below the tree line, collect only dead and downed wood. Use only sticks that can be broken by hand, not logs.

➡ If you make a campfire, keep it small and utilize existing fire rings only – don't build new ones.

Waste

➡ Discard all gray-water at least 100ft from all water sources. Don't put any soap in the water (even biodegradable soap pollutes).

➡ Carry out all trash, including toilet paper. Toilet paper burns poorly, and animals will dig up anything scented.

➡ Relieve yourself at least 200ft from any water source. For solid waste, dig a hole 6in deep (in snow, dig down to the soil).

Come summer, many climbers relocate to gentler, high-elevation Tioga Rd, especially around Tuolumne Meadows, where temperatures are cooler than in the Valley and where there's an abundance of glacially polished granite domes.

With so much glacial debris scattered about, Yosemite is also outstanding for bouldering, the sport of climbing without a rope at short distances above the ground. The only equipment necessary are shoes, a chalk bag and a bouldering mat, so it's a great way to enter the sport of climbing. Yosemite Valley and along Tioga Rd, including at Tuolumne Meadows, are the park's most popular bouldering spots.

Yosemite doesn't have a monopoly on rock climbing: Sequoia and Kings Canyon National Parks have some outstanding climbing with a fraction of the crowds, although some spots require a long backcountry hike to access. In the Eastern Sierra, Mammoth Lakes and the Owens River Valley and Buttermilks Country near Bishop are top climbing areas. There's also plenty of high-altitude climbing between Saddlebag Lake and Yosemite's Tioga Pass Entrance. In winter, Lee Vining Canyon is popular with ice climbers.

➡ **Yosemite Mountaineering School & Guide Service** (www.yosemitemountaineering.com) If you're new to climbing, or want to build on your techniques and knowledge, come to the Curry Village Mountain Shop between April and November. Ask about big-wall weekend climbing seminars and 'Girls on Granite' boot camps.

➡ **Sierra Rock Climbing School** (www.sierrarockclimbingschool.com) Check with this Mammoth Lakes–based outfitter for climbing courses and guides in the Eastern Sierra.

Rafting (p92), Yosemite Valley

Horseback Riding

There's ample opportunity to saddle up within the parks. But don't imagine yourself galloping across a meadow with the wind at your back – stock animals must stick to trails. Keep in mind that unless you're bringing your own horses, any 'horseback rides' offered within the parks are usually on tough, surefooted mules.

From late spring through early fall, the Yosemite Valley and Wawona Stables offer two-hour and half-day trail rides in Yosemite. In Kings Canyon, Grant Grove Stables and the Cedar Grove Pack Station offer short trail rides lasting one or two hours, as does the Horse Corral Pack Station in the Sequoia National Forest. If you want to get out into the wilderness, both the Cedar Grove Pack and Horse Corral Pack Station can arrange multiday backcountry trips, including for fishing.

The Eastern Sierra is ideal for horseback adventuring, with its mountain vistas, lakes and valleys. Several outfitters run trips out of Mammoth Lakes and Bishop, putting riders within easy reach of the gorgeous Ansel Adams Wilderness and John

Muir Wilderness. Pack trips also depart from Virginia Lakes, south of Bridgeport, and from June Lake, south of Lee Vining; at the latter, shorter trail rides last from one hour to all day.

Swimming

Few sensations top the joy of jumping into a river or swimming in a mountain lake. However, you'd better be able to tolerate cold water here: rivers swollen with spring snowmelt don't become safe enough for swimming until midsummer, and alpine lakes stay chilly year-round.

In rivers, always swim near other swimmers unless you're absolutely certain about the nature of the current. People drown every year in Sierra Nevada rivers. Watch out for slippery boulders, and never swim around, above or below a waterfall, as you could drown if the current carries you over the top or if you're hit by rockfall.

Public swimming pools with lifeguards are open in summer at Curry Village and Yosemite Lodge. The following are some good spots to swim:

➡ **Merced River** Yosemite's warmest waters are found along sandy beaches in the Valley; more swimming holes are hidden around Wawona, too.

➡ **Tenaya Lake** This high-elevation lake is bordered by a half-moon sandy beach.

➡ **Eastern Sierra** Take your pick between Lundy Lake or June Lake, or visit local hot springs.

➡ **Kaweah River** Families picnic by the rocks and swim in the Foothills and Lodgepole areas of Sequoia National Park.

➡ **Kings River** Near Cedar Grove in Kings Canyon, Muir Rock and the Red Bridge are popular swimming holes.

➡ **Hume Lake** Off the Kings Canyon Scenic Byway, find family-friendly swimming beaches and water-sports equipment rental.

Rafting

During the summer months, floating the Merced River in Yosemite Valley is a fun way to beat the heat (inflatable raft rentals available at Curry Village). All the whitewater action happens in late spring, when snowmelt runoff creates lots of rapids along the Merced River.

The Yosemite region's white-water rafting season usually kicks off in April. Typically, the Tuolumne River runs into early September, while the Merced wraps up by mid-July, and both are well suited for beginner to intermediate rafters. For experts, there's renowned Cherry Creek, a 9-mile stretch of the upper Tuolumne, offering nearly nonstop Class IV to V+ rapids marked by narrow shoots, huge boulders, sheer drops, ledges and vertical holes.

In the Sierra National Forest, Kings River offers a scenic 10-mile stretch of exciting, mostly Class III rapids that are good for beginners. With its headwaters in Sequoia National Park, the Kaweah River kicks out challenging Class III to V rapids west of the park. Depending on snowmelt, these rivers' rafting season runs from mid-April until mid-July, though in recent years drought has meant shorter seasons.

BUT WAIT, THERE'S MORE!

ACTIVITY	LOCATION	DESCRIPTION
Canoeing & Kayaking	Yosemite Valley	Bring your own kayak or canoe to paddle the Merced River during early summer.
	Tenaya Lake	Bring your own motorless watercraft to this alpine lake in Yosemite's high country.
	Tioga & Saddlebag Lakes	Easy DIY put-ins at an alpine lake off Tioga Rd, east of Yosemite.
	Mono Lake	Paddle past bizarre-looking tufa formations; rentals and guided tours available in summer and early fall.
	June Lake	Lakeshore marinas rent canoes and kayaks in the Eastern Sierra.
	Mammoth Lakes	Eastern Sierra's best paddling is at Crowley Lake, Convict Lake and Lakes Basin; marinas rent canoes and kayaks.
	Hume Lake	Rent a canoe or kayak and paddle across this forested lake off the Kings Canyon Scenic Byway.
Caving	Crystal Cave	Explore Sequoia's most famous marble cave, carved by an underground river; tours run from late spring through fall.
	Boyden Cavern	Go for a wet-and-wild guided walk deep in Kings Canyon; tours run from late spring through early fall.
Fishing*	Yosemite Valley	Catch trout on the Merced River between Happy Isles and Foresta Bridge.
	Tuolumne Meadows	Trout swim the Lyell and Dana Forks of the Tuolumne River.
	Wawona	Some of Yosemite's best stream fishing for trout.
	Hetch Hetchy	Trout fishing in the reservoir and along the Tuolumne River.
	Eastern Sierra	Trout fishing in lakes, rivers and streams, especially Saddlebag Lake, June Lake and Mammoth Lakes.
	Kings Canyon	Cast for trout at Hume Lake and along the Kings River.
Golf	Wawona	Yosemite's historic nine-hole 'organic' golf course, open spring through fall.
Hang Gliding	Yosemite	Advanced pilots with their own equipment can soar from Glacier Point to Yosemite Valley.
Stargazing	Glacier Point	Join amateur astronomers and park rangers high above Yosemite Valley on summer weekends.
Tennis	Wawona	Tree-shaded outdoor court in southern Yosemite, open late spring through fall.

* California fishing license required for anyone over 16 years; state fishing laws apply (see www.wildlife.ca.gov/fishing). Ask for local fishing regulations at visitor centers and ranger stations.

A backcountry skier in Yosemite National Park (p95)

Guided River Trips

Several outfitters offer one-day, overnight and multiday white-water rafting trips in the Sierra Nevada, with prices that vary by season and day of the week. All rafters should be strong swimmers and generally at least 12 years old.

➡ **All-Outdoors California Whitewater Rafting** (☑800-247-2387, 925-932-8993; www.aorafting.com) Veteran California outfitter runs Cherry Creek; also does the Merced, Tuolumne and Kaweah Rivers.

➡ **OARS** (☑209-736-4677, 800-346-6277; www.oars.com) ✐ Worldwide rafting operator with a solid reputation and admirable environmental ethics. Offers trips on the Tuolumne and Merced Rivers.

➡ **ARTA River Trips** (☑800-323-2782, 209-962-7873; www.arta.org) Nonprofit outfitter runs one-day and multiday Tuolumne River trips, as well as day trips on the Merced River.

➡ **Sierra Mac** (☑800-457-2580, 209-591-8027; www.sierramac.com) One of two outfitters running Cherry Creek; offers other Tuolumne and Merced River trips.

➡ **Whitewater Voyages** (☑800-400-7238, 760-376-1500; www.whitewatervoyages.com) Runs trips on the Tuolumne, Merced, Kaweah, Kings and Kern Rivers.

➡ **Zephyr Rafting** (☑800-431-3636, 209-532-6249; www.zrafting.com) Large, reputable outfitter offering trips on the Merced, Tuolumne and Kings Rivers.

➡ **Kings River Expeditions** (☑800-846-3674, 559-233-4881; www.kingsriver.com) Small local operator for one- and two-day Kings River trips.

Winter Activities

Downhill Skiing & Snowboarding

When it comes to downhill skiing and snowboarding, Mammoth Mountain in the Eastern Sierra reigns supreme. A top-rate mountain with excellent terrain for all levels of ability, Mammoth is known for its sunny skies, vertical chutes, airy snow and laid-back atmosphere. For a more local vibe, hit June Mountain nearby. Not for adrenaline junkies, Yosemite's Badger Pass is a historical spot: it's California's oldest ski resort. Gentle slopes, terrain parks, and an excellent ski school and rental gear for the whole family make it an incredible spot for beginners. In the Sequoia National Forest between Kings Canyon and Sequoia National Parks, novices can try out snowboarding at Montecito Sequoia Lodge

Cross-Country Skiing

Outstanding cross-country skiing is found throughout the Sierra Nevada. Yosemite is an invigorating place for skiers of all skill levels, with options ranging from short scenic loops to challenging backcountry trails. Cross-country skiers can take their pick of almost 350 miles of well-marked trails and roads, with over 25 miles of groomed trails accessed from Badger Pass. Other popular park ski trails are found at Crane Flat and Mariposa Grove (closed through spring 2017). With advance reservations, experienced skiers can overnight at the no-frills backcountry ski huts at Glacier Point, Ostrander Lake or Tuolumne Meadows.

In Sequoia and Kings Canyon, some 50 miles of marked but ungroomed trails crisscross the Giant Forest and Grant Grove areas, with rental skis available at Wuksachi Lodge and Grant Grove Village. Backcountry skiers can try the challenging Lakes Trail from Lodgepole to the Pear Lake Ski Hut (advance reservations required). In the Sequoia National Forest, ski rentals and groomed trails await at Montecito Sequoia Lodge.

In the Eastern Sierra, Mammoth Lakes has some top-rated cross-country skiing, with over 300 miles of ungroomed trails in town and in the Inyo National Forest. The Ansel Adams Wilderness, John Muir Wilderness and Saddlebag Lake area east of Yosemite's Tioga Pass offer endless exploring opportunities for experienced backcountry skiers.

➡ **Badger Pass Cross-Country Center & Ski School** (☏209-372-8444) Located in the Badger Pass Ski Area, this school offers beginner-lesson-plus-rental packages, group and private lessons, ski equipment rentals and guided tours. It also runs overnight trips to Glacier Point Ski Hut, a rustic stone-and-log cabin.

➡ **Montecito Sequoia Lodge** (p178) Old-fashioned family-oriented resort offers lessons, rents cross-country and skate skis, and maintains over 30 miles of groomed trails for all skill levels in the Sequoia National Forest.

➡ **Tamarack Cross-Country Ski Center** (p148) Hop on Mammoth Lakes' town shuttle to the Tamarack Lodge, where rentals and lessons are available. Almost 20 miles of groomed track run around Twin Lakes and the Lakes Basin.

Snowshoeing

One of the easiest ways to explore the winter wilderness is to strap on a pair of snowshoes and head out on any of the hiking or cross-country skiing trails. Just be sure not to tramp directly in ski tracks, which destroys them for any cross-country skiers who come after you.

You can rent snowshoes at Yosemite's Badger Pass and explore on your own or join a fun guided trip, ranging from two-hour moonlight walks to an all-day trek out to Dewey Point and back. If you bring your own snowshoes, Yosemite Valley, Mariposa Grove (closed through spring 2017) and Crane Flat are all scenic spots. Near Hetch Hetchy, Evergreen Lodge rents snowshoes and offers guided snowshoe hikes inside the park.

In Sequoia National Park, ranger-led snowshoe walks depart from Wuksachi Lodge, so reserve a spot by calling ahead or signing up in person in advance. Rental snowshoes are available at Sequoia's Wuksachi Lodge and Kings Canyon's Grant Grove Village. For a backcountry adventure, score overnight reservations for Pear Lake Ski Hut, accessible on snowshoes and cross-country skis.

Most cross-country ski centers rent snowshoes, as does Mammoth Mountain in the Eastern Sierra.

Skating, Sledding, Tubing & Snow Play

One of the most memorable winter activities for families in Yosemite is skating on Curry Village's outdoor rink (rentals available). Or rent a snow tube and send yourself spinning downhill at Yosemite's Badger Pass. At Montecito Sequoia Lodge in the Sequoia National Forest and at Mammoth Mountain in the Eastern Sierra, you can rent a snow tube or a sled and go rocketing downhill. Sledding and tubing are also popular at designated snow-play areas throughout all three parks and in nearby national forests, but you'll have to bring your own snow-play gear. Just south of Yosemite, Tenaya Lodge has a small outdoor ice-skating rink (rentals available) and horse-drawn sleigh rides.

Plan Your Trip
Travel with Children

Kids love the parks, and bringing them along is a no-brainer. Spend days swimming, biking and hiking. How about spying on the wildlife, marveling at waterfalls, peering over tall cliffs and exploring crazy-cool caves? For many kids, just sleeping in a tent for the first time is the biggest adventure.

Best Regions for Kids

Yosemite National Park
Drop by the Happy Isles Nature Center, be awestruck by Yosemite Valley's waterfalls, drink in views of Half Dome from Glacier Point and picnic by wildflower-strewn Tuolumne Meadows. When your kids get tired of traipsing around the valley, simply hop on the bus and head back to your car, campsite or lodge.

Around Yosemite
Ride a historic narrow-gauge railroad through pine forests, explore an Old West mining ghost town and ski the powder slopes of Mammoth Mountain or June Lake.

Sequoia & Kings Canyon National Parks
In Sequoia, learn all about giant sequoias in the Giant Forest, then scramble up Moro Rock and explore the creepy-crawly underground at Crystal Cave. In Kings Canyon, duck inside the Fallen Monarch tree in Grant Grove, cool off at Hume Lake, tour Boyden Cavern and spot wildlife in Zumwalt Meadow.

National Parks for Kids

The Sierra Nevada region is a fantastic destination for a family trip, whether you're traveling with a toddler or teenagers. All three national parks organize lots of children's activities and programs. To find kid-oriented events going on now, check the free seasonal park newspapers or consult the daily or weekly program calendars posted at visitor centers and some park lodgings and campgrounds.

Children's Highlights
Classes

➡ **Yosemite Conservancy** Park partner offers outdoor classes and indoor programs that teach kids about ecology, history and more. (p231)

➡ **Yosemite Art Center** Low-cost art classes are taught in Yosemite Valley (sign up at least one day in advance); children under 12 must be accompanied by an adult. (p101)

➡ **Ansel Adams Gallery** Photography walks for budding shutterbugs explore Yosemite Valley. (p101)

➡ **Yosemite Mountaineering School** Kids aged 10 and up can take a beginning 'Go Climb a Rock' class in Yosemite Valley. (p91)

Cycling & Mountain Biking

➡ **Yosemite Valley** Rent bikes or bring your own to pedal along paved, mostly level bike paths.

➡ **Mammoth Mountain** Older kids and teens will go bananas over this giant mountain-biking park, open during summer.

Hiking
Yosemite

➡ **Yosemite Valley Loop** Hike along primarily paved, flat trails, then hop the shuttle bus back to where you started. (p52)

➡ **Vernal Fall** It's less than a mile to the footbridge below one of Yosemite Valley's most famous falls. (p55)

➡ **Mirror Lake** Best in spring or early summer, when the lake's waters reflect iconic Half Dome. (p53)

➡ **Nature Center at Happy Isles** Guided junior ranger walks start here during summer. (p103)

➡ **Sentinel Dome** Yosemite's easiest granite-dome scramble, worth it for 360-degree views. (p57)

➡ **McGurk Meadow** An easy-as-pie walk among wildflowers, just off Glacier Point Rd. (p56)

➡ **Mariposa Grove** Ramble among majestic giant sequoia trees (note the grove is closed through spring 2017). (p109)

➡ **Tuolumne Meadows** Stroll by wildflowers and the Tuolumne River to Soda Springs, or climb nearby granite domes. (p65)

Sequoia & Kings Canyon

➡ **Big Trees Trail** Marvel at giant sequoia trees along a short nature loop. (p163)

➡ **Moro Rock** Climb with older kids up a granite dome for spectacular panoramas. (p162)

➡ **Crescent Meadow Loop** Spy on black bears and peer inside the Chimney Tree. (p164)

➡ **Tokopah Falls** Scenic riverside hike to a 1200ft cascade tumbling down cliffs. (p164)

➡ **General Grant Tree Trail** Stare up at giant sequoias and step inside the Fallen Monarch. (p167)

➡ **Zumwalt Meadow** A peaceful riverside ramble, with a good chance of spotting wildlife. (p167)

BE A JUNIOR RANGER!

The junior ranger program is a national-park-specific activity book that helps children of different ages learn about wildlife, history and conservation. It's one of the best all-in-one bundles of things for kids to do, and includes scavenger hunts, crossword puzzles and do-good assignments like picking up a bag of trash on the trail or interviewing a real park ranger. Upon completion, kids get a souvenir badge. It's a neat way for families to experience and learn about the parks, and it's open to all ages (even adults!). Booklets are available for a nominal fee from park visitor centers and bookstores.

In the Eastern Sierra, the Inyo National Forest has its own junior ranger program, with activity booklets stocked at USFS ranger stations and visitor centers.

History

➡ **Yosemite Valley Visitor Center** Child-friendly, interactive natural and cultural history exhibits, plus afternoon junior ranger talks and evening programs for little ones in the outdoor theater during summer. (p130)

➡ **Yosemite Museum** Explore Yosemite's indigenous heritage, including the reconstructed Native American village. Don't miss the cross-section of a giant sequoia (count the rings!) out front. (p100)

➡ **Pioneer Yosemite History Center** Wawona's atmospheric old buildings, stagecoaches and covered bridge are worth a look. In summer, hop on a stagecoach for a short ride. (p109)

➡ **Yosemite Mountain Sugar Pine Railroad** South of Yosemite, ride historic narrow-gauge trains into the forest. (p140)

➡ **Sequoia Natural History Association** In summer, this park partner puts on family-oriented living history programs, with a BBQ cookout at Wolverton Meadow and campfire storytelling at Wuksachi Lodge. (p231)

➡ **Hospital Rock** Inspect ancient pictographs and Native American grinding holes in the Foothills area of Sequoia National Park. (p180)

➡ **Bodie State Historic Park** Explore the ghostly ruins of a real 19th-century mining town that went from boom to bust in the Eastern Sierra. (p144)

➡ **Laws Railroad Museum** A fun whistle-stop for train enthusiasts in the Eastern Sierra, with family-friendly special events. (p153)

Horseback Riding

➡ **Yosemite** Hitch up in summer for a scenic two-hour trip to Mirror Lake in Yosemite Valley, or a two-hour ride along a pioneer-era wagon road in Wawona. (p91)

➡ **Yosemite Trails Pack Station** Just south of the park, this outfit offers one- and two-hour creekside trail rides from April through early November, weather permitting. (p91)

➡ **Kings Canyon** In summer, one- or two-hour horseback trips trek among giant sequoias in Grant Grove and along the Kings River from Cedar Grove. (p176)

Nature Centers

➡ **Nature Center at Happy Isles** In Yosemite Valley, you'll find great hands-on exhibits and dioramas depicting natural environments. Kids can learn about pine cones, rub their hands across granite, check out different animal tracks and even snicker at the display on animal scat. (p103)

➡ **Giant Forest Museum** In Sequoia's Giant Forest, this family-friendly educational center has lots of stuff to touch, play with and explore, with a walkway outside that dramatically shows how tall these giant trees are. (p179)

➡ **Discovery Room** In Kings Canyon, at the back of Grant Grove's visitor center, kids can practice pine-cone identification and play a spot-the-species game with bilingual (Spanish/English) murals. (p194)

Swimming & Water Sports

➡ **Merced River** In summer, go rafting or kayaking in Yosemite Valley, or just splash around by the sandy shore.

➡ **Curry Village & Yosemite Lodge** Yosemite Valley's outdoor public swimming pools let families cool off.

➡ **Tenaya Lake** Build sandcastles on the beach of Yosemite's roadside high-altitude lake (warning: the water is chilly, even in summer!).

KEEPING KIDS SAFE & HEALTHY OUTDOORS

Travel with kids always requires extra safety measures, but with a little preparation and common sense, your family can make the most of your park visit.

➡ Dress children (and yourself) in layers so they can peel clothing on or off as needed – mountain weather can change suddenly.

➡ Bring along lots of high-energy snacks and drinks, even for short outings and easy hikes. Remember kids dehydrate more quickly than adults. See p244 for more advice on dehydration.

➡ When hiking, make sure your kids stay within earshot (if not sight). They may want to rush ahead, but it's easy to miss a trail junction or take a wrong turn.

➡ As an extra precaution while hiking, have each kid wear brightly colored clothes and carry a flashlight and safety whistle.

➡ Make sure kids know what to do if they get lost on the trail (eg stay put, periodically blow the whistle) or anywhere else in the parks (eg ask a ranger for help).

➡ Be extra cautious with kids around waterfalls, cliff edges and at viewpoints, not all of which have barrier railings; the same goes for any peaks or domes.

➡ At higher elevations, kids may experience altitude sickness. Watch them for symptoms, especially while active outdoors. Descend to lower elevations immediately if any symptoms arise.

➡ Ensure your kids know what to do if they see a bear (see the boxed text on p243).

➡ Children are more vulnerable to spider and snake bites. Remind them not to pick up or provoke snakes (eg with sticks), and never put their hands anywhere they can't see.

➡ Teach children to identify poison oak (see the boxed text on p30).

Swimmers at Merced River (p92), Yosemite National Park

➡ **Hume Lake** Along the Kings Canyon Scenic Byway, take a dip in this pretty forest lake with sandy beaches, always crowded with families.

➡ **Kaweah River** Big families picnic, sunbathe on the rocks and splash around summertime swimming holes in Sequoia's Foothills and Lodgepole areas.

➡ **Muir Rock** Later in summer, this swimming spot along the Kings River near Roads End in Cedar Grove offers a small, sandy beach.

➡ **June Lake** In the Eastern Sierra, hang out by the beach in summer, or launch a canoe, kayak or paddleboat.

Winter Sports

➡ **Badger Pass** In Yosemite, gentle slopes and groomed cross-country tracks are excellent for beginners. The 'Badger Pups' kids downhill program offers lessons for little skiers and boarders from four to six years old. Childcare is available for ages three to nine. (p96)

➡ **Curry Village** Go ice-skating on an outdoor rink with superb scenery in Yosemite Valley. There's a smaller outdoor rink at Tenaya Lodge, just south of the park. (p97)

➡ **Wuksachi Lodge** In Sequoia National Park, rent snowshoes and take the whole family for a hike around giant sequoia groves, or join a ranger-guided snowshoe walk. (p176)

➡ **Mammoth Mountain** In the Eastern Sierra near Mammoth Lakes, this superb skiing and snowboarding resort offers kids lessons and childcare services. Families also love tamer and less-crowded June Mountain ski resort nearby. (p148)

➡ **Montecito Sequoia Lodge** In the Giant Sequoia National Monument, this family camp offers cross-country ski trails, snowboarding, snow tubing and sledding, and daily children's activities. (p178)

Planning

Packing too much into your national-parks trip can cause frustration and spoil the adventure. Try to include the kids in the trip planning from the get-go. If they have a hand in choosing activities, they'll be much more interested and excited when you finally arrive.

RAINY DAYS AROUND THE PARKS

It's raining, it's pouring – will the kids think it's superboring? A little weather doesn't have to spoil your trip. In fact, it might prod you to explore some cool indoor activities you might not have noticed otherwise.

Yosemite National Park

➡ **LeConte Memorial Lodge** (p235) The cozy children's corner is stuffed full of ecofriendly books, games, puzzles, stuffed animals, fake bugs, crayons and an activity table.

➡ **Nature Center at Happy Isles** (p103) Hands-on animal displays and identification activities (including everyone's favorites, animal tracks and scat); will interest adult amateur naturalists, too.

➡ **Yosemite Art Center** (p101) Don't overlook the creative classes and drop-in family crafts program offered in Yosemite Valley.

➡ **Camp Curry Lounge** (p102) If you just need somewhere to sit out the storm, head to where the kids can play games by the fire (bring the cards!).

Sequoia & Kings Canyon National Parks

➡ **Kings Canyon Visitor Center** (p194) Fun nature-themed activity stations for kids are hidden at the back of the park's main visitor center in Grant Grove Village.

➡ **Boyden Cavern** (p184) A little rain usually won't stop folks from spelunking these labyrinths, just off the Kings Canyon Scenic Byway.

For more advice and anecdotes, especially for families hitting the road together for the first time, read Lonely Planet's *Travel with Children*. With helpful checklists, the *Sierra Club Family Outdoors Guide,* by Marlyn Doan, is handy for parents who are new to the outdoors.

To easily find family lodgings, restaurants, activities, attractions and more throughout this guide, just look for the family-friendly icon (⬛).

Before You Go

Some great resources for getting kids psyched-up about your trip:

➡ Yosemite's official website (www.nps.gov/ yose/learn/kidsyouth) links to all kinds of junior ranger and educational online activities, as does the 'Park Fun' page (www.nps.gov/yose/learn/ kidsyouth/parkfun.htm).

➡ Sequoia and Kings Canyon's official website (www.nps.gov/seki/learn/kidsyouth) lists free ranger-led programs, and also includes a link to the *Sequoia Seeds* kids' newspaper.

➡ The National Park Service (NPS) WebRangers portal (www.nps.gov/kids) has dozens of fun, educational activities for aspiring junior rangers.

➡ Phil Frank's comic-strip books *Fur and Loafing in Yosemite* and *Eat, Drink & Be Hairy*

are compilations of hilarious, bear-filled park adventures.

Useful Planning Websites

➡ **Lonelyplanet.com** (www.lonelyplanet. com) Ask questions and get advice from other travelers in the Thorn Tree's 'Kids to Go' and 'USA' forums.

➡ **Travel for Kids – High Sierra** (www. travelforkids.com/Funtodo/California/high-sierra.htm) Loads of tips for family activities, sightseeing, hiking and accommodations, plus recommended children's books.

Sleeping & Eating

The parks and nearby gateway towns all cater for families. Most lodgings allow kids under 12 years old to sleep for free in the same room as their parents, though a rollaway cot may cost extra. If you bring your own bedding, a child-sized inflatable mattress or portable sleeping crib will fit into most motel or hotel rooms. Almost all restaurants in and around the parks have kids' menus with smaller portions and significantly lower prices. Dress codes are casual almost everywhere (except at Yosemite's Ahwahnee Hotel dining room).

Plan Your Trip
Travel with Pets

If you bring your pets, it's crucial that they stay comfortable and safe. Consider the availability of pet-friendly lodgings, potential interactions with other pets and wildlife, and local restrictions on recreational use, especially hiking. Be sure to check the different regulations governing each of the areas you plan to visit, too.

Policies & Regulations

Pets are allowed in the parks, though restrictions are limiting. Dogs aren't allowed on park shuttles, inside any buildings or lodgings, on (almost any) hiking trails or in wilderness areas. Dogs are generally permitted in campgrounds and picnic areas, but must be kept on a 6ft leash and accompanied at all times. Don't sneak dogs

SAFE & HEALTHY PETS
➡ Pets are extremely susceptible to overheating. Never leave your pet alone in a hot car, where they may experience brain and organ damage after only five minutes.

➡ Follow park regulations and keep your dog leashed at all times. Off-leash there's more opportunity for your dog to roll in poison oak or fight with another pet or a wild animal.

➡ Keep your dog healthy by periodically checking for ticks and being prepared for weather extremes. Bring plenty of water on hot days and blankets for chilly evenings.

➡ Remember that pet food is potentially bear food. Store your pet's food properly at all times (eg use bear lockers at campgrounds, trailheads and parking lots).

Best Regions for Pets

Yosemite National Park
Dogs are allowed on most paved paths, including the scenic Yosemite Valley Loop, but *not* on hiking trails (with one or two exceptions). Almost all park campgrounds accept pets, and a few have facilities for horses as well.

Around Yosemite
Mammoth Lakes and the Eastern Sierra offer an abundance of dog-friendly trails and scenic backcountry stock trips, especially in the Inyo National Forest.

Sequoia & Kings Canyon National Parks
Dogs are prohibited on all park trails, but are allowed at park campgrounds. Backcountry stock trips are popular, with scenic trails starting from Mineral King, Cedar Grove and the Sequoia National Forest nearby. The national forest allows dogs on hiking trails and in campgrounds.

into backcountry or leave them tied up and unattended at campgrounds; it's illegal and you will be cited. Remember to clean up your pooch's poop, too.

In the Sequoia National Forest, leashed dogs are permitted on trails and at campgrounds (maximum two pets per campsite), but they must sleep inside a tent or vehicle at night. Dogs aren't allowed at developed swimming areas.

Up-to-date policies are at the following:

➡ **Yosemite** www.nps.gov/yose/planyourvisit/pets.htm

➡ **Sequoia & Kings Canyon** www.nps.gov/seki/planyourvisit/pets.htm

➡ **Sequoia National Forest FAQ** www.fs.usda.gov/sequoia/

Service animals (eg guide dogs) are welcome in the parks. They may accompany visitors with documented disabilities on park shuttles, inside museums and visitor centers, and on hiking trails and into the backcountry. Ask about current regulations to see if any special permits are required or if any areas are off-limits. Ensure your service animal always wears its official vest and is kept on a 6ft-long leash.

Camping & Hiking with Dogs

In Yosemite National Park, dogs are allowed on paved paths, unless otherwise signposted – they're prohibited on paved trails leaving the Valley floor, for instance. Dogs are not allowed on any unpaved roads or trails, except for the Wawona Meadow Loop and parts of Old Big Oak Flat Rd. You can bring pets into most developed campgrounds in Yosemite, except walk-in campgrounds (eg Camp 4 in Yosemite Valley).

In Sequoia and Kings Canyon National Parks, dogs are allowed in all developed campgrounds, but never on any trails, paved or unpaved.

Most national forests allow dogs at campgrounds and on hiking trails, with the possible exception of wilderness areas; inquire at the nearest USFS ranger station.

Bodie State Historic Park in the Eastern Sierra allows leashed dogs into the town site.

Dog-Friendly Lodgings & Kennels

Except for service animals, dogs are not allowed inside any park lodgings. Some hotels and motels outside the parks accept pets, although a nightly surcharge, weight limits and breed restrictions may apply. Not far from Yosemite's South Entrance, Tenaya Lodge (p141) offers dog-sitting and kennel services (surcharge applies) for hotel guests.

Yosemite Valley has a **dog kennel** (☏20 9-372-8348; www.yosemitepark.com; per dog per day $9.50; ☉late May-early Sep), though it's basic. Dogs are kept in outdoor cages (no food allowed, due to wildlife concerns) and stay unattended. Boarding fees are per day (no overnight stays allowed). You must provide a written copy of vet immunization records. Reservations are strongly recommended.

Horse Trails & Facilities

On backcountry trails, stock users must follow strict guidelines on group size, grazing and dispersal of manure, as well as feed restrictions to prevent the introduction of invasive plant species. Many trails are horse-friendly unless posted otherwise, but you'll need a special wilderness stock-use permit to use them.

Sequoia and Kings Canyon National Parks have several trails for stock trips, including those starting from the Mineral King and Cedar Grove areas. If you don't bring your own animals, talk to pack outfits in and around the parks about stock rentals and guided trips.

In Yosemite, a handful of developed campgrounds have stock facilities, and the **park concessionaire** (☏209-372-4386; www.yosemitepark.com) may have overnight boarding facilities available by advance reservation. There's a primitive Horse Camp (p188) in the Sequoia National Forest. There are more horse camps in the Eastern Sierra.

Up-to-date policies, permit regulations and camping and trails information are at the following:

➡ **Yosemite** www.nps.gov/yose/planyourvisit/stock.htm

➡ **Sequoia & Kings Canyon** www.nps.gov/seki/planyourvisit/stockuse.htm

➡ **Sequoia National Forest** www.fs.usda.gov/recmain/sequoia/recreation

On the Road

Yosemite National Park

Why Go?

The jaw-dropping head-turner of USA national parks, Yosemite (yo-*sem*-it-tee) garners the devotion of all who enter. From the waterfall-striped granite walls buttressing emerald green Yosemite Valley to the skyscraping giant sequoias catapulting into the air at Mariposa Grove, you feel a sense of awe and reverence that so much natural beauty exists in one place. It is a Unesco World Heritage site that makes even Switzerland look like God's practice run. As far as we can tell, America's third-oldest national park has only one downside: the impact of the four million visitors annually who wend their way here. But lift your eyes ever so slightly above the crowds, seek out the park's serene corners or explore its miles of roadless wilderness and you'll feel your heart instantly moved by unrivaled splendors.

Best Hikes

➡ Panorama Trail (p58)

➡ Tueeulala & Wapama Falls (p70)

➡ May Lake & Mt Hoffmann (p63)

➡ Taft Point & The Fissures (p57)

➡ Lyell Canyon (p79)

Off the Beaten Track

➡ Hetch Hetchy (p70)

➡ Yosemite Valley Loop Trail (p52)

➡ Mono Pass (p69)

➡ Chilnualna Falls (p60)

➡ Gaylor Lakes (p68)

Road Distances (miles)

	Big Oak Flat Entrance	Arch Rock Entrance	Wawona	Yosemite Village
Arch Rock Entrance	20			
Wawona	40	30		
Yosemite Village	25	10	25	
Tuolumne Meadows	45	50	75	55

Note: Distances are approximate

Entrances

The park has four main gates: Big Oak Flat Entrance (Hwy 120 West) and Arch Rock Entrance (Hwy 140) from the west, South Entrance (Hwy 41) near Wawona, and Tioga Pass Entrance (Hwy 120 East) from the east.

Tioga Pass (9945ft) is the highest roadway across the Sierra, and Tioga Rd/Hwy 120 East is usually open only between early June and mid-November, though the dates vary every year. In high snow years, the road may not open until July, so check the status of the road before driving across the park in springtime.

DON'T MISS

For two of the best views over Yosemite Valley, you don't even need to stroll far from your car. The best all-around photo op of the Valley can be had from Tunnel View, a large, busy parking lot and viewpoint at the east end of Wawona Tunnel, on Hwy 41. It's just a short drive from the Valley floor. The vista encompasses most of the Valley's greatest hits: El Capitan on the left, Bridalveil Fall on the right, the green Valley floor below, and glorious Half Dome front and center. This viewpoint is often mistakenly called Inspiration Point. That point was on an old park road and is now reachable via a steep hike from the Tunnel View parking lot.

The second view, known as Valley View, is a good one to hit on your way out. It offers a bottom-up (rather than top-down) view of the Valley and is a lovely spot to dip your toes in the Merced River and bid farewell to sights like Bridalveil Fall, Cathedral Rocks and El Capitan. Look carefully to spot the tip-top of Half Dome in the distance. As you head west out of the Valley on Northside Dr, look for the Valley View turnout (roadside marker V11), just over a mile past El Capitan Meadow.

When You Arrive

➡ The $30 vehicle entrance fee is valid for one week; keep your receipt to show when you exit the park.

➡ You'll receive a park map and the seasonal *Yosemite Guide* newspaper with information on activities, campgrounds, lodging, shuttles, visitor services and more.

➡ The park is open 24 hours daily. If you arrive at night and the gate is unattended, pay the entrance fee when you leave.

PLANNING TIPS

For 24-hour recorded information, including winter road conditions and summer road-construction updates, call ☑ 209-372-0200.

The **park website** (www.nps.gov/yose) offers free downloads of the park newspaper and helpful trip-planning tips.

Fast Facts

➡ Total area: 1169 sq miles

➡ Designated wilderness area: 1101 sq miles (95% of park)

➡ Yosemite Valley elevation: 3955ft

Reservations

➡ **Recreation.gov**
(☑ 518-885-3639, 877-444-6777; www.recreation.gov) Handles reservations for all of Yosemite's reservable campgrounds and those in the surrounding national forests. At press time, the concessionaire handling all non-camping accommodations within Yosemite National Park was in transition. See the 'Plan your visit' section of the park website (www.nps.gov/yose) for more information.

Resources

➡ **Yosemite Conservancy**
(☑ 209-379-2317; www.yosemiteconservancy.org) A nonprofit educational organization, it organizes educational and recreational programs and activities and operates the wilderness permit reservation system.

Yosemite National Park

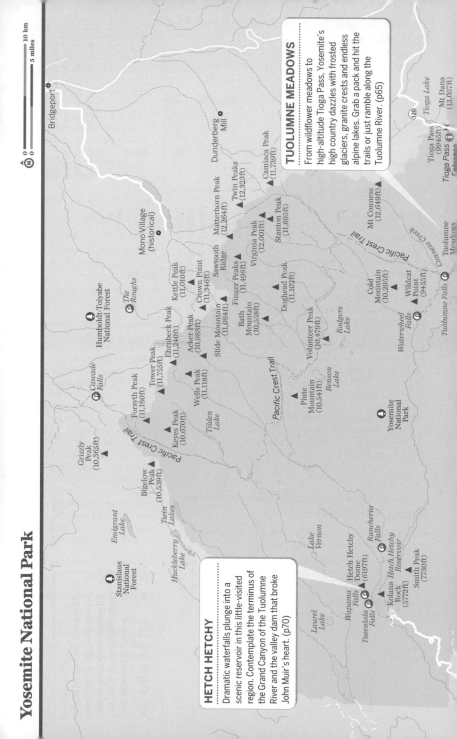

HETCH HETCHY

Dramatic waterfalls plunge into a scenic reservoir in this little-visited region. Contemplate the terminus of the Grand Canyon of the Tuolumne River and the valley dam that broke John Muir's heart. (p70)

TUOLUMNE MEADOWS

From wildflower meadows to high-altitude Tioga Pass, Yosemite's high country dazzles with frosted glaciers, granite crests and endless alpine lakes. Grab a pack and hit the trails or just ramble along the Tuolumne River. (p65)

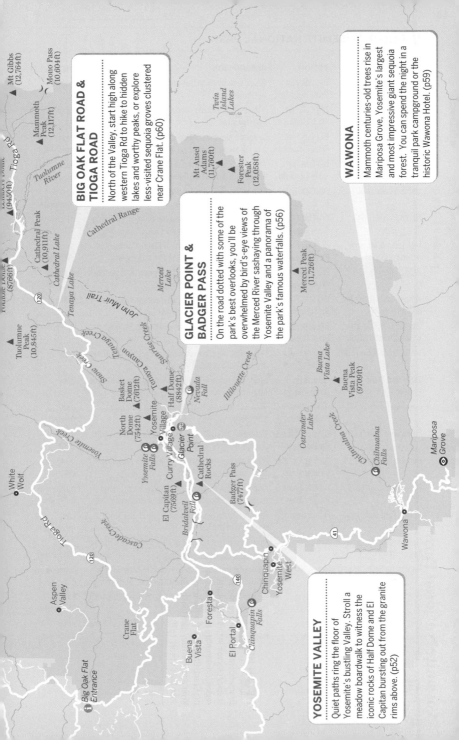

BIG OAK FLAT ROAD & TIOGA ROAD

North of the Valley, start high along western Tioga Rd to hike to hidden lakes and worthy peaks, or explore less-visited sequoia groves clustered near Crane Flat. (p60)

WAWONA

Mammoth centuries-old trees rise in Mariposa Grove, Yosemite's largest and most impressive giant sequoia forest. You can spend the night in a tranquil park campground or the historic Wawona Hotel. (p59)

GLACIER POINT & BADGER PASS

On the road dotted with some of the park's best overlooks, you'll be overwhelmed by bird's-eye views of the Merced River sashaying through Yosemite Valley and a panorama of the park's famous waterfalls. (p56)

YOSEMITE VALLEY

Quiet paths ring the floor of Yosemite's bustling Valley. Stroll a meadow boardwalk to witness the iconic rocks of Half Dome and El Capitan bursting out from the granite rims above. (p52)

Mt Gibbs (12,764ft)

Mono Pass (10,604ft)

Mammoth Peak (12,117ft)

Tioga Rd

Tuolumne River

Tenaya Peak (9450ft)

Cathedral Peak (10,911ft)

Cathedral Lake

Twin Island Lakes

Cathedral Range

Mt Ansel Adams (11,760ft)

Forester Peak (12,058ft)

Tuolumne Peak (10,845ft)

Fairview Dome (8766ft)

120

Tenaya Lake

Tenaya Canyon

Tenaya Creek

Snow Creek

John Muir Trail

Sunrise Creek

Merced Lake

Merced Peak (11,726ft)

White Wolf

Yosemite Creek

Basket Dome

North Dome (7542ft)

Yosemite Village

Yosemite Falls

Curry Village

Half Dome (8842ft)

Nevada Fall

Illilouette Creek

Buena Vista Lake

Buena Vista Peak (9709ft)

Glacier Point

Ostrander Lake

Cascade Creek

El Capitan (7569ft)

Cathedral Rocks

Bridalveil Fall

Badger Pass

Badger Pass (7477ft)

Chilnualna Creek

Chilnualna Falls

Crane Flat

Tioga Rd

120

Aspen Valley

Big Oak Flat Entrance

Buena Vista

Foresta

El Portal

140

Chinquapin

Yosemite West

Chinquapin Falls

Wawona

41

Mariposa Grove

HIKING IN YOSEMITE NATIONAL PARK

NAME	REGION	DESCRIPTION	DIFFICULTY
Lukens Lake (p62)	Big Oak Flat Rd & Tioga Rd	Quick hike to small but attractive lake; lots of wildflowers	easy
Tenaya Lake (p62)	Big Oak Flat Rd & Tioga Rd	A level stroll around one of biggest lakes in the high country	easy
Tuolumne Grove (p61)	Big Oak Flat Rd & Tioga Rd	Descend along a portion of Old Big Oak Flat Rd to a small sequoia grove	easy-moderate
Merced Grove (p61)	Big Oak Flat Rd & Tioga Rd	The park's least visited sequoia grove; downhill with a stiff ascent on the return	easy-moderate
Harden Lake (p62)	Big Oak Flat Rd & Tioga Rd	Follow the old Tioga Rd and the Tuolumne River for a rare warm lake swim	easy-moderate
North Dome (p64)	Big Oak Flat Rd & Tioga Rd	Astounding views of Yosemite Valley, Half Dome and Tenaya Canyon; includes 1000ft descent	moderate
May Lake & Mt Hoffmann (p63)	Big Oak Flat Rd & Tioga Rd	Short hike to May Lake High Sierra Camp, plus more challenging summit to nearby peak	moderate-difficult
Clouds Rest (p63)	Big Oak Flat Rd & Tioga Rd	Yosemite's largest expanse of granite; arguably its finest panoramic viewpoint	difficult
Tenaya Lake to Yosemite Valley (p77)	Big Oak Flat Rd & Tioga Rd	Includes 6321ft cumulative descent, with the option to summit Clouds Rest	difficult
Old Big Oak Flat Rd to Yosemite Falls (p76)	Big Oak Flat Rd & Tioga Rd	Inspiring hike from the heights of the Valley's north rim	difficult
McGurk Meadow (p56)	Glacier Point & Badger Pass	Short, flat walk to lush meadow; lots of wildflowers and old log cabin	easy
Taft Point & the Fissures (p57)	Glacier Point & Badger Pass	Major Valley viewpoint with interesting geological features	easy
Sentinel Dome (p57)	Glacier Point & Badger Pass	Easiest hike to top of a dome with amazing 360-degree views	easy-moderate
Panorama Trail (p58)	Glacier Point & Badger Pass	Descends from Glacier Point to Valley floor, with postcard views the whole way down	moderate-difficult
Pohono Trail (p58)	Glacier Point & Badger Pass	Passes numerous Valley viewpoints; has waterfalls; requires car shuttle	moderate-difficult
Ostrander Lake (p75)	Glacier Point & Badger Pass	Out-and-back wildflower trail with distant views leads to a backcountry hut and amphitheater lake	moderate-difficult
Carlon Falls (p70)	Hetch Hetchy	Falls feed into two swimming spots on the western edge of the park	easy-moderate
Tueeulala & Wapama Falls (p70)	Hetch Hetchy	Undulating trail to base of Hetch Hetchy's roaring waterfalls; boasts views aplenty	easy-moderate
Rancheria Falls (p85)	Hetch Hetchy	A popular introduction to Hetch Hetchy's lower altitude backcountry and waterfalls; best in spring	moderate-difficult
Dog Lake (p66)	Tuolumne Meadows	Picnicking and brisk swimming await at the end of this pine-forest trail	easy-moderate
Lyell Canyon (p79)	Tuolumne Meadows	Flat trail; swimming; superb views of Mt Lyell and its eponymous glacier	easy-moderate

 Drinking Water
 Restrooms
 Ranger Station Nearby
 Public Transportation to Trailhead

DURATION	ROUND-TRIP DISTANCE	ELEVATION CHANGE	FEATURES	FACILITIES
1hr	1.6 miles	+200ft	Wildlife Watching, Great for Families	
1hr	2 miles	+50ft	View, Great for Families	Restroom, Bus, Picnic Tables
1½hr	2 miles	+500ft	Great for Families	Restroom, Picnic Tables
1½-2hr	3 miles	+600ft	Great for Families	
2-3hr	5.8 miles	+400ft	Great for Families	Restroom, Bus, Picnic Tables
4½-6hr	11 miles	-1000/+422ft	View	Backcountry Campsite
4-5hr	6 miles	+2004ft	Wildlife Watching, View	Restroom, Water
6-7hr	14.4 miles	+2205ft	Wildlife Watching, View	
2 days (one way)	17.1 miles (one way)	+2205ft	View	Restroom, Water, Backcountry Campsite
2 days (one way)	18.8 miles (one way)	+3080/-2700ft	View	Bus, Backcountry Campsite
1hr	1.6 miles	+150ft	Great for Families	
1hr	2.2 miles	+250ft	View, Great for Families	Restroom
1hr	2.2 miles	+370ft	View, Great for Families	Restroom
5hr (one way)	8.5 miles (one way)	-3200/+760ft	Wildlife Watching, View	Restroom, Water
7-9hr (one way)	13.8 miles (one way)	-2800ft	View	Restroom, Water
2 days	12.4 miles	+1550ft	View	Restroom, Backcountry Campsite
2hr	2.4 miles	+300ft	Great for Families	Restroom, Picnic Tables
2½-3hr	5.4 miles	+400ft	Wildlife Watching, View, Great for Families	Restroom, Water, Playground, Backcountry Campsite
7hr-2 days	13 miles	+786ft	Wildlife Watching, View, Great for Families	Restroom, Water, Playground, Backcountry Campsite
2hr	2.8 miles	+520ft	View, Great for Families	Restroom, Bus, Picnic Tables
2 days	17.6 miles	+200ft	Wildlife Watching, View, Great for Families	

View   Wildlife Watching   Backcountry Campsite   Great for Families   Picnic Tables

HIKING IN YOSEMITE NATIONAL PARK (CONTINUED)

NAME	REGION	DESCRIPTION
Lembert Dome (p66)	Tuolumne Meadows	One of the best places to watch the sun set in Yosemite is atop this granite dome
Gaylor Lakes (p68)	Tuolumne Meadows	Short, steep hike with epic scenery of high country and lakes above Tioga Pass
Elizabeth Lake (p66)	Tuolumne Meadows	Great jaunt for acclimatizing in Tuolumne; superb views; lots to explore
Cathedral Lakes (p67)	Tuolumne Meadows	Easily one of Yosemite's most spectacular hikes
Glen Aulin (p68)	Tuolumne Meadows	Follow Tuolumne River past waterfalls to one of the High Sierra Camps
Young Lakes (p80)	Tuolumne Meadows	Sweeping views of the Cathedral Range lead to a trio of lovely lakes
Mono Pass (p69)	Tuolumne Meadows	Outstanding day hike into high country above Tioga Pass
Vogelsang (p82)	Tuolumne Meadows	Multiday, high-country trip with astounding views of Cathedral Range
Mt Dana (p69)	Tuolumne Meadows	Lung-busting, thigh-burning hike to the park's second-highest peak
Waterwheel Falls (p84)	Tuolumne Meadows	Splendid series of waterfalls at head of Grand Canyon of the Tuolumne River
Wawona Meadow Loop (p59)	Wawona	Loop around meadow shaded and flat, but lots of horse manure
Chilnualna Falls (p60)	Wawona	Uncrowded trail along cascading creek to top of waterfalls over Wawona Dome's shoulder
Yosemite Valley Loop (p52)	Yosemite Valley	Surprisingly uncrowded trail that passes all the major Valley sights
Mirror Lake & Tenaya Canyon Loop (p53)	Yosemite Valley	Best in spring, a relaxed stroll to the lovely sight of reflective Mirror Lake and beyond
Inspiration Point (p54)	Yosemite Valley	Some of the finest views of Yosemite Valley; easily extended to include other viewpoints
Vernal & Nevada Falls (p55)	Yosemite Valley	Justifiably popular hike to two of Yosemite's finest falls; mind-blowing scenery
Four Mile Trail (p54)	Yosemite Valley	One of the grandest viewpoints in the entire country; also accessible by car or shuttle
Yosemite Falls (p54)	Yosemite Valley	Sweat yourself silly and enjoy the views hiking to the top of Yosemite's highest falls
Half Dome (p73)	Yosemite Valley	The park's most difficult day hike is a strenuous push to the top of Yosemite's iconic dome

 Drinking Water   *Restrooms*   *Waterfall*   *Public Transportation to Trailhead*

DIFFICULTY	DURATION	ROUND-TRIP DISTANCE	ELEVATION CHANGE	FEATURES	FACILITIES
moderate	2-3hr	2.4 miles	+850ft	[View] [Great for Families]	[Toilet] [Bus] [Picnic Tables]
moderate	2-3hr	3 miles	+560ft	[Wildlife Watching] [View]	[Bus]
moderate	2½-4hr	5.2 miles	+800ft	[View] [Great for Families]	
moderate	4-7hr	8 miles	+1000ft	[Wildlife Watching] [View] [Great for Families]	[Bus]
moderate	6-8hr	11 miles	-600ft	[Wildlife Watching] [View]	[Toilet] [Water] [Backcountry Campsite]
moderate	2 days	13 miles	+1300ft	[View] [Waves]	[Toilet] [Bus] [Backcountry Campsite] [Picnic Tables]
moderate-difficult	4hr	7.4 miles	+915ft	[Wildlife Watching] [View]	[Toilet]
moderate-difficult	3 days	27 miles	+3852ft	[Wildlife Watching] [View] [Waves]	[Toilet] [Water] [Backcountry Campsite]
difficult	4-7hr	5.8 miles	+3108ft	[Wildlife Watching] [View]	[Toilet]
difficult	2 days	18 miles	+2260ft	[View]	[Water] [Backcountry Campsite]
easy	1-1½hr	3.5 miles	+200ft	[Wildlife Watching]	[Toilet] [Water]
moderate-difficult	4-5hr	8.2 miles	+2240ft	[View] [Waves]	[Toilet] [Water]
easy	varies	varies	+330ft	[Great for Families] [Waves]	[Toilet] [Water]
easy-moderate	1-2hr	2-5 miles	+100ft	[Great for Families]	[Toilet] [Water]
moderate-difficult	1½-2½hr	2.6 miles	+1000ft	[View] [Waves]	
moderate-difficult	4-6hr	6.5 miles	+1900ft	[View] [Great for Families] [Waves]	[Toilet] [Water]
difficult	4-8hr	9.2 miles	+3200ft	[View] [Great for Families] [Waves]	[Toilet] [Water]
difficult	5-6hr	6.8 miles	+2400ft	[View] [Great for Families] [Waves]	[Toilet] [Water]
difficult	10-12hr/ 2 days	14-16 miles	+4800ft	[Wildlife Watching] [View] [Waves]	[Toilet] [Water] [Backcountry Campsite]

[Binoculars] View   [Deer] Wildlife Watching   [Triangle] Backcountry Campsite   [Family] Great for Families   [Picnic table] Picnic Tables

🥾 DAY HIKES

There's no better way – and often no other way – to see Yosemite than by hiking into it. It's impossible to say one area of the park is better for hiking than another. Really, it depends on the hiker's ability and interests and the time of year. For example, the vast wilderness surrounding Tuolumne Meadows is a hikers' mecca, but it's accessible only when Tioga Rd is open (usually late May through early November).

Hikes along Tioga Rd are likewise only accessible when the road is open, and when it is, the walking is phenomenal. There are easy hikes and day hikes to splendid lakes – including Harden, Lukens and May Lakes – all sans the heat and crowds of the Valley.

Offering what is likely the park's finest view, Glacier Point is also a good jumping-off point for hikes into the backcountry to the south. The area is also popular for the Valley rim walks along the Pohono Trail.

Yosemite Valley is accessible year-round, but in the height of summer the heat can be brutal and the trails get crowded. Spring is a great time for hiking in the Valley as well as at Hetch Hetchy, another low-elevation area that experiences harsh summer heat. Temperatures in Wawona are similar.

Yosemite Valley offers hikes for all levels. Those seeking gentle strolls can visit Mirror Lake and wander the Valley Loop trails as far as they wish. The rest of the Valley's trails involve significant elevation gains. At the far end of the spectrum is the trek to the summit of Half Dome, perhaps the single most difficult (and popular) day hike in the entire park. Just remember that the altitude can make you short of breath before you become acclimatized. To assist you to choose the best hike for you, we rate the hikes from easy to difficult (p29).

Yosemite Valley

Many of Yosemite's easiest hikes – some might call them strolls – are along the mostly flat floor of Yosemite Valley. It's a lovely place to wander, especially in the evenings when the day-trippers are gone and Half Dome glows against the sunset. Nearly all day hikes from Yosemite Valley require some ascent. Assuming you can score a wilderness permit, the popular Half Dome hike (p73) is more relaxed as an overnighter.

🥾 Yosemite Valley Loop

Duration Varies
Distance Varies
Difficulty Easy
Start/Finish Varies
Nearest Town Yosemite Village
Transportation Shuttle
Summary Generally flat and paved, these trails are a great way to acquaint yourself with Yosemite Valley and its many historic sites. Plaques along the way explain the Valley's natural and human history.

Whether you want to plot a route from your campsite to the nearest hot shower, or take in the views from the meadows and bridges around the Valley floor, the vaguely defined loop trails are an undeniably great way to get to know Yosemite Valley. Parts are even wheelchair- and stroller-friendly, and they connect the Valley's most important historic and natural features. In some places the trail joins the road, in other places it peters out only to reappear later. Generally, it follows alongside Northside and Southside Drives, with some sections tracing the routes of former wagon roads.

For the ambitious, a well-marked path leads up and down the entire Valley, but it's easily broken into segments, making the journey manageable for just about any level of hiker. Pick up a free Yosemite Valley hiking map at the Yosemite Valley Visitor Center for easy route-finding and labeled point-to-point distances.

You can walk a 2.6-mile loop around the eastern end of the Valley by starting at **Curry Village**. From here, head east along the edge of the day-use parking area, with the tent cabins on your right. When you hit the shuttle road, turn right and follow the road into and through the trailhead parking area. Southeast of the parking lot, two trails lead to **Happy Isles**: one skirts the shuttle road, and another leads into the trees and across a delicate meadow area known as the **Fen**. After visiting the **Nature Center at Happy Isles**, cross the Merced River and follow the trail alongside the road, veering left when you can to stay along the banks of the river. Just before you reach the stables, head left (southwest) on the road across the river, past the entrances to Lower and Upper Pines Campgrounds. Then look for the sign pointing to Curry Village.

Yosemite Valley Day Hikes

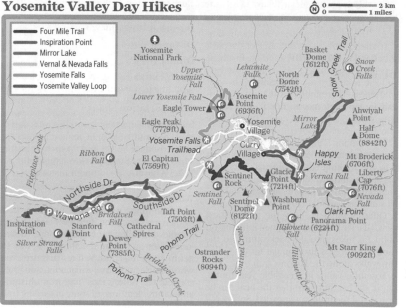

Legend:
- Four Mile Trail
- Inspiration Point
- Mirror Lake
- Vernal & Nevada Falls
- Yosemite Falls
- Yosemite Valley Loop

Further removed from the Valley's central commercial district, the 6.5-mile loop on the west end of the Valley passes good swimming spots on the Merced and offers fabulous views of El Capitan and Bridalveil Fall. The trail basically follows Northside and Southside Drives between the base of El Capitan and **Pohono Bridge**, the westernmost bridge over the Merced River.

🚶 Mirror Lake & Tenaya Canyon Loop

Duration 1–2 hours

Distance 2–5 miles round-trip

Difficulty Easy–Moderate

Start/Finish Mirror Lake Trailhead

Nearest Town Curry Village

Transportation Shuttle stop 17

Summary Shallow Mirror Lake, reflecting Mt Watkins and Half Dome on its tranquil surface, is one of the Valley's most photographed sites. Further northeast, Tenaya Canyon offers one of the quietest corners of Yosemite Valley.

Formed when a rockfall dammed a section of Tenaya Creek, Mirror Lake has been slowly reverting to 'Mirror Meadow' ever since the park service stopped dredging it in 1971. Only folks who visit in spring and early summer get the splendid sight that Mirror Lake is named for. By midsummer, it's just Tenaya Creek, and by fall, the creek has sometimes dried up altogether. Spring is also a great time to visit for other reasons: the dogwoods are in full bloom and Tenaya Creek becomes a lively torrent as you venture further up the canyon. The Ahwahneechee called Mirror Lake Ahwiyah, meaning 'quiet water.'

From the Mirror Lake Trailhead, near shuttle stop 17, follow the Mirror Lake road to **Tenaya Creek Bridge**. Cross Tenaya Creek and follow the paved service road one mile to **Mirror Lake**, where interpretive signs explain the area's natural history. From here you can return back to the shuttle stop, or journey up Tenaya Canyon for a little solitude.

The trail continues along Tenaya Creek into **Tenaya Canyon**, in 1 mile passing the Snow Creek Trail junction and soon after crossing two tranquil footbridges. In 2009 a 115,000-ton rockfall cascaded almost 2000ft from Ahwiyah Point near Half Dome, burying a large section of the trail beyond here. A path now traverses the rockfall, and your heart may skip a beat when you hear the pinging sound of loose rocks in that area.

From this opposite side of Tenaya Creek, the trail loops back through the canyon, passing Mirror Lake again.

🏃 Inspiration Point

Duration 1½–2½ hours
Distance 2.6-mile round-trip
Difficulty Moderate–Difficult
Start/Finish Tunnel View parking lot
Nearest Town Yosemite Village
Transportation Car
Summary Some of the best vistas in all Yosemite are granted to those who hike this steep trail to this classic viewpoint.

Sure, Tunnel View offers an amazing look into the Valley. But the view is even more impressive along the steep trail to Inspiration Point. Best of all, you'll leave the crowds behind.

Inspiration Point used to be a viewpoint along an old road into Yosemite Valley. The roadbed still exists, but this hike (actually the western end of the Pohono Trail) is now the only way to reach the point. You'll start by climbing a series of switchbacks from the upper Tunnel View parking lot (which is on Hwy 41 immediately east of the Wawona Tunnel). Almost immediately the view improves, with fewer trees and no bus tourists to battle for camera positions. Short spur trails lead to open viewpoints.

The climb is steep and steady but, thankfully, fairly short. The view from Inspiration Point itself – a large open area – isn't as spectacular as what you get on the way up, but it's a worthy destination nonetheless, quiet and perfect for a picnic. If you've got the energy, continue up the trail 2.5 miles further to **Stanford Point** and even on to **Crocker Point** (7090ft). Both offer epic views. The Inspiration Point trail is often doable in winter.

🏃 Yosemite Falls

Duration 5–6 hours
Distance 6.8-mile round-trip
Difficulty Difficult
Start/Finish Yosemite Falls Trailhead near Camp 4
Nearest Town Yosemite Village
Transportation Shuttle stop 7
Summary This classic hike along one of the park's oldest trails leads from the Valley

floor to the top of the three-step falls. The stiff ascent (and equivalent descent) make it a real thigh-burning, knee-busting haul.

The heart-stopping views from atop Upper Yosemite Fall will make you quickly forget any pain endured on the hike up. If it seems a bit much, you can always hike just the first mile (and 1000 vertical feet) to **Columbia Rock** (5031ft), a justifiably classic viewpoint.

From the northeastern side of Camp 4, the Yosemite Falls Trail immediately starts in on the four dozen short switchbacks that zigzag up a talus slope through canyon live oaks. After 0.8 miles, the grade eases as the trail follows more switchbacks east to Columbia Rock.

In another 0.4 miles, the trail approaches the top of **Lower Yosemite Fall**, where breezes may shower you with a fine, cooling mist. After admiring the view of Upper Yosemite Fall, brace yourself for the numerous switchbacks that run steadily up a rocky cleft to the Valley rim. The falls once ran down this cleft.

The trail tops out 3.2 miles from the trailhead and bends east. At the junction, the trail going straight leads to **Eagle Peak** (7779ft). Turn right at this junction and follow the trail two-tenths of a mile to the brink of Upper Yosemite Fall at the **Yosemite Falls Overlook** (6400ft). The view of the falls is impressive, but views of El Capitan and Half Dome are obscured. For a wider perspective, go the extra 1.6 miles (and nearly 600ft more in elevation gain) to **Yosemite Point** (6936ft), where you'll get incredible views of Half Dome, North Dome, Clouds Rest, Glacier Point, Cathedral Rocks and Lost Arrow.

Keep in mind the falls are often dry by midsummer, so late May and June (after the snow has cleared) are the best months to catch the scene in all its frothy glory. When you're done, retrace your steps to the trailhead.

🏃 Four Mile Trail

Duration 4–8 hours
Distance 9.2-mile round-trip
Difficulty Difficult
Start/Finish Four Mile Trailhead
Nearest Town Yosemite Village
Transportation El Capitan Shuttle stop 5; Shuttle stop 7
Summary A fulfilling day hike from Yosemite Valley that ascends the Valley's

southern wall to Glacier Point, the park's most famous viewpoint. The reward for the grunt is one of the finest vistas in the entire country.

Sure, you can easily get to Glacier Point by car or bus, but there's something supremely rewarding about making the journey on foot. If the El Capitan shuttle isn't running yet, take the Valley shuttle to stop 7, and walk south along a paved footpath leading across Swinging Bridge to Southside Dr. From here walk parallel to the road a short distance west to the Four Mile Trailhead. (This adds about another half-mile each way.)

Today the Four Mile Trail actually spans closer to 4.6 miles, having been rerouted since it was first completed in 1872. It was originally intended as a toll pathway, at the time being the quickest way into the Valley.

The trail climbs steadily, passing 2000ft **Sentinel Fall** and **Sentinel Rock** (7038ft). At **Union Point**, 3 miles from the trailhead, you'll first catch a glimpse of Half Dome. Continue climbing until the trail levels out for the final leg to **Glacier Point**. Take in the views, fill up with more water and check out the snack bar.

When you're ready, return the way you came. Hardy hikers can turn this into an excellent loop trail (and avoid retracing their steps) by continuing on the Panorama Trail to Nevada Fall, then down to Happy Isles.

🏃 Vernal & Nevada Falls

Duration 4–6 hours

Distance 6.5-mile round-trip

Difficulty Moderate–Difficult

Start/Finish Vernal & Nevada Falls/John Muir Trailhead

Nearest Junction Happy Isles

Transportation Shuttle stop 16

Summary Affording views that are unmatched anywhere else in the park, this well-trodden partial loop ascends the so-called Giant Staircase: the route of the Merced River as it plunges over Nevada and Vernal Falls.

If you can only do a single day hike in Yosemite – *and it's springtime* – make this the one. Not only are Vernal and Nevada Falls two of Yosemite's most spectacular waterfalls, but Yosemite Falls and Illilouette Fall both make appearances in the distance from select spots on the trail. If you prefer a shorter excursion, stop at the top of Vernal Fall.

There are two ways to hike this loop: up the **Mist Trail** and down the **John Muir Trail** (in a clockwise direction) or vice versa. It's easier on the knees to climb rather than descend the plethora of steep granite steps along the Mist Trail, so it's best to go for the clockwise route. Then you can lollygag along the John Muir Trail – which has astounding views of both falls – on the way down. The granite slabs atop Nevada Fall make for a superb lunch spot (as close to the edge as you want), with the granite dome of **Liberty Cap** (7076ft) towering above.

From the Happy Isles shuttle stop, cross the road bridge over the Merced River, turn right at the trailhead and follow the riverbank upstream. As the trail steepens, watch over your right shoulder for Illilouette Fall (often dry in summer), which peels over a 370ft cliff in the distance. From a lookout, you can gaze west and see Yosemite Falls. After 0.8 miles you arrive at the **Vernal Fall footbridge**, which offers the first view of 317ft Vernal Fall upstream.

Shortly beyond the Vernal Fall footbridge (just past the water fountain and restrooms), you'll reach the junction of the John Muir and Mist Trails. To do the trail clockwise, hang a left and shortly begin the steep 0.3-mile ascent to the top of **Vernal Fall** by way of the Mist Trail's granite steps. If it's springtime, prepare to get drenched in spray – wear some waterproof clothing! – and peer behind you as you near the top to see rainbows in the mist.

Above the falls, the Merced whizzes down a long ramp of granite known as the **Silver Apron** and into the deceptively serene Emerald Pool before plunging over the cliff. No matter how fun the apron looks on a hot day, *don't enter the water:* underwater currents in Emerald Pool have whipped many swimmers over the falls.

From above the apron, it's another 1.3 miles via granite steps and steep switchbacks to the top of the Mist Trail, which meets the John Muir Trail, about 0.2 miles northeast of the falls. From this junction, it's 2.5 miles back to Happy Isles via the Mist Trail or 4 miles via the John Muir Trail.

Shortly after joining the John Muir Trail, you'll cross a footbridge (elevation 5907ft) over the Merced. Beneath it, the river whizzes through a chute before plummeting 594ft over the edge of **Nevada Fall**. Nevada

Fall is the first of the series of steps in the Giant Staircase, a metaphor that becomes clear when viewed from afar at Glacier Point. Plant yourself on a slab of granite for lunch and views, and be prepared to fend off the ballsy Stellar jays and squirrels that will have your jerky in their jaws in no time, should you let down your guard.

Returning back from Nevada Fall along the John Muir Trail offers a fabulous glimpse of Yosemite Falls. The trail passes the Panorama Trail junction and traverses a cliff, offering awesome views of Nevada Fall as it winds down the canyon. Soon you'll reach **Clark Point** and a junction that leads down to the Mist Trail. From here it's just over 2 miles downhill, through Douglas firs and canyon live oaks to Happy Isles.

If you choose to do this hike in summertime, be sure to hit the trail early to avoid the crowds and afternoon heat.

Glacier Point & Badger Pass

If you're looking for bird's-eye views of Yosemite Valley, then several Glacier Point Rd hikes will fit the bill perfectly. Dewey Point, Taft Point and the Sentinel Dome hikes all lead to spectacular overlooks of Yosemite Valley.

Sentinel Dome hike offers perhaps the widest, finest view of all, and the hike to its summit takes a mere half-hour. Some of the hikes link up with other top-notch trails, such as the Four Mile Trail to Glacier Point and the trail from Wawona Tunnel to Inspiration Point (the westernmost leg of the Pohono Trail). Bask in views as you descend from Glacier Point and ogle some of Yosemite's best waterfalls.

If the service continues, these hikes may be reachable via the Badger Pass–Glacier Point shuttle.

🎿 McGurk Meadow

Duration 1 hour

Distance 1.6-mile round-trip

Difficulty Easy

Start/Finish McGurk Meadow Trailhead

Nearest Junction Bridalveil Creek Campground

Transportation Car

Summary An effortless and relaxing walk through grassy wildflower meadows, this is a nice choice for families or those who want an easier, less-crowded hike.

For a short stroll with solitude and tranquility, lush, open McGurk Meadow fits the bill.

Glacier Point & Badger Pass Day Hikes

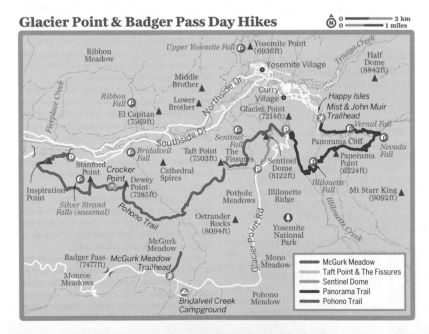

Park at a pullout along Glacier Point Rd just west of the Bridalveil Creek Campground entrance; the posted trailhead is about 100yd west of the parking area.

Shaded by lodgepole pines, a level and sun-dappled path meanders through quiet forest. After about a mile, a historic one-room **log cabin** appears on the left. Kids will love playing in and around this former seasonal shelter for cattle ranchers, and adults will need to double over to enter the low, half-scale doorway.

The meadow sits across a small footbridge just beyond the cabin, and its wildflowers peak in July, erupting in splashes of red, white and yellow. If you wish to continue on, another 3.2 miles takes you to **Dewey Point** (7385ft) and big, wide views down into the Valley.

🏃 Taft Point & The Fissures

Duration 1 hour

Distance 2.2-mile round-trip

Difficulty Easy

Start/Finish Sentinel Dome/Taft Point Trailhead

Nearest Junction Glacier Point

Transportation Car

Summary A hike over easy terrain leads to a spectacular overlook and drop-off at the edge of a sheer 3000ft cliff. Sizable boulders fill a series of enormous granite cracks.

Park in the Sentinel Dome/Taft Point lot on the north side of Glacier Point Rd, about 13 miles from Chinquapin. Note that the main parking area is not that large and often fills up by midmorning; it is less packed in the afternoons.

Taft Point (7503ft) is a fantastic, hair-raising viewpoint at the edge of a sheer 3000ft cliff, with impressive views of El Capitan and Yosemite Valley. On the same promontory are the Fissures, a series of deep, narrow cracks in the granite, many with large boulders wedged inside. Choose your steps carefully, especially when accompanying small children.

After a gentle descent through pleasant forest, you'll emerge on an open, rocky slope dotted with hardy wind-shaped trees. On your right are the **Fissures**, which drop hundreds of feet along the edge of Profile Cliff. Across Yosemite Valley, you'll see the Three Brothers, with similar yet longer cracks in the rock.

Ahead is **Taft Point**, guarded only by a short metal railing. Unless you have a profound fear of heights, approach and peer over the edge – the sheer drop is mind-boggling. Look west through binoculars to spot climbers on the southeast face and nose of El Capitan. After soaking up the views, which include a close-up look at Cathedral Spires, return on a gentle uphill climb to the parking lot.

🏃 Sentinel Dome

Duration 1 hour

Distance 2.2-mile round-trip

Difficulty Easy–Moderate

Start/Finish Sentinel Dome/Taft Point Trailhead

Nearest Junction Glacier Point

Transportation Car

Summary The easiest trail up one of the park's fabled granite domes will reward you with sprawling panoramic vistas of high peaks and falls. Ravaged and surreal trees strain to grow against the wind.

For those unable to visit Half Dome's summit, **Sentinel's summit** (8122ft) offers an equally outstanding 360-degree perspective of Yosemite's wonders. A visit at sunrise, sunset or during a full moon is spectacular. You can also combine a trip up Sentinel Dome with a walk to Taft Point and the Fissures, an equidistant hike from the same trailhead, or combine the two to form a loop via the solitary Pohono Trail.

Park in the Sentinel Dome/Taft Point lot on the north side of Glacier Point Rd. From the parking lot, take the trail's gently rising right fork and head northwest across open granite slabs to the dome's base. Skirt the base to an old service road, which leads to the dome's northeast shoulder. From here, head up the gentle granite slope to the top (wear good hiking shoes).

The gnarled, bleached bones of a wind-beaten Jeffrey pine once crowned the top. The photogenic tree died in a drought in the late 1970s, but caused heartbreak to many when it finally fell in 2003.

From the top, the views take in almost the entire park. To the west are Cathedral Rocks and El Capitan, while to the north you'll spot Yosemite Falls and, in the distance, Mt Hoffmann. North Dome, Basket Dome and Mt Watkins line the Valley's northeast side, and Clouds Rest and Half Dome rise dramatically above Tenaya Canyon. In the distance, above Nevada Fall, you'll see the notable peaks of the Cathedral and Ritter Ranges. To the east lie Mt Starr King and the peaks of the Clark Range.

🥾 Panorama Trail

Duration 5 hours

Distance 8.5 miles one way

Difficulty Moderate–Difficult

Start Glacier Point

Finish Happy Isles

Nearest Junction Glacier Point

Transportation Glacier Point hikers' bus or car

Summary Picture-postcard views accompany this trail and eye-popping sightlines of Half Dome are a highlight. Visit Nevada Fall as you descend down, down, down to the Valley floor.

Connecting Glacier Point and Nevada Fall, this trail is gorgeous, comprising several miles of Yosemite's most picture-perfect scenery. Hikers seeking a full loop from the Valley must first tackle the steep 3200ft ascent on the Four Mile Trail. Those starting from Glacier Point and heading down to the Valley must arrange a car shuttle or reserve a seat on the Glacier Point hikers' bus. Or you can simply hike to Nevada Fall and return to Glacier Point the way you came.

At Glacier Point, look for the Panorama Trail signpost near the snack bar. Descend a fire-scarred hillside south toward Illilouette Fall. The route down is largely easy, with magnificent views to your left – including Half Dome, which from here looks like the tip of a giant thumb. If you're lucky, you'll also find blue grouse on the trail, hooting and cooing in gentle, haunting tones. Make sure you bring sunscreen and a hat, as most of the tree cover has burned away.

After about 1.2 miles you'll meet the trail from Mono Meadow. Turn left and take a short series of switchbacks down to Illilouette Creek. The best place to admire 370ft **Illilouette Fall** is a well-worn viewpoint above the creek on the left.

At the 2-mile mark, a footbridge crosses **Illilouette Creek**, whose shaded banks invite a picnic. The trail leaves the creek and climbs east to **Panorama Point**, then **Pano-**

rama Cliff. This 760ft climb is the only significant elevation gain on the hike. Vantage points high above the Merced River afford amazing views of the Glacier Point apron, Half Dome, Mt Broderick (6706ft), Liberty Cap (7076ft) and Mt Starr King (9092ft).

The trail descends to a junction with the John Muir Trail. Turn right and follow the trail 0.2 miles to the top of **Nevada Fall**, 3.2 miles from Illilouette Creek.

To reach the Valley, descend the Mist Trail via Vernal Fall or take the slightly longer and gentler John Muir Trail. You'll emerge at Happy Isles on the Valley's east end (part of the Vernal & Nevada Falls hike).

🥾 Pohono Trail

Duration 7–9 hours

Distance 13.8 miles one way

Difficulty Moderate–Difficult

Start Glacier Point

Finish Tunnel View parking lot

Nearest Junction Glacier Point

Transportation Glacier Point hikers' bus or car

Summary A panoramic traverse of the southern Valley rim between Glacier Point and the Wawona Tunnel overlook, this hike descends along a scenic ridge above three waterfalls.

Romantically named Bridalveil Fall was called Pohono by the Ahwahneechee, who thought the fall bewitched. According to Native American legend, an evil spirit who breathed out a fatal wind lived at its base; to sleep near it meant certain death. Some claimed to hear the voices of those who had drowned, warning others to stay away.

As the trailheads are many miles apart, you'll need either two vehicles or to arrange for pickup following your hike. The Glacier Point hikers' bus can take you to Glacier Point from the Valley, but it doesn't stop at the Wawona Tunnel parking area.

It's best to go from east to west, starting at Glacier Point. (The trail descends more than 2800ft, so hiking the opposite direction would involve a strenuous climb.) Though it's generally downhill, the trail does make some noticeable climbs here and there. Highlights include Glacier Point (7214ft), Taft Point, Dewey Point, Crocker Point (7090ft), Stanford Point and Inspiration Point. The trail traverses an area high above three waterfalls – Sentinel, Bridalveil and Silver Strand.

Look for the well-marked trailhead near the snack bar at **Glacier Point**. After about a mile, you'll reach the trail junction for **Sentinel Dome**. You can either climb to the top or keep going, skirting just north of the dome along the Valley rim. After about 2 miles, you'll join the trail to **Taft Point**, which leads you across open rock, past the **Fissures** to the point itself. Peer over the railing before resuming your hike.

The trail continues west along the Valley rim, dipping to cross **Bridalveil Creek**. Past the creek, a trail veers left toward McGurk Meadow. Instead, bear right toward **Dewey Point** and another magnificent view (use extreme caution when peering over the edge). Across the Valley, you'll see 1612ft Ribbon Fall – when flowing, the highest single-tier waterfall in North America.

About a half-mile further west is **Crocker Point**, again worth a short detour for the view, which takes in Bridalveil Fall. Another short walk brings you to **Stanford Point**, the last cliff-edge viewpoint on this trail. Looking across the Valley from these western viewpoints, you can see the remains of the Old Big Oak Flat Rd, a white line traversing talus fields below on the north rim. Once you cross Meadow Brook and Artist Creek,

you'll begin the steep, 2.5-mile descent to **Inspiration Point**, an overgrown viewpoint along an old roadbed. The final 1.3-mile leg ends at the Tunnel View parking lot.

Wawona

Mariposa Grove features quite a few lovely hiking trails, and you could easily spend a half-day or more crisscrossing its 250 acres. A trail connects the grove with Wawona, where an easy loop circles Wawona Meadow and a more difficult trail leads to Chilnualna Falls, one of the park's lesser-known waterfalls. From there, long-distance trails head to such remote areas as the Buena Vista Crest and the Clark Range. Note that the majority of Mariposa Grove will be closed during a two-year restoration project that lasts through sometime in 2017.

🏃 Wawona Meadow Loop

Duration 1–1½ hours

Distance 3.5-mile round-trip

Difficulty Easy

Start/Finish Wawona Hotel

Nearest Town Wawona

Transportation Car

Wawona Day Hikes

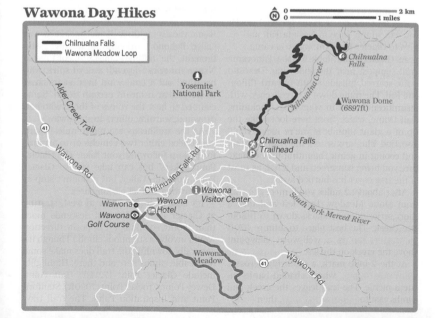

0 0 ———— 2 km
0 ———— 1 miles

— Chilnualna Falls
— Wawona Meadow Loop

Alder Creek Trail

Wawona Rd

(41)

Yosemite National Park

Chilnualna Falls Rd

Chilnualna Creek

Chilnualna Falls

▲ Wawona Dome (6897ft)

🅿 Chilnualna Falls Trailhead

ℹ Wawona Visitor Center

Wawona

Wawona Hotel

Wawona Golf Course

South Fork Merced River

Wawona Meadow

(41)

Wawona Rd

Summary A relaxed loop on a former stagecoach road, this level hike surveys a pretty meadow, with wildflowers raging in late spring and early summer.

Though you won't huff and puff too much on this gentle, shaded loop around pretty Wawona Meadow, you will have to dodge copious amounts of smelly horse manure plopped and squashed along the entire trail. Horseback riders and stagecoaches use the loop, throwing up lots of dust – another unpleasant element, especially on an already hot summer day.

On the other hand, this short, easy trail is a nice way to spend an hour or two beneath the trees beside the meadow. It's especially lovely when native wildflowers are in bloom. If you're lucky, you might even be alone most of the way – aside from the horses. Dogs are permitted here.

From the Wawona Hotel, cross Hwy 41 on a small road through the golf course. The trail starts a short distance down on your left and follows an old dirt road around the meadow perimeter. On the return, you'll cross Hwy 41 again and wind up on the hotel's back lawn. Plunk down in an Adirondack chair and soak up the scene.

🥾 Chilnualna Falls

Duration 4–5 hours

Distance 8.2-mile round-trip

Difficulty Moderate–Difficult

Start/Finish Chilnualna Falls Trailhead

Nearest Town Wawona

Transportation Car

Summary Chilnualna Creek tumbles over the north shoulder of forested Wawona Dome in an almost continuous series of cascades. The largest and most impressive of these, Chilnualna Falls, thunders into a deep, narrow chasm.

Unlike its Valley counterparts, this fall is not free-leaping, but its soothing, whitewater rush makes it an attractive day hike without lots of company. Carry lots of water or a filter, as the route can be hot. The top is a nice picnic spot. Like all Yosemite waterfalls, Chilnualna Falls is best between April and June when streams are at their fullest. July and August are often too hot for an afternoon hike, and by September the fall is limited by low water.

The trailhead is at the eastern end of Chilnualna Falls Rd. Follow Hwy 41 (Wawona Rd) a quarter-mile north of the Wawona Hotel and store, and take a right just over the bridge on Chilnualna Falls Rd; follow it for 1.7 miles. The parking area is on the right, and the trailhead is marked.

The trail follows the northwest bank of Chilnualna Creek 0.1 miles to the first series of tumbling cascades, which in spring shower the trail with a cool mist. Ascend several brief sets of granite steps beside the falls. Above, the stock trail joins the footpath along the Yosemite Wilderness boundary, a short but steep 0.2 miles and 600ft above the trailhead.

The trail rises gently yet continually through open, mixed-conifer forest, leveling out as it passes the rushing creek. It then moves away from the creek, taking you on long, sweeping switchbacks. The sheer granite curve of Wawona Dome fills the sky to the east as you rise above forested Wawona Valley. About halfway along the hike, you'll reach an unobstructed viewpoint from a granite overlook (5400ft); it offers the first good view of the fall. To the southwest are the forested Chowchilla Mountains.

The trail climbs several well-graded switchbacks, then a final dynamite-blasted switchback across a granite cliff to the top of Chilnualna Falls (6200ft). While you won't find any better view of the fall, it's worth continuing a quarter mile further to a nice picnic spot along Chilnualna Creek. If you're on an overnight trip, head for the campsites further up both Chilnualna and Deer Creeks.

Retrace your steps 4.3 miles to the trailhead in two hours or so, past a sign that reads '5.6 miles to Wawona' (referring to the Hotel and store, not your trailhead). At a junction 0.2 miles from the trailhead, avoid the tempting, broad horse trail (which comes out at a different trailhead) in favor of the footpath that bears left back down along the creek.

Big Oak Flat Road & Tioga Road

Two of the area's main hikes lead to groves of giant sequoias. Though neither grove is as magnificent as Wawona's Mariposa Grove, the crowds are mercifully thinner.

Day hikes and backcountry excursions are plentiful in Yosemite's subalpine wilderness, which stretches north and south

Big Oak Flat Road & Tioga Road Day Hikes

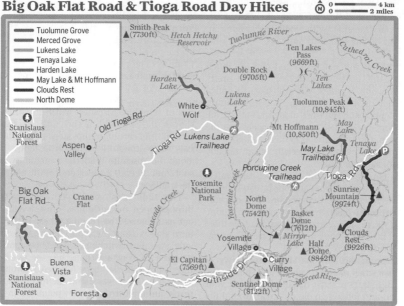

from either side of Tioga Rd. Like Tuolumne Meadows further east, this truly is a hikers' paradise. Several trails from the south side of the road lead to Yosemite Valley, and if you take the hikers' bus up from the Valley, they're more or less downhill all the way – an exquisite and rare treat.

🏃 Tuolumne Grove

Duration 1½ hours

Distance 2-mile round-trip

Difficulty Easy–Moderate

Start/Finish Tuolumne Grove Trailhead

Nearest Junction Crane Flat gas station

Transportation Car

Summary Descend into Yosemite's second-most-visited grove of giant sequoias (the walk back up is a bit of a haul). There's even a tree you can walk through.

You can reach this moderately sized grove of sequoias via a short, steep hike down a section of the Old Big Oak Flat Rd (closed to cars). Follow the road and a few switchbacks to the first trees, then meander through the grove and along an interpretive nature trail. The most popular attraction is the **Tunnel**

Tree (or 'Dead Giant'), already a stump when a tunnel was cut into it in 1878. Another interesting specimen is the **Leaning Towering Tree**. It fell over in 1983, and now looks like a huge set of cracked vertebrae. At one end, its roots shoot out like flares, and the hollowed-out core makes a fun tunnel for kids to explore.

The only bummer about this hike is the steady uphill climb back to the parking area. When it's hot, you'll be hurting – or panting at the very least. It's not awful though, and hikers of any age should be able to handle it given time and patience.

🏃 Merced Grove

Duration 1½–2 hours

Distance 3-mile round-trip

Difficulty Easy–Moderate

Start/Finish Merced Grove Trailhead

Nearest Junction Crane Flat gas station

Transportation Car

Summary This hike leads down to a beautiful sequoia grove, with crowds rarely present to break the solitude. The walk follows a dirt road to a dense cluster of giant trees.

The smallest sequoia grove in the park, Merced is also the quietest, thanks in part to its distance from major park sights. If you seek solitude amid the sequoias, this is for you. You'll start from a small parking lot along Big Oak Flat Rd midway between Crane Flat and the Big Oak Flat gate. The trail follows a dirt road (closed to cars), which remains flat for the first half-mile before dipping downhill into the grove. A handful of the trees surround a small log cabin. Reserve your energy for the hike out.

🏃 Lukens Lake

Duration 1 hour

Distance 1.6-mile round-trip

Difficulty Easy

Start/Finish Lukens Lake Trailhead

Nearest Town White Wolf

Transportation Tuolumne Meadows hikers' bus or car

Summary A gentle, quick jaunt along a wildflower meadow and a peaceful lake edged by shaded forest. Even small children can do this walk with ease.

Hike up here early in the morning or late in the afternoon, especially on a weekday, and you just might have the quiet blue lake, green meadow and surrounding sea of colorful wildflowers all to yourself. (Weekends are a different story.) Corn lilies trace the path leading up to the lake, and thousands of orange and black butterflies cluster on the ground in summer. If you hold still and listen, you can hear the low hum of omnipresent bees. Purple and white flowers erupt as you near the lakeshore, forming an exquisitely colored carpet. Revel in the idyllic setting and serenity in the 'golden hour' of early evening light. Even beginners can handle the short jaunt from Tioga Rd.

Start from the marked parking area a couple of miles east of the White Wolf turnoff. Cross the road and begin the trail in the soft woods. Climbing steadily, you'll reach a small ridge, then drop down to Lukens Lake. The trail follows the south shore to the west end, where you'll find plenty of shady spots to rest, picnic or simply sit in quiet contemplation.

An alternative 2.3-mile trail (one-way) leads to the lake's west side from White Wolf Lodge.

🏃 Tenaya Lake

Duration 1 hour

Distance 2-mile round-trip

Difficulty Easy

Start/Finish East Tenaya Lake parking lot

Nearest Town Tuolumne Meadows

Transportation Tuolumne Meadows shuttle stop 9

Summary A back-and-forth stroll along one of Yosemite's prettiest lakes, with no need to head high into the backcountry to reach it. A long sandy beach tempts you into trying the chilly blue water.

A pleasant stroll, this loop trail skirts the south shore of one of the park's biggest natural lakes. Begin from the parking lot on the lake's east end and take the new accessible boardwalk trail to the popular sandy beach. Walk south along the beach, and look for the trail amid the trees just ahead. As the path traces the shore, small spurs lead down to the water. Though the shoreline is rocky, there are several nice spots for a picnic. When you reach the west end (and the Sunrise Trailhead), it's best to either wait for the free shuttle bus back to the parking lot or simply return the way you came.

🏃 Harden Lake

Duration 2–3 hours

Distance 5.8-mile round-trip

Difficulty Easy–Moderate

Start/Finish White Wolf

Nearest Town White Wolf

Transportation Tuolumne Meadows hikers' bus or car

Summary Tracing a short section of the old Tioga Rd, this nicely forested out-and-back route is mostly level. Your reward is a tranquil and pretty lake basin that's good for a swim.

From the White Wolf Lodge parking area, start toward the direction of the White Wolf campground and follow the gravel road – a section of the old Tioga Rd – to the left of the campground entrance. The roadway passes a mixed forest of lodgepole pine and Jeffrey pine, running parallel to the Middle

Fork of the Tuolumne River. A few areas of fire damage are visible just before a discreet sewage-treatment facility appears off to the left. Continue on, and at the 2-mile mark take a right off the (now dirt) road and onto a foot trail. Jittery leaves of quaking aspens flutter in the breeze, and the occasional pinedrops plant can be spotted by its unusual red stalks. The 2013 Rim Fire came perilously close to here, and the many blackened trees you see resulted from backfires set to contain it.

Follow the trail for almost a mile to the lake. On the path toward the small boulder-littered shore, a meadow erupts with bulbous yellow Bigelow sneezeweed and white sprays of yampa. If you continue on a bit further north, feast on tremendous views of the Grand Canyon of the Tuolumne River and the peaks in the park's northern wilderness.

Harden Lake is an unusually warm-water lake for these parts, primarily because it evaporates rapidly during summer. So bring a towel and splash around without feeling like a polar bear. Retrace your steps to the parking lot.

🚶 May Lake & Mt Hoffmann

Duration 4–5 hours

Distance 6-mile round-trip

Difficulty Moderate–Difficult

Start/Finish May Lake Trailhead

Nearest Town Tuolumne Meadows

Transportation Tuolumne Meadows hikers' bus or car

Summary May Lake is a relatively easy uphill jaunt to instant backcountry. A new trail to Mt Hoffmann winds up its rocky slope, and the payoff is one of the best viewpoints of the park.

At the park's geographical center, **Mt Hoffmann** (10,850ft) commands outstanding views of Yosemite's entire high country. The broad summit plateau offers a superb perspective, a vista that drew the first California Geological Survey party in 1863. They named the peak after Charles F Hoffmann, the party's topographer and artist. The first peak climbed in Yosemite, Mt Hoffmann remains one of the park's most frequently visited summits.

Alternatively, some hikers go no further than **May Lake** (9350ft), on the High Sierra Camps loop, a pristine mountain lake that cries out for a shoreline picnic. It alone is a satisfying destination, with great views of Half Dome, Cathedral Peak and Mt Clark along the way. The hike takes only about 30 to 40 minutes in each direction, and if you have a wilderness permit you can overnight at the nice backpackers' campground next to the May Lake High Sierra Camp.

Start from the May Lake Trailhead (8846ft), 1.7 miles up a paved section of the old Tioga Rd. The turnoff from Tioga Rd is 2.2 miles west of Olmsted Point and 3.2 miles east of the Porcupine Flat Campground. Be sure to use the bear boxes in the parking lot. (Note that the May Lake stop on the Tuolumne Meadows shuttle is a different trailhead east of Olmsted Point.)

The 1.2-mile stretch to May Lake is fairly easy, although it's a steady 500ft climb. At the lake the trail splits; the right fork leads to May Lake High Sierra Camp, the left traces the lakeshore and then ascends to Mt Hoffmann. The Hoffmann trail winds through a talus field, where it follows a cairned path. Skirt the south edge of a meadow where the trail turns sharply toward Mt Hoffmann's east summit, and then aim for the higher west summit.

The last bit up involves some basic scrambling, so you'll want your hands free. Don't be surprised if some curious marmots pop their heads out of the rocks to check your progress. Be warned: the swarms of marmots living at the summit and in the rocks piles are not shy – they'll come right up to you. If you sit down, keep an eye on your day pack! Retrace your steps to the May Lake Trailhead.

🚶 Clouds Rest

Duration 6–7 hours

Distance 14.4-mile round-trip

Difficulty Difficult

Start/Finish Sunrise Lakes Trailhead

Nearest Town Tuolumne Meadows

Transportation Tuolumne Meadows shuttle stop 10 or car

Summary A fair amount of effort and distance is required for this classic hike, but you'll be amply rewarded with phenomenal 360-degree views from one of the park's best vantage points.

Yosemite's largest granite peak, Clouds Rest (9926ft) rises 4500ft above Tenaya Creek, with spectacular views from the summit and along the trail. More than 1000ft higher than nearby Half Dome, Clouds Rest may well be the park's best panoramic viewpoint. The hike involves a strenuous ascent and equally significant descent (make sure you have a cold drink waiting for you!), but getting here is definitely worth the effort. This hike forms part of the Tenaya Lake to Yosemite Valley hike.

Start from the Sunrise Lakes Trailhead at the west end of Tenaya Lake. Trailhead parking is limited, and the lot fills early. If you're staying in Tuolumne Meadows, it's easier to take the free shuttle bus to the trailhead.

Follow the trail along **Tenaya Creek** for your first glimpse of Clouds Rest and Tenaya Canyon's shining granite walls. As the trail climbs steadily up well-constructed switchbacks, the view expands to include prominent Mt Hoffmann (10,850ft) to the northwest and Tuolumne Peak (10,845ft) to the north. After a steady ascent, the grade eases atop soft earth amid large red firs. At 2.5 miles, continue straight past the Sunrise Lakes junction and descend southwest. As Yosemite Valley and Sentinel Dome come into view, the trail reaches the level floor west of Sunrise Mountain (9974ft). Paintbrushes, lupines and wandering daisies bloom here, alongside mats of pink heather and bushes of poisonous white-flowered Labrador tea. About 2 miles from the Sunrise trail junction you'll reach a creek that's the last water source en route to the summit – so fill up here (and filter it).

At approximately 5 miles you'll reach the Forsyth Trail junction, although it's not labeled as such on the sign. Bear southwest and ascend the ridgeline that culminates in **Clouds Rest**. To the southeast are fabulous views of wedge-shaped Mt Clark (11,522ft), the Cascade Cliffs and Bunnell Point in Merced Canyon. The granite swell of Mt Starr King (9092ft) rises to the southwest. The trail soon passes over a low rise and through a slight but obvious saddle. At a large white pine about a mile beyond the saddle, a small unmarked trail forks left; this is recommended for those not willing or able to hike the more exposed summit path.

A sign reading 'Clouds Rest Foot Trail' directs you along the granite ridge, which narrows rather thrillingly in one place. Never less than 5ft wide, the narrowest section might look intimidating but takes only five to 10 seconds to cross. The summit itself offers breathtaking views of Half Dome and the Valley. The view stretches from the Sawtooth Ridge and Matterhorn Peak along the park's north border to Mt Ritter and Banner Peak, standing dark and prominent to the southeast. Mts Conness and Dana on the Sierra Crest and the closer Cathedral Range are all outstanding. This is one of the Sierra Nevada's most inspiring viewpoints – savor the sights before retracing your steps to the trailhead.

You can extend your hike by continuing down to Yosemite Valley (as part of the Tenaya Lake to Yosemite Valley hike).

🚶 North Dome

Duration 4½–6 hours

Distance 11-mile round-trip

Difficulty Moderate

Start/Finish Porcupine Creek Trailhead

Nearest Town White Wolf

Transportation Tuolumne Meadows hikers' bus or car

Summary Perhaps the best vantage point along the Valley rim, this trail sees relatively few hikers. It's a downhill trek outbound, so you'll be doing the ascent on the return.

The trail descends 1000ft and rises 422ft on the way there, so be ready for a climb on the return trip. A side trip to the natural arch on Indian Ridge adds another 240ft climb. Note that North Dome is an exposed and hazardous place to be in a thunderstorm, and the final approach is not recommended in wet conditions.

From Tioga Rd, start at the Porcupine Creek Trailhead (8120ft), 1.2 miles east of Porcupine Flat Campground. To reach the trailhead from the campground, walk to the southern side of the highway from the camp entrance and follow the footpath that parallels the road.

An abandoned road leads beneath red firs until the pavement ends at 0.7 miles and the trail crosses Porcupine Creek via a log. After an easy ascent into the forest, you'll reach a few trail junctions in quick succession. Follow each in the signed direction of North Dome.

The trail climbs gently up Indian Ridge to an inviting view across the Valley to Sentinel Dome and Taft Point. The trail soon turns sharply and ascends steadily, leading to the marked Indian Rock trail junction at 3.6 miles from the trailhead.

A worthwhile but optional 0.60 mile (round-trip, included in hike mileage) side trip leads to **Indian Rock** (8360ft), Yosemite's only visible natural arch. Follow the short, steep spur trail to the arch. From the trail you can see the arch from all sorts of angles, and the arch affords good views of Clouds Rest, the Clark Range, Mt Starr King and Sentinel Dome. Clamber onto the rock for a view of Half Dome framed by the arch.

At the Indian Rock trail junction, the main trail continues south, leading to a spectacular viewpoint at the end of the ridge: front and center is Half Dome, and across the Valley is hard-to-see Illilouette Fall. North Dome lies directly below to the south, and Basket Dome's rounded peak (7612ft) lies to the southeast.

Hikers have created a number of indistinct use trails from here. The main trail curves around a large Jeffrey pine and drops southeast (left) off the ridgeline in the direction of Half Dome and then descends on switchbacks across open granite. Cairns lead to the marked North Dome Trail junction. Turn east for the final half-mile stretch. The rough trail descends steeply on a worn rock slab (that is dangerously slippery when wet) before a short final ascent to the **summit**.

West are the Sentinels, Cathedrals, El Capitan, the Three Brothers and Yosemite Point (Yosemite Falls lie hidden). To the northeast are Basket Dome, Mt Watkins and the distant peaks of the Cathedral Range. Horse Ridge rims the horizon to the south, while dominating the scene is the sheer north face of Half Dome – surely one of Yosemite's most

impressive sights. Clouds Rest rises on the far side of granite-walled Tenaya Canyon.

Retrace your steps along Indian Ridge to return to the trailhead. You can extend the hike by descending to the Valley on either the Snow Creek Trail (which heads down to Tenaya Canyon and Mirror Lake) or on the trail west to Yosemite Point and Yosemite Falls Overlook. From the latter, take the Yosemite Falls Trail down to Camp 4.

Use the hikers' bus from the Valley to reach the North Dome Trailhead in the morning. You can also start hiking from the Valley and visit North Dome on a very demanding round-trip of eight to 10 hours. For an especially vigorous day hike, traverse the Valley's north rim via North Dome by ascending the Snow Creek Trail's 100-plus switchbacks and returning via the Yosemite Falls Trail.

Tuolumne Meadows

The many day hikes out of Tuolumne Meadows are some of the finest in all of Yosemite, especially in July, when colorful wildflowers – poking up wherever they can – bring the high country to life. If you don't need to return to the Valley the same day using public transportation, all of these hikes are reachable via the Tuolumne Meadows hikers' bus or the YARTS Hwy 120/395 bus.

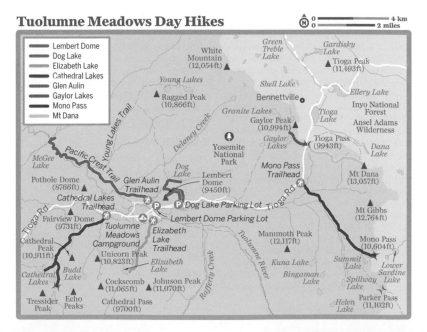

Tuolumne Meadows Day Hikes

🚶 Lembert Dome

Duration 2–3 hours

Distance 2.4-mile round-trip

Difficulty Moderate

Start/Finish Dog Lake parking lot

Nearest Town Tuolumne Meadows

Transportation Tuolumne Meadows shuttle stop 2

Summary The short hike (and scramble) to the top of Tuolumne's most iconic dome offers fun on granite and fantastic views in all directions, especially at sunset.

Lembert Dome (9450ft) rises from the meadows' east end, opposite the campground. Scrambling around the base of the dome's steep southwest face is a favorite Tuolumne pastime, but the real pleasure is hiking up the backside and standing atop the summit, where the views are staggering. Mt Dana, the Cathedral Range, Tuolumne Meadows, Pothole Dome, Fairview Dome and the Lyell Fork Tuolumne are all visible from the top. To the east, the Sierra Crest stretches from Mt Conness to the Kuna Crest. It's magical just before sunset.

This hike is doable for most walkers, but reaching the summit requires scrambling up the granite at the end – not recommended for the slippery-footed or faint at heart. Once you're on top, however, you can picnic upon a ledge or walk the ridge, scramble down some rock and cross a tree-filled saddle to the section of Lembert Dome that's so prominent from the road below.

Two similarly named trails lead to Lembert Dome. The one from the Lembert Dome parking lot, at the very base of the dome, is a steep, borderline unpleasant trail that's been damaged by storms. To reach the preferred Dog Lake Trail by car, drive east from the Tuolumne Meadows Campground and turn right onto the road leading to Tuolumne Meadows Lodge. Park in the Dog Lake parking lot, about a half-mile up this road. From the north side of the lot, follow the signed Dog Lake/Young Lakes trail up and across Tioga Rd.

This trail, almost entirely shaded in pine forest, is the quickest way up the backside of the dome. From the top of the trail, you can scramble up the granite to the dome's summit.

🚶 Dog Lake

Duration 2 hours

Distance 2.8-mile round-trip

Difficulty Easy–Moderate

Start/Finish Dog Lake or Lembert Dome parking lots

Nearest Town Tuolumne Meadows

Transportation Tuolumne Meadows hikers' bus; Tuolumne Meadows shuttle stop 2

Summary This short hike skirts the base of Lembert Dome and climbs gently through lodgepole pine forest to scenic Dog Lake, a great spot for an afternoon picnic and, if you can take it, a chilly dip.

Pine tree–ringed Dog Lake (9170ft) is accessible via the same trails that head to Lembert Dome. The better one leaves from the appropriately named Dog Lake parking lot, near Tuolumne Meadows Lodge. Follow this trail to the base of Lembert Dome. When you reach the turnoff for the summit, continue straight. A half-mile or so up the fairly flat trail is another junction; turn right toward Dog Lake (left is a steep downhill to the Lembert Dome parking lot). It's about another half-mile to the lake. Although most topo maps don't show it, a trail circles the lake, allowing you to hike around it before heading home.

Be prepared to share this subalpine gem with fellow hikers – on weekends it may resemble your local reservoir, as people lug abundant picnic supplies and even inflatable rafts up to the lake's forested shores.

🚶 Elizabeth Lake

Duration 2½–4 hours

Distance 5.2-mile round-trip

Difficulty Moderate

Start/Finish Elizabeth Lake Trailhead, Tuolumne Meadows Campground

Nearest Town Tuolumne Meadows

Transportation Tuolumne Meadows hikers' bus; Tuolumne Meadows shuttle stop 5

Summary At the foot of jagged Unicorn Peak, this easily reached alpine lake offers spectacular views and plenty of opportunity for exploration beyond the lake itself.

Any time is a good time for a hike to this beautiful lake, but it's particularly good choice if you've just rolled into the Tuolumne Meadows area and need a short acclimatization hike before sunset. Because it's fairly short, the trail gets busy, but heading up in the late afternoon means you'll encounter fewer people. That said, you could easily stretch a day out of this hike by exploring the saddles and ridges around the lake or, if you're experienced, by attempting the summit of **Unicorn Peak** (10,823ft), a class 3–4 climb.

The trailhead lies in the upper 'B' section of Tuolumne Meadows Campground. When you pull in, ask the ranger on duty for a campground map, or follow the sign to Elizabeth Lake. Once you're on the trail, the climbing kicks in immediately, and most of the elevation gain is out of the way within the first mile or so. Most of this section is shaded by lodgepole pines. The first real treat is the trail's encounter with **Unicorn Creek**, which drains into **Elizabeth Lake**. After that, the trail widens and levels off, and finally meets a fork at the northeast end of the lake. Turn right, and you'll hit the water. Otherwise, you'll follow Unicorn Creek into a meadow (a reward in itself), where several side trails also lead to the lakeshore. Climbing the slopes on the south side of the lake affords views of Lembert Dome and, far beyond, 12,649ft Mt Conness. To return to the trailhead, retrace your steps.

If you choose to come earlier in the day, Elizabeth Lake makes a nice spot for a picnic lunch.

🎒 Cathedral Lakes

Duration 4–7 hours

Distance 8-mile round-trip (upper lake)

Difficulty Moderate

Start/Finish Cathedral Lakes Trailhead

Nearest Town Tuolumne Meadows

Transportation Tuolumne Meadows hikers' bus; Tuolumne Meadows shuttle stop 7

Summary Easily one of Yosemite's most spectacular hikes, this steady climb through mixed conifer forest ends with glorious views of Cathedral Peak from the shores of two shimmering alpine lakes.

If you can only manage one hike in Tuolumne, this should probably be it. Cathedral Lake (9588ft), the lower of the two lakes, sits within a mind-blowing glacial cirque, a perfect amphitheater of granite capped by the iconic spire of nearby **Cathedral Peak** (10,911ft). From the lake's southwest side, the granite drops steeply away, affording views as far as Tenaya Lake, whose blue waters shimmer in the distance. Although it's only about two hours to this lower lake, you could easily spend an entire day exploring the granite slopes, meadows and peaks surrounding it. Continuing to the **upper lake** (9585ft) adds less than an hour to the hike and puts the round-trip walk at 8 miles, including the stop at Cathedral Lake. Admittedly, the upper lake is less spectacular when measured against the lower lake, but by all other standards it's utterly sublime.

Parking for the Cathedral Lake Trailhead is along the shoulder of Tioga Rd, 0.5 miles west of Tuolumne Meadows Visitor Center. Due to the popularity of this hike, parking spaces fill up fast, so arrive early or take the free shuttle. Camping is allowed at the lower lake (despite what some maps show), but be absolutely certain you're 100ft from the water *and* the trail, and that you choose an already impacted site to prevent further damage. Better yet, camp somewhere near the upper lake or off the pass.

From the Cathedral Lake Trailhead on Tioga Rd, the hike heads southwest along the John Muir Trail. Almost immediately, it begins to climb through forest of lodgepole pine, mountain hemlock and the occasional whitebark pine. After ascending over 400ft, the trail levels out and a massive slab of granite – the northern flank of Cathedral Peak – slopes up from the left side of the trail. Soon you'll see Fairview Dome (9731ft) through the trees to your right.

Before long, the trail begins its second ascent, climbing nearly 600ft before leveling off and affording outstanding views of Cathedral Peak. Three miles from the trailhead, you'll hit the junction that leads 0.5 miles southwest to Cathedral Lake. This trail crosses a stunning **meadow** (turn around as you cross it for the head-on view of Cathedral Peak) before arriving at the granite shores of the lake. Be sure to follow the trail around the lake and take in the views from the southwest side.

To visit the upper lake, backtrack to the main trail, turn right (southeast) and, after about 0.5 miles, you'll hit the lake. If you wish to stretch the hike out even further, you can continue past the upper lake to Cathedral Pass (9700ft), where you'll be rewarded with a stellar side-view of Cathedral Peak and Eichorn Pinnacle (Cathedral's fin-like west peak). This side trip adds about 0.6 miles to the trip.

🚶 Glen Aulin

Duration 6–8 hours

Distance 11-mile round-trip

Difficulty Moderate

Start/Finish Glen Aulin Trailhead near Lembert Dome parking lot

Nearest Town Tuolumne Meadows

Transportation Tuolumne Meadows shuttle stop 4

Summary The first leg of the multiday hike through the Grand Canyon of the Tuolumne makes for a great day hike, offering stunning views of the Cathedral Range before reaching Glen Aulin High Sierra Camp.

Except for the dip in the final stretch, most of the elevation change along this hike is gradual. It's an uphill return, so save energy for the climb home. The hike follows a section of the Pacific Crest Trail (PCT), the same stretch that horse packers use to supply the High Sierra Camp. It's a beautiful walk, though it's well worn and there can be plenty of aromatic horse dung along the way.

The trailhead lies behind the Lembert Dome parking lot, which is immediately east of the Tuolumne Meadows Campground and bridge. Follow the dirt road northwest. When you reach the gate, swing west toward Soda Springs, watching for the Glen Aulin Trail signs to the right of Parsons Lodge.

The trail leads through open lodgepole pine forest, crosses shallow Delaney Creek, then continues to a signed junction with the Young Lakes Trail, 1.3 miles from Soda Springs. Take the left fork, heading northwest through lodgepole pines. You'll emerge on riverside meadows with outstanding views of Fairview Dome (9731ft), Cathedral Peak (10,911ft) and Unicorn Peak (10,823ft).

Continuing on, the level, cairn-dotted trail crosses a vast, glacially polished granite slab over which the Tuolumne River flows. The river's roar signals the end of Tuolumne Meadows and the start of a series of cas-cades that tumble toward the Grand Canyon of the Tuolumne.

The trail climbs briefly over a granite rib, affording distant views of Matterhorn Peak (12,264ft) and Virginia Peak (12,001ft) on Yosemite's north border and a first view of the huge, orange-tinged granite cliff above Glen Aulin. Descend through forest to a two-part wooden footbridge spanning the river, 2.3 miles from the Young Lakes Trail junction.

The trail descends steadily, alternating between forest and riverside before reaching Tuolumne Falls. Continue along the plunging river to a signed junction with the May Lake Trail and then a steel girder footbridge spanning the river. Cross it and you'll reach two trail junctions in close succession. To the right is the Glen Aulin High Sierra Camp. At the second junction, the PCT continues north (straight) to a backpackers' campground and on to Cold and Virginia Canyons.

You can hang out here, or turn west (toward Waterwheel Falls) and continue a short distance into Glen Aulin itself – a long, level forested valley where the river flows green and tranquil beneath a massive water-stained granite wall.

To extend this into an overnight excursion, consider taking the Waterwheel Falls hike.

🚶 Gaylor Lakes

Duration 2–3 hours

Distance 3-mile round-trip

Difficulty Moderate

Start/Finish Gaylor Lakes Trailhead and parking lot

Nearest Town Tuolumne Meadows

Transportation Tuolumne Meadows–Tioga Pass shuttle

Summary This spectacular and popular trail climbs gently up to Gaylor Lakes, set in pristine alpine territory just inside the park boundary near Tioga Pass.

The hike to Gaylor Lakes is a high-altitude hike, so prior acclimatization (such as a day in Tuolumne) is a good idea. There can be snow any time of the year. Sound good? It is.

The trail begins from the parking lot, immediately west of Tioga Pass Entrance, and wastes no time in starting its steep ascent. At the crest, Lower Gaylor Lake (10,334ft) lies in a basin below you, with great views everywhere you turn. The trail skirts the lower lake and then climbs to **Upper Gaylor Lake** (10,510ft).

For an extra bonus, head past the lake and climb again to the site of the old **Great Sierra Mine**, where the views are even wider and more stunning. All told, the alpine countryside here is knockout beautiful, so budget some time for poking around.

🏃 Mono Pass

Duration 4 hours

Distance 7.4-mile round-trip

Difficulty Moderate–Difficult

Start/Finish Mono Pass Trailhead

Nearest Town Tuolumne Meadows

Transportation Tuolumne Meadows–Tioga Pass shuttle

Summary This outrageously scenic, high-altitude hike from Dana Meadows starts at 9689ft and follows an ancient Native American trail past meadows and through open forest to the vast, lake-crowned Mono Pass.

A saddle on the Sierra Crest between the rounded summits of Mts Gibbs (12,764ft) and Lewis (12,296ft), Mono Pass was the highest point on an ancient Native American trade route that linked the Mono Lake area with Tuolumne and continued to Yosemite Valley via Cathedral Pass. Remnants of late-19th-century log buildings – relics of the mining years – remain along the trail among subalpine meadows and lakes. It's a fantastic walk through some of the highest of Tuolumne's readily accessible high country.

The Mono Pass Trailhead and parking lot is at road marker T37, 1.4 miles south of Tioga Pass. The trail leads southeast through open forest within the shadow of 13,057ft Mt Dana to the northeast. After an easy half-mile hike alongside **Dana Meadows**, the trail crosses the Dana Fork of the Tuolumne River, then crosses two small ridges before passing beneath lodgepole pines beside several small, buttercup-filled meadows. Emerging from the pines, the trail makes a gentle ascent along **Parker Pass Creek**, with the reddish bulk of Mt Gibbs above and to the east.

When you reach the signed Spillway Lake trail junction, follow the left fork toward Mono and Parker Passes. The trail passes the remains of a log cabin and opens onto a large meadow beside a small creek, with impressive views of Kuna Crest and Mammoth Peak (12,117ft). Thirty minutes (1.4 miles) past the Spillway Lake junction, a small trail branches right toward Parker Pass. Keep going straight, however, past twisted whitebark pines and two small lakes to **Mono Pass** (10,604ft).

Tiny Summit Lake lies to the west, while east of the pass are Upper and Lower Sardine Lakes. Further down, Walker Lake lies in an area known as Bloody Canyon. Tree frogs chirp from the banks of Summit Lake in early summer. Flourishing in meadows along its north side are scrub willows, Sierra onions and yellow potentillas. At the south end of the pass sit three historic log cabins.

Retrace your steps to the trailhead. To make this an overnight trip, you must camp outside the park in the Ansel Adams Wilderness. Two worthy destinations are Upper Sardine Lake, just east of Mono Pass, and a more strenuous hike to Alger Lakes via Parker Pass and Koip Peak Pass.

🏃 Mt Dana

Duration 4–7 hours

Distance 5.8-mile round-trip

Difficulty Difficult

Start/Finish Unmarked trailhead immediately east of Tioga Pass Entrance

Nearest Town Tuolumne Meadows

Transportation Tuolumne Meadows–Tioga Pass shuttle or car

Summary Starting at 9945ft, this strenuous hike is a leg-working, lung-busting climb to the top of Yosemite's second-highest peak, which, at 13,057ft, offers stunning views in every direction.

Mt Dana, which takes its name from American geologist James Dwight Dana, offers unrivaled views of Mono Lake, the Grand Canyon of the Tuolumne and the rest of the Yosemite high country from its summit. Remember, though, that this is a steep, high-altitude hike which *starts* at nearly 10,000ft. Prior acclimatization will ease your struggle.

The hiking season runs from July to mid-September, though snow may block the trail in early summer. Don't even start the hike if a storm threatens.

Parking is available at the Gaylor Lakes trailhead just inside the Tioga Pass Entrance. From a small employee parking area beside the Tioga Pass Entrance kiosk, the trail heads east, passing between two broad, shallow pools before the ascent begins. At almost 2 miles, the trail passes through flower-filled meadows on a wide ridge, a natural place to pause and brace yourself for the final 1400ft ascent in the last mile.

There's no mapped trail to the top, but the many use trails here previously have been consolidated into one obvious path, with frequent cairns 2ft to 3ft tall leading the way up the rocky slope to the summit. The views from the summit of Mt Dana are outstanding enough to invite lingering, but no camping is permitted. From the summit, retrace your steps downhill to the trailhead.

Hetch Hetchy

Hetch Hetchy offers some outstanding hiking, but day hikers are essentially limited to the Wapama Falls Trail, which traces the reservoir's scenic north shore, a fairly easy hike for just about anyone. You'll see some trees blackened by the 2013 Rim Fire.

🏃 Tueeulala & Wapama Falls

Duration 2½–3 hours

Distance 5.4-mile round-trip

Difficulty Easy–Moderate

Start/Finish Rancheria Falls Trailhead, O'Shaughnessy Dam

Nearest Junction Evergreen Lodge

Transportation Car

Summary This hike along the north shore of Hetch Hetchy Reservoir leads to the base of two neighboring falls: the free-leaping, seasonal Tueeulala Falls and the enormous triple cascades of year-round Wapama Falls.

Few – if any – trails in Yosemite bring you as close to the shower and roar of a giant waterfall as this one does to Wapama Falls. In springtime, after a good snowmelt, the falls can rage so mightily that the park occasionally has to close the trail itself as water rolls over the bridges. On your way, you'll pass the wispy Tueeulala Falls (*twee*-la-la), which spring spectacularly from the cliffs

from more than 1000ft above the trail. All the while, Hetch Hetchy Dome (6197ft), on the north shore, and the mighty **Kolana Rock** (5772ft), on the south shore, loom over the entire scene. You can capture both falls and adjacent Hetch Hetchy Dome in a single striking photo. Kolana Rock's vertical north face provides nesting sites for peregrine falcons, once close to extinction but now present in healthier numbers.

The gentle north shore trail is fairly flat, but does have a few ups and downs that will challenge unfit hikers in the summer heat. Plan the hike for mid- to late spring, when temperatures are cooler, butterflies are abundant, wildflowers are in bloom and the falls are full.

From the parking lot (3813ft), cross **O'Shaughnessy Dam** and pass through the tunnel on its far side. The broad, oak-shaded trail then heads northeast, above and parallel to the north shore of Hetch Hetchy Reservoir. In just over a mile, after rising gradually past several small seasonal streams, you'll reach a signed trail junction (4050ft).

Take the right (east) fork, following the sign to Wapama Falls. The trail descends gently, then bears left onto broad granite slabs before reaching **Tueeulala Falls**. Most of the falls end up flowing beneath the footbridge, but in spring a small section of the trail can fill with runoff. By June, the falls are usually dry.

The trail continues down a staircase that switchbacks gently to the base of thundering **Wapama Falls** (3900ft), where wooden footbridges span Falls Creek. In spring, water cascades over the trail beyond the first footbridge and almost covers the second. When the water is high, crossing is dangerous (two hikers were swept to their deaths in 2011), but at other times the flow is ankle-deep. The frothy, gushing torrents create billowing clouds of mist that drench the entire area and make for a cool bath on a warm afternoon.

Return to the trailhead via the same route.

🏃 Carlon Falls

Duration 2 hours

Distance 2.4-mile round-trip

Difficulty Easy–Moderate

Start/Finish Carlon Day Use Area

Hetch Hetchy Day Hikes

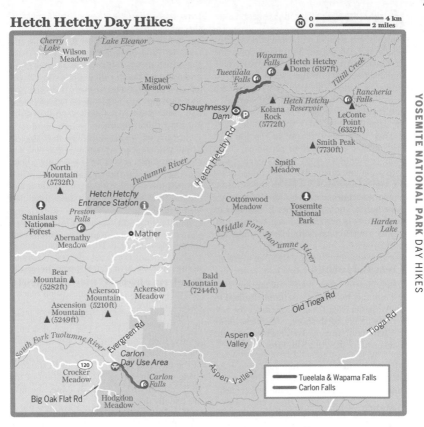

Nearest Junction Evergreen Lodge

Transportation Car

Summary This short but sweet hike follows the South Fork Tuolumne River up to Carlon Falls, which cascade down granite slabs into perfect swimming holes.

Most people blow right by Carlon Falls on their way to Hetch Hetchy, but a quick stop for this short venture is well worthwhile. The hike is especially satisfying on a hot day, when the swimming holes beneath the falls are paradisaical. Folks who stay at Evergreen Lodge and Camp Mather frequent the falls, so arrive early to have the place to yourself. The only thing making this hike 'moderate' is a section of washed-out trail that requires surefootedness.

To get to the trailhead, drive northwest on Evergreen Rd, which departs Hwy 120 about 1 mile before the Big Oak Flat Entrance. About 1 mile after turning off, you'll see the Carlon Day Use Area at a bridge across the river. Park in the pullout on the far (north) side of the bridge and hike upstream from there. Although the trailhead is outside the Yosemite park boundary, you enter the park after about 0.1 miles.

Shaded by ponderosa pines, incense-cedars and the occasional dogwood, the trail winds along the north bank of the river, through patches of fragrant kitkitdizze (an exceptionally pungent shrub also known as Sierran Mountain Misery) and finally arrives at **Carlon Falls**. Better described as a cascade, the falls tumble nearly 40ft across moss- and fern-draped granite into two separate **swimming holes**. There's plenty of granite around for sunning, so be sure to bring lunch.

🏃 OVERNIGHT HIKES

Backcountry hiking and sleeping beneath the stars is one of Yosemite's finest adventures. The vast majority of the almost four million people who visit Yosemite every year never leave the Valley floor, meaning the park's 1101 sq miles of wilderness is, relatively speaking, empty. There are a few painless bureaucratic hurdles to jump before heading out, however, but a little planning will make your trek a triumph.

Wilderness Permits

Wilderness permits are required for all overnight backcountry trips (not for day hikes). To stem overuse of the backcountry, a quota system is in effect for each trailhead. You must spend your first night in the area noted on your permit – from there, you're free to roam.

Permits are available either in advance (between 26 weeks and two days ahead) or on a first-come, first-served basis from the nearest wilderness center. The park reserves 40% of its wilderness permits for walk-ups; these become available at 11am one day before the hike-in date. If you show up early the day before your hike, you should have no problem getting a permit. For popular hikes (such as Little Yosemite Valley, Cathedral Lakes or the High Sierra Camp routes), you should show up and get in line before the permit offices open the day before you hike. Always have a backup plan, as some spots fill very quickly.

Hikers who turn up at the wilderness center nearest the trailhead get priority over someone at another wilderness center. For example, if there is one permit left for Lyell Canyon, the Yosemite Valley Wilderness Center will call the Tuolumne Meadows Wilderness Center to make sure that no one breezing in to the Tuolumne office wants it before giving it to someone who has been waiting overnight in the Valley.

Reserving a **wilderness permit** (☑209-372-0740; www.nps.gov/yose/planyourvisit/wpres.htm; advance reservation fee $5, plus $5 per person, free for walk-ins; ☻8:30am-4:30pm Mon-Fri Dec-Sep, extended hours late May-early Sep) is the best way to ensure you get one, and you can do so by fax, phone or through the mail. Faxes received between 5pm (the previous day) and 7:30am (the first morning you can reserve) get first priority. Reservations are not available from October to April, but you'll still need to get a permit.

In winter, wilderness permits are available at the Yosemite Valley Visitor Center, the Hetch Hetchy Entrance Station and the seasonal ranger station at the Badger Pass A-frame building. Self-registration permits are available 24 hours a day outside the Wawona and Big Oak Flat Information Stations and the Tuolumne Meadows Ranger Station. See www.nps.gov/yose/planyourvisit/permitstations.htm for more information.

Study your maps, read up and decide where you want to go before registering for a permit. Rangers can offer guidance about starting points and trail conditions, but they will not recommend one area over another because they don't know hikers' skills. See the National Park Service (NPS) website for updated trail conditions (www.nps.gov/yose/planyourvisit/wildcond.htm) or contact the wilderness centers.

Backpackers' Campgrounds

To accommodate backpackers heading into or out of the wilderness, the park offers walk-in backpackers' campgrounds in Yosemite Valley, Tuolumne Meadows, White Wolf and Hetch Hetchy. If you hold a valid wilderness permit, you may spend the night before and the night after your trip in one of these campgrounds. The cost is $6 per person per night, and reservations are unnecessary.

Long-distance cyclists may also use these campgrounds for one-night stays.

Wilderness Regulations

For the sake of the bears more than your food, approved bear-resistant food canisters are required for all overnight hikes in the park. When you pick up your wilderness permit, you'll have to rent a bear canister or show that you have one. They're also sold at stores throughout the park. These canisters weigh just under 3lb each and, when carefully packed, can store three to five days' worth of food for one or two people. Keep the canisters closed when cooking.

Campfires are forbidden above 9600ft. Where available, use pre-existing campsites to reduce your impact, and camp at least 100ft from water sources and trails. Never put soap in the water, even 'biodegradable' types. Properly filter all drinking water or boil it for three to five minutes, and don't burn trash. Pack out everything you bring, including toilet paper.

Wilderness camping is prohibited within 4 trail-miles of Yosemite Valley, Tuolumne Meadows, Glacier Point, Hetch Hetchy and Wawona, and you must be at least one 'air mile' from any road. No one is actually going to bust out the measuring tape – the idea is to keep people from simply wandering into the trees and camping when they can't find open campsites in the park. When you get a wilderness permit, you'll be asked to list the approximate location of your first campsite.

Yosemite Valley

Most hikes within and around Yosemite Valley proper are day hikes. Most overnight hikes from the Valley will take you out of its confines entirely. The hike to the top of Half Dome, Yosemite's most famous trek, is one major exception.

🚶 Half Dome

Duration 10–12 hours/2 days

Distance 14- to 16-mile round-trip

Difficulty Difficult

Start/Finish Vernal & Nevada Falls/John Muir Trailhead near Happy Isles

Nearest Junction Happy Isles

Transportation Shuttle stop 16

Summary Ideally done over two days, but doable as a grueling day hike, the demanding trek to the top of Yosemite's signature peak offers views (and crowds and sore muscles) like you wouldn't believe.

For many visitors, this is the ultimate Yosemite hike, an achievement to boast about to the grandkids some day. The stand-alone summit of this glacier-carved chunk of granite offers awesome 360-degree views, and peering down its sheer 2000ft north face offers a thrill you'll remember the rest of your life. But, unless you get a crack-of-dawn start, you'll have people aplenty to deal with. Most importantly, advance permits are now required for all hikers, making a Half Dome summit even harder to arrange.

Ideally, Half Dome is best tackled in two days, allowing you more time to rest up and enjoy the gorgeous surroundings. But since it's so popular, you'll have a hard time getting a wilderness permit to sleep overnight at the limited legal camping areas on the route (the most popular being Little Yosemite Valley). If you do attempt this hike in a single day (and many people do), and have a coveted permit, be ready for some serious exertion. Get an early start (like 6am – though the shuttle doesn't start until 7am), pack lots of water and bring a flashlight, because you may wind up hiking home in the dark.

Climbing gear is unnecessary. Instead, hikers haul themselves up the final 650ft to the summit between two steel cables. Climbing this stretch is only allowed when the cable route is open, usually late May to mid-October, depending on snow

---

❶ MANDATORY HALF DOME PERMITS

To stem lengthy lines (and increasingly dangerous conditions) on the vertiginous cables of Half Dome, the park now requires that all hikers obtain an advance permit to climb the cables. There are currently three ways to do this, though check www.nps.gov/yose/planyourvisit/hdpermits.htm for the latest information. Rangers check permits at the base of the cables.

Preseason permit lottery (☏ 877-444-6777; www.recreation.gov; application fee online/by phone $4.50/6.50) Lottery applications for 225 day-hiking spots must be completed in March, with confirmation notification sent in mid-April; an additional $8 per person charge confirms the permit. Applications can include up to six people and seven alternate dates.

Daily lottery Approximately 50 additional day-hiking permits are distributed by lottery two days before each hiking date. Apply online or by phone between midnight and 1pm Pacific Time; notification available late that same evening. It's easier to score weekday permits.

Backpackers Those with Yosemite-issued wilderness permits that *reasonably include* Half Dome can request Half Dome permits ($8 per person) without going through the lottery process. Backpackers with wilderness permits from a National Forest or another park can use that permit to climb the cables as long as their route also reasonably includes the area.

Half Dome and Vernal & Nevada Falls

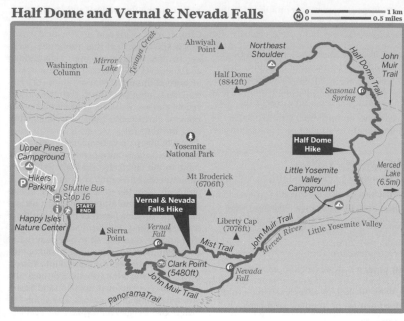

conditions. If planning an early-season or late-season trip, confirm ahead that the cables are in place.

Start at Happy Isles and ascend to the top of **Nevada Fall** on either the John Muir or Mist Trails. Continue over a low rise to level **Little Yosemite Valley**, which boasts views of Half Dome's south side. You'll also find solar composting toilets, bear boxes and a seasonal ranger station, all welcome features at the well-used campground, which is one of the park's most heavily visited areas.

From the west end of Little Yosemite Valley, the Merced Lake Trail heads east along the river to the Merced Lake High Sierra Camp. Stay on the John Muir Trail, which turns north and climbs steeply through forest 1.3 miles to the Half Dome Trail junction, just 2 miles from the summit.

Take the left fork onto the Half Dome Trail. Just above the junction on the left is a hard-to-spot seasonal spring – the last source of water en route (filter or treat it). Continue on through forest and then up switchbacks to the northeast shoulder (7600ft), an alternative camping spot with spectacular views. Visit the summit at sunset and sunrise for exquisite solitude.

From here, a rocky trail snakes 650ft up two dozen switchbacks to a notch at the base of the **cables**. The twin steel cables are draped from posts bolted into the granite on the final 600ft ascent up an exposed 45-degree rock face. There are gloves available to protect your hands, and intermittent wooden cross-boards provide footholds. A trip in light crowds takes only 15 minutes, but on crowded cables (or if you're jittery), expect it to take much longer. 'Sharing the road' will be your biggest challenge.

A word of caution: do *not* ascend the cables if there's any chance of a storm. The exposed summit is no place to be when lightning strikes (should you have any doubts, read Bob Madgic's *Shattered Air;* 2005), nor do you want to get stuck halfway up with your hands wrapped around virtual lightning rods.

The **summit** is fairly flat and about five acres in size. From here, enjoy amazing views of Yosemite Valley, Mt Starr King, Clouds Rest, the Cathedral Range and the Sierra Crest. Camping on the summit is prohibited, and as tempting as it is to linger, watch the time carefully to avoid a hazardous descent in darkness.

If no wilderness permits are available from Happy Isles, other good starting points include Tenaya Lake and Glacier Point, the latter leading you along the gorgeous Panorama Trail.

Glacier Point & Badger Pass

Trails from the south and east side of Glacier Point Rd wind into some of Yosemite's largest wilderness tracts. Serious backpackers interested in longer hauls can explore such rugged areas as the Merced headwaters or the Clark Range, along the park's southeast border.

🕅 Ostrander Lake

Duration 2 days

Distance 12.4-mile round-trip

Difficulty Moderate–Difficult

Start/Finish Ostrander Lake Trailhead

Nearest Junction Bridalveil Creek Campground

Transportation Car

Summary A deservedly popular out-and-back trek to an atmospheric stone ski hut. A gorgeous granite-bowl lake cuts into the forest, with water perfect for a brisk dip.

Sure this trail is doable as a day hike, but what's the rush? Doing the trek over two days gives you the chance to check out regenerating forest, enjoy wildflowers and spy some wild strawberries.

Park at the Ostrander Lake Trailhead lot (just over a mile east of Bridalveil Creek Campground road) and use the bear boxes to stockpile any food that you're not packing in. You soon cross over a footbridge and the level trail starts through a swath of burned-through **lodgepole forest**. The trail, remaining level, fords through purple, yellow and white banks of waist-high wildflowers, ecstatic bees and ground-hugging wild strawberries.

The hiking path that you're following was once a jeep road, but it is now also a winter route to the Ostrander Ski Hut, and yellow and orange cross-country ski markings are posted on trees the whole way there.

At almost 2 miles, bear left at a signed junction. Another junction comes within a mile, and once again bear left, following the trail sign to Ostrander Lake. The right-hand side trail goes to Wawona, among other places. A climb gears up slowly, and Horizon Ridge appears to your left (east) through the skeletons of burned-out trees and the dainty little puffs of young fir trees. The climb becomes steeper, but a clearing just past the ridge offers energizing views, just when you need the extra encouragement. The jagged Clark Range perches to the northeast, and you can spy on Basket Dome, North Dome and Half Dome as well. In approximately a

Ostrander Lake

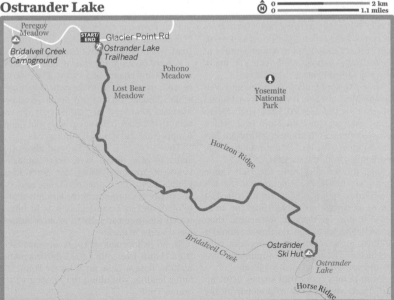

half-mile, the pitched roof of the handcrafted stone **Ostrander Ski Hut** comes into view, framed by **Ostrander Lake** with a slope of rock boulders tumbling down its far shore from Horse Ridge.

You can trace the lake's western bank to find established campsites, and then cool off with a refreshing dip in the lake. When you're ready, you can return following the same trail.

Big Oak Flat Road & Tioga Road

Sometimes the best way to appreciate the beauty of Yosemite Valley is to sneak up on it from above. The Old Big Oak Flat Rd to Yosemite Falls hike skirts the Valley's northern perimeter, while the Tenaya Lake to Yosemite Valley hike drops down from Tioga Rd.

🥾 Old Big Oak Flat Road to Yosemite Falls

Duration 2 days

Distance 18.8 miles one way

Difficulty Difficult

Start Old Big Oak Flat Trailhead

Finish Yosemite Falls Trailhead

Nearest Junction Crane Flat gas station

Transportation Tuolumne Meadows hikers' bus

Summary Climb up to bird's-eye views of Yosemite Valley, Half Dome and the Clark Range on a trail that never gets crowded. Spend the night on top of El Capitan before descending Yosemite Falls.

When planning for this hike, note that some creeks along the way can be difficult to cross during peak spring runoff (Tamarack is the hardest), but run dry in summer. Unless you don't mind carrying in *all* your water, this is best done as a late-spring trip. Ask at the Yosemite Valley or Big Oak Flat wilderness centers about the status of water sources and creek levels en route.

DAY 1: OLD BIG OAK FLAT ROAD TRAILHEAD TO EL CAPITAN
7–8 HOURS / 10.1 MILES

From Yosemite Valley, get the Tuolumne Meadows hikers' bus to drop you a quarter-mile west of Foresta turnoff on Big Oak Flat Rd, in the 'Old Big Oak Flat Rd' parking lot. The trailhead (across the street) begins with switchbacks, climbing through an area charred first by the 1990 Foresta fire and then retorched for good measure by the 2009 Big Meadow fire.

Old Big Oak Flat Road to Yosemite Falls

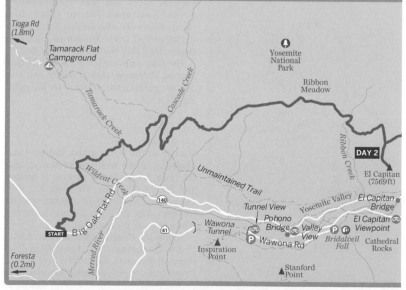

Over 4 miles, cross Wildcat Creek and then Tamarack Creek (a more challenging crossing with heavy runoff) before coming to a junction at a footbridge. To the left, it's just over 2 miles to Tamarack Flat Campground via the Old Big Oak Flat Rd. Instead continue right (southeast), crossing the footbridge over Cascade Creek. In a half mile, go left (northeast) at a junction and leave the spotty asphalt remains of the Old Big Oak Flat Rd, which continues fitfully down to the Valley through the Rockslides area, and is not maintained. The path is forested with red fir, Jeffrey pine and canyon live oak. Pass through **Ribbon Meadow**, with corn lilies and, in wet years, many mosquitoes. Cross Ribbon Creek and veer a quarter-mile south off the trail to camp on the sandy top of **El Capitan** (at just over 10 miles). Camp at an existing site to avoid trampling the undergrowth. At eye level, the surrounding peaks look like frothy waves, with the iconic Half Dome to the east. It's a stunning viewpoint to see the evening alpenglow.

DAY 2: EL CAPITAN TO YOSEMITE FALLS
6–7 HOURS / 8.7 MILES

Rejoin the trail and continue east for 1.7 miles to the **Three Brothers**. A half-mile jut takes you to **Eagle Peak** (7779ft), the upper of the trio, with more awesome and dizzying

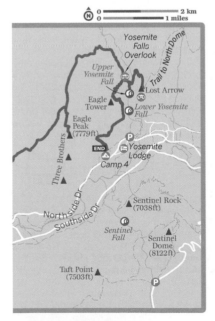

views of the Valley and the Clark Range. Continue northeast and, at the junction of the Yosemite Creek Trail, turn south to reach the top of **Yosemite Falls** in about a half-mile. It's 3.6 miles down more than a hundred switchbacks and 2700ft of knee-knocking descent to the Valley floor.

Tenaya Lake to Yosemite Valley

Duration 2 days

Distance 17.1 miles one way

Difficulty Difficult

Start Sunrise Lakes Trailhead

Finish Happy Isles

Nearest Town Tuolumne Meadows

Transportation Tuolumne Meadows hikers' bus; Tuolumne Meadows shuttle stop 10; YARTS Hwy 120/395 bus

Summary Instead of driving between Tioga Rd and Yosemite Valley, why not hike it? The Tenaya Lake to Yosemite Valley hike is one of the classics, allowing you an up-close look at the major landscape changes.

The most spectacular trail from Tioga Rd to Yosemite Valley traverses the summit of **Clouds Rest** (9926ft), arguably Yosemite's finest panoramic viewpoint. An easier variation bypasses Clouds Rest and follows Sunrise Creek. Both hikes descend through Little Yosemite Valley and pass world-renowned Nevada and Vernal Falls to Happy Isles. Hearty hikers can also include a side trip to the top of Half Dome. On stormy days, steer clear of both Half Dome and Clouds Rest.

The trailheads are almost 50 miles apart by road. Unless you plan to shuttle two vehicles, use public transportation for the uphill leg of the hike.

DAY 1: TENAYA LAKE TO LITTLE YOSEMITE VALLEY
8–10 HOURS / 12.3 MILES

Start from the well-marked Sunrise Lakes Trailhead, at the west end of Tenaya Lake off Tioga Rd. Trailhead parking is limited, and the lot fills early. Those leaving from Tuolumne Meadows can instead use the free Tuolumne to Olmsted Point shuttle bus, which stops at the trailhead.

Follow the Clouds Rest hike (p63) for the trail to the summit. From there, head down steps off the south side to the ridge below. In 0.6 miles there's a signed junction with

Tenaya Lake to Yosemite Valley

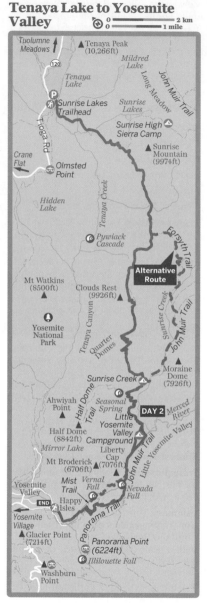

At 3.8 miles from the summit of Clouds Rest, you'll reach the marked junction with the John Muir Trail (7200ft). Nearby **Sunrise Creek** offers several forested campsites and provides the first water since well before Clouds Rest. Turn west onto the John Muir Trail and descend a half-mile to the signed junction with the heavily traveled Half Dome Trail. Go south 1.3 miles to the established and busy campsites in **Little Yosemite Valley** (6100ft) along the Merced River. Beware: both Sunrise Creek and Little Yosemite Valley experience chronic problems with bears.

ALTERNATIVE ROUTE: TENAYA LAKE TO LITTLE YOSEMITE VALLEY VIA FORSYTH & JOHN MUIR TRAILS
7–9 HOURS / 10.9 MILES

Those not inclined to visit the Clouds Rest summit can follow an easier, forested alternative trail along Sunrise Creek, which eventually meets the trail from Clouds Rest and descends to Little Yosemite Valley.

To begin, follow the Day 1 description for 4.7 miles to the signed junction (9100ft) with the Clouds Rest and Forsyth Trails. Bear southeast and follow the Forsyth Trail across a meadow into the pine and granite landscape. The trail leads down a slope of red firs, offering good views of the Clark Range, Merced Canyon and Mt Starr King. Follow Sunrise Creek until a slight ascent takes you to the marked junction (8000ft) with the John Muir Trail, also known here as the Sunrise Trail. Go southwest on the John Muir Trail 0.1 miles to another junction, where a trail to Merced Lake heads east. Stay on the John Muir Trail, heading west along Sunrise Creek, then descend switchbacks to the junction (7200ft) with the Clouds Rest Trail. Continue a half-mile to the busy Half Dome Trail, then turn south and descend the John Muir Trail to Little Yosemite Valley.

DAY 2: LITTLE YOSEMITE VALLEY TO HAPPY ISLES VIA THE JOHN MUIR TRAIL
2–3 HOURS / 4.8 MILES

Today you can follow either the Mist Trail or the John Muir Trail some 1065ft down to Happy Isles in Yosemite Valley. We recommend the John Muir Trail because the granite steps on the Mist Trail tend to pound your knees on the descent. If you do take the Mist Trail, it's 3.9 miles to Happy Isles.

From Little Yosemite Valley, follow the John Muir Trail for 0.5 miles, where it traces the Merced River and then contours to the

a bypass trail for horses. Continue straight, down through pines, chinquapins and manzanitas. Pass beneath granite domes and continue the descent on switchbacks. Near the bottom of the 2726ft descent, the trail enters shady forest.

Lyell Canyon

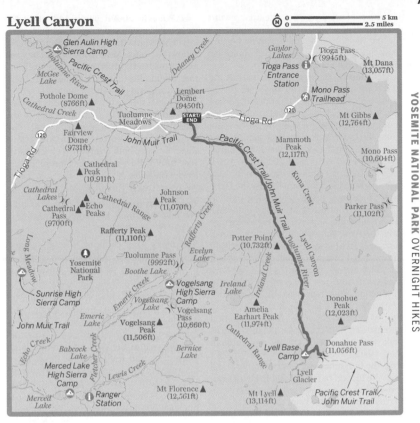

south of Liberty Cap. At 1.1 miles, meet the Mist Trail (and follow it to the right, if you wish). Continue southwest along the John Muir Trail, fording the footbridge over the rushing Merced at **Nevada Fall**. Pass the junction with the Panorama Trail and, at approximately 4 miles, cross the river again. From here it's less than a mile to the trailhead, walking along the eastern riverbank.

Tuolumne Meadows

Several of day hikes can also be extended into overnight excursions, including Cathedral Lakes and Glen Aulin.

🏃 Lyell Canyon

Duration 2 days

Distance 17.6-mile round-trip

Difficulty Easy–Moderate

Start/Finish Lyell Canyon Trailhead at Dog Lake parking lot

Nearest Town Tuolumne Meadows

Transportation Tuolumne Meadows hikers' bus; Tuolumne Meadows shuttle stop 1 or 3; YARTS Hwy 120/395 bus

Summary This flat section of the John Muir Trail meanders deep into Lyell Canyon to the base of Mt Lyell, the park's highest peak. Fishing, relaxing, views and side trips are all excellent.

If destinations such as Cathedral Lake and Nevada Fall slap you in the face with their shockingly good looks, Lyell Canyon gently rolls its beauty over you like a blanket on a cool day. The Lyell Canyon trail takes you through a special place, along a section of the John Muir Trail as it follows the Lyell Fork of the Tuolumne River through a gorgeous subalpine meadow hemmed in by tree-covered granite peaks. The final reward is the view of Lyell Peak and its eponymous glacier, towering over the meadow beyond Donohue Pass. This is also a great choice for those who loathe uphill climbs.

If you drove, the best place to park is the Dog Lake parking lot, off the road to Tuolumne Meadows Lodge. If that's full, park in the Tuolumne Meadows Wilderness Center parking lot, further west on the same road. From the latter, look for a trail sign reading 'John Muir Trail' and walk southeast, paralleling the road. After about 0.2 miles, you'll pass the trail that comes down from the Dog Lake parking lot. Soon, you'll cross the Dana Fork (Tuolumne River) by bearing right at a junction (continuing straight would take you to the lodge) and crossing the footbridge over the river. Soon you'll hit another junction; veer right toward Donohue Pass (hint: always head toward Donohue Pass). About 0.5 miles further, you'll cross the Lyell Fork over two footbridges and come to yet another junction. This time, bear left.

Another 0.5 miles on, the trail passes the Vogelsang/Yosemite Valley junction and crosses Rafferty Creek. Finally it turns southeast into **Lyell Canyon**, and you can start paying attention to the scenery rather than the trail junctions. After 4.2 miles you'll pass the turnoff to Ireland and Evelyn Lakes, cross Ireland Creek and pass beneath the inverted cone of Potter Point (10,732ft).

If you wish to camp in Lyell Canyon – a highlight of any Yosemite trip – you'll find several campsites alongside the river; just make sure you're at least 4 miles from the trailhead. Basically, anything south of Ireland Creek is fine. Some of the best campsites are about 0.5 miles before the head of the canyon, where you can see Mt Lyell (13,114ft) looming over the southeast end of the meadow. There are campsites on both sides of the river and above the trail. Once you start heading up the 'staircase' at the head of the canyon, campsites are few until you reach Lyell Base Camp, a busy climbers' camp below Donohue Pass.

You can take a day-long side trip to the summit of **Mt Lyell**, but only experienced climbers should attempt it. The ascent alone gains over 4000ft, and the difficult route traverses a glacier, involves steep and complex climbs, and requires safety ropes. Another option is setting up your own base camp in the canyon and continuing another few miles up the John Muir Trail to **Dono-hue Pass** (a 2000ft climb), admiring the impressive peaks and glaciers along the way.

On your second day, the task is simple: follow the John Muir Trail along the Lyell Fork back to the trailhead.

🏃 Young Lakes

Duration 2 days

Distance 13-mile round-trip

Difficulty Moderate

Start/Finish Dog Lake Trailhead near Lembert Dome parking lot

Nearest Town Tuolumne Meadows

Transportation Tuolumne Meadows hikers' bus; Tuolumne Meadows shuttle stop 4; YARTS Hwy 120/395 bus

Summary After climbing through forests of lodgepole pines, this trail opens up to offer sweeping views of the Cathedral Range before reaching shimmering Young Lakes, at the base of gnarly Ragged Peak.

DAY 1: TRAILHEAD TO YOUNG LAKES
3–4 HOURS / 6.2 MILES

Set at elevations between 9950ft and 10,050ft, the three Young Lakes make for a vigorous day hike but offer much more – particularly at sunrise and sunset – to those who make an overnight journey out of it. If the permit quota for Cathedral Lakes is full, this is a good alternative. Some walkers knock this off their favorite-hikes list because much of it is through pine forest, meaning fewer vistas. But the rewards at the lakes above make up for this tenfold.

Starting from the Lembert Dome parking lot, follow the Dog Lake trail into the trees, with Lembert Dome on your right. After 1.3 miles you'll pass the trail to Lembert Dome. After another 0.3 miles, you'll hit the junction to 9240ft **Dog Lake**, good for a quick detour and snack stop.

Back on the Young Lakes trail, you'll ascend gradually to about 9400ft before descending to **Delaney Creek**, which burbles along the edge of a lovely meadow. Cross Delaney Creek and follow the trail across the meadow and around the western side of a granite peak. Shortly thereafter, the trail meanders into a clearing and you'll see snarled Ragged Peak to the north. After entering a gently sloping meadow spotted with wildflowers and stunted whitebark pines, you're presented with a magnificent view to the south: the entire Cathedral Range and all its

Young Lakes

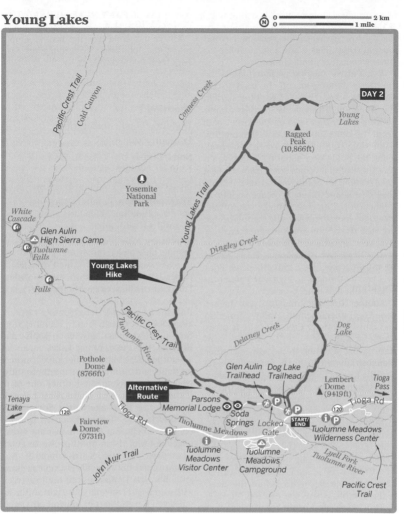

major peaks, including Cathedral Peak, Unicorn Peak and Echo Peaks (with Cockscomb just behind Unicorn). To the far left stands Mt Lyell (13,114ft), Yosemite's highest peak.

Cross **Dingley Creek** (a good spot to fill up the water bottles), and follow the trail over a small crest, with Ragged Peak on your right. The trail winds down through the pines and boulders to meet a junction (the return route). Keep to your right and continue around the northwest shoulder of Ragged Peak until, after 1.5 miles from the junction, you arrive at the lowest of the **Young Lakes**. There are numerous places to

camp along the northwest shore, and trees offer shade and shelter from any wind that might pick up. The lake itself sits within a sort of granite amphitheater formed by the northern flanks of Ragged Peak, which takes on a fiery golden glow at sunset, lighting up the lake with its reflection in the water.

From the northeast side of the lake, a trail leads up to **middle Young Lake**. From the middle lake's eastern shore, the trail climbs alongside a pretty waterfall – with one short section of easy scrambling alongside it – before reaching a meadow and gently sloping down to the third, **upper Young Lake**. It's a truly stunning alpine setting boasting marvelous views in every direction. There are a couple of campsites eked out above the northwestern shore.

DAY 2: YOUNG LAKES TO TRAILHEAD
3–4 HOURS / 6.8 MILES

To return from lower Young Lake, follow the same trail out until, after 1.5 miles from Young Lake, you reach the junction you passed on the way up. Stay to your right. The views are less impressive along the return trail, but it makes for variation. After 3.7 miles of mostly downhill walking you'll join the Pacific Crest Trail (PCT). After crossing Delaney Creek, the trail becomes extremely worn, sandy and mule-trodden. At a junction you can either stay to your left to reach the Lembert Dome parking lot, or head to your right to visit Soda Springs.

🚶 Vogelsang

Duration 3 days

Distance 27-mile round-trip

Difficulty Moderate–Difficult

Start/Finish Lyell Canyon Trailhead from Dog Lake parking lot

Nearest Town Tuolumne Meadows

Transportation Tuolumne Meadows hikers' bus; Tuolumne Meadows shuttle stop 1 or 3

Summary This exquisite but very popular semi-loop crosses Tuolumne and Vogelsang Passes through Yosemite's Cathedral Range, offering a remarkable circuit through John Muir's 'Range of Light.'

The sloping subalpine meadows and streams on either side of gentle Tuolumne Pass (9992ft) provide a scenic backdrop for some of the Sierra Nevada's most delightful hiking. The trail takes in multiple cascades and sweeping views of distant peaks in several mountain ranges, including the hard-to-see Clark Range. Camping at Vogelsang Lake and crossing the alpine Vogelsang Pass (10,660ft) rank among the highlights of this journey around Vogelsang Peak.

Vogelsang Peak, Lake and Pass, and High Sierra Camp, all take their name from the Vogelsang brothers, who headed the California Fish and Game Board from 1896 to 1910. The name itself translates aptly from German as 'a meadow where birds sing.'

DAY 1: LYELL CANYON TRAILHEAD TO VOGELSANG LAKE
4–6 HOURS / 7.2 MILES

On Day 1, follow the Lyell Canyon hike to the Pacific Crest/John Muir Trail. After 0.8 miles, at Rafferty Creek, turn south, leaving the John Muir Trail; the 2½-hour, 4.9-mile ascent along Rafferty Creek begins with a rugged uphill climb. Gouged out by the steel-shod hooves of packhorses and mules that supply the Vogelsang High Sierra Camp, the trail clambers over granite steps and cobblestones through forest for some 20 to 30 minutes before it eases and nears Rafferty Creek's left bank. To the north you'll see Mt Conness and White Mountain, while the Lyell Fork Meadows spread out some 500ft below to the east.

With the steepest part of the trail now behind you, you'll gradually ascend an attractive little valley, following the west bank of Rafferty Creek. The forested trail gently climbs, then enters a small open meadow. Passing beneath lodgepole pines and crossing several smaller streams, the well-worn trail finally emerges into a lovely meadow along Rafferty Creek. Finally, 6.1 miles from the trailhead, you'll arrive at gentle **Tuolumne Pass** (9992ft).

At the signed Tuolumne Pass junction, take the left fork and head southeast. The trail offers enticing views of Boothe Lake and the granite ridge above it as it travels 0.8 miles to Vogelsang High Sierra Camp (10,130ft). At a signed junction, a backpackers' campground lies to the left (east), while the trail to the right (west) descends to Merced Lake High Sierra Camp. Instead, continue straight (south) toward Vogelsang Pass. About 0.5 miles beyond the High Sierra Camp you'll reach large **Vogelsang Lake** (10,341ft), set in a picture-perfect cirque beneath Fletcher and Vogelsang Peaks. Above the northeast shore are campsites set among whitebark pines.

DAY 2: VOGELSANG LAKE TO EMERIC LAKE
5–7 HOURS / 10.2 MILES

The trail ascends above the southwest end of Vogelsang Lake, eventually crossing a large, cold stream just below its spring-fed source. The view of the lake below and Cathedral Range beyond is sublime. Five minutes' walk further you'll reach **Vogelsang Pass** (10,660ft), in the serrated granite ridge that descends from Vogelsang Peak (11,506ft).

Vogelsang

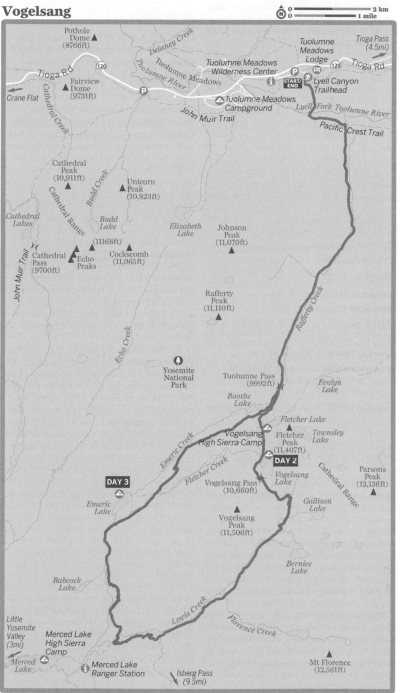

From here the trail rises a bit and provides a long view of the upper Lewis Creek Basin. Lovely Gallison Lake, surrounded by meadow, issues forth a cascading stream. Large Bernice Lake spreads out at the base of a massive granite ridge beneath Mt Florence (12,561ft). Half a dozen more lakes lie hidden in a chain above Gallison Lake, fed by permanent snow from the slopes of Simmons Peak (12,503ft) at the valley's head. To the southwest is the more distant Clark Range, sweeping from the west to the southeast.

Descend the switchbacks that follow the course of a small stream. At the base, enter a forest along the level valley floor. Streams course across the meadow, involving a few crossings. Continue straight past the Bernice Lake junction, heading downstream along Lewis Creek as the descent grows steeper.

Three miles from Bernice Lake trail junction, you'll pass the Isberg Pass trail junction. Continue on 1 mile through a dramatic canyon for a view of distant Half Dome before passing the signed Merced Lake trail junction (8160ft). Turn north at the junction and follow the trail up Fletcher Creek. After crossing a footbridge, the trail climbs beside the creek, crosses several side streams and climbs high above the left bank of Fletcher Creek. The trail levels out about one hour past the footbridge, offering a fabulous vista over Merced Canyon and the Clark Range.

Leaving the views behind, head beneath lodgepole pines past the signed Babcock Lake trail junction. In 2 miles, the trail emerges in a lovely meadow and finally hits a four-way trail junction. Turn northwest and head 0.4 miles to the large Emeric Lake (9338ft). Cross its inlet to reach good campsites above the northwest shore.

DAY 3: EMERIC LAKE TO LYELL CANYON TRAILHEAD
4½–5 HOURS / 9.1 MILES

On Day 3, retrace your steps to the four-way junction. Turn north on the route to Boothe Lake (rather than the heavily used trail to Vogelsang High Sierra Camp). This lovely lake, which lies 2.7 miles from the junction, was the original site of the High Sierra Camp before the camp was moved and renamed Vogelsang. The trail stays well above the lake, where camping is prohibited. Arrive once again at Tuolumne Pass, 0.4 miles beyond Boothe Lake. From here, retrace your steps: 4.9 miles down Rafferty Creek to the John Muir Trail and 1.1 miles to the Lyell Canyon Trailhead.

🏃 Waterwheel Falls

Duration 2 days

Distance 18-mile round-trip

Difficulty Difficult

Start/Finish Glen Aulin Trailhead near Lembert Dome parking lot

Nearest Town Tuolumne Meadows

Transportation Tuolumne Meadows hikers' bus; Tuolumne Meadows shuttle stop 4; YARTS Hwy 120/395 bus

Summary Follow this hike along the Grand Canyon of the Tuolumne River to Waterwheel Falls. It's the last and most impressive of six cascades along the river, before it plunges into the canyon on its descent toward Hetch Hetchy Reservoir.

For the first several miles of the hike, follow the Pacific Crest Trail (PCT) to Glen Aulin. About 0.2 miles after Tuolumne Falls, head northwest along the trail to Waterwheel Falls, which is 3.3 miles downstream from where you leave the PCT. The trail meanders through ghost forest to the river's edge, inviting a dip in the placid waters, then crosses an area made marshy by a stream that descends from Cold Mountain to the north.

In just over a mile, you'll reach the far end of the peaceful glen, where the river flows briskly to the brink of the first in a series of near continual cascades. The trail, too, plunges along the river, dropping over gorgeous orange-tinted granite. Ahead, the Grand Canyon of the Tuolumne stretches as far as the eye can see. The trail continues between the sheer, polished granite walls of Wildcat Point (9455ft) to the north and the 8000ft granite wall of Falls Ridge on the opposite bank. California Falls and LeConte Falls are the most prominent cascades in this section; most are unnamed. If you have to ask yourself, 'Is this Waterwheel Falls?' keep going – you'll know it when you see it.

About 2 miles beyond the glen, you'll reach a small unsigned junction where a spur trail branches southwest to a viewpoint of Waterwheel Falls. The obvious roar tells you this is the spot, although the falls remain hidden from view. From the main trail, walk to the edge of the massive falls, named for the distinctive 15ft- to 20ft-high plumes of water that curl into the air like a wheel midway down the more than 600ft-long falls.

Waterwheel Falls

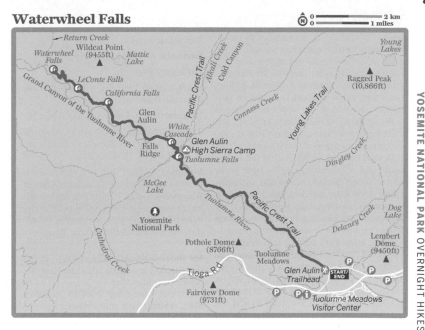

After admiring the cascade, return to the main trail, turn west, and descend another 10 minutes. As you approach the scattered junipers beside an obvious dark granite rib perpendicular to the trail, turn south and head down a sandy slope through manzanita, following a trail that parallels the rocky rib. It leads to a large, forested campsite (6440ft) that's partly visible from the main trail above. Camp beneath big ponderosa pines and incense cedars, about 0.3 miles below Waterwheel Falls, with the green and tranquil Tuolumne River about 200ft away.

On day two, retrace your steps 9 miles to the trailhead.

Hetch Hetchy

Hetch Hetchy offers some excellent backpacking opportunities, as well as access to some of the park's most remote areas, north of the reservoir. Summers can be brutally hot, which is why the trails out here are busiest in spring and fall.

🚶 Rancheria Falls

Duration 7 hours–2 days

Distance 13-mile round-trip

Difficulty Moderate–Difficult

Start/Finish Rancheria Falls Trailhead, O'Shaughnessy Dam

Nearest Junction Evergreen Lodge

Transportation Car

Summary This classic Hetch Hetchy hike passes the spectacular Tueeulala and Wapama Falls, then takes you to the gentler Rancheria Falls, where swimming holes abound and the scenery is outrageous.

Rancheria Falls is doable as a day hike, but it's best enjoyed as an overnighter, allowing you to experience sunset over Rancheria Creek and Hetch Hetchy Reservoir. This part of Yosemite can be brutally hot in summer and, like the Tueeulala and Wapama Falls hike, is best in the spring. Still, it can be rewarding in July and even August, despite the heat, thanks to fewer people and the excellent swimming holes near the falls. Watch out for poison oak along the trail.

Follow the hike to **Wapama Falls**. After the falls, the trail climbs into the shade of black oaks and laurels, offering relief from the sun. It then ascends a series of switchbacks and skirts around the base of **Hetch Hetchy Dome** (6197ft), passing two epic viewpoints over the reservoir on the way. Alternately

Rancheria Falls

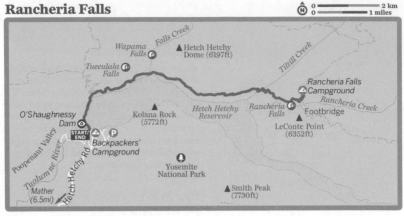

climbing and falling through shaded oak forest and hot, exposed stretches, the trail finally arrives at two footbridges over **Tiltill Creek**, which mark the end of the no-camping zone.

After climbing up from Tiltill Creek, you'll get your first glimpse of **Rancheria Falls** as they shoot down a granite apron into the reservoir below. Camping below the falls looks inviting but, because the area has become so impacted, it's best to continue 0.25 miles further to the established Rancheria Falls Campground.

After chucking your sack and pitching your tent, walk further up the trail, past the Tiltill Valley junction (stay to your right) to the footbridge over **Rancheria Creek**. During summer, when the water levels are low, there are two superb emerald-green swimming holes set in a chasm of granite, both with rock- and bridge-jumping opportunities for the adventurous. The views of Rancheria Creek and the reservoir from here are sublime. To return on day two, retrace your steps.

🚗 DRIVING

Driving is hardly the proper way to see Yosemite Valley (unless you enjoy craning your neck in traffic to see the sights otherwise blocked by your roof), but it's an undeniably superb way to experience the high country – and beyond – via the spectacular Tioga Rd. This is the only road that bisects the park between its eastern and western borders. All park roads, however, are lined with beautiful scenery, so really you can't go wrong. If you're going to drive within Yosemite Valley, try to avoid doing it on weekends.

🚗 Yosemite Valley

Duration Varies depending on traffic

Distance 12.5-mile round-trip

Start/Finish Yosemite Village

Nearest Town Yosemite Village

Transportation Shuttle or car

Summary The only driving route in Yosemite Valley takes you past the Valley's classic sights and viewpoints, including Bridalveil Fall and Yosemite Falls.

This entire route is covered by the free Valley and El Capitan shuttles, so consider parking the car, freeing up your hands, and doing this by public transportation so you're not adding to the Valley gridlock. Note that the El Capitan shuttle has more limited service – every 30 minutes – but a set schedule.

This loop follows the only two roads in and out of Yosemite Valley: Northside Dr and Southside Dr. Each is (mostly) one way and, as their names suggest, they sit on either side of the Merced River. Without traffic, you can easily drive this loop in less than an hour, but budget more time as you'll want to stop frequently.

Starting in Yosemite Village, head west on Northside Dr, which leads past Yosemite Falls, the Three Brothers (Lower, Middle and Eagle Peak) and El Capitan to **Valley View** (roadside marker V11), a great viewpoint along the Merced River. To complete the loop, turn left (south) at the Pohono Bridge, just past Valley View, and cross the Merced River. Then head east on Southside

Yosemite Valley

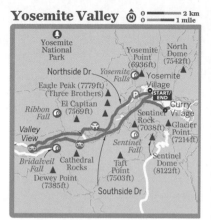

N 0 — 2 km
0 — 1 mile

Yosemite National Park

Yosemite Point (6936ft)

North Dome (7542ft)

Northside Dr *Yosemite Falls* START/END Yosemite Village

Eagle Peak (7779ft) (Three Brothers)

El Capitan (7569ft)

Ribbon Fall

Curry Village

Sentinel Rock (7038ft)

Glacier Point (7214ft)

Valley View

Sentinel Fall

Bridalveil Fall Cathedral Rocks

Taft Point (7503ft)

Sentinel Dome (8122ft)

Dewey Point (7385ft)

Southside Dr

Dr back toward Yosemite Village. From that road you get wider views of Yosemite Falls and El Capitan on the north rim and a closer look at south rim features such as Cathedral Rocks, Sentinel Rock and Bridalveil Fall. You also drive by the site of **old Yosemite Village**, near where Yosemite Valley Chapel now sits. The road dead-ends just past Curry Village, or you can turn at Sentinel Bridge back toward Yosemite Village.

CYCLING

Bikes are prohibited from all hiking trails within Yosemite, so you'll need to stick to roads and bike paths. Moderate-level bike rides within Yosemite, which is dominated by steep grades except in Yosemite Valley, are few and far between. Generally it's either easy (ie the Valley) or difficult (everywhere else).

Many people bicycle along formidable **Tioga Rd**, though it's not a route for the casual cyclist. If you succumb to the temptation, keep in mind that this winding, climbing route has many blind spots and often fields a lot of traffic. It's a tough, relentless grind, so start riding early in the morning and keep well hydrated. From Crane Flat, it's just under 100 miles to Tioga Pass and back. In late spring, before plowing is complete at Olmsted Point, the road on either side of it is usually open to cyclists for a week or so before the road reopens to cars.

Glacier Point Rd, a 32-mile round-trip from the Chinquapin junction, is another option for a longer ride. The pavement's smooth,

the traffic is usually not too heavy and the vistas at Glacier Point are worth the climbs.

Bicycle Rentals

If you can't bring your own bike, stands at Yosemite Lodge and Curry Village rent single-speed beach cruisers (per hour/day $12/34) or bikes with an attached child trailer (per hour/day $20.50/63). You're required to leave either a driver's license or credit card for collateral. Neither location accepts reservations, but you should be fine if you arrive before 11am or so.

Yosemite Valley Loops

Duration 1–3 hours

Distance Up to 12 miles round-trip

Difficulty Easy

Start/Finish Yosemite Lodge

Nearest Town Yosemite Village

Transportation Shuttle stop 8

Summary Whether done in segments or in its entirety, this easy pedal around the floor of Yosemite Valley is as relaxing as it gets – and the views are amazing.

Twelve miles of paved, mostly flat bicycle paths run up and down the length of Yosemite Valley, making for some very relaxed and superbly enjoyable peddling, whether you're solo or a family of five. The free Yosemite Valley hiking map provided at the Yosemite Valley Visitor Center shows the bike route in detail, and it's easy to whip out while riding.

You can pick up the bike path near just about anywhere you're staying in the Valley. Most people start where they rent bikes at either Curry Village or Yosemite Lodge. From the latter, follow the path down to the riverside, past the lodge buildings, across a meadow and west to **Swinging Bridge** (which actually doesn't swing at all). Cross over the Merced River, veer east along Southside Dr, take in the magnificent view of Yosemite Falls, then Half Dome. Soon you'll pass Curry Village, the Royal Arches will appear on your left and you'll finally hit the road to Happy Isles. Pass the **Nature Center at Happy Isles** and continue along the road to loop around to North Pines Campground. Cross the Merced again, then cut north to Northside Dr, which you can follow back to Yosemite Lodge.

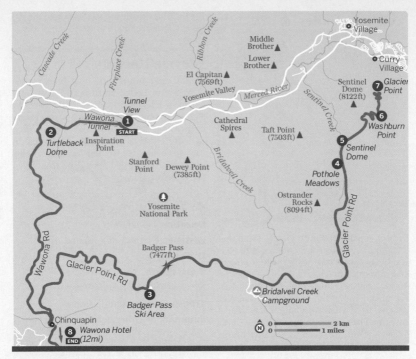

Driving Tour
Wawona Road & Glacier Point Road

START TUNNEL VIEW
END WAWONA HOTEL
LENGTH 52 MILES; TWO HOURS

Start your expedition from the east side of the Wawona Tunnel in the spectacular pull-off point of **1 Tunnel View**. No, you will not be staring slack-jawed at a dark traffic structure, but at the magnificent landscape to the east. Best in the spring when snowmelt has it gushing, 620ft Bridalveil Fall leaps off a plateau. When it thins out in summer, it sways like a string in the wind. The sheer wall of El Capitan rises to the north side of the Valley, and Half Dome pops out in the background past deep green forest.

Buckle up and head west through Wawona Tunnel, which is almost a mile long. Two miles after your return to daylight, you approach **2 Turtleback Dome**, a slab of exfoliating granite that looks like it's been sliced horizontally into pieces of crumbling bread.

In six more miles you'll come to the Chinquapin junction; turn left onto Glacier Point Rd to begin the forested 16-mile stretch to Glacier Point. In 2 miles is the wide western view of Merced Canyon, which descends 4500ft below you. The **3 Badger Pass Ski Area** appears in three more miles, though the lifts and lodge will be deserted in warm weather. In winter, the road is closed beyond here. Pass Bridalveil Creek Campground, with nearby views of the Clark Range to the east.

The road turns abruptly north near Mono Meadow, reaching **4 Pothole Meadows**, where strangely small bowls of water collect during wet months. A quarter-mile more lands you at the parking area for **5 Sentinel Dome** (8122ft), one of the park's easiest-to-hike granite domes. Switchbacks descend through red fir forest to **6 Washburn Point**, which has views *almost* as good as those from Glacier Point. Winding through into **7 Glacier Point**, the peak of Half Dome parades before you.

Double back to the Chinquapin junction, and turn left to continue south on the Wawona Rd (Hwy 41). The final 12-mile stretch crosses the South Fork of the Merced River before reaching the **8 Wawona Hotel**, a landmark lodging dating from 1879.

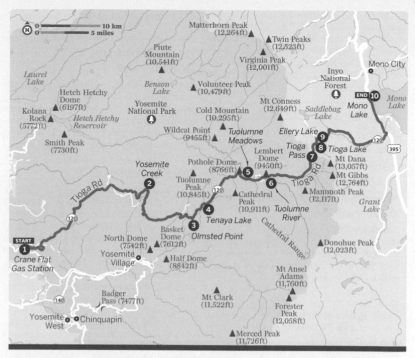

Driving Tour
Tioga Road to Mono Lake

START CRANE FLAT GAS STATION
END MONO LAKE
LENGTH 60 MILES; TWO TO FOUR HOURS

The highest elevation trans-Sierra highway and one of California's ultimate drives, Tioga Rd is open only during summer and fall, usually from late May to early November. Beginning at the ❶ **Crane Flat Gas Station**, follow signs for Hwy 120 East. Gas up if you need to, as the next opportunity isn't until the very end of this drive.

In half a mile you'll see the trailhead lot for Tuolumne Grove, one of the park's giant sequoia groves. The road begins to climb through evergreen forest, gaining almost 2000ft over 14 miles to the White Wolf turnoff road, a section of the crooked old Tioga Rd, completed in 1883. Cross over a segment of ❷ **Yosemite Creek** and imagine the flow you see leaping off Yosemite Falls a few miles downstream.

Almost 10 miles on is the spacious must-do overlook of ❸ **Olmsted Point**, with magnificent views of Half Dome and Tenaya Canyon

and interpretive displays about the geological masterpiece surrounding you. Granite domes buffer shimmering ❹ **Tenaya Lake**, with climbers dangling like spiders.

At 8600ft and the beauty queen of Yosemite's high country, wildflowers carpet verdant ❺ **Tuolumne Meadows**, and the spiky peaks of the Cathedral Range silhouette endless sky. Wedge-like Lembert Dome sits astride the ❻ **Tuolumne River**, whose waters make a lengthy journey to slake the thirst of San Francisco.

The road bears north in approximately 5 miles, skirting beautiful Dana Meadows at the approach to the road's dizzying apex, ❼ **Tioga Pass** (9945ft). The pinnacle of Mt Dana looms to the east as you exit the park, where you quickly pass the chilly waters of ❽ **Tioga Lake** and ❾ **Ellery Lake**.

The road straightens and reorients to the east as it descends relentlessly along the abyss of Lee Vining Canyon. Downshift to preserve your brakes. As you reach road's end at Hwy 395, surreal ❿ **Mono Lake** comes into view.

If you only have time for one section, the route from Yosemite Village to the Mirror Lake road is especially serene after it splits from Northside Dr. Widening, it passes through thick woods and travels over the Merced, out of sight of any traffic and most people.

⏚ Carlon to Hetch Hetchy

Duration 3–4 hours

Distance 34-mile round-trip

Difficulty Moderate

Start/Finish Carlon Falls Day Use Area

Nearest Junction Evergreen Lodge

Transportation Car

Summary With a gentle ascent to the Hetch Hetchy Entrance Station and an adrenaline-spiking descent to the reservoir, this ride offers fabulous views and a spectacular destination.

With relatively little traffic, this ride to Hetch Hetchy Reservoir offers a splendid way to take in the scenery along the northwest boundary of the park. Fuel up with a good picnic lunch at the reservoir: the return climb is much more strenuous than the exciting drop on the way there. In summer, it can get extremely hot out here, so get an early start. In spring, it's divine.

To get to the starting point, drive northwest on Evergreen Rd, which departs Hwy 120 about 1 mile west of the Big Oak Flat Entrance. About 1 mile after turning off, you'll see the **Carlon Day Use Area** at a bridge across the South Fork Tuolumne River. Park in the parking lot and ride out to Evergreen Rd, cross the bridge and you're off. The first 9.5 miles rise and fall fairly gently with a modest overall elevation gain of about 550ft, and you'll pass by wildflower meadows, weathered wooden farmhouses and intermittent forest char remaining from the 2013 Rim Fire. About 1.5 miles after the park entrance (which lies about 7 miles from Carlon), you'll hit the crest of the ride (topping out around 5000ft) and begin the 1205ft descent to the reservoir. The views over the Poopenaut Valley are outstanding – be sure to stop for a breather at one of the viewpoints.

After you reach the reservoir, gobble down your energy bars, take a deep breath and slog your way back to the car.

OTHER ACTIVITIES

Rock Climbing & Bouldering

When it comes to rock climbing, Yosemite reigns supreme. If you're new to climbing, consider taking a class at the Yosemite Mountaineering School. For more information on climbing within the park, see www.nps.gov/yose/planyourvisit/climbing.htm.

Yosemite Valley

First, know this: all ropes lead to Camp 4. Most of the Valley's climbing activity revolves around this walk-in campground and historic hangout for climbing's most legendary figures. Camp 4 is where you go when you want to stop reading and start asking real people questions about where to climb, what to carry and what to expect. It's also where you find climbing partners, pick up used gear (among other things) and find the car keys you left sitting at the base of the climb.

For many climbers, reaching the summit of El Capitan is a lifetime achievement, and hopefuls from around the world arrive to tackle its fabled routes.

As for bouldering, the possibilities are limitless. Popular areas include the west end of Camp 4, Sentinel Rock, the Four Mile Trail Trailhead, and the rocks near Housekeeping Camp and around Mirror Lake, to name only a few.

Big Oak Flat Road & Tioga Road

The big draw in these parts is Polly Dome, right next to Tenaya Lake. Stately Pleasure Dome, on the side of Polly adjacent to the lake, is the most popular spot, offering a good mix of easy and moderate routes. The granite rocks in this part of the park are well suited for slab and friction climbing, and both are well represented here.

For more difficult climbing, try the backside of Pywiack and Medlicott Domes, both just northeast of the lake toward Tuolumne Meadows. The beach at the east end of Tenaya Lake is an ideal spot for watching climbers.

For good bouldering, head to the Knobs, just over a mile north of Tenaya Lake on the west side of the road. Beginners will find excellent climbing on nearby Low-Profile Dome, particularly along the Golfer's Route.

Tuolumne Meadows

Come summertime, when temperatures in the Valley regularly top 90°F, climbers head to Tuolumne Meadows where the cool, high-country air is much more conducive to climbing. Thanks to the altitude, the air is also thinner, so climbing here requires at least a day's acclimatization for most people.

Cathedral Peak and its fin-shaped west peak, the frightening Eichorn Pinnacle, are both epic and extremely popular climbs. It's fun watching climbers tackle these peaks from the Cathedral Lakes trail. The Northwest Books route on Lembert Dome is one of the most popular climbs on that iconic dome. Mt Conness, on the park's eastern border, is a challenging all-day climb.

Horseback Riding

Guided Trail Rides

There's ample opportunity to ride in Yosemite, but unless you bring your own horse you'll probably be on the back of a mule. For kids, it's a great way to take in the scenery, breathe some dust and have a little fun. Guided mule rides are offered at three stables within the park from roughly spring through fall.

For guided rides throughout the park, no experience is necessary, but riders must be at least seven years old and 44in tall and weigh less than 225lb. Don't sign on for a full-day trip unless you're in good physical shape – you'll regret it. Prices at all of the park-operated stables are the same: $65 for two hours and $88.50 for a half-day trip. The season runs from May to October, although this varies slightly by location. During the popular summer months, you should make a reservation, particularly for longer rides, by calling the stable directly.

Yosemite Stables
Yosemite Valley   HORSEBACK RIDING
(Map p100; ☏ 209-372-8348) Located near North Pines Campground, with rides to Mirror Lake and Clark's Point (for views of Vernal Fall).

Yosemite Stables
Wawona   HORSEBACK RIDING
(☏ 209-375-6502) Located behind the Pioneer Yosemite History Center, it offers rides around Wawona Meadow and to Chilnualna Falls.

Yosemite Trails
Pack Station   HORSEBACK RIDING
(☏ 559-683-7611; www.yosemitetrails.com) Just outside the park's South Entrance, offers rides to the Mariposa Grove of big trees (per person half-day $160), and sleigh rides (adult/child $30/20) in winter. Until the restoration project ends in 2017, Mariposa Grove rides will be limited to the outer grove.

YOSEMITE MOUNTAINEERING SCHOOL

Since 1969 **Yosemite Mountaineering School** (Map p100; ☏ 209-372-8344; Curry Village; ⊙ Apr-Oct) has been teaching and guiding rock climbers, mountaineers and back-country skiers of all levels. While you can learn everything from basic backpacking skills to building a snow cave, the school's specialty is teaching folks how to move their bodies up slabs of granite. Whether you're a 12-year-old who wants to learn the basics of climbing, belaying and rappeling or a sport climber who wants to learn the art of big walls, you'll find this school a gold mine of opportunity. Beginners over the age of 10 can sign up for the Go Climb a Rock seminar ($148 per person), which is pretty much guaranteed to inspire participants to go on for more. For parents, it's a great and constructive way to turn the kids loose for a day.

Other class offerings include anchoring, leading/multipitch climbing, self-rescue/aid and crack climbing, for which Yosemite, of course, is famous. You can even create your own custom climbing trip or hire guides to take you climbing.

The school is based out of the Curry Village Mountain Shop from April through November; it relocates to Badger Pass in winter. With the closure of the Tuolumne Meadows Sport Shop, it's unclear whether it will have a summer outpost at Tuolumne Meadows. The friendly and knowledgeable staff will offer suggestions based on your skill level and objectives.

High Sierra Camps

Yosemite High Sierra Camps

Saddle Trips HORSEBACK RIDING
(☑559-253-5672, freight 209-372-8348; trip per person adult/child from $1172/937, freight per lb $5) These are far and away the most popular (though definitely not the cheapest) ways to see the park from a saddle, with mules schlepping you and all the supplies. These four- to six-day trips include all meals and visit the spectacular High Sierra Camps circuit. They fill up months in advance; check the park concessionaire website for details.

Stock Camps

If you're bringing your own pack animals, you can use the stock camps at Tuolumne Meadows, Wawona and Bridalveil Creek campgrounds. Each site accommodates six people and six animals. You can reserve sites up to five months in advance by phone only through Recreation.gov (p45). Stock are allowed on all Yosemite trails except those posted on the Stock Closure list (www.nps.gov/yose/planyourvisit/stock.htm).

Rafting & Kayaking

The Merced River flows lazily through Yosemite Valley, offering rafters and kayakers a marvelous way to take in the scenery on a hot summer day. That said, you do have to share the water with a plethora of other boats, but with the right sense of humor and a little Merced River water running down your face, it's undeniably fun. Accommodations are available for those with mobility impairments.

Rafts, kayaks, air mattresses and inner tubes (or whatever strange, nonmotorized flotation device you're using) are allowed only along the 3-mile stretch between Stoneman Bridge (near Curry Village) and Sentinel Beach. The waters are gentle enough for children, and **raft rentals** (Map p100; ☑209-372-4386; per person $31) are available at Curry Village. Rates include all equipment and a return shuttle to the rental kiosk. No permit is required to use your own raft, canoe or kayak on the Merced. Shuttles depart every 30 minutes and cost $5.50 for those bringing their own flotation devices.

Serious paddlers are salivating over the **new Merced River plan**, which opens up the *entire* river to boaters with appropriate watercraft and personal flotation devices. River advocates swear that the best one-day river trip in California is between Clark's Bridge (near the stables) and the Pohono Bridge, especially in spring when the dogwoods are blooming overhead. A stretch of class IV whitewater from El Capitan Meadow and Pohono Bridge is certain to get your adrenaline pumping. For route descriptions and a complete overview of the new policies, go to www.americanwhitewater.org and find the Merced in its 'river search.'

Whenever you disembark, be sure to do so only on sand or gravel bars – *not* vegetated riparian areas which cannot handle the human impact.

Rafting is also fun in Wawona on the South Fork of the Merced, between the campground and Swinging Bridge. On Tioga Rd, near Tuolumne Meadows, Tenaya Lake is a great place for a float and especially good for kayaking.

Swimming

River swimming throughout Yosemite is best mid- to late summer, when the water levels are low and the current gentler. The Merced River is Yosemite's biggest killer, so never swim where you're not certain the current is safe.

FINDING SOLITUDE

If you've come to Yosemite looking for peace and solitude, there are plenty of places to find it. Sure, the park gets packed every summer, but with a little effort you can find near-empty trails, quiet riverside hangouts and other hideaways tucked throughout the park. If solitude is a priority, avoid summer (especially August weekends). Winter and spring are both excellent times to visit. A good rule is to hit the trail just after sunrise or late in the day, when the crowds are either sleeping or running off to supper. Yosemite Valley is where most visitors throng, and roads, campgrounds and popular trails (such as that to Vernal Fall) are predictably packed. Even in summer, though, you may find peace and quiet along the Yosemite Valley Loop trails, which few Valley visitors seem to know about.

Yosemite Valley

On a hot summer day in Yosemite Valley, nothing beats the heat like lounging in the gentle Merced River. Provided you don't trample the riparian life on your way, you can jump in just about anywhere, but there are several locations proving particularly good: at the beach just behind Housekeeping Camp; on the stretch behind Yosemite Lodge; and at the Cathedral Beach and Devil's Elbow areas opposite the El Capitan Picnic Area. The beach immediately below Swinging Bridge is hugely popular and, thanks to calm waters, great for families. Tenaya Creek offers good swimming as well, especially near the bridge leading toward Mirror Lake.

Skin too thin? Curry Village and Yosemite Lodge provide public outdoor **swimming pools** (admission adult/child $5/4). The price includes towels and showers.

Wawona

You'll find nice swimming holes near the campground and by Swinging Bridge. The latter is reached via a 2-mile drive east along Forest Dr, which parallels the south bank of the Merced River. Park in a lot beyond private Camp Wawona and walk the short distance to the river.

Big Oak Flat Road & Tioga Road

If you can handle cold water, Tenaya Lake offers some of the most enjoyable swimming in the park. It's hard to resist this glistening lake that beckons with sapphire waters. A sandy half-moon beach wraps around the east end. Sunbathers and picnickers are also drawn to the rocks that rim its north and west sides.

Want to work a little for that dip? May Lake is an easy hike and gorgeous, if a bit chilly. You can swim anywhere except a signed section of the western side where the May Lake High Camp draws its drinking water. Further west, Harden Lake is unusually warm compared with other nearby lakes because much of its volume evaporates in summer. A late- or even mid-season swim is practically balmy.

Tuolumne Meadows

The Tuolumne River is an excellent choice for high-country swimming, with many easy-to-reach sandy-bottomed pools and slightly warmer temperatures than other High Sierra rivers. From the pullout at the west end of Tuolumne Meadows, follow the trail along Pothole Dome and the river for about a mile to a gorgeous waterfall and hidden swimming spot.

You'll also find a couple of small but good swimming holes at the twin bridges crossing the chipper Lyell Fork Tuolumne; to get there, head out on the trail to Lyell Canyon. If you don't mind hiking a bit further, the Lyell Fork also has some great (albeit shallow) swimming areas. Elizabeth Lake can be a bit bone-chilling, but on a hot summer day, plenty of people take the plunge and love it.

Fishing

Yosemite may not be the sort of place you go to catch whopping trophy trout, but the setting is fabulous, and wettin' a line, so to say, in the Merced or Tuolumne River is pretty darn satisfying. Stream and river fishing is permitted only from the last Saturday in April until mid-November; lake fishing is OK year-round. In Wawona the South Fork of the Merced offers some of the best stream fishing in the park. In and around the park you can fish the Merced River between Happy Isles and the Foresta Bridge in El Portal, although if you catch a rainbow trout, you'll have to throw it back. In Yosemite Valley, you're allowed only five brown trout per day, and bait is prohibited (artificial lures or barbless flies only).

The park's most satisfying fishing, especially for fly casters, is undoubtedly in Tuolumne Meadows. Although the fish aren't big, they're still out there, and the setting is unbeatable. The Dana Fork Tuolumne and

---

WATERFALL WARNING

On a blistering day, the park's waterways are a siren song for sweaty hikers with aching feet. But no matter how inviting, *never* enter rivers or creeks near a waterfall. Pay attention to posted warning signs (they're there because of prior fatalities), and use common sense if there aren't any. All it takes is one slip and within seconds you could be barreling toward a waterfall's precipice. More than a dozen visitors have died at Vernal Fall – please don't increase that statistic.

especially the Lyell Fork Tuolumne are good, with easy access from shore and no wading required. As for lakes, Elizabeth Lake is the most easily accessible. If you're heading up to Young Lakes, bring a pole. Some of the best lake fishing is on Saddlebag Lake, just outside the park, east of the Tioga Pass entrance, off Hwy 120.

Hetch Hetchy Reservoir is said to house a trove of very large trout; casting is permitted from the shore only, though no live bait is allowed. Above the reservoir, the Tuolumne River is supposedly very good.

You can pick up tackle and supplies at the Yosemite Village Sport Shop and the stores in Tuolumne Meadows, Wawona and Crane Flat. For more information on fishing in the park, see www.nps.gov/yose/planyourvisit/fishing.htm.

Hang Gliding

You can actually hang glide from Glacier Point for a mere $5, provided you're an active member of the US Hang Gliding & Paragliding Association (USHPA; ☑ 719-632-8300; www.ushpa.aero), have a level 4 (advanced standing) certification, and you preregister online with the Yosemite Hang Gliders Association (YHGA; www.yhga.org). On weekend mornings from late May to early September, weather permitting, qualified hang gliders can launch from the overlook between 7am and 9am, well before any thermal activity rolls in, and float down to Leidig Meadow, just west of Yosemite Lodge. One of the best free shows in the park is watching the colorful gliders sprint off the edge and soar over the Valley like tiny paper airplanes.

ⓘ COFFEE WITH A RANGER

Rise and shine and schmooze with a perky park ranger at one of the morning Coffee with a Ranger sessions held at campgrounds throughout the park. A chance to get some quality time with the best sources of park information, you can solicit suggestions for your day's adventures while getting a complimentary caffeine fix. Check the *Yosemite Guide* for locations and times, and don't forget to bring a mug!

Boating

Motorless boats of any kind can use beautiful and easy-to-access Tenaya Lake – hands down the best place to boat in the park. Lounging at the foot of John Muir's beloved Mt Hoffmann is tranquil May Lake, a lovely place to paddle an inflatable; that is, unless you want to hoof anything heavier for the 1.2 miles from the trailhead along Tioga Rd.

Golf

If you find the need to smack the ol' tiny white ball around, head to Yosemite's nine-hole, par-35 Wawona Golf Course (☑ 209-375-6572; green fees per 9/18 holes from $21.50/36), which was built in 1917. The course hails itself as one of the country's few 'organic' golf courses, meaning no pesticides are used on the lawn and everything is irrigated with gray water. Cart and club rentals are available.

Campfire & Public Programs

There's something almost universally enjoyable about group campfire programs. Pull a bench around a roaring bonfire, with stars above, big trees behind you and lots of friendly folks all around, and it's as if you've left the world's troubles behind.

During the summer, free campfire programs are held at the following Yosemite campgrounds: Tuolumne Meadows, Wawona, Bridalveil Creek, Crane Flat, White Wolf and Lower Pines. Check the *Yosemite Guide* for the week's programs and times. Rangers, naturalists and other park staff lead the programs, and topics include the history, ecology and geology of the local region, a few tips on dealing with bears, and maybe some stories and songs. They're geared toward families and people of all ages.

Similar evening programs are also held at amphitheaters behind Yosemite Lodge and Curry Village – even in the absence of an actual campfire, the mood remains the same. These programs include general talks about the area, with occasional slide shows and films.

The Sierra Club's LeConte Memorial also hosts programs on Fridays and Saturdays. More in-depth than the average campfire talk, these cover such topics as the founding of the John Muir Trail and the history of Hetch Hetchy.

WORTH A TRIP

WINTER SKI HUTS

When Yosemite National park is hushed and white, three classic ski huts are open for overnight guests who make the trek on snowshoes or cross-country skis. The journeys aren't easy, but certainly worth the work. Make sure to self-register for a wilderness permit before you head out.

In winter, the concession stand at Glacier Point fills with bunk beds and becomes the **Glacier Point Ski Hut** (Map p100; ☏ 209-372-8444). It's operated by the park concessionaire and reached by a 10.5-mile trip on an intermediate trail. Guided trips are led by the Cross-Country Ski Center; one-night trips cost $350 per person, two nights $550. These tariffs include meals, wine, accommodations and guides. Or you can get there without a guide (reservation required) and pay $146 per day for meals and lodging.

The handcrafted stone **Ostrander Lake Ski Hut** (www.yosemiteconservancy.org; bunk weekday/weekend $35/55), operated by the Yosemite Conservancy, can accommodate up to 15 skiers in a gorgeous lakeside spot beneath Horse Ridge. Cooking facilities are provided, but you must ski in with all of your supplies. The 10-mile trip requires experience and a high fitness level. Staffed throughout winter, the hut is open to backcountry skiers and snowshoers, and a drawing is held for reservations in November.

Are you up to a 16-mile trek from the eastern side of the park, summiting Tioga Pass? In winter, the Tuolumne Meadows Campground reservation office reinvents itself as the free **Tuolumne Meadows Ski Hut**. It has a wood-burning stove, sleeps 10, and is first come, first served. Tuolumne winter rangers post helpful conditions updates at www.nps.gov/yose/blogs/tmconditions.htm. If you're hesitant to try this on your own, the Cross-Country Ski Center runs infrequent six-day tours for $876 per person. A stone building facing Tioga Rd, just west of the bridge across the Tuolumne River, it's right at the entrance to the campground.

Glacier Point rangers lead weekly programs at a lovely stone amphitheater near the snack bar, and sometimes offer sunset talks along the railing overlooking the Valley. Over at Tuolumne Meadows, talks take place at **Parsons Memorial Lodge**, reachable via an easy half-mile hike.

The busiest time is, of course, during the summer, usually June to September. Limited programs are offered in the low season, and they're held during cold weather at indoor locations such as Yosemite Lodge and the Ahwahnee Hotel.

Monthly **Yosemite Forum** lectures focus on nature and science within the Sierra Nevada and take place in the auditorium of the Yosemite Valley Visitor Center.

WINTER ACTIVITIES

The white coat of winter opens up a different set of things to do, as the Valley becomes a quiet, frosty world of snow-draped evergreens, ice-coated lakes and vivid vistas of gleaming white mountains sparkling against blue skies. Winter tends to arrive in full force by mid-November and whimper out in early April.

Cross-Country Skiing

Glacier Point & Badger Pass

Twenty-five miles of groomed track and 90 miles of marked trails fan out from Badger Pass. From here, you can schuss out to the Clark Range Vista and Glacier Point, an invigorating 21-mile round-trip. Pick up a trail map or download one from the Yosemite National Park (www.nps.gov/yose) website.

The **Yosemite Cross-Country Ski Center** (☏ 209-372-8444) offers learn-to-ski packages ($46), guided tours (from $102 per person), telemark instruction ($49), private lessons (starting at $37) and equipment rental ($25 for skis, boots and poles). It also leads very popular overnight trips to the Glacier Point Ski Hut (p95).

Wawona

Mariposa Grove contains a series of well-marked cross-country skiing trails, including an 8-mile loop trail from the South Entrance. Trail maps can be purchased at the park or printed from the park website at www.fs.usda.gov/activity/sierra/recreation/wintersports. The trails also connect to marked Sierra National Forest trails just south of the park in Goat Meadow and along Beasore Rd.

Big Oak Flat Road & Tioga Road

You'll find good marked cross-country skiing and snowshoeing trails in the Crane Flat area, including Old Big Oak Flat Rd, which leads to Tuolumne Grove and Hodgdon Meadow. Trail maps are available at the park and at www.yosemitepark.com/cflat-winter-trails.pdf. When Tioga Rd is closed in winter, it becomes a popular, though ungroomed, ski route.

Downhill Skiing & Snowboarding

California's oldest ski slope, **Badger Pass Ski Area** (☑209-372-8430; www.badgerpass.com; lift ticket adult/child $49/25; ⊙9am-4pm mid-Dec–Mar) sits at 7300ft on Glacier Point Rd, about 22 miles from the Valley. Known as a family-friendly mountain geared toward beginners and intermediates, it features an 800ft vertical drop, nine runs, two terrain parks, five lifts, a full-service lodge and equipment rental ($37 for a full set of gear). For great money-saving deals, check out the stay-and-ski packages at the Wawo-

---

YOSEMITE'S ARTISTS
....

From its very beginnings as a park, Yosemite has inspired a body of art nearly as impressive as the landscape itself. The artists who came to Yosemite with the first generation of tourists revealed a world of extraordinary beauty, even as miners, ranchers and lumbermen were tearing it apart in their lust for profit. From the illustrations of Thomas Ayres to the photographs of Carleton Watkins, art played a key role in the bid to establish Yosemite as a national park.

In the mid-19th century, the Hudson River School and related movements in American art strived to capture the face of God in the wild magnificence of nature. A parallel trend in literature expressed a distinctly American spiritualism tied to the wilderness; writers who explored such transcendental themes included Ralph Waldo Emerson, Walt Whitman, Emily Dickinson and Henry David Thoreau. Into this intellectual moment, which flourished on the East Coast, came the first paintings of Yosemite by a recognized artist, Albert Bierstadt, in 1863.

At that time, San Francisco was becoming the epicenter for a distinctly Californian school of art. Inspired by the vistas that Bierstadt and the photographers were capturing in Yosemite, many other artists embraced the Sierra as a subject matter. Mountain landscapes by Charles Nahl, Thomas Hill and William Keith soon adorned Victorian mansions in San Francisco and Sacramento, and painters became a regular fixture in the haunts of John Muir, who occasionally led groups of them on sketching expeditions into remote locations. Hill set up a studio at Wawona in 1884, beginning the tradition of resident artists and galleries in the park.

While the painters were often content to set up their easels in the meadows, photographers became known for seeking out more inaccessible regions. Sierra Club photographer-mountaineers such as Joseph LeConte and Norman Clyde captured extremely remote areas of the park. Yosemite's best-known photographer, of course, was Ansel Adams, who developed a level of craft not seen in the work of his predecessors. An early proponent of the idea that photography could adhere to the same aesthetic principles used by fine artists, he also became a strong advocate for the preservation of the wilderness, working on the frontlines of the growing conservation movement.

In 1929 Adams married Virginia Best, whose father's gallery in Yosemite Valley was the precursor to the Ansel Adams Gallery, found today in Yosemite Village. In 1940 Adams held a photography workshop at the gallery with fellow photographer Edward Weston, beginning a tradition of photography education that continues to this day.

Three of Adams' assistants – John Sexton, Alan Ross and Ted Orland – are lesser known but equally important to the greater body of Yosemite photography. Photographer-mountaineer Galen Rowell, who Adams himself highly regarded, took some of the most extreme photos of the park, continuing to expose those faraway places to the public eye.

na Hotel, Yosemite Lodge and Ahwahnee Hotel, and note that lift-ticket prices drop considerably during midweek. It also rents tubes for snow tubing.

The excellent on-site Yosemite Ski School is highly regarded for its top-notch instruction, particularly for beginners. Group lessons are $47, private lessons start at $89.50 per hour and the 'Guaranteed Learn to Ski/Snowboard' package costs $82 to $95. Badger's gentle slopes are well suited for first-time snowboarders.

In winter, a free daily shuttle runs from the Valley to Badger Pass in the morning, returning to the Valley in the afternoon.

Snowshoeing

It wouldn't be difficult to argue that Yosemite Valley is at its very best just after a fresh snowfall. Snowshoeing around the Valley, past icy monoliths, frozen waterfalls and meadows blanketed in snow, is a truly magical activity. The John Muir Trail, which begins at Happy Isles, is a popular destination.

You can rent snowshoes ($24/21 per half-/full day) at Badger Pass (and sometimes at the Curry Village Ice Rink), where rangers lead two-hour naturalist treks that are informative, fun and almost free ($5). Check the *Yosemite Guide* for schedules. Rentals are also available at the Crane Flat gas station. From January to March, rangers offer two-hour 'Full Moon Snowshoe Walks' (with/without equipment rental $20/5) on nights of, and leading up to, a full moon. Sign up at the Yosemite Lodge Tour Desk or call ☎ 209-372-1240.

Ice-Skating

A delightful way to spend a winter's afternoon is twirling about on the large outdoor **Curry Village Ice Rink** (Map p100; 2½hr session adult/child $10.50/10, skate rental $4; ☺ Nov-Mar). Daily sessions begin at 3:30pm and 7pm, with additional sessions at 8:30am and noon on weekends and holidays.

Snow Camping

There are no quotas or reservations for winter camping, but you still need to get a wilderness permit (p72).

Destinations accessed from Glacier Point Rd are some of the most popular places to enjoy snow camping. There are restrictions on staying at overlooks, and you must camp at least 1.5 miles from Badger Pass. See www.nps.gov/yose/planyourvisit/wildwinter.htm for more information as well as a winter trail map.

Off-limits in summer, Wawona's peaceful and protected Mariposa Grove is open for camping from December to mid-April when snow closes the road, though it's unlikely to be accessible during the grove restoration (through spring 2017) – check with the park for closures and conditions. You must set up your tent uphill from Clothespin Tree. The Wawona Campground also stays open for winter camping on a first-come, first-served basis.

The Yosemite Cross-Country Ski Center (p95) offers an overnight trip at Badger Pass ($292 per person, including meals), with instruction in snow camping fundamentals and survival skills.

Sledding & Tubing

If tubing down a hill is more your fancy, there's a snow-play area located in Crane Flat. Badger Pass also has a tubing area for younger kids, with two-hour sessions ($17) starting at 11:30am and 2pm, tubes included. In the Sierra National Forest a mile south of the South Entrance, the free Goat Meadow Snow Play Area is another good location if you have gear.

⊙ SIGHTS

⊙ Yosemite Valley

Yosemite Valley is the park's crown jewel. It's home to what most people think of when they imagine Yosemite: Half Dome, Yosemite Falls, El Capitan, the Royal Arches – all those mind-boggling sights that draw over four million people to the park each year. But the numbers can be deceiving. Most visitors come in July and August, and many of them stay only for the day. Sure, the stores, the dining rooms and the food stands at Yosemite Village and Curry Village are a complete nightmare, and the traffic is maddening, but come sundown, when the day-trippers and tour buses disappear, you can stroll the loop trails along the Valley floor and feel the tranquil magic that has always been here. Of

Yosemite Valley Region

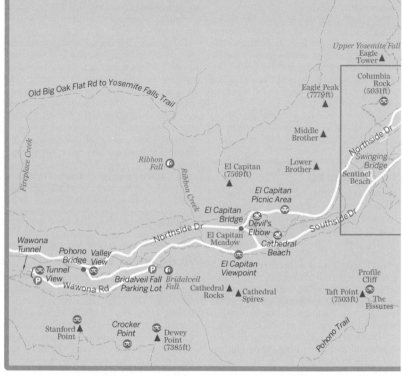

course, visiting the Valley outside of summer makes finding solitude a cinch. If you don't mind nippy nights, then springtime, when the waterfalls are raging, is one of the very best times to visit. Winter is quiet, and the snow lends a serenity to the Valley that few people experience.

❶ Orientation

Meadow-carpeted Yosemite Valley is 7 miles long and 1 mile wide (at its widest point). The Merced River meanders down its middle, within sight of Half Dome on the east end, westward past El Capitan, and out of the park into the Merced River Canyon.

Northside and Southside Drives parallel the valley on either side of the river, each one way for most of its route (the former heads west, the latter heads east). Four bridges span the river, including Sentinel Bridge, which leads to Yosemite Village, the Valley's commercial center.

The Ahwahnee Hotel sits about a half-mile east of the village, while Yosemite Lodge is near the base of Yosemite Falls, less than a mile west of the village. Curry Village and the three Pines campgrounds lie south of the river, about a mile east of Sentinel Bridge.

Three highways diverge at the west end of the Valley. Big Oak Flat Rd leads north to Crane Flat (where it meets Hwy 120), Hetch Hetchy and Tuolumne Meadows; Hwy 140 heads west out of the park to El Portal and Mariposa; and Hwy 41 runs south to Glacier Point Rd, Wawona and Mariposa Grove.

Yosemite Village & Around

Regardless of your feelings toward commercial development in one of the world's natural wonders, you'll probably wind up here at one point or another, as the village offers just about every amenity – from pizzas and ice cream to firewood and wilderness permits.

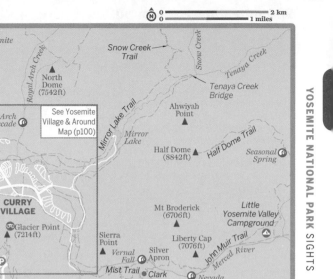

Commercial development began in the Valley almost as soon as the public became aware of the park. Quite a few hotels opened around the turn of the 20th century, and by the 1920s a collection of businesses – including hotels, photo studios, a dance pavilion and even a cinema – had risen just south of the river near Sentinel Bridge. This was the original Yosemite Village. By the 1950s, however, it was downgraded to the 'Old Village,' as businesses moved north of the river. The site of the Old Village has since reverted to meadow (look for road marker V20), though the chapel remains, albeit in a slightly different spot. A few buildings were moved to the Pioneer History Center in Wawona, and Best's Studio was moved to the present-day village and eventually renamed the Ansel Adams Gallery.

The Village Store has a huge range of groceries – including produce, vegetarian items and deli foods. It's more expensive than your local store but has a surprisingly good selection. It also carries camp supplies, booze, maps and an overwhelming supply of Yosemite-emblazoned souvenirs. Head to the **Yosemite Village Sport Shop** (Map p100; ⊗9am-6pm, reduced hours in winter) for last-minute camping supplies.

Rarely do visitors spend much time in the Valley without a stop at the park's main visitor center (p130). If you've never been to Yosemite, it's an excellent place to load up on information.

At the main desk, rangers answer tourists' questions (remaining amazingly friendly amid the barrage) and can pretty much settle any query you might have. An excellent free Valley hiking map is available, and weather reports, campground availability, and trail and road conditions are posted behind the desk.

Yosemite Village & Around

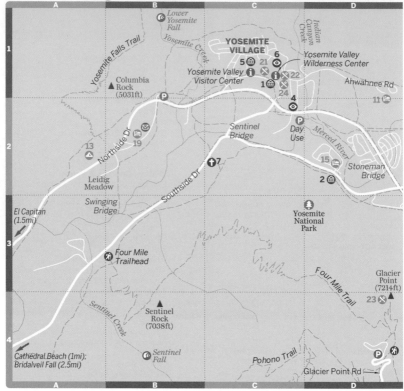

To the right of the help desk is the exhibit hall, which offers an interactive walk through Yosemite's history from the dinosaurs to the present.

To the left of the visitor center help desk, the **Yosemite Conservancy Bookstore** (www.yosemiteconservancystore.com) stocks an outstanding assortment of Yosemite-related books and maps and a smattering of Yosemite paraphernalia.

Yosemite Theater   THEATER
(Map p100; performances adult/child $8/4; ☺9:30am-5pm) Behind the Yosemite Valley Visitor Center, this theater screens two films: Ken Burns' *Yosemite: A Gathering of Spirit,* a celebration of the Yosemite Grant's 150th anniversary, and the painfully dramatic but beautifully photographed *Spirit of Yosemite.* The movies alternate, starting every half-hour between 9:30am and 4:30pm (from noon on Sundays), and offer a free, air-conditioned respite from the summer heat.

In the evening, take your pick from a rotating cast of performers, including actor Lee Stetson, who portrays the fascinating life and philosophy of John Muir, and Park Ranger Shelton Johnson, who re-creates the experiences of a Buffalo Soldier. There are also special children's shows.

Yosemite Museum   MUSEUM
(Map p100; ☺9am-5pm summer, 10am-4pm winter, often closed noon-1pm) **FREE** This museum has Miwok and Paiute artifacts, including woven baskets, beaded buckskin dresses and dance capes made from feathers, and Indian cultural demonstrators engage visitors with traditional basket weaving, tool-making and crafts. There's also an **art gallery** with paintings and photographs from the museum's permanent collection. Behind the museum, a self-guided interpretive trail winds past a reconstructed c 1870 **Indian village** with pounding stones, an acorn granary, a ceremonial roundhouse and a conical bark house.

YOSEMITE NATIONAL PARK SIGHTS

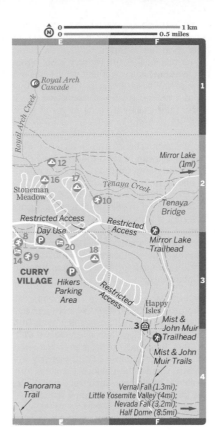

0 / 1 km
0 / 0.5 miles

Yosemite Village & Around

Ansel Adams Gallery   GALLERY
(Map p100; ☎209-372-4413; www.anseladams.com; ☺9am-6pm summer, shorter winter hours) Few know about it, but *original* Ansel Adams photographic prints are shown at Yosemite Valley's Ansel Adams Gallery. The curator-led 'Fine Print' tour is limited to five people; call in advance to reserve a spot. For budding photographers, free guided 'Camera Walks' are offered at 8:30am thrice weekly in summer; space is limited to 15 people.

Yosemite Art Center   ARTS CENTER
(Map p100; ☎209-372-1442; www.yosemiteconservancy.org/yosemite-art-center; art classes $10; ☺9am-noon & 1-4:30pm Apr-Oct, art classes 9:45am-2pm Mon-Sat, 1:30-3:30pm Sun) In late spring, summer and fall, this center holds art classes nearly every day that feature a different artist and medium (watercolor, pastel, acrylic etc) each week. Classes usually take place outside, and students must

bring their own supplies or purchase them at the center. No experience is necessary. Children under 12 must be accompanied by an adult. Sign up at least a day ahead to ensure a spot.

Yosemite Valley Chapel CHURCH
(Map p100; www.yosemitevalleychapel.org) Built in 1879, this chapel is Yosemite's oldest structure that still remains in use. The church originally stood near the base of Four Mile Trail, and in 1901 was moved about a mile to its present site. Sunday morning services are nondenominational.

Curry Village & Around

Lying directly below Glacier Point, Curry Village is home to Yosemite Valley's second-biggest collection of restaurants, stores and overnight accommodations. Originally called Camp Curry, it was founded in 1899 by David and Jennie Curry as a place where everyday visitors could find 'a good bed and a clean napkin at every meal.' Starting with just a handful of tents, the camp quickly grew, thanks in large part to David Curry's entrepreneurial drive and booming personality. One of his biggest promotional schemes was the Firefall, a nightly event and significant tourist draw.

More than 100 years later, the Camp Curry sign still hangs over the entrance, but this sprawling complex retains few traces of its turn-of-the-20th-century roots. From the parking lot, a sea of tent cabins fans out toward the base of Glacier Point, radiating from a central cluster of stores and snack bars – not exactly a vision of rustic glory. Still, it's pleasant to settle in for pizza and beer on the patio that faces the amphitheater out back. There's even a small cocktail bar. Or you can head to the charming deck of the old Camp Curry Lounge for a catnap in one of the rocking chairs.

Curry Village Mountain Shop (Map p100; ☎ 209-372-8396; ◷ 8am-8pm summer, shorter hours rest of year) offers the Valley's best selection of camping, mountaineering and backpacking supplies and is the home of the Yosemite Mountaineering School. It's also world-renowned for its selection of big-wall climbing gear.

LeConte Memorial Lodge HISTORIC BUILDING
(Map p100; ☎ 209-372-4542; www.sierraclub.org/education/leconte; ◷ 10am-4pm Wed-Sun & Fri & Sat evenings May-Sep) Built by the Sierra Club in 1903, this small, rustic, granite-and-wood lodge offers a glimpse into a relatively unknown chapter of California architecture. Designed by Berkeley architect John White, the building sits firmly within a style known

---

THE FIREFALL

Imagine the ruckus that would ensue today if someone built a bonfire and sent it toppling over Glacier Point. Rangers and fire crews would swarm the scene, and rangers would no doubt press arson charges. So it's hard to believe that this was a Yosemite evening tradition for 88 years, inciting public rapture and no official park condemnation. It sounds horrific to those schooled in the 'leave no trace' wilderness ethic, but countless Valley campers still testify to the beauty and excitement of the Firefall, regarded as a sublime summer moment in the enchantment of a summer's evening. Even the echoing signal call to Glacier Point from the Camp Curry campfire, 'Let the fire fall!' became a spine-tingling element of the tradition.

The Firefall originated around 1872, when a hotel was being built at the top of James McCauley's new 4-mile toll trail to Glacier Point. Perhaps as an advertisement for his enterprise, McCauley pushed his campfire off the cliff, creating a glowing waterfall of sparks that was so appealing that tourists in Yosemite Valley called on McCauley to repeat it. His sons transformed the Firefall into a family business, collecting $1.50 from each person who wanted to see it happen. When they found enough takers, a fire builder went up the trail to build a large fire of fir bark and pushed it off the cliff just after nightfall.

The McCauleys left Yosemite in 1897, but two years later David Curry reintroduced the Firefall as a way to draw business to his newly created Camp Curry. Apart from two brief hiatuses, one in 1913 and the other during WWII, the Firefall continued to hold a place in Yosemite evening activities until the National Park Service (NPS) ended it in 1968, finally declaring the tradition to be incompatible with natural land management.

To read a compilation of Firefall memories, visit http://firefall.info.

as the First Bay Tradition, a movement that was intimately linked with the 20th-century Arts and Crafts Movement. The First Bay Tradition placed great importance on reflecting the natural world and insisted each work of architecture be specific to its surroundings.

Nature Center at Happy Isles   MUSEUM
(Map p100; ⏱ 9am-5pm late May-Sep; 🚼) A great hands-on nature museum, the Nature Center displays explain the differences between the park's various pinecones, rocks, animal tracks and (everyone's favorite subject) scat. Out back, don't miss an exhibit on the 1996 rock fall, when an 80,000-ton rock slab plunged 2000ft to the nearby valley floor, killing a man and felling about 1000 trees.

Ahwahnee Hotel

Almost as iconic as Half Dome itself, the elegant **Ahwahnee Hotel** (Map p100) has drawn well-heeled tourists through its towering doors since 1927. Of course, you needn't be wealthy in the least to partake of its many charms. In fact, a visit to Yosemite Valley is hardly complete without a stroll through the **Great Lounge** (aka the lobby), which is handsomely decorated with leaded glass, sculpted tile, Native American rugs and Turkish kilims. You can relax on the plush but aging couches and stare out the 10 floor-to-ceiling windows, wander into the **Solarium**, or send the kids into the walk-in fireplace (no longer in use) for a photo. You can even sneak up the back stairs for a peek into the private **Tudor Room**, which has excellent views over the Great Lounge.

Take a wander around the outside, too. The hotel was built entirely from local granite, pine and cedar – against the backdrop of the Royal Arches it's truly a sight to see. There's no mistaking the reasoning behind its National Historic Landmark designation. Dropping in for a meal at the restaurant or a drink and a snack at the bar are great ways to experience this historic hotel without coughing up three car payments' worth of cash in order to spend the night.

The Ahwahnee was built on the site of a former Ahwahnee–Miwok village. In order to promote the relatively young national park, National Park Service (NPS) director Stephen Mather dreamed up the idea of a majestic hotel to attract wealthy guests. The site was chosen for its exposure to the sun and its views of Half Dome, Yosemite Falls

DON'T MISS

HORSETAIL FALL

For two weeks in late February, if the sky's clear and the water flow is just right, visitors can behold a fiery spectacle at Horsetail Fall. A seasonal ribbon of water dropping off the eastern edge of El Capitan (p105), when the fall catches the sunset during this time of year its thin flow blazes like a stream of molten lava. Many compare it to witnessing the Glacier Point Firefall, and photographers flock to the El Capitan Picnic Area to get the best views.

and Glacier Point. The hotel was designed by American architect Gilbert Stanley Underwood, who also designed Zion Lodge, Bryce Canyon Lodge and Grand Canyon North Rim Lodge. If the Ahwahnee's lobby looks familiar, perhaps it's because it inspired the lobby of the Overlook Hotel, the ill-fated inn from Stanley Kubrick's *The Shining*.

Yosemite Lodge at the Falls

Near the base of Yosemite Falls, the collection of buildings known as Yosemite Lodge includes modern, motel-like accommodations, restaurants, shops, a bar, a bicycle-rental stand, a public pool, a tour desk and other amenities. The amphitheater hosts regular evening programs, and the pool is open to the public.

Unlike the Ahwahnee Hotel, it's not a very striking development. Despite efforts to blend it into the natural surroundings, the place feels strangely like a suburban condo development. Though it doesn't appear very old, the lodge dates back to 1915. It underwent extensive redesign and remodeling in 1956 and 1998, retaining little to suggest its history.

The Yosemite Valley shuttle bus stops right out front, as do Yosemite Area Regional Transport System (YARTS) buses. All guided tram tours, ski shuttles and hiker buses also leave from here; tickets are available from the tour desk in the lobby.

Yosemite Falls

One of the world's most dramatic natural spectacles, Yosemite Falls is a marvel to behold. Naturalist John Muir devoted entire pages to its changing personality, its

YOSEMITE NATIONAL PARK SIGHTS

myriad sounds, its movement with the wind and its transformations between the seasons. No matter where you are when you see it (and it regularly pops into view from all over the Valley), the falls will stop you in your tracks.

In spring, when snowmelt gets Yosemite Creek really pumping, the sight is astounding. On those nights when the falls are full and the moon is bright, you might spot a 'moonbow.' In winter, as the spray freezes midair, an ice cone forms at the base of the falls.

Dropping 2425ft, Yosemite Falls is considered the tallest in North America. Some question that claim, however, as Yosemite Falls comprises three distinct tiers: towering 1430ft Upper Yosemite Fall, tumbling 675ft Middle Cascade and the final 320ft drop of Lower Yosemite Fall. It's also possible to make the grueling hike to the top. The easternmost route of the loop trail is wheelchair-accessible.

To get to the base of Lower Yosemite Fall, get off at shuttle stop 6 (or park in the lot just north of Yosemite Lodge) and join the legions of visitors for the easy quarter-mile stroll. Note that in midsummer, when the snowmelt has dissipated, both the upper and lower falls usually dry up – sometimes to a trickle, other times stopping altogether.

THE LEGEND OF HALF DOME

According to Native American legend, one of Yosemite's early inhabitants came down from the mountains to Mono Lake, where he married a Paiute named Tesaiyac. The journey back to the Valley was difficult, and by the time they reached what was to become Mirror Lake, Tesaiyac decided she wanted to return to her people at Mono Lake. Her husband refused to live on such barren, arid land with no oak trees where he could get acorns. With a heart full of despair, Tesaiyac fled toward Mono Lake, her husband in pursuit. When the spirits heard the couple quarreling, they grew angry and turned the two into stone: he became North Dome and she became Half Dome. The tears she cried made marks as they ran down her face, forming Mirror Lake.

Half Dome

Rising 8842ft above sea level, and nearly a mile above the Valley floor, Half Dome serves as the park's spiritual centerpiece and stands as one of the most glorious and monumental (not to mention best-known) domes on earth.

Its namesake shape is, in fact, an illusion. While from the Valley the dome appears to have been neatly sliced in half, from Glacier or Washburn Points you'll see that it's actually a thin ridge with a back slope nearly as steep as its fabled facade. As you travel through the park, witness Half Dome's many faces. For example, from Mirror Lake it presents a powerful form, while from the Panorama Trail it looks somewhat like a big toe poking out above the rocks and trees.

Half Dome towers above Tenaya Canyon, a classic, glacially carved gorge. Across this canyon rise North Dome and Basket Dome, examples of fully intact domes. In contrast, Half Dome's north face shattered along cracks as a small glacier undercut the dome's base. The resulting cliff boasts a 93% vertical grade (the sheerest in North America), attracting climbers from around the world. Hikers with a permit can reach its summit from the Valley via a long series of trails. The final 45-degree stretch to the top was first made accessible by George Anderson, a local blacksmith who drilled holes in the granite in 1875 and installed a rope system (later replaced by the steel cables in use today).

Bridalveil Fall

In the southwest end of Yosemite Valley, Bridalveil Fall tumbles 620ft. The Ahwahneechee people call it Pohono (Spirit of the Puffing Wind), as gusts often blow the fall from side to side, even lifting water back up into the air. This waterfall usually runs year-round, though it's reduced to a whisper by midsummer. Bring rain gear or expect to get soaked when the fall is heavy.

Take the seasonal El Capitan shuttle or park at the large lot where Wawona Rd (Hwy 41) meets Southside Dr. From the lot, it's a quarter-mile walk to the base of the fall. The path is paved, but probably too rough for wheelchairs, and there's a somewhat steep climb at the very end. Avoid climbing on the slippery rocks at its base – no one likes a broken bone.

If you'd rather walk from the Valley, a trail (part of the Loop Trails) follows Southside

DON'T MISS

SUMMER STARGAZING

On many Friday and Saturday nights in summer, the Glacier Point amphitheater hosts various astronomy clubs, which set up telescopes and let the public take a closer-than-usual look at what's deep in the night sky – from the moon's mottled surface to fuzzy, faraway star clusters. These programs are accompanied by 'Stars Over Yosemite' discussions, during which rangers point out constellations in the sky above Glacier Point. Bring the kids.

On most summer nights, there are also four-hour **stargazing tours** (☑ 209-372-4386, 209-372-1240; adult/senior/child over 4yr/child under 4yr $41/35/23/free) from the Valley to Glacier Point that include an hour-long astronomy program.

Throughout the summer, astronomy walks are also regularly hosted by amateur astronomers in Tuolumne Meadows, Yosemite Valley and Wawona. In Tuolumne you get to walk out into the meadow, lay on granite still warm from the afternoon sun and gaze up at the star-blazoned sky.

Check the *Yosemite Guide* for schedules.

Dr, beginning near the LeConte Memorial Lodge and running about 3.8 miles west to the falls.

El Capitan

At nearly 3600ft from base to summit, El Capitan ranks as one of the world's largest granite monoliths. Its sheer face makes it a world-class destination for experienced climbers, and one that wasn't 'conquered' until 1958. Since then, it's been inundated. Look closely and you'll probably spot climbers reckoning with El Cap's series of cracks and ledges, including the famous 'Nose.' At night, park along the road and dim your headlights; once your eyes adjust, you'll easily make out the pinpricks of headlamps dotting the rock face. Listen, too, for voices.

The meadow across from El Capitan is good for watching climbers dangle from granite (you need binoculars for a really good view). Look for the haul bags first – they're bigger, more colorful and move around more than the climbers, making them easier to spot. As part of the excellent 'Ask a Climber' program, climbing rangers set up telescopes at El Capitan Bridge for a few hours (mid-May through mid-October) and answers visitors' questions. See the *Yosemite Guide* listing for schedule.

⊙ Glacier Point & Badger Pass

Constructed to replace an 1882 wagon road, the modern 16-mile stretch of Glacier Point Rd leads to what many people consider the finest viewpoint in Yosemite. A year-round destination, winter attracts skiers galore who whoosh down the Badger Pass slopes and traverse the unplowed road as a cross-country route. In warmer months, gawkers flock to the end of the road for its satiating Half Dome views and hikers file out from its many trailheads.

ⓘ Orientation

From Yosemite Valley, it's 30 miles (about an hour's drive) to Glacier Point. Glacier Point Rd runs east from the Chinquapin junction on Hwy 41, dead-ending at Glacier Point itself. The road rises from about 6000ft at Chinquapin to 7700ft at the Sentinel Dome parking lot, then down again to 7214ft at Glacier Point. From the Chinquapin turnoff, Badger Pass Ski Area lies about 5 miles to the east; in winter, Glacier Point Rd is closed east of the ski area.

Glacier Point lies at the far eastern end of winding Glacier Point Rd. Along the road, hiking trails lead to more spectacular viewpoints such as Dewey Point and Sentinel Dome. The road also passes Bridalveil Creek Campground, adjacent to Bridalveil Creek, which runs north and drops into Yosemite Valley as Bridalveil Fall.

The only services in the area are at Glacier Point, where there's a small snack bar and gift shop. Rangers are stationed at viewpoint areas but the closest visitor center is in Yosemite Valley. No wilderness permits are available in the vicinity (except at Badger Pass in winter); you must backtrack to either Yosemite Valley or Wawona if you develop warm-weather backcountry urges.

A Valley–Glacier Point bus service operates in summer, and a mandatory Badger Pass–Glacier Point shuttle may operate at peak times. There's also a Valley–Badger Pass service in winter.

Glacier Point & Badger Pass Region

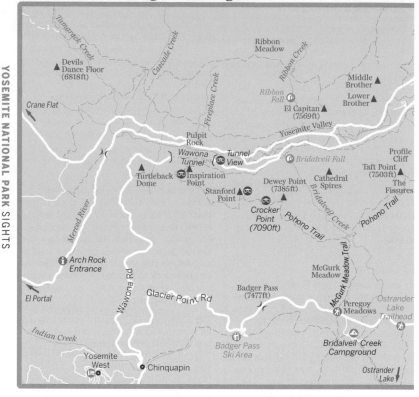

Glacier Point

The views from 7214ft Glacier Point can make you feel like you cheated somehow – a huge array of superstar sights present themselves without any physical effort. A quick mosey up from the parking lot and you'll find the entire eastern Yosemite Valley spread out before you, from Yosemite Falls to Half Dome, as well as the distant peaks that ring Tuolumne Meadows. Half Dome looms practically at eye level, and if you look closely you can spot ant-sized hikers on its summit. The cable approach is not visible, however.

To the left of Half Dome lies the glacially carved Tenaya Canyon, and to its right are the wavy white ribbons of Nevada and Vernal Falls. On the Valley floor, the Merced River snakes through green meadows and groves of trees. Sidle up to the railing, hold on tight and peer 3200ft straight down at

Curry Village. The aqua rectangle of its swimming pool is clearly visible, as is the Ahwahnee Hotel just to the north. Basket Dome and North Dome also rise to the north of the Valley, and Liberty Cap and the Clark Range can be seen to the right of Half Dome.

Almost from the park's inception, Glacier Point has been a popular destination. It used to be that getting up here was a major undertaking. That changed once the Four Mile Trail opened in 1872. While not exactly an easy climb – neither then nor today – the trail did offer a more direct route to the point. James McCauley, an early Yosemite pioneer, financed the formation of the trail, for which he charged a toll; he later took over the reins of the Mountain House hotel, built in 1873 atop Glacier Point. In the 1870s he also conceived the famous Firefall, though Curry Village later picked up and heavily promoted the event.

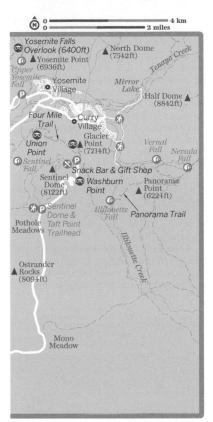

A wagon road to the point was completed in 1882, and the current Glacier Point Rd was built in 1936. As far back as 1929 (and again in the 1970s), there was talk of building an aerial tramway to ferry tourists from Yosemite Valley to Glacier Point. But since the cables would be an eyesore and the system would disturb fragile ecosystems, plans thankfully were abandoned. The spectacularly situated Glacier Point Hotel stood on the point from 1917 until 1969, when it burned down along with the adjacent McCauley Mountain House.

At the tip of the point is **Overhanging Rock**, a huge granite slab protruding from the cliff edge like an outstretched tongue, defying gravity and once providing a scenic stage for daredevil extroverts. Through the years, many famous photos have been taken of folks performing handstands, high kicks and other wacky stunts on the rock. You'll

have to stick to the pictures though, as the precipice is now off-limits.

To escape the crowds, consider a short hike down the first half-mile or so of the Four Mile Trail, which drops gently into a quiet forest and – at this point at least – isn't too steep. After about 10 or 15 minutes, you'll round a corner to a view of El Capitan and Yosemite Valley's western half. Serious switchbacks begin below this point.

Unless the Badger Pass shuttle is continued, drivers should go in the morning to avoid the idling afternoon backup from the parking lot.

Washburn Point

Named for the brothers who built the Wawona Hotel, this viewpoint along Glacier Point Rd is magnificent, though not quite as expansive as Glacier Point. The point faces east toward the Clark Range and lacks the sweeping view of Yosemite Valley. Still, a stop here serves as a great warm-up to Glacier Point, less than a mile down the road.

Badger Pass

The California ski industry essentially got its start in Yosemite Valley, and Badger Pass was California's first alpine ski resort. After Yosemite's All-Year Highway (now Hwy 140) was completed in 1926 and the Ahwahnee Hotel opened its doors the following year, Yosemite Valley quickly became a popular winter destination.

As the 1929 Winter Olympics approached, the newly formed Curry Company and the Yosemite Winter Club submitted an impassioned bid to host the games. They lost, and instead the events were held at Lake Placid, New York – where, in a freakish irony, no snow fell that winter. Bales of hay were used in lieu of snow, while the Sierra saw record snowfalls.

When Wawona Tunnel opened in 1933, skiers began congregating at Badger Pass. In 1935 a new lodge opened on Glacier Point Rd, and a newfangled device called 'the upski' was installed at the pass. The crude lift consisted of nothing more than two counterbalanced sleds, but it worked, and Badger Pass became California's first alpine ski resort.

In winter a free shuttle bus runs between the Valley and Badger Pass. Also in winter, wilderness permits are available by self-registration at the **A-frame building**

(☎209-372-0409), where the first-aid station and ski patrol are also situated. Rangers usually staff the office from 8am to 5pm.

☉ Wawona

Yosemite's historical center, Wawona was home to the park's first headquarters (supervised by Captain AE Wood on the site of the Wawona Campground) and its first tourist facilities. The latter was a simple wayside station run by Galen Clark, who homesteaded in Wawona in 1856. A decade later, Clark was appointed state guardian of the Yosemite Grant, which protected Yosemite Valley and the Mariposa Grove. In 1875 he sold his lodge to the Washburn brothers, who built what's known today as the Wawona Hotel. The Washburns also renamed the area Wawona – thought to be the local Native American word for 'big trees.'

Completed in 1875, the original Wawona Rd opened the floodgates for tourists curious to see the big trees – as well as wondrous Yosemite Valley to the north. The road was modernized in 1933, following construction of the Wawona Tunnel.

From 1891 to 1906, the current Wawona Campground site was home base for the US cavalry, who were appointed as the first official protectors of the newly formed national park. The cavalry moved its headquarters to Yosemite Valley in 1906. Curiously, considering its significant role in the park's history, Wawona remained private property for decades and wasn't incorporated into the boundaries of Yosemite National Park until 1932. Some parts of the area are still in private hands, including the houses that line Chilnualna Falls Rd.

A blend of Victorian elegance and utilitarian New England charm, the Wawona Hotel is the commercial hub of the area. The unassuming white wooden building sits behind a

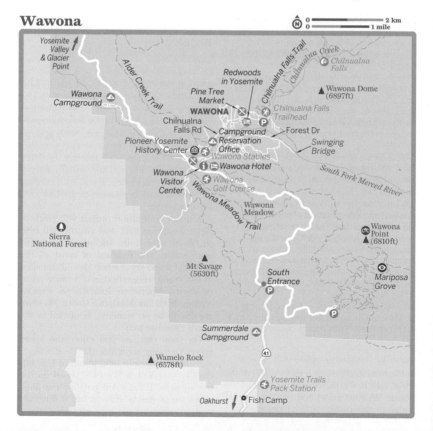

large, manicured green lawn and a fountain inhabited by very vocal frogs.

The Wawona Visitor Center (p130) doubles as the area's visitor center and wilderness center. It issues wilderness permits and bear canisters, answers general park questions and sells some maps and books. The station is located inside Hill's Studio, a historic 1886 building (it was the studio of landscape painter Thomas Hill) adjacent to the Wawona Hotel. Small exhibits in the studio include reproductions of his work. When the office is open for the season, it issues wilderness permits for all areas of the park. During the months it's closed, backcountry-bound visitors can self-register for wilderness permits for trailheads in Wawona and Glacier Point Rd only. Bear canisters can be rented at the general store when the office is closed.

ℹ️ Orientation

Wawona lies on Hwy 41 (Wawona Rd), 4 miles north of the park's South Entrance, which is about 63 miles north of Fresno. Yosemite Valley is a 27-mile drive north. From the Wawona Hotel, the new YARTS Hwy 41 bus route services Yosemite Valley (round-trip adult/child under 13 years $13/9) a few times daily.

The South Fork of the Merced River passes through Wawona, running northwest out of the park. Most visitor services lie just to its south. Across Hwy 41, there's the Wawona Golf Course and the expansive Wawona Meadow, which doubled as the local airport in the early 20th century.

At the corner of Hwy 41 and Forest Dr, just north of the hotel, are a general store, post office, ATM and gas station (24 hours with credit card).

North of the river is Chilnualna Falls Rd, which runs east into a development of private homes and rental properties. The horse stables, the Pioneer Yosemite History Center and a small Campground Reservation Office are along Chilnualna Falls Rd, as are the Bassett Memorial Library (with free internet access) and the year-round Pine Tree Market, about a mile northeast of Hwy 41.

Some 6 miles southeast of Wawona stands the Mariposa Grove of giant sequoias, the park's largest and deservedly popular sequoia grove.

Pioneer Yosemite History Center

In Wawona itself, about 6 miles north of the grove, take in the manicured grounds of the elegant Wawona Hotel and cross a covered bridge to this rustic center (rides adult/child

---

ℹ️ MARIPOSA GROVE CLOSURE

Mariposa Grove will be closed for a major restoration project through approximately spring 2017. The park will remove paved roads from the grove, add trails, enhance trail signage, improve accessibility options and relocate most parking to a new lot with free shuttle transportation at the South Entrance. If you're determined to visit the grove during the closure, a strenuous out-and-back trek from Wawona to the outer loop of Mariposa Grove may be your only option (minimum 12 miles round-trip, 2400ft elevation gain). Check www.nps.gov/yose/planyourvisit/mariposagrove.htm for status updates and the possibility of winter access.

$5/4; ⊙24hr, rides Wed-Sun Jun-Sep; ♿) FREE, where some of the park's oldest buildings were relocated. It also features stagecoaches that brought early tourists to Yosemite, and offers short horse-drawn stagecoach rides.

Mariposa Grove

With their massive stature and multi-millennium maturity, the chunky high-rise sequoias of Mariposa Grove will make you feel rather insignificant. It's the largest grove of giant sequoias in the park, with approximately 500 mature trees towering over 250 acres. Walking trails wind through this very popular grove, and you can usually have a more solitary experience if you come during the early evening in summer or anytime outside of summer.

A major restoration project will be completed in spring 2017, and visitors will benefit from new trails, including accessible boardwalks. The removal of most of the parking lot and grove roads should translate to less traffic congestion and a more natural visitor experience. Exhibits on sequoia ecology from the Mariposa Grove Museum are due to be permanently relocated to the South Entrance hub.

On your right as you enter the lower grove, you may recognize the Fallen Monarch from an iconic 1899 photo of U.S. 6th Cavalry – and their horses – posed on the tree's length. Its exposed root system illustrates the sequoias' shallow but diffuse life support system.

Walk a half-mile up to the 1800-year-old **Grizzly Giant**, a bloated beast of a tree with branches that are bigger in circumference than most of the pine trees in this forest. The walk-through **California Tunnel Tree** is close by, and the favored spot for 'I visited the tall forest' photos. Incredibly, this tree continues to survive, even though its heart was hacked out back in 1895.

In the upper grove, the more famous **Fallen Wawona Tunnel Tree**, however, fell over in a heap in 1969 – its 10ft-high hole gouged from a fire scar in 1881. Other notable specimens include the **Telescope Tree** and the **Clothespin Tree**. Three miles from the parking lot, the wide-open overlook at **Wawona Point** (6810ft) takes in the entire area. It's about a mile round-trip from the Fallen Wawona Tunnel Tree.

Depending on your energy level, you could spend half an hour or a few hours exploring the forest. Between the new shuttle stop and the Wawona Tunnel Tree in the upper grove, the elevation gain is about 1000ft, but the trail is gentle.

In summer, weekends and holidays, parking at the grove is limited to visitors with accessible placards; others must take the free shuttle bus from the South Entrance unless they arrive outside of the to-be-determined shuttle hours. It takes at least an hour to drive from Yosemite Valley to the grove shuttle at the South Entrance. Snowfall closes the Mariposa Grove Rd to cars from about November to April, but you can always hike, ski or snowshoe in (2 miles, 500ft of elevation gain) and experience it in its quiet hibernation.

ⓘ CHANGES IN TUOLUMNE MEADOWS
....

With the implementation of a new management plan for the Tuolumne River corridor, the Tuolumne Meadows (p113) gas station and sports shop have closed, and stable rides will probably end.

Much of the roadside parking along the meadow is due to be eliminated soon, so expect to park at the lots near Lembert Dome, the visitor center or the wilderness center and take the shuttle bus. Future plans include moving the visitor center and possibly repositioning some trailheads, though this timeline is still in progress.

◉ Big Oak Flat Road & Tioga Road

Those arriving on Hwy 120 first encounter this section of the park. While not the most spectacular part of Yosemite, it has a steady flow of visitors. Many just pass through, but the campgrounds at Hodgdon Meadow and Crane Flat keep the area humming with people.

Big Oak Flat Rd was the second route into the park, completed in 1874, just a month after Coulterville Rd. Both were toll roads. Today, Big Oak Flat Rd follows a modified route into the Valley, though a portion of the old road remains open to cyclists and hikers headed for Tuolumne Grove. In winter the road is popular with cross-country skiers.

Going east on Big Oak Flat Rd (Hwy 120) past the Big Oak Flat Entrance, you'll find the Big Oak Flat Information Station (p130). It serves as a mini visitor center with a good variety of books, maps and postcards for sale. The staff can answer questions and there is a courtesy phone inside to check available concessionaire-run lodging inside the park. In the same office is the **wilderness permit desk** (☺8am-5pm May-Sep), which issues permits and doles out bear boxes ($5 per week).

At Crane Flat junction, the **Crane Flat Service Station & General Store** (☺8am-8pm summer, approx 9am-5pm winter) sells firewood, ice, beer, and a smattering of groceries and last-minute camping supplies. Perhaps most importantly, it also has decent fresh coffee. The gas station operates 24 hours year-round with a credit card, and there's a pay phone outside.

ⓘ Orientation

From the entrance, Big Oak Flat Rd descends southeast into the Valley, passing through several tunnels that offer great overlooks of the Merced River Canyon.

Going north, Tioga Rd (Hwy 120 East) rises from 6200ft at Crane Flat to 9945ft at Tioga Pass. Because of the high elevation, snow closes the road (and everything along it) in winter; the road's generally plowed and open from late May or mid-June to mid-November. Exact dates are impossible to predetermine, so always call ahead. From the Crane Flat junction until Tenaya Lake, there are few visitor services.

A half-mile from Crane Flat (going east on Tioga Rd toward Tuolumne Meadows) is the turnoff for Tuolumne Grove, a small grove containing two dozen mature giant sequoias.

Big Oak Flat Road & Crane Flat

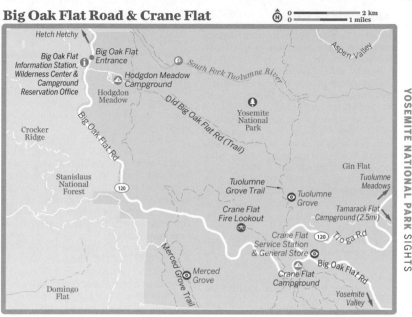

Crane Flat

Throngs of sandhill cranes once rested here as they crisscrossed the Sierra Nevada, and the birds gave the meadow (and surrounding area) its name. About 4 miles east of the entrance is the road to the **Merced Grove**, a seldom-visited giant sequoia grove. At 6000ft, a springtime Valley rainstorm often translates to snow flurries here. In winter, the area is a hub for cross-country skiing and snow play.

Along Tioga Road

The only road that bisects the park is Tioga Rd, a 56-mile scenic highway that runs between Crane Flat in the west (starting from Crane Flat junction) and Hwy 395 at Lee Vining, about 12 miles east of Tioga Pass, the park's easternmost gate. Along the way it traverses a superb High Sierra landscape. Be prepared to pull over regularly to gawk at sights such as glorious Tenaya Lake, mighty Clouds Rest and Half Dome from Olmsted Point.

Initially called the Great Sierra Wagon Rd, the road was built by the Great Sierra Consolidated Silver Company in 1882–83 to supply a mine at Bennettville near Tioga

Pass. Ironically, no significant silver was ever found, and the mine closed soon after the road was completed. Tioga Rd was realigned and modernized in 1961. Only a few sections of the original roadbed remain, including the rough, 4.5-mile stretch that leads to Yosemite Creek Campground. Head down this narrow, tortuous road for a glimpse of how much more treacherous park roads used to be – and not even that long ago. You'll return to Tioga Rd with new-found respect for this engineering marvel.

As Tioga Rd heads east toward Tuolumne Meadows, it passes four campgrounds. Some 15 miles northeast of Crane Flat is White Wolf, with a small lodge with tent cabins and a store that sells mostly snacks and drinks. White Wolf sits on a short spur road a mile north of Tioga Rd.

During summer, a Yosemite Valley–Tuolumne Meadows bus run by the park concessionaire is an excellent transportation option for one-way hikes that depart from Tioga Rd. Schedules and fares have been in flux, so check updates on the park website or *Yosemite Guide*.

Olmsted Point
VIEWPOINT
This jaw-dropping viewpoint is a lunar landscape of glaciated granite with a stunning

Along Tioga Road

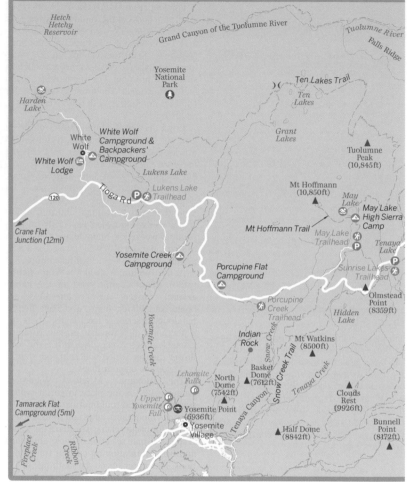

view down Tenaya Canyon to the backside of **Half Dome**. Midway between the May Lake turnoff and Tenaya Lake, the point was named for Frederick Law Olmsted (1822–1903), who was appointed chairman of the first Board of Commissioners to manage the newly established Yosemite Grant in 1864. Olmsted also helped to design Central Park in New York City and did some landscaping for the University of California and Stanford University.

To experience an even better view, and without the company of your awestruck compatriots, stroll a quarter-mile down to the overlook, where you can get past the tree cover and see even deeper into the canyon. Because of extreme avalanche hazards, Olmsted Point is the last area of Hwy 120 to be plowed before the road opens.

Tenaya Lake LAKE

Just east of Olmsted Point, Tenaya Lake (8150ft) takes its name from Chief Tenaya, the Ahwahneechee chief who aided white soldiers, only to be driven from the land by white militias in the early 1850s. Tenaya allegedly protested use of his name, pointing out that the lake already had a name –

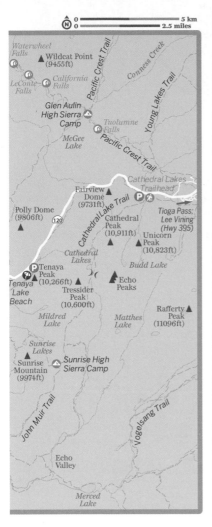

Pywiack ('Lake of Shining Rocks') for the polished granite that surrounds it.

⊙ Tuolumne Meadows

Arriving at Tuolumne (too-*ahl*-uh-mee) Meadows after the drive up from Yosemite Valley is like stepping into another world, even though the two areas are only about 55 miles apart. Instead of being surrounded by waterfalls and sheer granite walls, you emerge in a subalpine wonderland marked by jagged peaks, smooth granite domes, brilliant blue lakes and the meadows' lush grasses and wildflowers. The flowers, which peak in July, are truly a highlight of any visit to Yosemite.

Flowing from the Sierra Crest, the Lyell and Dana Forks of the Tuolumne River – not to mention creeks such as Budd, Unicorn and Delaney – all converge at Tuolumne Meadows (8600ft elevation). At 2.5 miles long, the main flat cradles the Sierra's largest subalpine meadow. The surrounding peaks and domes make Tuolumne a paradise for climbers and hikers, with trails stretching in all directions.

Lying deep in the high country of the Sierra, the Tuolumne Meadows region enjoys a brief but glorious summer and, depending on weather conditions, is only accessible roughly between June and November. Despite the short season, Tuolumne is far quieter than the Valley, although the area around the store, campground and visitor center can get crowded, especially on mid-summer weekends. Many hiking trails, such as Dog Lake, are also well traveled, but with a little effort you'll quickly find solitude.

At the Tuolumne Meadows Visitor Center (p130), about a mile west of the campground, rangers answer questions, sell books and hiking maps, and have helpful handouts describing local trails. There are a few good displays that explain common glacial features. Especially handy is the wildflower display, which will help you identify what you see on your hikes.

The Tuolumne Meadows Wilderness Center (p130) is the place to go for wilderness permits and trail information. Since Tuolumne's mountains, lakes and trails are such a draw for backpackers, it's often a busy spot. It stocks a small selection of books and maps, and has information on current trail conditions. The center sits on the south side of Tioga Rd just east of Lembert Dome, on the spur road leading to Tuolumne Meadows Lodge.

The Tuolumne Meadows Store stocks groceries and supplies and has a post office.

❶ Orientation

Tuolumne Meadows sits along Tioga Rd (Hwy 120) west of the park's Tioga Pass Entrance.

Temperatures in Tuolumne Meadows and the surrounding high country are 15°F to 20°F cooler than in Yosemite Valley, a benefit for hikers and anyone else who struggles in the heat. At the same time, nights are much chillier up here, so pack warm clothes. And remember, snow can fall here in any month of the year, though typically no later than June and no earlier than September.

YOSEMITE NATIONAL PARK SIGHTS

Tuolumne Meadows Region

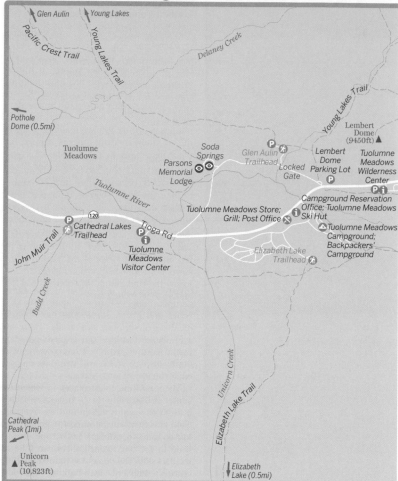

Main Meadow

Stretching nearly 3 miles from Pothole Dome in the west to Lembert Dome in the east, Tuolumne's main meadow is a beautiful sight to behold, especially during sunset, when golden light ripples across the green grass and lashes up the sides of distant peaks into the still blue sky. Grab a fishing pole and dip into the gently rolling **Tuolumne River** as the sunlight drifts away, or just find a quiet spot to sit and stare at the landscape as the mood shifts and the colors shimmer.

While the meadow is a perfect place for quiet contemplation, there's actually a lot of activity going on here. Blanketed in snow for most of the year, the meadow explodes to life in summer, when the wildflowers, taking full advantage of the short growing season, fill the grassy expanse with color. For an explanation of what's happening beneath the meadow's deceptively still surface, check out the interpretive signs that line the dirt road between the Lembert Dome parking lot and Soda Springs.

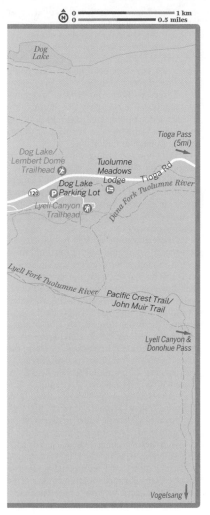

long. The first starts opposite the visitor center on Tioga Rd. The other begins in the Lembert Dome parking area.

Parsons Memorial Lodge   HISTORIC BUILDING
(⊙10am-4pm) Nearby Soda Springs stands this simple but beautifully rugged cabin built in 1915 from local granite. It initially served as a Sierra Club meeting room and was named for Edward Taylor Parsons (1861–1914), an adventurer and active Sierra Club member who helped found the club's outings program. Today it opens as a shelter during thunderstorms (there's a huge fireplace inside), as well as for special events, ranger talks and other programs. See *Yosemite Guide* for the current schedule.

Pothole Dome

Pothole Dome marks the west end of Tuolumne Meadows. It's small by Yosemite standards, but the short, 200ft climb to the top offers great views of the meadows and surrounding peaks. Park along Tioga Rd, then follow the trail around the dome's west side and up to its modest summit.

Lembert Dome

Prominently marking the eastern end of the main meadow, Lembert Dome towers about 800ft above the Tuolumne River. Its summit, which chalks in at 9450ft above sea level, is easily one of the finest places to watch the sunset in Yosemite. Its steep western face is a de facto granite playground for everyone from kids (who stick around the gently sloping bottom) to climbers (who rope up and head to the top). Nonclimbers can hike up the backside. The dome was named for 19th-century shepherd Jean-Baptiste Lembert, who homesteaded in Tuolumne Meadows.

Soda Springs   NATURAL SPRINGS
Above the northern shore of the Tuolumne River, carbonated mineral water burbles silently out of Soda Springs, a small natural spring that turns its surroundings into a cluster of mineral-crusted, rust-red puddles. People used to drink the stuff, though the park service now discourages the practice due to possible contamination – it's not exactly an appealing water source anyway.

The springs are a short, pleasant walk across the flat middle of the meadow. There are two approaches, both about 0.5 miles

Cathedral Range

Dominating the views to the south of Tuolumne Meadows, the jagged Cathedral Range runs roughly northwest from the Sierra Crest, marking the divide between the Tuolumne and Merced Rivers. Its granite pinnacles are immediately striking, in particular **Cathedral Peak** (10,911ft), visible from numerous spots in the region, including along Tioga Rd. At certain angles, its summit appears to be a near-perfect pinpoint, though in reality it's a craggy, double-pronged affair. Other mountains in the range include Tresidder Peak, Echo Peaks, the Matthes Crest and Unicorn Peak (10,823ft), another standout with a horn-shaped protuberance, just east of Cathedral Peak. Soda Springs offers a particularly good vantage point for viewing the range, as does the trail up to Young Lakes. The Cathedral Lakes hike is the classic must-do hike into the range itself.

Tioga Pass

East of Tuolumne Meadows, Tioga Rd (Hwy 120) climbs steadily toward Tioga Pass, which at 9945ft is the highest auto route over the Sierra. The short ride by car or free shuttle bus from Tuolumne Meadows takes you across dramatic, wide open spaces – a stretch of stark, windswept countryside near the timberline. You'll notice a temperature drop, and possibly widespread patches of snow.

Tioga Rd parallels the Dana Fork of the Tuolumne River, then turns north, where it borders the beautiful Dana Meadows all the way to Tioga Pass. To the east you'll see great views of Mt Gibbs (12,764ft) and 13,057ft Mt Dana, the park's second-highest peak after Mt Lyell (13,114ft).

⊙ Hetch Hetchy

No developed part of Yosemite feels as removed from the rest of the park as Hetch Hetchy. Despite the fact that 'Hetchy's' soaring waterfalls, granite domes and sheer cliffs rival its more glamorous counterparts in Yosemite Valley, Hetch Hetchy receives but a fraction of the visitors that the Valley does. This is mainly because Hetch Hetchy Valley is filled with water – the **Hetch Hetchy Reservoir** – and because, save for a couple of drinking fountains, a parking lot and a backpacker campground, there are practically no visitor services. Hetch Hetchy is a magical place, and is definitely worth the detour north from the much busier Big Oak Flat Entrance.

Hetch Hetchy Valley was filled with water only after a long political and environmental battle that lasted a dozen years during the early 20th century. Despite the best efforts of John Muir, who led the fight against it, the US Congress approved the 1913 *Raker Act,* which allowed the city of San Francisco to construct O'Shaughnessy Dam in the Hetch Hetchy Valley. This blocked the Tuolumne River and created Hetch Hetchy Reservoir.

Muir's spirit was crushed, and he died a year later, supposedly of a broken heart.

Today the reservoir and dam supply water and hydroelectric power to much of the Bay Area, including Silicon Valley. When you turn on a tap in San Francisco, out pours Tuolumne River water from the Hetch Hetchy Reservoir. Some politicians and environmentalists (particularly the Sierra Club) still argue for pulling the cork and draining the valley. And who knows? Stranger things have happened in California.

There's one good thing you can say about the dam: by filling in the valley, it has prevented the overdevelopment that plagues Yosemite Valley. Hetch Hetchy remains a lovely, quiet spot – good for a quick day trip or as a jumping-off point for a serious backcountry experience.

Its low elevation makes Hetch Hetchy an especially suitable hiking destination in spring and fall, when much of the high country is still blanketed by ice and snow. In summer, however, it can be very hot and dry – bring a hat, sunscreen and plenty of water. Tueeulala and Wapama Falls are best in spring. The former dries up by late summer.

The 8-mile-long Hetch Hetchy Reservoir stretches behind **O'Shaughnessy Dam**, the site of the area's trailheads, parking area and backpackers' campground (available only to those with a valid wilderness permit).

Hetch Hetchy is a 40-mile drive from Yosemite Valley. From the park's Big Oak Flat Entrance, drive a mile or two west on Hwy 120 and look for the signed turnoff to Hetch Hetchy along Evergreen Rd; turn right (north), drive 8 miles to Mather and turn right (east) on Hetch Hetchy Rd. The Hetch Hetchy Entrance Station (p130) is just a mile beyond the junction; here backpackers can pick up wilderness permits and rent bear canisters.

From the entrance, it's about 9 miles to the parking lot beside O'Shaughnessy Dam. About 5.7 miles past the entrance, at roadside marker H3, you'll pass an overlook of the reservoir to the east and lovely Poopenaut Valley some 1200ft below.

The road to Hetch Hetchy is open only during daylight hours – approximately 7am to 9pm in summer, 8am to 7pm in spring and fall, and 8am to 5pm in winter. Hours vary year to year and season to season; they're posted on a sign at the Evergreen Rd turnoff. The gate is locked at night, and the road may close in winter due to heavy snows

Hetch Hetchy Region

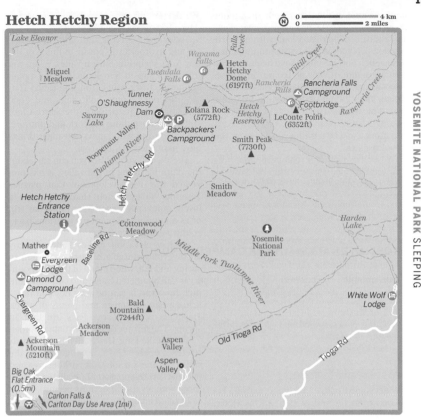

(carry chains). Vehicles over 25ft are not permitted on the narrow, winding road.

The closest convenience supplies and lodging are at Evergreen Lodge, just south of Mather.

🛏 SLEEPING

One of the biggest questions facing Yosemite visitors is where to spend the night. More than four million people visit Yosemite each year, many as day visitors but many also vying for one of the approximately 1500 campsites or 1300 rooms and tent cabins available in the park. During the height of summer, visitors fill open reservations faster than blue jays descend on a picnic. Newcomers with visions of sleeping soundly under the stars often find that campsites and rooms are full, having been reserved months in advance.

Most lodges and campgrounds both inside and outside the park open and close at slightly different times each year, depending on weather. Always check before you go. If you're stuck without a place to sleep inside the park, look outside its borders.

Those hoping to get in touch with nature may find they're more in touch with their neighbors, who are often clanging pans, slurping beer by the fire or snoring in their tents just 10ft or 20ft away. It gets especially crowded in Yosemite Valley. Overnighters looking for a quieter, more rugged experience are better off in spots like Bridalveil Creek, Yosemite Creek and Porcupine Flat.

Campgrounds in Yosemite range from primitive tent-only sites to developed ones that can accommodate large RVs. Most have flush toilets and potable water. The exceptions are the park's three primitive sites (Tamarack Flat, Yosemite Creek and Porcupine Flat) and the Yosemite Valley backpackers' campground, which have vault (pit) toilets and require you to bring your own water or a means of purifying water from nearby streams. None of the campgrounds have showers.

Campground elevations are important to consider. For instance, the campgrounds along Tioga Rd and in Tuolumne Meadows, some of which sit above 8000ft, may boast warm weather during the day, but come nightfall you'll be wishing you'd packed that wool sweater.

Yosemite has four campgrounds open all year: Upper Pines, Camp 4, Wawona and Hodgdon Meadow. The rest are open seasonally.

Yosemite Valley

While Yosemite Valley campgrounds are convenient to many of the park's major sights and activities, they're also very crowded, often noisy and definitely lacking in privacy. Don't camp here expecting to get away from it all – for solitude, you're better off in less-visited areas of the park.

Yosemite Valley's three Pines campgrounds (North Pines, Upper Pines and Lower Pines) are all located east of Yosemite Village at the far end of the Valley and are open to both RVs and tent campers.

YOSEMITE NATIONAL PARK CAMPGROUNDS

CAMPGROUND	LOCATION	DESCRIPTION	NO OF SITES
Hodgdon Meadow (p124)	Big Oak Flat Rd	Close to park entrance; utilitarian, can be crowded & noisy; easy drive to Yosemite Valley	105
Crane Flat (p124)	Crane Flat	Large family campground across five loops; varied sites; easy drive to Yosemite Valley	166
Bridalveil Creek (p121)	Glacier Point Rd	Near Glacier Point; some attractive sites; removed from Valley crowds	110
Porcupine Flat (p124)	Tioga Rd	Primitive, close to road but relatively quiet; RV access front half only	52
Tamarack Flat (p123)	Tioga Rd	Quiet, secluded, primitive; accessed via rough 3-mile road; tent only	52
White Wolf (p124)	Tioga Rd	Only nonprimitive campground in area; walking distance to store and restaurant	74
Yosemite Creek (p123)	Tioga Rd	Park's most secluded, quiet, primitive campground; accessed via rough 4.5-mile road; tent only	75
Tuolumne Meadows (p124)	Tuolumne Meadows	Park's biggest campground, many sites well dispersed over large, forested area	304
Wawona (p122)	Wawona	Located along river; nicer sites in back section (open summer only); short drive to store	93
Camp 4 (p119)	Yosemite Valley	Walk-in campground, popular with climbers; fee is per person; campers share sites; tent-only	35
Lower Pines (p119)	Yosemite Valley	Smaller Valley campground; minimum privacy	60
North Pines (p119)	Yosemite Valley	Smaller Valley campground; pleasant sites, slightly removed from development; adjacent to stables	81
Upper Pines (p121)	Yosemite Valley	Largest Valley campground, expect little privacy, especially in summer; close to Happy Isles	238

All of the above campgrounds have: bear-proof boxes, parking, picnic tables, fire pits and trash cans.

 Drinking Water   *Rest-rooms*   *Ranger Station Nearby*   *Payphone*

Camping

Camp 4   CAMPGROUND $
(Map p100; shared tent sites per person $6; ☺year-round) Legendary Camp 4 is Yosemite's only first-come, first-served campground and, for over half a century, has been a hub and home for Valley climbers. Each of the 35 walk-in sites holds six people, so be ready to share with others. It's a fun, low-key place, though not necessarily conducive to sleep.

The check-in kiosk opens at 8:30am; from Thursday through Saturday in summer, be in line by 6:30am.

Backpackers' Campground   CAMPGROUND $
(Map p100; tent sites per person $6; ☺Apr–mid-Oct) The 20 quiet, wooded sites here are open only to backpackers holding valid wilderness permits. It's a walk-in, self-registration campground, reached via a bridge over Tenaya Creek from the west end of North Pines Campground. It has vault toilets, and campers must treat water.

Lower Pines Campground   CAMPGROUND $
(Map p100; tent & RV sites $26; ☺Apr-Oct; 🐾) Set amid the trees on the south shore of the Merced River, this is the smallest of the Pines campgrounds, with 60 crammed and noisy sites. Reservations required.

North Pines Campground   CAMPGROUND $
(Map p100; tent & RV sites $26; ☺Apr-Oct; 🐾) A bit off the beaten path with 81 sites near Mirror Lake, North Pines campground is

YOSEMITE NATIONAL PARK SLEEPING

ELEVATION	OPEN	RESERVATION REQUIRED?	DAY FEE	FACILITIES /FEATURES
4872ft	year-round	mid-Apr–mid-Oct	$18-26	
6192ft	Jun–mid-Oct	yes	$26	
7200ft	Jul-early Sep	no	$14	
8100ft	Jul-Sep	no	$12	
6315ft	late Jun-Sep	no	$12	
8000ft	Jul-early Sep	no	$18	
7659ft	Jul-early Sep	no	$12	
8600ft	Jul-Sep	half reserved	$26	
4000ft	year-round	Apr-Sep	$18-26	
4000ft	year-round	no	$6 per person	
4000ft	Apr-Oct	yes	$26	
4000ft	Apr-Sep	yes	$26	
4000ft	year-round	mid-Mar–Nov	$26	

 RV Dump Station

 Dogs Allowed (On Leash)

 Grocery Store Nearby

Wheelchair Accessible

HOW TO SCORE A CAMPSITE IN YOSEMITE

If you're one of those folks who can't bear the thought of driving four hours or more without knowing whether there's a campsite waiting for you, you'd better make a reservation if you want to camp in Yosemite. It's the only way to ensure you'll have a place to lay your head. However, if you'd rather chance it – or if you couldn't get (or never got around to making) a reservation before you came – there are options.

Reservations

Reservations for all campgrounds within the park are handled by Recreation.gov (p45). Campsites can be reserved up to five months in advance. Reservations become available on the 15th of every month in one-month blocks. Be sure to act quickly (preferably online), as most dates in summer fill up the first day reservations become available – usually within minutes!

If you still have questions regarding the whole process or simply wish to speak with a human being in Yosemite, call the Yosemite Valley Campground Reservation Office (information only ☏209-372-8502). Also, check the website of Yosemite National Park (www.nps.gov/yose).

If you already have a reservation, proceed directly to the campground gate to check in. If you're going to be more than 24 hours late, call the campground office; otherwise you may lose your reservation. At check-in, the person listed on the reservation is required to be present and show identification (at least by the following day if they arrive late), and it is no longer possible to change the name on a camping reservation without canceling it.

Trying Your Luck

If you arrive at Yosemite without a reservation, there are several options. Practically every day, reservation-only campsites become available due to cancellations or early departures, and these are sold on a first-come, first-served basis from the reservation offices. If nothing's available when they open, you can put your name on a waiting list and return at the prescribed time (usually 3pm) to find out if you've gotten one.

YOSEMITE VALLEY

If you want to stay in Yosemite Valley, you have two options, though in summer you'll need to be there before opening time for either. Option one is the first-come, first-served, walk-in campground at Camp 4. A lawn chair line starts forming by 6:30am for summer weekends, and the benefit of getting a site here is that you can stay for up to seven nights.

Option two is the Yosemite Valley Campground Reservation Office (Map p100; ☏209-372-8502 information only; Curry Village parking lot; ⊘8am-5pm) in the day-use parking lot near Camp Curry. It rarely has multiple-night cancellations, but it has more potential sites available than Camp 4.

OTHER PARK AREAS

Outside the Valley, the first-come, first-served campgrounds are Bridalveil Creek, Tamarack Flat, White Wolf, Yosemite Creek, Porcupine Flat and half the sites at Tuolumne Meadows. Or you can stop by one of the other reservation offices:

Big Oak Flat (p123) Next to the Big Oak Information Station; no waiting list so be here when it opens to scoop up cancellations.

Tuolumne Meadows (☏209-372-4025; ⊘8am-5pm Jul-Sep) Near the campground entrance.

Wawona (☏209-375-9535; ⊘8am-5pm late May-early Oct) On Chilnualna Falls Rd.

probably the quietest of the valley's campgrounds. Reservations required.

Upper Pines Campground CAMPGROUND $
(Map p100; tent & RV sites $26; ☺ year-round; ☒) With 238 sites spread under a forest of pine, Yosemite's second-largest campground is close-quarters camping at its finest. It sits along the bus and pedestrian road to the Nature Center at Happy Isles and trailhead, only a short walk away from Curry Village. Reservations required mid-March through November.

Lodging

Yosemite Valley offers a fair range of accommodations, from simple tent cabins to comfortable motel units to luxurious accommodations. Tent cabins at Curry Village and Housekeeping Camp are great for families who wish to avoid both exorbitant hotel costs and the labor of setting up camp.

Housekeeping Camp CABINS $$
(Map p100; q $106; ☺ Apr-Oct) This cluster of 266 cabins, each walled in by concrete on three sides and lidded by a canvas roof, is crammed and noisy, but the setting along the Merced River has its merits. Each unit can sleep up to six and has electricity, light, a table and chairs, and a covered patio with picnic tables.

Curry Village CABINS $$
(Map p100; tent cabin $121-126, cabin $193, without bath $146; ☎☒) Founded in 1899 as a summer camp, Curry has hundreds of units squished tightly together beneath towering evergreens. The canvas cabins are basically glorified tents, so for more comfort, quiet and privacy get one of the cozy wood cabins, which have bedspreads, drapes and vintage posters. There are also 18 attractive motel-style rooms in the **Stoneman House** (r $202), including a loft suite sleeping up to six.

Yosemite Lodge at the Falls MOTEL $$$
(Map p100; r from $235; @☎☒) ✈ Situated a short walk from Yosemite Falls, this multi-building complex contains a wide range of eateries, a lively bar, big pool and other handy amenities. Delightful rooms, thanks to a recent eco-conscious renovation, now feel properly lodge-like, with rustic wooden furniture and striking nature photography. All have cable TV, telephone, fridge and coffeemaker, and great patio or balcony panoramas.

Ahwahnee Hotel HISTORIC HOTEL $$$
(Map p100; r from $458; @☎☒) The crème de la crème of Yosemite's lodging, this sumptuous historic property dazzles with soaring ceilings, Turkish kilims lining the hallways and atmospheric lounges with mammoth stone fireplaces. It's the gold standard for upscale lodges, though if you're not blessed with bullion, you can still soak up the ambiance during afternoon tea, a drink in the bar or a gourmet meal.

Other options include 24 cottages out back and a handful of suites.

🛏 Glacier Point & Badger Pass

Camping

Bridalveil Creek Campground CAMPGROUND $
(tent & RV sites $18; ☺ Jul-early Sep; ☒) Tucked 25 miles (a mere 40 minutes) away from the Valley buzz, this 110-site campground is the only developed place to stay in the Glacier Point Rd area. Sites are well spaced beneath pretty pine forest, and the ones near the amphitheater front a long granite outcropping that's perfect for watching the sunset in solitude.

CAMPFIRES

Everyone loves a campfire, but take note of a few rules. Fires in Yosemite campgrounds are allowed only within established fire rings or barbecue pits. Wood and kindling gathering is illegal in the Valley, so you'll have to buy firewood. To improve air quality, from May through September campfires in the Valley are allowed only between 5pm and 10pm. Those staying in campgrounds outside the Valley are allowed to gather wood, but it must be downed (on the ground) and dead. It's often easier (and always more environmentally sound) to simply buy a bundle, preferably from within a 50-mile radius to thwart invasive pests.

After having a campfire, make sure it's completely out. Stir the fire and coals with water a half-hour before going to bed or leaving the site, then hold your hand close to check for any lingering hot spots.

LODGING RESERVATIONS IN YOSEMITE

Nearly all the lodging in Yosemite National Park, from tent cabins and High Sierra Camps to the Ahwahnee Hotel, is managed by the park concessionaire. The concessionaire was in the process of changing at press time, so check the park website (www.nps.gov/yose/planyourvisit/eatingsleeping.htm) for reservations contact information. The only accommodations outside that system are the Ostrander Ski Hut and the homes and cabins in Foresta (a private vacation settlement south of Big Oak Flat Rd), Yosemite West and the Redwoods in Yosemite.

Reservations are available 366 days in advance of your arrival date. Places get snapped up early for summer months, especially on weekends and holidays, but if you're flexible, there's often some space available on short notice, especially midweek. You can go on the website and easily view everything that's available.

If you roll into the park without a reservation, the Yosemite Valley Visitor Center and all the lodging front desks have courtesy phones so you can inquire about room availability throughout the park. That said, it's important to remember that rooms *rarely* become available midsummer.

Located 8 miles up from Hwy 41, it's first-come, first-served, has drinking water and flush toilets, and there's a horse camp at the back. The altitude here (7200ft) keeps things much cooler than the Valley.

Lodging

This private development rents contemporary accommodations in a community just west of Hwy 41. Although it is outside the park proper, Yosemite West is accessible only from inside the park. Look for the turnoff about half a mile south of the intersection with Glacier Point Rd. Drive about a mile and you'll reach a sign, where there are maps and phone numbers of the local establishments.

Scenic Wonders   ACCOMMODATION SERVICES $$$
(📞888-967-3648; www.scenicwonders.com; condo from $210, cabin from $265) This Yosemite West management company rents out over three dozen houses, cabins and studios.

Yosemite West High Sierra B&B   B&B $$$
(📞209-372-4808; www.yosemitehighsierra.com; 7460 Henness Ridge Rd; r $270-340, apt $360-520; 🛜) Choose from five B&B lodge rooms (for up to three people) or an apartment that sleeps up to five. Minimum stay of two to three nights. The owners have been sharing their love and knowledge of Yosemite for over 20 years, and guests swoon over the sunsets from the view deck.

🛏 Wawona

Camping

Wawona Campground   CAMPGROUND $
(tent & RV sites $18-26; ⊙year-round; 🐾) The south fork of the Merced River cuts through this southernmost section of Yosemite, and this campground includes some sites situated right alongside its banks. It's a pleasant place to set up your tent or RV, though some of the nicer spots are in the back section and only open in summer, when the whole campground goes on the reservation system.

Between October and April, the campground is first-come, first-served.

Lodging

Wawona Hotel   HISTORIC HOTEL $$
(r $226, without bath $155; ⊙mid-Mar–Dec; 🛜🏊) This National Historic Landmark, dating from 1879, is a collection of six graceful, white-washed New England–style buildings flanked by wide porches. The 104 rooms – with no phone or TV – come with Victorian-style furniture and other period items, and about half the rooms share bathrooms, with nice robes provided for the walk there.

Redwoods in Yosemite   ACCOMMODATIONS SERVICES $$$
(📞209-375-6666, 877-753-8566; www.redwoodsinyosemite.com; 8038 Chilnualna Falls Rd; homes per night $243-1480; 🛜🏊) This private enterprise rents over 130 fully furnished ac-

commodations of various sizes and levels of comfort, from rustic log cabins to spacious six-bedroom vacation homes. (Hot tub, anyone?) The main office (where there is free coffee and tantalizing fresh popcorn) is 2 miles east of Hwy 41 on Chilnualna Falls Rd; look for the junction just north of the Wawona General Store.

There's a three-night minimum stay in summer and during holidays; two nights otherwise.

🛏 Big Oak Flat Road & Tioga Road

Camping

If you're in the mood for some solitude and crisper evening air, you'll find a number of options along Tioga Rd (Hwy 120) as it heads east from Crane Flat to Tuolumne Meadows. When it's been a light snow season, early birds may get the place all to themselves. The four campgrounds along Tioga Rd operate on a first-come, first-served basis, and two of them are the most rugged, quiet and beautiful in the park. White Wolf offers flush toilets and running water, while the other three are primitive, with only vault toilets and no water tap, so be sure to bring your own water or be prepared to purify it from adjacent streams.

Next door to the Big Oak Flat Information Station, the staff at the small **Campground Reservation Office** (☏209-379-2123; ☺8am-5pm, mid-Apr–mid-Oct) offers advice on camping options and posts information on site availability at the first-come, first-served

campgrounds at Tamarack, Yosemite Creek, Porcupine Flat and White Wolf, though they don't assign sites. Come in at 8am to see if there are any cancellations at Hodgdon Meadow or Crane Flat campgrounds.

Tamarack Flat Campground CAMPGROUND $ (tent sites $12; ☺late Jun-Sep; 🐾) One of the most serene and spacious places in the park to set up your tent is 3 miles down a rough road that's as steep and narrow as it is woodsy and beautiful. Expect about a 15-minute drive off Tioga Rd each way (RVs and trailers aren't recommended). The 52 tent-only sites are well dispersed among trees, with some near a creek – which lends the campground a very open feel, with lots of sun and sky. The parts of the park accessible by road are rarely this quiet.

White Wolf Campground CAMPGROUND $ (tent & RV sites $18; ☺Jul-early Sep; 🐾) Located north of Tioga Rd on a mile-long spur road, this 74-site campground, adjacent to the White Wolf Lodge and store, enjoys a relaxed setting among pine trees and granite boulders beside a lazy stream. It's an attractive and convenient alternative to the Valley without forsaking all the creature comforts of civilization. There's also a backpackers' campground.

Ambitious hikers can hike from here to the top of El Capitan.

Yosemite Creek Campground CAMPGROUND $ (tent sites $12; ☺Jul-early Sep; 🐾) Drive 4.5 miles (about 20 minutes) down a rough stretch of the old Tioga Rd – a narrow, winding piece of roadway that's no good for RVs or trailers – and you find yourself in the most secluded, spacious and serene

---

SHOWERING IN & AROUND YOSEMITE

Yosemite campers have one thing in common: they all need a wash. No campgrounds in the park have showers. Should you feel the need to remove that four-day layer of grime or wash your hair, head to the public showers at Curry Village or Housekeeping Camp. Both places have hot showers and charge about $5 for non-guests. And after a few years of turning away non-guests, the Tuolumne Meadows Lodge is scheduled to reopen a new shower house and welcome members of the public. No public shower facilities exist at Wawona.

Following are some handy pay showers outside the park:

High Sierra RV Park (☏559-683-7662; www.highsierrarv.com; 40389 Hwy 41, Oakhurst; shower $5; ☺8-11:30am & 1-6pm year-round)

Indian Flat RV Park (☏209-379-2339; www.indianflatrvpark.com; 9988 Hwy 140; tent sites $30, RV sites $42-48, tent cabins $89-129, cottages $149-169; 🐾🐾)

Mono Vista RV Park (☏760-647-6401; www.monovistarvpark.net; Hwy 395, Lee Vining; shower $3; ☺9am-6pm Apr-Oct)

car-accessible campground in the park. The 75 primitive sites are surprisingly well dispersed: some in the trees, others in the open.

A trail from here leads to the top of Yosemite Falls.

Porcupine Flat Campground CAMPGROUND $
(tent & RV sites $12; ☺ Jul–mid-Oct; 🍴) If you want easy access to Tioga Rd and don't mind treating or bringing your own water, try this 52-site campground, which sits about halfway between Crane Flat and Tuolumne Meadows, the latter only a 20-minute drive away. The sites up front can handle RVs and campers, but the quieter and more rustic back half is for tents only.

At 8100ft, it's the second-highest developed campground in the park, and a good place to spend the night acclimatizing before hitting the high country. There's some road noise in the daytime, but it dissipates after dark.

Hodgdon Meadow Campground CAMPGROUND $
(Big Oak Flat Rd; tent & RV sites $18-26; ☺ year-round; 🍴) Just east of the Big Oak Flat Entrance, this popular campground has 105 mostly crowded sites; a few of the nicer ones are walk-ins, though you won't have to go more than 20yd. All campsites here must be reserved during summer (mid-April to mid-October) but are first-come, first-served the rest of the year.

FOOD STORAGE

Store all food and scented items – cosmetics, toothpaste, soda cans and any other food-related trash – in the bear-proof storage lockers provided at each campsite and in major parking lots. Never leave anything in your car, including canned goods. Bears have a powerful sense of smell and are adept at breaking into locked vehicles. They also recognize coolers and grocery bags, so even if these are empty and clean, at least cover them with a blanket. Failure to follow these rules can lead to a citation (or the trashing of your car). When cooking at your campsite, avoid leaving the locker hanging open and the food spread out. Treat the locker like a fridge – pull out only what you need, then shut and latch the door.

Crane Flat Campground CAMPGROUND $
(Big Oak Flat Rd; tent & RV sites $26; ☺ Jun–mid-Oct; 🍴) Around 8 miles east of the Big Oak Flat Entrance is this large campground (166 sites), located near the Crane Flat store and the junction with Tioga Rd. Sites lie along five different loops, most in the trees and some very nicely dispersed. The central location is great for those wanting to split their time between Tuolumne Meadows and Yosemite Valley.

Reservations are required year-round; the campground can open late during high snow years.

Lodging

White Wolf Lodge CABINS, TENT CABINS $$
(tent cabin $126, cabin with bath $158; ☺ Jul–mid-Sep) This complex enjoys its own little world a mile up a spur road, away from the hubbub and traffic of Hwy 120 and the Valley. There are 24 spartan four-bedded tent cabins without electricity and four very-in-demand hard-walled cabins that feel like rustic motel rooms. The generator cuts out at 11pm, so you'll need a flashlight until early morning.

🛏 Tuolumne Meadows

Camping

Tuolumne Meadows Campground CAMPGROUND $
(tent & RV sites $26; ☺ Jul-Sep; 🍴) This is the largest campground in the park, with 304 sites for tents or RVs (35ft limit). Despite its size, many of the sites are tucked into the trees, making the place feel far less crowded than other park campgrounds. Some of the sites in the 'E' and 'F' sections are delightfully peaceful, and 'A' is adjacent to the Tuolumne River.

At 8600ft, it also includes a horse camp, group camp and walk-in backpackers' campground for those with wilderness permits. Half the sites here are on the reservation system, while the other half are kept first-come, first-served. The evening campfire program is excellent.

Lodging

Tuolumne Meadows Lodge TENT CABINS $$
(tent cabin $123; ☺ mid-Jun–mid-Sep) In the high country, about 55 miles from the valley, this 'lodge' consists of 69 wood-framed,

WORTH A TRIP

HIGH SIERRA CAMPS

In the backcountry near Tuolumne Meadows, the exceptionally popular High Sierra Camps provide shelter and sustenance to hikers who'd rather not carry food or a tent. The camps – called **Vogelsang**, **Merced Lake**, **Sunrise**, **May Lake** and **Glen Aulin** – are set 6 to 10 miles apart along a loop trail. They consist of dormitory-style canvas tent cabins with beds, blankets or comforters, plus showers (at May Lake, Sunrise and Merced Lake – subject to water availability) and a central dining tent. Guests bring their own sheets and towels. The rate is $180 per adult ($109 for children aged seven to 12) per night, including breakfast and dinner. Organized hiking or saddle trips led by ranger naturalists are also available (from $1172).

A short season (roughly late June to September) and high demand mean that there's a lottery for reservations. **Applications** (☎559-253-5672; www.yosemitepark.com) are currently accepted in September and October only. If you don't have a reservation, call from February to check for cancellations. Dates vary year to year, so watch the website for updates.

While the camp lodgings are only for reserved guests, each has an adjacent backpackers' campsite available to anyone with a wilderness permit. The backpackers' campsites come complete with bear boxes, toilets and potable water taps. It's also possible to reserve meals at a High Sierra Camp, which can ease the burden of carrying your own food. Meals-only spaces are limited to six per camp; use the above lottery application to reserve.

canvas-covered tent cabins, each set on a cement floor and boasting a prehistoric wood-burning stove, card table, roll-up canvas window and candles (no electricity). Bathrooms and showers are shared, and each cabin has four twin beds or two twins and a double.

Linens are included, but bring your sleeping bag if you want to be extra warm. The lodge complex – which is part of the original High Sierra Camp loop – also includes a dining hall serving great breakfasts, box lunches and dinner. Cooking is prohibited. To guarantee you get a room, book *366* days in advance.

Hetch Hetchy

Camping

The only place to stay in this area is the **backpackers' campground** (tent sites per person $6; ⏲year-round), which is one of the park's nicest. But it's brutally hot in summer and available only to holders of valid wilderness permits for Hetch Hetchy.

Once you leave the park, the nearest official campground is the pleasant **Dimond O Campground** (☎877-444-6777; www.recreation.gov; Evergreen Rd; tent & RV sites $24; ⏲May-Sep), which lies 6 miles north of Hwy 120 on Evergreen Rd, in the Stanislaus National Forest. Some sites can be reserved; others are first-come, first-served.

Lodging

There is no park lodging in Hetch Hetchy. The nearest accommodations are at the lovely Evergreen Lodge, about 1.5 miles outside the park border, just south of Camp Mather (a summer camp open to San Francisco residents by lottery).

★**Evergreen Lodge** CABINS, CAMPGROUND **$$$**
(☎209-379-2606; www.evergreenlodge.com; 33160 Evergreen Rd; tents $90-125, cabins $180-415; @☎≋) Outside Yosemite National Park near the entrance to Hetch Hetchy, this classic 90-year-old resort consists of a series of lovingly decorated and comfy cabins (each with its own cache of board games) spread out among the trees. Accommodations run from rustic to deluxe, and all cabins have private porches without distracting phone or TV. Roughing-it guests can cheat with comfy, prefurnished tents.

The place has just about everything you could ask for, including a tavern (complete with pool table), a general store, a fantastic restaurant serving all meals, live music, horseshoe pits, ping-pong, a giant outdoor chess set, a kids' zip line, and all sorts of guided hikes and outdoor activities – many of them family-oriented. Seasonal equipment rentals are also available.

Rush Creek Lodge LODGE **$$$**
(☎209-379-2373; www.rushcreeklodge.com; 34001 Hwy 120, Groveland; q/2-bedroom villa from $295/350; @☎≋) Opening in summer

2016 a mere half mile from the Big Oak Flat Entrance, Evergreen Lodge's new sister resort promises to be an exciting overnight option. 'Contemporary rustic' lodge rooms fit four and spacious hillside and forest villas sleep up to six people, all with view decks.

A recreation concierge will be on hand to help visitors sort through what to see and do. There will be free family-friendly activities on-site daily, plus a games room, nature playground, gold panning, bike paths and a zipline for kids. A full **restaurant** (breakfast & lunch $7-16, dinner mains $11-34; ☺ 7-10:30am, noon-3pm, 5:30-10pm May-Oct, 5-9pm Nov-Apr) serving Californian cuisine will offer all meals.

✖ EATING & DRINKING

With the exception of dining at the Mountain Room Restaurant or the Wawona and Ahwahnee Hotels, Yosemite is hardly defined by its culinary wonders – except, of course, when setting comes into play. As for the food, content yourself with reliably prepared, fill-the-stomach type meals that are slightly overpriced but certainly do the trick after a good hike. Some places, such as the Tuolumne Meadows Grill (where the French fries are undoubtedly phenomenal) or the Wawona Hotel (for brunch), do have a sort of cult following among visitors in the know. Whether you're looking for a sit-down meal or a sandwich for the road, just about every option is available in Yosemite.

All Yosemite restaurants in the park are run by the park concessionaire, and everything (except dinner at the Ahwahnee) is child-friendly.

✖ Yosemite Valley

Yosemite Village and Curry Village are the best options for relatively cheap eats and to-go items.

Yosemite Village

Village Store   SUPERMARKET $
(Map p100; Yosemite Village; ☺8am-8pm, to 10pm summer) The biggest and best grocery store in the park is located smack in the center of Yosemite Village. Whether you're after last-minute items or full-fledged dinners, there's no denying the place comes in handy. The store carries decent produce, fresh meat and fish, and even some surprising items like tofu hot dogs, hummus, udon noodles and polenta.

You'll also find a small section of camping supplies along with plenty of souvenirs.

Degnan's Deli   DELI $
(Map p100; Yosemite Village; sandwiches $7.25-8.25; ☺7am-5pm; 🖉) Likely the best of the bunch in the Yosemite Village complex, this store-cum deli whips up excellent made-to-order sandwiches, breakfast items and snack foods. Picnic table seating outside.

Degnan's Cafe   CAFE $
(Map p100; Yosemite Village; sandwiches & salads $5-10; ☺11am-6pm Apr-Sep; 🖫) Beside Degnan's Deli, this cafe serves espresso drinks, smoothies and pastries, which you can guzzle down over a newspaper purchased at one of the stands outside.

Degnan's Loft   PIZZA $
(Map p100; Yosemite Village; mains $8-12.50; ☺11am-9pm late May-Sep; 🖉🖫) Head upstairs to this convivial place with high-beamed ceilings and a many-sided fireplace, and kick back under the dangling lift chair for decent salads, lasagna and pizza.

Village Grill   FAST FOOD $
(Map p100; Yosemite Village; mains $6-13; ☺11am-5pm Apr-Oct; 🖉) Fight the chipmunks for burgers, hot sandwiches, salads and fries alfresco. The housemade salsa is divine.

Curry Village

Curry Village's dining choices are hardly exciting, but they're convenient if you're staying in one of the Curry tent cabins or returning hungry from a grueling hike via the nearby Happy Isles Trailhead.

Meadow Grill   FAST FOOD $
(Map p100; Curry Village; mains $5.50-8; ☺11am-5pm Apr-Oct, to 7pm summer) Hot dogs, burgers and a few salads on a deck near the parking area.

Curry Village Pizza Patio   PIZZA $
(Map p100; Curry Village; pizzas from $9; ☺noon-10pm, shorter winter hours) Enjoy tasty pizza at this buzzing eatery that becomes a chatty après-hike hangout in the late afternoon.

Curry Village Coffee Corner   CAFE $
(Map p100; Curry Village; pastries $2-5; ☺6am-10pm, shorter winter hours) For a coffee jolt or sugar fix.

Curry Village Store
MARKET **$**

(Map p100; Curry Village; ⊘8am-10pm summer, shorter winter hours) The Curry Village store is undoubtedly handy if you're in the neighborhood and need snacks, sodas, gifts or beer.

Curry Village Dining Pavilion
CAFETERIA **$$**

(Map p100; Curry Village; breakfast adult/child $9.75/6, dinner adult/child $15.50/7.50; ⊘7-10am & 5:30-8:30pm Mar-Oct; ⓘ) The main restaurant in Curry Village, the cafeteria-style setting has all the charm of a train-station waiting room. The quality of food has improved a tad since the restaurant transitioned from a buffet format, though it's still pretty unexciting.

Curry Village Bar
BAR

(Map p100; Curry Village; ⊘noon-10pm) Directly beside the Curry Village Pizza Patio window, this tiny bar pulls a couple of decent microbrews and pours a full range of cocktails.

Ahwahnee Hotel

Ahwahnee Coffee Bar
CAFE **$**

(Ahwahnee Hotel; pastries $4-6, breakfast items $12; ⊘7-10:30am; ⓘ) In the morning, the Ahwahnee Bar transforms into a café serving espresso drinks, pastries and continental breakfast items.

★Ahwahnee Dining Room
CALIFORNIAN **$$$**

(Map p100; ☏209-372-1489; Ahwahnee Hotel; breakfast $7-22.50, lunch $15-22, dinner $26-46; ⊘7-10am, 11:30am-3pm & 5:30-9pm; ⓘ) ⚘ The formal ambiance (mind your manners) may not be for everybody, but few would not be awed by the sumptuous decor, soaring beamed ceiling and palatial chandeliers. The menu is constantly in flux, but most dishes have perfect pitch and are beautifully presented. There's a dress code at dinner, but otherwise shorts and sneakers are OK.

Sunday **brunch** (adult/child $45/15; ⊘7am to 3pm) is amazing. Reservations highly recommended for brunch and dinner.

Ahwahnee Bar
BAR

(Map p100; Ahwahnee Hotel; ⊘11:30am-11pm) The perfect way to experience the Ahwahnee without dipping too deep into your pockets; settle in for a drink at this cozy bar, complete with pianist. Appetizers and light meals ($10.50 to $25) provide sustenance.

RICK HYMAN / GETTY IMAGES ©

Ahwahnee Hotel

Yosemite Lodge at the Falls

★Yosemite Lodge Food Court
CAFETERIA **$**

(Map p100; Yosemite Lodge; mains $5.50-13.50; ⊘6:30am-9pm, to 8pm winter; ⓘ) This self-service restaurant has several tummy-filling stations serving a large choice of pastas, burgers, pizza and sandwiches, either made to order or served from beneath heat lamps. Proceed to the cashier and find a table inside or on the patio.

★Mountain Room Restaurant
AMERICAN **$$$**

(Map p100; ☏209-372-1403; Yosemite Lodge; mains $17-36; ⊘5:30-9:30pm; ⓘⓘ) ⚘ With a killer view of Yosemite Falls, the window tables at this casual and elegant contemporary steakhouse are a hot commodity. The chefs whip up the best meals in the park, with flat-iron steak and locally caught mountain trout wooing diners under a rotating display of nature photographs. Reservations accepted only for groups larger than eight; casual dress is OK.

Mountain Room Lounge
BAR

(Map p100; Yosemite Lodge; ⊘noon-11pm Sat & Sun, 4:30-11pm Mon-Fri) Catch up on the latest sports news while knocking back draft brews at this large bar that buzzes in wintertime. Order a s'mores kit (graham crackers, chocolate squares and marshmallows) to roast in the open-pit fireplace. Kids welcome until 10pm.

✕ Glacier Point & Badger Pass

When the road is open, the unexciting **snack bar** (Map p100; ⊙10am-5pm) at Glacier Point is your only food option.

In the wintertime (until 4pm), Badger Pass runs a **fast food grill** (mains $5-8) serving pizza, burgers, nachos and chicken strips. Upstairs, the walls of the **Snowflake Room** (mains under $10; ⊙11am-4pm) are covered with cool old ski photos and pieces of vintage ski equipment. On weekends and holidays, the cozy wood-beamed room offers sandwiches and salads, a bar and a view of the lifts.

✕ Wawona

The Wawona General Store, a short walk from the Wawona Hotel, offers a few picnic and camping items but focuses more on snacks and gifts.

Pine Tree Market   MARKET $
(7995 Chilnualna Falls Rd; ⊙8am-8pm summer, 8:30am-6:30pm rest of year) This tiny and super-friendly market sells groceries and bags of divine locally roasted coffee (take a deep breath in the aisles), and in summer it sells flats of seasonal fruit grown by regional farmers. It's located a mile east of Hwy 41 amid the redwoods in Yosemite; turn east off Chilnualna Falls Rd, which is just north of the Pioneer History Center.

Wawona Hotel Dining Room   AMERICAN $$$
(Wawona Hotel; breakfast & lunch $11-16, dinner $19-31; ⊙7:30-10am, 11:30am-2pm & 5:30-9pm Easter-Dec; 🅿🚼) 🍴 Beautiful sequoia-painted lamps light this old-fashioned white-tablecloth dining room, and the Victorian detail makes it an enchanting place to have an upscale (though somewhat overpriced) meal. 'Tasteful, casual attire' is the rule for dinner dress, and there's a barbecue on the lawn every Saturday during summer.

✕ Big Oak Flat Road & Tioga Road

A mile north of Tioga Rd, the White Wolf Lodge area has a miniscule store that sells snacks, ice-cream bars and coffee. At lunchtime, it has prepared sandwiches available, and there's always a vegetarian option available. The small, rustic **dining room** (🅿209-372-8416; breakfast $12, dinner adult/child $29/10; ⊙7:30-9:30am & 6-8pm; 🅿) is open for a buffet breakfast and in the evening for family-style dinners inside or on the front porch. Reservations are highly advised for dinner, with four seating times available.

✕Tuolumne Meadows

As with everything else along Tioga Rd, the eating establishments in Tuolumne Meadows are open roughly late June to mid-September only. Exact dates depend on snowfall.

Tuolumne Meadows Store   MARKET $
(⊙8am-8pm mid-Jun-mid-Sep) Browse the busy aisles of the Tuolumne Meadows Store, which stocks just about every necessity item you could have possibly forgotten: wine, beer, chips, dehydrated backpacking food, a smattering of produce, tofu dogs, dorky hats, camp cups, firewood, candy bars, fishing tackle and camping supplies, all at marked-up prices.

Tuolumne Meadows Grill   FAST FOOD $
(Tioga Rd; mains $7-12; ⊙8am-5pm mid-Jun-mid-Sep) You can hardly say you've visited Tuolumne without smacking down a burger and a basket of fries in the parking lot in front of the Tuolumne Meadows Grill. The soft-serve ice-cream cones and hearty breakfasts – not to mention the people-watching at the picnic tables – are equally mandatory.

Tuolumne Meadows Lodge   AMERICAN $$
(🅿209-372-8413; breakfast $6-12, dinner $10-$26; ⊙7-9am & 5:45-8pm; 🚼) For a classic Yosemite experience, make a dinner reservation (for breakfast, just show up) at the Tuolumne Meadows Lodge. The place is as basic-looking as they come, but the breakfasts are hearty and the dinners are good. Best of all, good company is pretty much guaranteed (or at least required): tables are shared. Snacks and cold drinks are sold all day at the lodge lobby.

✕ Hetch Hetchy

There are no eating establishments or stores in Hetch Hetchy, just one excellent place a mile outside the park border.

★ **Evergreen Lodge**   CALIFORNIAN $$
(📞 209-379-2606; www.evergreenlodge.com; 33160 Evergreen Rd; breakfast & lunch $12-18, dinner $20-34; ⊘ 7-10:30am & noon-3pm & 5-9pm; ➤☷) Creative and satisfying, the Evergreen's restaurant serves some of the best meals around, with big and delicious breakfasts, three types of burgers (Black Angus beef, buffalo and veggie) and dinner choices including dishes like rib-eye steak, grilled venison and vegan tamales. The homey wooden tavern is a perennial favorite forevening cocktails, beers on tap over a game of pool and live music on select weekends. A general store fills the gaps with to-go sandwiches, snacks and dreamy gelato.

ⓘ Information

BOOKSTORES

Almost every park store, from the gift shop at Yosemite Lodge to the convenience stores at Wawona and Crane Flat, offers a variety of books and park maps. For the best selection of information about the park and Sierra Nevada region, visit the **Yosemite Conservancy Bookstore** (www.yosemiteconservancystore.com), adjacent to the Yosemite Valley Visitor Center. The store is operated by the nonprofit Yosemite Conservancy, and proceeds benefit the park.

Hiking maps and guides can be found in all the park's sports shops, visitor centers and wilderness centers.

The Ansel Adams Gallery in Yosemite Village also carries a great selection of books, including fine-art and photography volumes.

DANGERS & ANNOYANCES

Yosemite is prime black bear habitat. Follow park rules on proper food storage and utilize bear-proof food lockers when parked overnight. Mosquitoes can be pesky in summer, so bug spray's not a bad idea.

Valley traffic can be oppressive in late spring and summer. Getting around by shuttle or bicycle is highly recommended.

INTERNET ACCESS

Degnan's Cafe (Yosemite Village; per min 25¢; ⊘ 7am-6pm) Pay terminals in this café adjacent to Degnan's Deli.

Mariposa County Public Library (📞 209-375-6510; Bassett Memorial Library, Chilnualna Falls Rd, Wawona; ⊘ 1-6pm Mon-Fri, 10am-3pm Sat; ☷) Free internet terminals and wi-fi available.

Mariposa County Public Library (📞 209-372-4552; 58 Cedar Ct, Girls Club Bldg, Yosemite Valley; ⊘ 9am-noon Mon & Tue, 9am-1pm Wed & Thu; ☷) Free internet terminals and wi-fi available.

Yosemite Lodge at the Falls (Yosemite Valley; ⊘ 24hr; ☷) Wi-fi costs $6 per day for non-guests.

MEDIA

For newspapers in Yosemite Valley, hit the coin-operated boxes outside Degnan's Deli, in front of the stores at Curry Village and at Housekeeping Camp. In Tuolumne Meadows, they're sold in front of the store and at the Tuolumne Meadows Lodge.

MEDICAL SERVICES

Yosemite Medical Clinic (📞 209-372-4637; 9000 Ahwahnee Dr, Yosemite Village; ⊘ 9am-7pm daily late-May–late Sep, 9am-5pm Mon-Fri late-Sep–late-May) A 24-hour emergency service is available.

MONEY

Stores in Yosemite Village, Curry Village and Wawona all have ATMs, as does the Ahwahnee Hotel and Yosemite Lodge.

POST

Tuolumne Meadows Post Office (⊘ 9am-5pm Mon-Fri, to 1pm Sat, closed mid-Sep–mid-Jun) Inside the Tuolumne Meadows Store.

Wawona Post Office (⊘ 9am-5pm Mon-Fri, to noon Sat) At Wawona General Store.

Yosemite Lodge Post Office (⊘ 12:30-2:45pm Mon-Fri) Next to the pool.

Yosemite Village Post Office (Map p100; ⊘ 8:30am-5pm Mon-Fri, 10am-noon Sat)

TELEPHONE

There are pay phones at every developed location throughout the park. Cell phone reception is sketchy, depending on your location, and AT&T, Verizon and Sprint have the best coverage.

USEFUL WEBSITES

Discussion forums with good local advice can be found at www.yosemite.ca.us/forum and www.yosemitenews.info.

Yosemite Conservancy (www.yosemiteconservancy.org) Information and educational programs offered by the nonprofit park-support organization.

Yosemite National Park (www.nps.gov/yose) Official Yosemite National Park Service site with the most comprehensive and current information. News and road closures/openings are often posted first on its Facebook page (www.facebook.com/YosemiteNPS).

ℹ️ ROADSIDE KNOWLEDGE

Ever wonder what those little wooden roadside markers are? You know, the ones with the Half Dome symbol and a code like H15 or T32. Well, wonder no longer. They demarcate sights along roadways throughout Yosemite. But in order to decipher the code, you have to carry a copy of the handy little *Yosemite Road Guide*, a booklet featuring descriptions that correspond to the codes on the signs. Also packed with some great park history, the booklet is a must-have for any drive through the park. Pick one up at a visitor center or Yosemite Conservancy bookstores anywhere in the park.

VISITOR CENTERS

Rangers staff the park visitor centers, and can answer questions and suggest suitable hiking trails, activities and sights. The visitor centers offer excellent displays on park history and the local environment, as well as a range of maps, hiking and climbing guides, geology and ecology books, and gift items. While less extensive, the centers at Big Oak Flat and Wawona are still good places to ask questions, get your bearings and purchase useful books and maps.

Big Oak Flat Information Station (☑209-379-1899; ⊗8am-5pm late May-Sep) Also has a wilderness permit desk.

Tuolumne Meadows Visitor Center (☑209-372-0263; ⊗9am-6pm Jun-Sep)

Wawona Visitor Center (☑209-375-9531; ⊗8:30am-5pm May-Sep) Issues wilderness permits.

Yosemite Valley Visitor Center (Map p100; ☑209-372-0200; Yosemite Village; ⊗9am-5pm) The main office, with exhibits and free film screenings in the theater.

WILDERNESS CENTERS

Yosemite's two main wilderness centers are in Yosemite Valley and Tuolumne Meadows. At both, hikers can buy maps and guidebooks, check current weather and trail conditions, get helpful tips on planning and packing, and – most importantly – obtain wilderness permits. You can also rent the all-important bear-proof food canisters ($5 per week).

Advance reservations for wilderness permits (p72) cannot be made through the wilderness centers themselves. Note also that reservations are not necessary for winter camping, but you still need to get a wilderness permit during wintertime.

The **Wawona Visitor Center** (p130) also issues wilderness permits.

Big Oak Flat Wilderness Center (☑209-379-1967) Inside the Big Oak Flat Information Station.

Hetch Hetchy Entrance (☑209-379-1922; ⊗7am-9pm summer, 8am-5pm winter)

Tuolumne Meadows Wilderness Center (☑209-372-0309; ⊗8am-5pm Jun-Sep) Issues wilderness permits.

Yosemite Valley Wilderness Center (Map p100; ☑209-372-0745; Yosemite Village; ⊗8am-5pm May-Sep) Wilderness permits, maps and backcountry advice.

ℹ️ Getting Around

BICYCLE

Twelve miles of mostly flat, paved bicycle trails run up and down Yosemite Valley, making biking a fantastic way to get around. If you've ever sat in Valley traffic on a summer day, you know the merits of strapping a couple of bikes to the car. Since the Valley is flat, single-speed bikes are great. If you don't have your own bike, rentals (p87) are available at Yosemite Lodge and Curry Village.

CAR & MOTORCYCLE

The park speed limit is 35mph, except in Yosemite Valley and by Tenaya Lake, where it drops to 25mph. Resist the urge to speed – bears don't look before crossing the road!

You'll find gas stations in Crane Flat and Wawona. (The long-time station in Tuolumne Meadows has closed.) The stations generally close after dark, but you can gas up anytime by paying at the pump with a credit card. Gas is not available in Yosemite Valley; the closest gas station to the Valley is in El Portal.

If you're in Yosemite and happen upon the unfortunate need for automotive repairs, you can call the **Village Garage** (☑209-372-8320; ⊗8am-5pm), which is across the street from the Village Store. It also offers 24-hour roadside service.

Most trailheads have free parking areas where you can leave your vehicle for several days. Make sure to put all food and scented items in a bear box. In Yosemite Valley, backpackers must park in the hikers' parking area between Curry Village and Happy Isles. Day-use visitors can use the parking lots either at Curry Village or near Yosemite Village, and take the free shuttle bus around the Valley.

Overnight parking is not permitted on Tioga or Glacier Point Rds after October 15.

SHUTTLES & BUSES

Yosemite offers very good public transportation within the hubs of Yosemite Valley and along

Tioga Rd in the Tuolumne Meadows area. Some of the following transportation options were in flux at press time, so confirm information, schedules and departure points with the *Yosemite Guide* or the park's website at www.nps.gov/yose/planyourvisit/publictransportation.htm.

Yosemite Valley

The free Yosemite Valley Visitor Shuttle stops year-round at 21 numbered locations, from Happy Isles and Mirror Lake in the east (both closed to car without accessible parking placards) to Yosemite Lodge in the west, with stops at all popular sites. This excellent, easy-to-use, hybrid-fuel bus service operates 7am to 10pm daily at 10- to 20-minute intervals. Small, fold-up route maps are available free at most stores and lobby desks throughout the park.

El Capitan

From mid-June through early October, this free bus runs a western loop from the Yosemite Valley Visitor Center to Bridalveil Fall, stopping at El Capitan, Camp 4 and the Four Mile Trailhead. Service is from 9am to 6pm, at 30-minute intervals.

Yosemite–Badger Pass

From approximately mid-December through March (when the Badger Pass Ski Area is open), a free Badger Pass shuttle bus runs daily from Yosemite Valley in the morning, returning from the Badger Pass ski area in the afternoon at 2pm and 4:30pm.

Mariposa Grove

The Mariposa Grove restoration includes removal of most of its parking lot. When the grove reopens in 2017, visitors during peak visitation periods will access it using a free shuttle that will run from a new South Entrance transit hub.

A more limited shuttle connecting the Wawona Hotel and campground to the South Entrance hub may be instituted as well.

Wawona–Yosemite Valley

There is no longer a free daily shuttle between Wawona and Yosemite Valley. From the Wawona Hotel, visitors can take the new YARTS (www.yarts.com) Hwy 41 bus to Yosemite Valley (round-trip adult/child under 13 years $13/9), with departures a few times daily.

Glacier Point

Yosemite Valley–Glacier Point From about mid-June to mid-September, the **Glacier Point Sightseeing Bus** (✐ 209-372-4386; round-trip adult/senior/child $41/35/23) loops from Yosemite Valley to Glacier Point and back, stopping at various points along the way and taking about four hours for the whole trip. It runs three times daily from about June to October. Hikers can pay for a one-way journey and return to the Valley under their own steam. This is a very popular bus, so reservations must be made a day or two in advance.

Badger Pass–Glacier Point In the summer 2015, the park began a free peak season shuttle from Badger Pass to cut down on traffic congestion at Glacier Point, with stops at most trailheads. It's unclear whether this mandatory shuttle service (running from 10am at Badger Pass, with the last return departing Glacier Point at 5:30pm) will continue, though it would be a welcome development to anyone who's experienced gridlock while waiting for a parking spot to open up at Glacier Point. Drivers with accessibility placards or area wilderness permits and campers at Bridalveil Creek Campground are still permitted to drive.

Yosemite Valley–Tuolumne Meadows

Tuolumne Meadows Hikers' Bus In summer, the park concessionaire traditionally runs a morning tour **bus** (one way adult/child 5-12 yr $14.50/7.25; ☉ Jul–early Sep) that leaves from multiple stops in the Valley and can drop off or pick up hikers at trailheads along the way to Tuolumne Meadows. It returns in the afternoon. Fares vary according to your trip, and reservations are strongly recommended. They can be made up to one week in advance, or stop by the tour desk at Yosemite Lodge.

But in 2015, the park began a thrice-daily *free* hikers' bus along that route, and there was no word on whether the free option or fee-based tour bus would be used in subsequent years. Check for updates.

YARTS To get from the Valley to Tuolumne and other points along Tioga Rd, you can also ride the YARTS Hwy 120/395 buses heading to Mammoth Lakes. The 5pm YARTS bus is the only eastbound evening service from the Valley to Tuolumne. Check the website www.yarts.com for details.

Around Tuolumne Meadows

Tuolumne Meadows–Olmsted Point The free Tuolumne Meadows shuttle bus plies part of Tioga Rd daily from about mid-June to mid-September (the exact schedule varies annually). The shuttle travels between Tuolumne Meadows Lodge and Olmsted Point, starting at the lodge at 7am and operating at roughly 30-minute intervals until 7pm. The last eastbound shuttle departs Olmsted Point at 6pm.

Tuolumne Meadows–Tioga Pass A free shuttle travels between Tuolumne Meadows Lodge and Tioga Pass, stopping at the Mono Pass trailhead. It departs the lodge at 9am, noon, 3pm and 5pm and returns from Tioga Pass at 9:15am, 12:15pm, 3:15pm and 5:15pm.

TOM GRUBBE / GETTY IMAGES ©

1. Tuolumne Meadows (p113)
Tuolumne Meadows is a paradise for climbers and hikers, with trails stretching in all directions.

2. Bridalveil Creek (p59)
A wildfire burns in the distance, on the trail over Bridalveil Creek.

3. Liberty Cap and Nevada Fall (p55)
Nevada Fall is the first of the series of steps in the Giant Staircase.

4. Indian Rock (p64)
Indian Rock, Yosemite's only visible natural arch, can be visited on a sidetrip from the North Dome hike.

JON ARNOLD IMAGES / GETTY IMAGES ©

Around Yosemite National Park

Best Views

➡ Minaret Vista (p152)

➡ Conway Summit (p144)

➡ Alabama Hills (p156)

➡ Merced River Canyon (p136)

➡ Mono Lake (p146)

➡ Little Lakes Valley (p152)

Best Places to Stay

➡ Tioga Pass Resort (p143)

➡ Yosemite Bug Rustic Mountain Resort (p137)

➡ Blackberry Inn Bed & Breakfast (p139)

➡ Yosemite Gateway Motel (p145)

Why Go?

Though many consider Yosemite the crème de la crème of the Sierras, you may just find you prefer the flavor of other regions around it. You'll find many who'd argue the unbeatable merits of the Eastern Sierra, which is home to sights such as Mono Lake, Mammoth Lakes, hidden hot springs, shimmering alpine lakes and some of the state's most dramatic mountain scenery.

Heading to Yosemite by car or bus, you'll travel along one of four primary approaches. To the west, Hwys 120 and 140 provide the main access routes, with wonderful little gold-rush-era towns and groovy old-time saloons. To the south, Hwy 41 passes by pastoral fishing lakes and mountain roads, and the eastern route over Tioga Pass is the highest auto pass in California.

Road Distances (miles)

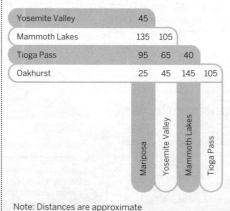

	Mariposa	Yosemite Valley	Mammoth Lakes	Tioga Pass
Yosemite Valley	45			
Mammoth Lakes	135	105		
Tioga Pass	95	65	40	
Oakhurst	25	45	145	105

Note: Distances are approximate

Around Yosemite National Park

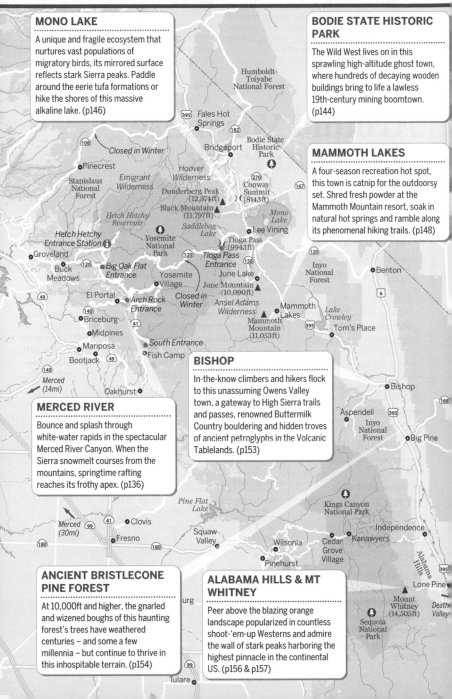

◎ 0 ————— 50 km
0 ————— 25 miles

MONO LAKE

A unique and fragile ecosystem that nurtures vast populations of migratory birds, its mirrored surface reflects stark Sierra peaks. Paddle around the eerie tufa formations or hike the shores of this massive alkaline lake. (p146)

BODIE STATE HISTORIC PARK

The Wild West lives on in this sprawling high-altitude ghost town, where hundreds of decaying wooden buildings bring to life a lawless 19th-century mining boomtown. (p144)

MAMMOTH LAKES

A four-season recreation hot spot, this town is catnip for the outdoorsy set. Shred fresh powder at the Mammoth Mountain resort, soak in natural hot springs and ramble along its phenomenal hiking trails. (p148)

BISHOP

In-the-know climbers and hikers flock to this unassuming Owens Valley town, a gateway to High Sierra trails and passes, renowned Buttermilk Country bouldering and hidden troves of ancient petroglyphs in the Volcanic Tablelands. (p153)

MERCED RIVER

Bounce and splash through white-water rapids in the spectacular Merced River Canyon. When the Sierra snowmelt courses from the mountains, springtime rafting reaches its frothy apex. (p136)

ANCIENT BRISTLECONE PINE FOREST

At 10,000ft and higher, the gnarled and wizened boughs of this haunting forest's trees have weathered centuries — and some a few millennia — but continue to thrive in this inhospitable terrain. (p154)

ALABAMA HILLS & MT WHITNEY

Peer above the blazing orange landscape popularized in countless shoot-'em-up Westerns and admire the wall of stark peaks harboring the highest pinnacle in the continental US. (p156 & p157)

Humboldt-Toiyabe National Forest

Fales Hot Springs

Bridgeport

Pinecrest

Closed in Winter

Stanislaus National Forest

Emigrant Wilderness

Hoover Wilderness

Dunderberg Peak (12,374ft)

Black Mountain (11,797ft)

Hetch Hetchy Reservoir

Saddlebag Lake

Conway Summit (8143ft)

Mono Lake

Lee Vining

Tioga Pass (9943ft)

Hetch Hetchy Entrance Station

Groveland

Yosemite National Park

Tioga Pass Entrance

Buck Meadows

Big Oak Flat Entrance

Yosemite Village

El Portal

Arch Rock Entrance

Closed in Winter

June Lake

June Mountain (10,090ft)

Ansel Adams Wilderness

Mammoth Lakes

Mammoth Mountain (11,053ft)

Inyo National Forest

Benton

Tom's Place

Lake Crowley

Briceburg

Midpines

Mariposa

Bootjack

South Entrance

Fish Camp

Merced (14mi)

Oakhurst

Bishop

Aspendell

Inyo National Forest

Big Pine

Pine Flat Lake

Merced (30mi)

Clovis

Fresno

Squaw Valley

Wilsonia

Pinehurst

Cedar Grove Village

Kings Canyon National Park

Kanawyers

Independence

Alabama Hills

Lone Pine

Mount Whitney (14,505ft)

Sequoia National Park

Death Valley

Tulare

urg

ⓘ Getting Around

Hwys 120 and 108 both lead over the Sierra Nevada range to Hwy 395, the main north–south artery through the Eastern Sierra. Due to heavy snowfall, both are only open roughly May or June through September. The **Yosemite Area Regional Transportation System** (YARTS; ☑ 877-989-2787; www.yarts.com) provides bus service to/from Yosemite. The **Eastern Sierra Transit Authority** (☑ 760-872-1901, 800-922-1930; www.estransit.com) runs year-round bus service along the Hwy 395 corridor.

WEST OF YOSEMITE

The two most important arteries into Yosemite – Hwy 140 and Hwy 120 – lie to the west. Aside from offering easy access to the national park, the highways are home to some marvelous little historic towns resting along their dusty shoulders.

Highway 140

The approach to Yosemite via Hwy 140, which parallels the bed of the long-defunct Yosemite Valley Railroad, is one of the most scenic, especially the section that meanders through **Merced River Canyon**. The springtime runoff makes this a spectacular spot for **river rafting**, with many miles of class III and IV rapids.

A major transportation hub, Merced is the end of the line for Amtrak train and Greyhound bus passengers. From here, passengers can take the year-round YARTS Hwy 140 bus (www.yarts.com) into the park, making this route an easy option for travelers without cars. The bus includes the park fee, and makes stops at Mariposa, Midpines and El Portal.

Mariposa

About halfway between Merced and Yosemite Valley, Mariposa (Spanish for 'butterfly') is the largest and most interesting town near the park. Established as a mining and railroad town during the gold rush, it has the oldest courthouse in continuous use (since 1854) west of the Mississippi, loads of Old West pioneer character and a friendly feel.

Rock hounds should drive to the Mariposa County Fairgrounds, 2 miles south of town on Hwy 49, to see the 13-pound 'Fricot Nugget' – the largest crystallized gold specimen from the California gold rush era – and other gems and machinery at the **California State Mining & Mineral Museum** (☑ 209-742-7625; www.parks.ca.gov/?page_id=588; admission adult/child under 13 $4/free; ◷ 10am-5pm Thu-Sun May-Sep, to 4pm Oct-Apr). An exhibit on glow-in-the-dark minerals is also very cool.

🛏 Sleeping

★ River Rock Inn   MOTEL $$
(☑ 209-966-5793; www.riverrockmariposa.com; 4993 7th St; r $135-179; ✳ 🛜 ❄) A bold splash of psychedelic purple and dusty-orange exterior paint jazzes up what claims to be the oldest motel in town. Recently updated kitchenette rooms done up in artsy earth tones have TVs and calming ceiling fans resembling lily pads. A block removed from Hwy 140 on a quiet side street, it features a courtyard deck and deli cafe serving beer, espresso and wine, with live acoustic music some summer evenings.

Mariposa Lodge   MOTEL $$
(☑ 209-966-3607, 800-966-8819; www.mariposalodge.com; 5052 Hwy 140; r $129-159; ✳ 🛜 ❄ 🐾) More of a generic motel, the simple, well-kept Mariposa sports clean, quiet rooms with triple-sheeted beds and friendly staff. It earns pluses for the good-sized kitchenette rooms and for the blooming flowers that border the grounds.

Mariposa Hotel Inn   HISTORIC HOTEL $$
(☑ 209-966-7500; www.mariposahotelinn.com; 5029 Hwy 140; r $139-169; ✳ 🛜) This creaky 1901 building has six king or queen rooms with old-time quilts and period-style furniture, and a corridor crammed with old town photos and newspaper clippings. Room 6 has an original claw-foot tub. Hummingbirds love the flowery back patio where breakfast is served.

✕ Eating

Happy Burger   DINER $
(www.happyburgerdiner.com; Hwy 140 at 12th St; mains $8-14; ◷ 5:30am-9pm; 🛜 🅿 ♿ 🐾) Boasting the largest menu in the Sierra, this buzzing roadside joint decorated with old LP album covers serves the cheapest meals in Mariposa. Its all-American cuisine means burgers, sandwiches, Mexican food and a ton of sinful ice-cream desserts. Free computer terminal inside and a 'doggy dining area' outdoors.

> ### ℹ CAMPING OUTSIDE YOSEMITE
>
> You'll find more camping options outside Yosemite than within the park itself – both US Forest Service (USFS) campgrounds and dispersed camping, which is allowed in most national forests. Dispersed camping is a great way to go if you crave solitude (no nearby campers) and affordability (it's free) – but remember, you're entirely on your own, which means no toilets or potable water (bring your own or come with a means to filter or purify stream water). If you're going to build a fire, you'll also need a free fire permit, which you can pick up at USFS ranger stations or print from www.preventwildfireca.org. Ranger stations also sell detailed USFS maps, which are helpful for navigating the maze of dirt roads. Finally, note that some areas (along Tioga Rd east of the park, for instance) don't allow dispersed camping; watch for signs.

Savoury's   NEW AMERICAN $$
(☑ 209-966-7677; www.savouryrestaurant.com; 5034 Hwy 140; mains $17-32; ☺ 5-9pm, closed Wed in winter; ℐ) Upscale yet casual Savoury's is still the best restaurant in town. Black lacquered tables and contemporary art create a tranquil window dressing for dishes like chipotle-and-orange-glazed chicken, hearty pastas and steak Diane.

Sugar Pine Cafe   AMERICAN $$
(www.sugarpinecafe.com; 5038 Hwy 140; breakfast $6-9, dinner $8-21; ☺ 7am-8:30pm Tue-Sat, to 3pm Sun & Mon) Gussied up with chrome soda counter stools and red circular booths, this 1940s-era diner serves yummy breakfast items, hot or cold sandwiches and burgers on whole-wheat buns. Dinner fare is pure comfort food like spaghetti and meatballs and pork chops.

ℹ Information

Mariposa County Visitor Center (☑ 209-966-7081, 866-425-3366; www.yosemite experience.com; cnr Hwys 140 & 49; ☺ 9am-6pm) Helpful staff and racks of brochures; public restrooms.

Midpines

There's not much to see or do in Midpines, a rural community about 25 miles west of Yosemite's Arch Rock Entrance. From Midpines, Hwy 140 drops down into the beautiful Merced River Canyon.

🛏 Sleeping & Eating

★ **Yosemite Bug Rustic Mountain Resort**   HOSTEL, CABIN $
(☑ 209-966-6666, 866-826-7108; www.yosemite bug.com; 6979 Hwy 140, Midpines; dm $30, tent cabins $45-75, r with/without bath from $150/75; @ 🛜) 𝄐 The highlight of this almost non-existent town is this folksy oasis, tucked away on a forested hillside about 25 miles from Yosemite. It's more like a convivial mountain retreat than a hostel: at night, friendly folks of all ages and backgrounds share stories, music, delicious, freshly prepared meals and beer and wine in the woodsy **cafe** (mains $10-22; ☺ 7-10am, 11:30am-3pm & 6-9pm; ℐ).

Dorm dwellers have access to a communal kitchen, and the resort has a spa with a hot tub; yoga lessons and massages are also available. The YARTS bus stops a quarter mile up the driveway.

Midpines Country Store   MARKET $
(6428 Hwy 140; ☺ 8am-6pm winter, until 7pm summer) An old-fashioned store with creaky wood floors and a (daytime only) gas station, it's been run by the current owners for over 35 years.

Briceburg

Some 20 miles outside the park, right where the Merced River meets Hwy 140, Briceburg consists of a **visitors center** (☑ 209-379-9414; www.blm.gov/ca/st/en/fo/folsom/mercedriverrec. html; ☺ 1-5pm Fri, from 9am Sat & Sun late Apr-early Sep) and three primitive **Bureau of Land Management campgrounds** (BLM; www.blm.gov/ca/st/en/fo/folsom/mercedriverrec. html; tent & RV sites $10; 🛋) with a to-die-for location right on the river. To reach them, you cross a beautiful 1920s wooden suspension bridge; long trailers and large RVs are not recommended.

El Portal

Right outside the Arch Rock Entrance, and primarily inhabited by park employees, El Portal stretches 7 miles alongside the Merced River and makes a convenient

DANITA DELIMONT / GETTY IMAGES ©

Mono Lake (p146)

Yosemite base. The town was once the terminus of the Yosemite Valley Railroad.

🛏 Sleeping & Eating

USFS Campgrounds   CAMPGROUND $
(☑ 877-444-6777; www.recreation.gov; Incline Rd; tent sites $24; 🐕) Dry Gulch and Dirt Flat are small but reservable tent-only campgrounds on the north shore of the Merced River. No potable water available.

Indian Flat RV Park   CAMPGROUND, CABIN $
(☑ 209-379-2339; www.indianflatrvpark.com; 9988 Hwy 140; tent sites $30, RV sites $42-48, tent cabins $89-129, cottages $149-169; ❋🐕) Primarily an inexpensive private campground, Indian Flat RV Park also has a number of interesting housing options, including two pretty stone cabin cottages with air-conditioning and roomy tent cabins with ceiling fans and private porches. Guests can use the pool and pay for wi-fi at its sister property next door, and nonguests can pay to shower.

Cedar Lodge   MOTEL $$
(☑ 209-379-2612, 888-742-4371; www.stayyosemite cedarlodge.com; 9966 Hwy 140; r $149-189; ❋🕸🏊) Approximately 9 miles west of the Arch Rock Entrance, the Cedar is a sprawling establishment with more than 200 adequate rooms, an indoor pool, a seasonal outdoor pool and a couple of restaurants. Balcony rooms are the best of the bunch. No cell service; sluggish wi-fi costs $10 per day.

Yosemite View Lodge   MOTEL $$$
(☑ 209-379-2681, 888-742-4371; www.stay yosemiteviewlodge.com; 11136 Hwy 140; r $189-269, ste $329-559; ❋@🕸🏊🐕) Less than 2 miles from the park entrance, Yosemite View Lodge is a big, modern complex with hot tubs, two restaurants and four pools. All the 300-plus rooms feature kitchenettes, some have gas fireplaces and views of the Merced River, and the ground-floor rooms have big patios. No cell reception; wi-fi is $10 per day.

The souped-up 'majestic suites' are massive, with opulent bathrooms featuring waterfall showers and plasma-TV entertainment centers.

Highway 120 (West)

Most folks visiting from the San Francisco Bay area take Hwy 120 into the park, entering Yosemite at the Big Oak Flat Entrance. This is also the main route to Hetch Hetchy; instead of entering at Big Oak Flat, you head north on Evergreen Rd, just before entering the park. YARTS Hwy 120 buses service Yosemite Valley from Sonora between mid-May and mid-September, with stops in Groveland and Buck Meadows.

Groveland

From the Big Oak Flat entrance, it's 22 miles to Groveland, an adorable town with restored gold-rush-era buildings and lots of visitor services. About 15 miles east of town, **Rainbow Pool** (www.fs.usda.gov/stanislaus) is a popular swimming hole with a small cascade; it's signed on the south side of Hwy 120.

🛏 Sleeping & Eating

Both hotels listed here include fantastic breakfasts. Summer dinner reservations are highly recommended.

Hotel Charlotte   HOTEL $$
(☑ 209-962-6455; www.hotelcharlotte.com; 18736 Main St; r $179-269; ❋@🕸🏊) A friendly, 13-room 1921 confection with beds adorned in

patchwork quilts, the Hotel Charlotte keeps the vintage flair alive but still has modern conveniences like individual heating controls. Room 13 is a cozy mini-cabin out back. A sophisticated **bistro** (small plates $10-28; ☺6-9pm May-Sep) and bar serves a creative small-plates menu.

Groveland Hotel   HOTEL $$

(☑800-273-3314, 209-962-4000; www.groveland. com; 18767 Main St; r $199-329; ❉@🛜🐕) The historic Groveland Hotel dates from 1850 and now houses a small bar, an excellent upscale **restaurant** (☑209-962-4000; www. groveland.com; 18767 Main St; mains $15-29; ☺7:30-10am & 5:30-9pm) 🍴 with a renowned 600-label wine list, and 17 bright, lovingly decorated rooms with wraparound verandas and resident teddy bears.

Mountain Sage   CAFE $

(www.mtsage.com; 18653 Main St; snacks $2.50-8; ☺7am-3pm, to 5pm May-Sep; 🛜) 🍴 This popular cafe is also an art gallery, nursery and live-music venue all rolled into one, with Fair Trade coffee, tasty baked treats and an excellent summer concert series (www.mountain sagemusic.org). A percentage of its coffee sales is donated to the local food bank.

Iron Door Grill & Saloon   AMERICAN $$

(☑209-962-6244; www.iron-door-saloon.com; 18761 Main St; mains $9.50-25; ☺restaurant 7am-10pm & bar 11am-2am, shorter winter hrs; 🍴) Claiming to be the oldest bar in the state, the Iron Door is a dusty, atmospheric old place, with big swinging doors, a giant bar, high ceilings, mounted animal heads and hundreds of dollar bills tacked to the ceiling. The adjacent, more contemporary, dining room serves good steaks, ribs and pasta dishes, and there's live music every weekend night in summer.

❶ Information

USFS Groveland Ranger Station (☑209-962-7825; www.fs.usda.gov/stanislaus; 24545 Hwy 120; ☺8am-4:30pm Mon-Sat Jun-Aug, reduced hrs Sep-May) About 8 miles east of Groveland, offers recreation information for the surrounding Stanislaus National Forest and nearby Tuolumne Wild and Scenic River Area.

Buck Meadows & Around

A former stagecoach stop en route to Yosemite, tiny Buck Meadows is only 20 minutes'

drive from the park entrance, and a good alternative to staying inside the park.

🛏 Sleeping & Eating

There are three convenient campgrounds in the **Stanislaus National Forest** between Groveland and Buck Meadows.

The Pines   CAMPGROUND $

(www.fs.usda.gov/stanislaus; Old Hwy 120; tent & RV sites $19 May-Sep, free Oct-Apr; 🐕) A first-come, first-served campground 9 miles east of Groveland.

Lost Claim   CAMPGROUND $

(www.recreation.gov; Hwy 120; tent sites $19; ☺May–mid-Sep; 🐕) Ten shady tent-only sites located 12 miles east of Groveland; reservable.

Sweetwater   CAMPGROUND $

(www.fs.usda.gov/stanislaus; Hwy 120; tent & RV sites $22; ☺May-early Sep; 🐕) A first-come, first-served campground 15 miles east of Groveland.

★ Blackberry Inn
Bed & Breakfast   B&B $$$

(☑209-962-4663, 888-867-5001; www.black berry-inn.com; 7567 Hamilton Station Loop; r $205-295; ❉@🛜) On a rural road right off Hwy 120, this stunningly converted house and newer wing offer 10 sumptuous rooms showcasing stained glass scenes of Yosemite, soaking tubs and electric fireplaces that give off real heat or just cozy ambiance. Its *big* breakfasts can be delivered to your room or patio so you can spy on the hummingbirds. Two-night minimum stay.

Yosemite Westgate Lodge   MOTEL $$$

(☑209-962-5281, 800-253-9673; www.yosemite westgate.com; 7633 Hwy 120; r $179-299; ❉🐕) A pleasant place to lay your head, these kitchenette motel rooms have been updated with flat-screen TVs and new bedding. Unwind in the small pool after a day of hiking and sightseeing. No wi-fi or cell service.

Buck Meadows
Restaurant & Bar   AMERICAN $$

(www.buckmeadowsrestaurant.com; 7647 Hwy 120; mains $9-23; ☺7am-10pm summer, shorter hrs otherwise) After a long day at the park, the half-pound 49er burgers (or more manageable third-pounders), steak dinners and the big pasta dishes hit the spot.

SOUTH OF YOSEMITE (HIGHWAY 41)

If you're heading up from Los Angeles or other Southern California points, this is the highway you'll likely wind up driving. Hwy 41 is generally open year-round, and a new YARTS Hwy 41 bus service connects Fresno to Yosemite Valley year-round via Oakhurst.

Oakhurst

At the junction of Hwys 41 and 49, about 15 miles south of the park entrance, Oakhurst functions primarily as a service town. This is your last chance to stock up on reasonably priced groceries, camping supplies and gas.

🛏 Sleeping & Eating

★ Sierra Sky Ranch   LODGE **$$**
(☑ 559-683-8040;   www.sierraskyranch.com; 50552 Rd 632; r $199-279; ❄ 🛜 🏊 🐾) This former ranch dates back to 1875 and encompasses 14 attractive acres. The homespun rooms are phone-free and pet-friendly, with double doors that open onto shady verandahs. The rambling and beautiful old lodge features a **restaurant** (☑ 559-658-2644; dinner mains $28-35) and a rustic saloon, and has loads of comfortable lounging areas. At the time of research, a major remodel was spiffing up the entire property.

With a storied history including previous uses as a TB hospital and a bordello, its past guests include Marilyn Monroe and John Wayne. Many swear that it's cheerfully haunted by former residents.

Oakhurst Lodge   MOTEL **$$**
(☑ 800-655-6343, 559-683-4417; www.oakhurstlodge.com; 40302 Hwy 41; r $149-199; ❄ 🛜 🐾) Right in the center of town, this older 33-unit motel presents a good no-frills budget option, with quiet and clean rooms, some with kitchenettes. Friendly new management is in the process of updating the property, adding flat-screen TVs, soundproof windows and lots of electrical outlets.

Hounds Tooth Inn   B&B **$$**
(☑ 559-642-6600; www.houndstoothinn.com; 42071 Hwy 41; r $149-259; ❄ 🛜) A few miles north of Oakhurst, this gorgeous garden B&B is swimming in rosebushes and Victorianesque charm. Its 12 airy rooms and two cottages, some with spas and fireplaces, feel a bit like an English manor house. Complimentary wine and hot drinks are available in the afternoon.

Château du Sureau   BOUTIQUE HOTEL **$$$**
(☑ 559-683-6860;   www.chateaudusureau.com; 48688 Victoria Ln; r incl breakfast $385-585, 2-bedroom villa $2950; ❄ @ 🛜 🏊 🐾) Never in a billion years would you expect to find this in Oakhurst. A luxe and discreet full-service European-style hotel and world-class spa, this serene destination property boasts an exceptional level of service. With wall tapestries, oil paintings and ornate chandeliers, its Californian-French **restaurant** (☑ 559-683-6860; www.chateausureau.com/restaurant.html; prix-fixe dinner $108, Sun brunch $64; ☺ dinner daily, plus 11am-1pm Sun; 🍴) could be a countryside castle.

South Gate Brewing Company   PUB FOOD **$**
(www.southgatebrewco.com;   40233 Enterprise Dr, off Hwy 49; mains $10-14; ☺ 11am-10pm Mon-Thu, 11am-11pm Fri & Sat, 10am-9pm Sun; 🛜 🍴) About a quarter mile west from the Hwy 41/49 junction, this popular microbrewery pub serves primo burgers, brick oven pizzas, sandwiches and salads. Try a Glacier Point Pale ale with a bacon and jalapeño-laden Jesse burger or the fish and chips.

❶ Information

Yosemite Sierra Visitors Bureau (☑ 559-683-4636; www.yosemitethisyear.com; 40637 Hwy 41; ☺ 8:30am-5pm Mon-Sat & 9am-1pm Sun summer, 8:30am-4:30pm Mon-Sat winter) A half-mile north of the Hwy 41/Hwy 49 intersection; free direct-dial lodgings phone. A seasonal Forest Service desk (☑ 559-658-7588; www.fs.usda.gov/sierra; ☺ 8:30am-5pm Mon-Sat Apr-Oct) issues wilderness permits.

Fish Camp

Fish Camp, just south of the park on Hwy 41, is more of a bend in the road, but it does have some good lodging options as well as the ever-popular **Sugar Pine Railroad** (☑ 559-683-7273; www.ymsprr.com; rides adult/child $22/11; ☺ approx Mar-Oct; 🚼), a historic steam train that chugs through the woods on a 4-mile loop.

🛏 Sleeping & Eating

Summerdale Campground   CAMPGROUND **$**
(☑ 877-444-6677; www.recreation.gov; tent & RV sites $28; ☺ May-Sep; 🐾) The closest campground to the park, it's a pleasant spot along Big Creek, with 28 well-dispersed sites in a grassy meadow with shade trees.

Sugar Pine Railroad steam train

White Chief Mountain Lodge　　MOTEL **$$**
(☑559-683-5444; www.whitechiefmountainlodge.
com; 7776 White Chief Mountain Rd; r $159-179;
☺Apr-Oct; ☎) The cheapest and most basic
option in town, this 1950s-era motel has
simple kitchenette rooms. New owners have
upgraded the exterior and some furniture,
but the rooms are still pretty blah. It's lo-
cated a few hundred yards east of Hwy 41;
watch for the sign and go up the wooded
country road. An on-site restaurant usually
serves breakfast and dinner in summer.

★**Narrow Gauge Inn**　　INN **$$$**
(☑559-683-7720;　　www.narrowgaugeinn.com;
48571 Hwy 41; r Nov-Mar $89-134, Apr-Oct $229-
369; ✳☎☎) Next door to the Sugar Pine
Railroad, this friendly, beautiful and supremely comfortable 26-room inn has a
seasonal hot tub, small bar, and the finest
restaurant in the area. Each tastefully appointed room features unique decor and a
pleasant deck facing the trees and mountains, and all have flat-screen TVs.

Big Creek Inn B&B　　B&B **$$$**
(☑559-641-2828; www.bigcreekinn.com; 1221 Hwy
41; r $239-299; ☎) Each of the three white-pal-
ette rooms has peaceful creek views and a
private balcony, and two have gas fireplaces.
From the comfortable rooms or the back pa-
tio, you can often spot deer and beavers, or
hummingbirds lining up at the patio feed-
er. Amenities include in-room DVD/Blu-ray
players and a large movie library, kitchenette
use and big soaking tubs with bath salts.

Tenaya Lodge　　HOTEL **$$$**
(☑559-683-6555, 888-514-2167; www.tenayalodge.
com; 1122 Hwy 41; r from $365; ✳@☎☎☎)
A hulking, modern hotel and conference
center just 2 miles from Yosemite's south entrance, this large resort and full spa feels like
a convention hotel.

★**Narrow Gauge Inn**　　NEW AMERICAN **$$$**
(☑559-683-6446; mains $15-39; ☺5-9pm mid-
Apr–Oct) Excellent food coupled with knock-
out views make the dining experience at the
Narrow Gauge Inn one of the finest in the
Yosemite region. The dinners are creative-
ly prepared, the lodge-like atmosphere is
casual but elegant, and windows look out on
lush mountain vistas.

Cozy up to the fireplace on colder eve-
nings or warm yourself up at the small
Buffalo Bar, perfect for a cocktail or glass of
chardonnay. Reservations recommended.

EASTERN SIERRA

Compared with the western side, the Eastern Sierra is another world. While rolling oak-covered foothills grace the Western Sierra and impede views of the mountains from a distance, a sweeping, nearly treeless desert basin abuts the steep eastern slopes. The result? Views – whether from the basin floor or from high in the mountains – like you wouldn't believe. Within this dramatic setting, National Forest roads lead to marvelously uncrowded campgrounds, hiking areas and undeveloped hot springs.

ℹ Getting Around

HIGHWAY 395

Eastern Sierra Transit Authority (p136) buses connect the Hwy 395 corridor between Lone Pine and Reno as well as Mammoth Lakes to Lancaster (an Amtrak stop between LA and southern Hwy 395). Fares depend on distance, and reservations are recommended. Weekday express buses link Bishop to Lone Pine and Mammoth Lakes.

HIGHWAY 120

YARTS Hwy 120/395 buses run from Yosemite Valley east over Tioga Pass (Hwy 120/Tioga Rd) and south to Mammoth Lakes via Crane Flat, White Wolf, Tuolumne Meadows, Lee Vining and June Lake, stopping on demand so you can get off (but not on) at any trailhead or campground along Tioga Rd. This route runs during summer only, with daily buses in July and August, but only Saturday and Sunday service during June (after Tioga Pass opens) and September. The Mammoth-bound bus leaves the Valley Visitor Center at 5pm; buses from Mammoth depart in the morning. Confirm the schedule, as it can change year-to-year.

Tioga Pass & Around

The stretch of Hwy 120 between Tioga Pass and Lee Vining is the most epic route into or out of Yosemite National Park – and one of the most stunning anywhere in California. The roadbed is scratched into the side of steep, dramatic Lee Vining Canyon, with sheer drop-offs, rugged rock walls and sweeping views. It's incredible to witness how quickly and significantly the scenery changes from one side of Tioga Pass to the other. Once you cross the pass heading east and start downhill, you'll leave behind the lush grasses and tall pines of Tuolumne and Dana Meadows for the dry, sagebrush-coated landscape of the Great Basin Desert. At the end of Hwy 120 lies Mono Lake, a massive expanse of saltwater at the edge of the Great Basin Desert.

Reflecting its bleak, high-alpine surroundings at an elevation of 10,087ft, **Saddlebag Lake** (actually a reservoir) lies at the end of a 2.5-mile dirt road that branches north from Hwy 120, about 2 miles east of Yosemite's Tioga Pass Entrance. With countless lakes and stunning views of North Peak (12,242ft) and Mt Conness (12,590ft) on the Yosemite border and pointy Tioga Peak (11,526ft) to the southeast, the area is utterly spectacular. Saddlebag Lake is California's highest car-accessible lake and a favorite haunt for anglers.

In September, check out the **Tioga Pass Run** (www.tiogapassrun.com), a footrace from Lee Vining to Tioga Pass: 12.4 miles – and only one (3100ft) hill!

🏃 Hiking

From Saddlebag Lake, one of the most popular hikes is a loop of the high altitude **20 Lakes Basin**. Never dropping below 10,000ft, this mostly level trail meanders past some of the most breathtaking scenery in the entire Yosemite region. If you backpack (overnight) here, you can pick up a wilderness permit from either the Tuolumne Meadows Wilderness Center (p130) or the Mono Basin Scenic Area Visitor Center (p146).

From Junction Campground (at the Saddlebag Lake turnoff from Hwy 120), a mile-long trail leads to the former site of **Bennettville**, a one-time mining town. About a mile north on Saddlebag Lake Rd you'll find a trailhead for **Gardisky Lake**, an oft-overlooked gem tucked beneath Tioga Peak. The hike is short but steep, with an elevation gain of almost 800ft in about a mile.

🛏 Sleeping & Eating

The **Inyo National Forest** (☎760-647-3044; www.fs.usda.gov/inyo) runs a number of excellent first-come, first-served campgrounds along Saddlebag Rd and Tioga Rd along Lee Vining Creek, including the following four listed here.

Junction   CAMPGROUND **$**
(cnr Hwy 120 & Saddlebag Lake Rd; tent & RV sites $16) Named for its location at the intersection of Hwy 120 and the Saddlebag Lake road, this 13-site campground offers sunny sites near Lee Vining Creek.

WORTH A TRIP

TWIN LAKES

These exquisite lakes are shadowed by the jagged Sawtooth Ridge, which includes 12,279ft Matterhorn Peak. Primarily a **fishing** resort, Twin Lakes is also a good access point for hikes into the Hoover Wilderness and Yosemite's lake-riddled northeastern reaches. The main trailhead is at the end of Twin Lakes Rd just past Annett's Mono Village; weekly overnight parking is $10 per vehicle. From here, hikers can set off along Robinson Creek for day hikes or overnight backpacking trips (wilderness permit required). The hike to lovely **Barney Lake** (8 miles round-trip) takes in magnificent views of jagged granite spires in Little Slide Canyon.

The road to Twin Lakes intersects Hwy 395 at the north end of Bridgeport and crosses rolling pastures and foothills, passing five good forest service campgrounds on Robinson Creek.

Also check out **Buckeye Hot Spring**, where piping hot water emerges from atop a steep hillside and cools as it trickles down into several rock pools right by the side of lively Buckeye Creek. Clothing is optional. To get here, turn right at Doc & Al's Resort (7 miles from Hwy 395), and drive 3 miles on a graded dirt road. Cross the bridge at Buckeye Creek (2.5 miles on), and bear right at the Y-junction, following signs to the hot spring. Go uphill a half-mile until you see a flattish parking area on your right. Follow the hillside trail down to the pools.

Sawmill Walk-in CAMPGROUND $
(Saddlebag Lake Rd; tent sites $16) One of the most scenic established campgrounds in the entire Sierra Nevada, Sawmill offers 12 sites on the edge of the beautiful Monroe Hall Research Area. It's about a quarter-mile walk to the campground.

Saddlebag Lake CAMPGROUND $
(Saddlebag Lake; tent & small RV sites $21) Perched atop a hill overlooking the reservoir, this is a favorite with anglers. All sites are small and well kept and some have splendid views over the lake.

Tioga Lake CAMPGROUND $
(Hwy 120; tent & small RV sites $21; 🌐) The campground closest to Tioga Pass is at Tioga Lake, and has a handful of sunny, exposed sites right on the lake but visible from the road.

★**Tioga Pass Resort** CABIN $$
(www.tiogapassresort.com; Hwy 120; d $125, cabin $170-260; ☉ Jun-Sep) Founded in 1914 and located 2 miles east of Tioga Pass, this resort attracts a fiercely loyal clientele to its quiet and comfortable woodsy cabins (most with full kitchen) beside Lee Vining Creek. Walk-ins can sometimes snag a cancellation.

The thimble-sized cafe serves excellent fare all day at a few tables and a broken horseshoe counter, with a house pastry chef concocting dozens of freshly made desserts.

Saddlebag Lake Resort DINER $
(www.saddlebaglakeresort.com; Saddlebag Lake; mains under $10; ☉ 7am-7pm mid-Jul–Sep) On the southeast shore of Saddlebag Lake, this diner-cum-general store (no lodging) serves up egg and pancake breakfasts, burgers, sandwiches and homemade pie.

Bridgeport

Barely three blocks long, set amid open high valley and in view of the peaks of Sawtooth Ridge, Bridgeport flaunts classic western flair with charming old storefronts and a homey ambience. Most everything shuts down or cuts back hours for the brutal winters, but the rest of the year the town is a magnet for anglers, hikers, climbers and hot-spring devotees.

◉ Sights & Activities

**Mono County
Courthouse** HISTORIC BUILDING
(☉ 9am-5pm Mon-Fri) The gavel has been dropped since 1880 at this courthouse, an all-white italianate dreamboat surrounded by a gracious lawn and a wrought-iron fence. On the street behind it, look for the Old County Jail, a spartan facility fashioned with iron latticework doors and stone walls 2ft thick. Unlucky inmates overnighted in its six cells from 1883 until 1964.

★ **Travertine Hot Spring**　HOT SPRING

FREE A bit south of town, head here to watch a panoramic Sierra sunset from three hot pools set amid impressive rock formations. To get here, turn east on Jack Sawyer Rd just before the ranger station, then follow the dirt road uphill for about 1 mile.

🛏 Sleeping & Eating

Bodie Victorian Hotel　HISTORIC HOTEL $

(📞760-616-1977; www.bodievictorianhotel.com; 85 Main St; r $60-125; ⊘May-Oct; ✳🔊) Go back to the 1800s in this curious building transplanted from Bodie that's completely furnished with antiques and rumored to be haunted. The bold Victorian wallpaper and striking bordello accoutrements more than make up for the slightly run-down feel. If no one's here, poke your head inside the Sportsmens Bar & Grill next door to rustle up an employee.

Redwood Motel　MOTEL $

(📞760-932-7060; www.redwoodmotel.net; 425 Main St; d from $89-99; ⊘Apr-Nov; ✳🔊🐾) A bucking bronco, an ox in a Hawaiian shirt and other wacky farm animal sculptures provide a cheerful welcome to this little kitchenette motel. Rooms are spotless and your dog-friendly host is super helpful in dispensing local area tips.

Bridgeport Inn　AMERICAN $$

(www.thebridgeportinn.com; 205 Main St; mains $10-30; ⊘7am-9pm mid-Mar–Oct; 🔊) Stop in at the country kitchen dining room of this whitewashed 1877 building for burgers, pot roast, steaks and seafood, and a dip into its modest wine list. Watch the world stream by from a classic soda-fountain stool on the long front porch.

❶ Information

Bridgeport Ranger Station & Visitor Center
(📞760-932-7070; www.fs.usda.gov/htnf; Hwy 395; ⊘8am-4:30pm daily Jun–mid-Sep, 8am-12:30pm & 1-4:30pm Mon-Fri mid-Sep–May) The local office for maps, information and Hoover Wilderness permits.

Bodie State Historic Park

For a time warp back to the gold-rush era, swing by **Bodie** (📞760-647-6445; www.parks.ca.gov/bodie; Rte 270; adult/child $5/3; ⊘9am-6pm mid-May–Oct, to 4pm Nov–mid-May), one of the West's most authentic and best-preserved ghost towns. Gold was first discovered here in 1859, and within 20 years the place grew from a rough mining camp to an even rougher boomtown with a population of 10,000 and a reputation for unbridled lawlessness. Fights and murders took place almost daily, the violence no doubt fueled by liquor dispensed in the town's 65 saloons, some of which did double duty as brothels, gambling halls or opium dens. The hills disgorged some $35 million worth of gold and silver in the 1870s and '80s, but when production plummeted, so did the population and eventually the town was abandoned to the elements.

About 200 weather-beaten buildings still sit frozen in time in this cold, barren and windswept valley heaped with tailing piles. Peering through dusty windows you'll see stocked stores, furnished homes, desks and books in a schoolhouse, and workshops filled with tools. The jail is still there, as are the fire station, churches, a bank vault and many other buildings. The former Miners' Union Hall now houses a **museum** and **visitors center** (⊘9am to one hour before park closes). Rangers conduct free general tours. In summertime, they also offer tours of the landscape and the cemetery; call for details.

Bodie is about 13 miles east of Hwy 395 via Rte 270; the last 3 miles are unpaved. Although the park is open year-round, the road is usually closed in winter and early spring, so you'd have to don snowshoes or cross-country skis to get there.

Virginia Lakes

South of Bridgeport, Hwy 395 gradually arrives at its highest point, **Conway Summit** (8143ft), where you'll be whipping out your camera to capture the awe-inspiring panorama of Mono Lake, backed by the Mono Craters, and June and Mammoth Mountains.

Also at the top is the turnout for Virginia Lakes Rd, which parallels Virginia Creek for about 6 miles to Virginia Lakes, a cluster of angler-worshipped lakes flanked by **Dunderberg Peak** (12,374ft) and **Black Mountain** (11,797ft). A trailhead at the end of the road gives access to the **Hoover Wilderness** and the **Pacific Crest Trail**. The trail continues down Cold Canyon through to Yosemite National Park. Check with the folks at the 1923 **Virginia Lakes Resort** (📞760-647-6484; www.virginialakesresort.com; cabins from $112; ⊘mid-May–mid-Oct; 🐾) for maps and tips about specific trails and fishing lures. The resort itself has snug cabins with kitchens, a cafe and a general store. Cabins sleep two to 12 people, and usually have a minimum stay.

There's also the option of camping at **Trumbull Lake Campground** (☎800-444-7275; www.recreation.gov; tent & RV sites $22; ⊙ mid-Jun–mid-Oct). The shady sites here are located among lodgepole pines. Nearby, **Virginia Lakes Pack Outfit** (☎760-937-0326; www.virginialakes.com) offers horseback-riding trips.

Lundy Lake

After Conway Summit, Hwy 395 twists down steeply into the Mono Basin. Before reaching Mono Lake, Lundy Lake Rd meanders west of the highway for about 5 miles to Lundy Lake. This is a gorgeous spot, especially in spring when wildflowers carpet the canyon along Mill Creek, or in fall when it is brightened by colorful foliage. Before reaching the lake, the road skirts first-come, first-served **Lundy Canyon Campground** (tent & RV sites $16; ⊙ late Apr-Oct; 🐾), with vault toilets; there's water available, but it must be boiled or treated. At the end of the lake, there's a ramshackle resort on the site of an 1880s mining town, plus a small store and boat rentals.

Past the resort, a dirt road leads into **Lundy Canyon** where, in 2 miles, it dead-ends at the trailhead for the Hoover Wilderness Area. A fantastic hike follows Mill Creek to a 200ft-high waterfall in the back of the canyon (approximately 5 miles round-trip), passing other worthy falls along the way. Industrious beavers define the landscape along the trail, with gnawed aspens scattered on the ground and a number of huge dams barricading the creek. Ambitious types can continue on via Lundy Pass to Saddlebag Lake and the Twenty Lakes Basin, though the final climb out of the canyon uses a very steep talus chute.

Lee Vining

Hwy 395 skirts the western bank of Mono Lake, rolling into the gateway town of Lee Vining where you can eat, sleep, gas up (for a pretty penny) and catch Hwy 120 to Yosemite National Park when the road's open. A superb base for exploring Mono Lake, Lee Vining is only 12 miles (about a 30-minute drive) from Yosemite's Tioga Pass entrance. **Lee Vining Canyon** is a popular location for **ice climbing**.

In town, take a quick look at the **Upside-Down House**, a kooky tourist attraction created by silent film actress Nellie Bly O'Bryan. Originally situated along Tioga Rd, it now resides in a park in front of the tiny **Mono Basin Historical Society Museum** (www.monobasinhs.org; donation $2; ⊙ 10am-4pm Thu-Mon mid-May–early Oct). To find it, turn east on 1st St and go one block to Mattley Ave.

🛏 Sleeping

El Mono Motel   MOTEL $
(☎ 760-647-6310; www.elmonomotel.com; 51 Hwy 395, Lee Vining; r $69-99; ⊙ mid-May–Oct; 🛜) Grab a board game or soak up some mountain sunshine in this friendly flower-ringed place attached to an excellent cafe. In operation since 1927, it's often booked solid, and each of its 11 simple rooms (a few share bathrooms) is unique, decorated with vibrant and colorful art and fabrics.

Lee Vining Motel   MOTEL $
(☎ 760-647-6440; Hwy 395; r $60-88; ⊙ mid-May–Oct; 🛜) If you didn't make a reservation and everything else is booked, try this first-come, first-served budget motel. It's a tad musty but fine for a night. Reception opens at 4pm.

★ Yosemite Gateway Motel   MOTEL $$
(☎ 760-647-6467; www.yosemitegatewaymotel.com; 51340 Hwy 395; r $119-159; ❉🛜) Think vistas. This is the only motel on the east side of the highway, and the views from some of the rooms are phenomenal. Its boutique-style rooms have comfortable beds with thick duvets and swank bathrooms.

Murphey's Motel   MOTEL $$
(☎ 800-334-6316, 760-647-6316; www.murpheysyosemite.com; 51493 Hwy 395; r $73-143; ❉🛜🐾) At the north end of town, this large and friendly motel offers comfy rooms with all mod cons.

🍴 Eating

Mono Market   MARKET $
(51303 Hwy 395; ⊙ 7am-10pm summer, shorter hrs in winter; 🅿) Stock up on quality groceries at the local market, whose diverse selection seems more like that of a big city grocery store. The deli serves delicious breakfast burritos, pastries and coffee, all to go.

Whoa Nellie Deli
CALIFORNIAN **$$**

(📞760-647-1088; www.whoanelliedeli.com; Tioga Gas Mart, Hwys 120 & 395, Lee Vining; mains $10-22; ⏱6:30am-9pm late Apr-Oct; 🔊) After putting this unexpected gas station restaurant on the map, its famed chef has moved on to Mammoth, but locals think the food is still damn good. Stop in for delicious fish tacos, wild buffalo meatloaf and other tasty morsels, and live bands two nights a week.

Mono Inn
NEW AMERICAN **$$**

(📞760-647-6581; www.themonoinn.com; 55620 Hwy 395; mains $9-35; ⏱5-9pm Tue-Sat, 10am-3pm Sun, Apr–mid-Nov) A restored 1922 lodge owned by the family of photographer Ansel Adams, this elegant yet casual lakefront restaurant makes everything from scratch and has delectable views to match. Stop in for the occasional live band on the creekside terrace. It's located about 5 miles north of Lee Vining.

Mono Lake

North America's second-oldest lake is a quiet and mysterious expanse of deep blue water whose glassy surface reflects jagged Sierra peaks, young volcanic cones and the unearthly tufa (*too*-fah) towers that make Mono Lake so distinctive. Jutting from the water like drip sand castles, the tufas form when calcium bubbles up from subterranean springs and combines with carbonate in the alkaline lake waters.

In *Roughing It*, Mark Twain described Mono Lake as California's 'dead sea.' Hardly. The brackish water teems with buzzing alkali flies and brine shrimp, both considered delicacies by dozens of migratory bird species that return here year after year. So do about 85% of the state's nesting population of California gulls, which take over the lake's volcanic islands from April to August. Like the Owens Valley, Mono Lake has also been a political football in the state's historical battle over water rights.

◉ Sights & Activities

South Tufa
NATURE RESERVE

(adult/child $3/free) Tufa spires ring the lake, but the biggest grove is on the south rim with a mile-long interpretive trail. Ask about ranger-led tours at the Mono Basin Scenic Area Visitor Center. To get to the reserve, head south from Lee Vining on Hwy 395 for

6 miles, then east on Hwy 120 for 5 miles to the dirt road leading to a parking lot.

Navy Beach
BEACH

The best place for swimming is at Navy Beach, just east of the South Tufa reserve. It's also the best place to put in canoes or kayaks. From late June to early September, the **Mono Lake Committee** (📞760-647-6595; www.monolake.org/visit/canoe; tours $25; ⏱8am, 9:30am & 11am Sat & Sun late Jun-early Sep) operates one-hour canoe tours around the tufas. Half-day kayak tours along the shore or out to Paoha Island are also offered by **Caldera Kayaks** (📞760-934-1691; www.calderakayak.com; tours $75; ⏱mid-May–early Oct). Both require reservations.

Panum Crater
NATURAL FEATURE

Rising above the south shore, Panum Crater is the youngest (about 640 years old), smallest and most accessible of the craters that string south toward Mammoth Mountain. A panoramic trail circles the crater rim (about 30 to 45 minutes), and a short but steep 'plug trail' puts you at the crater's core. A dirt road leads to the trailhead from Hwy 120, about 3 miles east of the junction with Hwy 395.

Black Point Fissures
NATURAL FEATURE

On the north shore of the lake are the Black Point Fissures, narrow crags that opened when lava mass cooled and contracted about 13,000 years ago. Access is from three places: east of Mono Lake County Park, from the west shore off Hwy 395, or south off Hwy 167. Check at the Mono Basin Scenic Area Visitor Center for specific directions.

❶ Information

Mono Basin Scenic Area Visitor Center
(📞760-647-3044; www.fs.usda.gov/inyo; ⏱8am-5pm, shorter spring & fall hours, closed Dec-Mar) Half a mile north of Lee Vining, this center has maps, interpretive displays, Inyo National Forest wilderness permits, bear-canister rentals, a bookstore and a 20-minute movie about Mono Lake.

Mono Lake Committee Information Center
(📞760-647-6595; www.monolake.org; cnr Hwy 395 & 3rd St; ⏱9am-5pm late-Oct–mid-Jun, 8am-9pm mid-Jun–Sep) Internet access ($2 per 15 minutes), maps, books, free 30-minute video about Mono Lake and passionate, preservation-minded staff. Public restroom too.

June Lake Loop

Under the shadow of massive **Carson Peak** (10,909ft), the stunning 16-mile June Lake Loop (Hwy 158) meanders through a picture-perfect horseshoe canyon, past the relaxed resort town of **June Lake** and four sparkling, fish-rich lakes: Grant, Silver, Gull and June. It's especially scenic in fall when the basin is ablaze with golden aspens. Catch the loop a few miles south of Lee Vining.

🏃 Activities

Hiking

The area is backed by the Ansel Adams Wilderness, which runs into Yosemite National Park. From Silver Lake, Gem and Agnew Lakes make spectacular day hikes, while Thousand Island and Emerald Lake (both on the Pacific Crest/John Muir Trails) are stunning overnight destinations (wilderness permit required).

Other Activities

Cyclists can zip around the entire loop, a moderate 22-mile circle including a section of Hwy 395. Boat and tackle rentals, as well as fishing licenses, are available at five marinas. In June Lake village, **Ernie's Tackle & Ski Shop** (☑760-648-7756; 2604 Hwy 158; ⊙6am-7pm) can get you geared up.

In wintertime, ice climbers flock to the area's frozen waterfalls.

June Mountain Ski Area   SKIING
(☑888-586-3686, 24hr snow info 760-934-2224; www.junemountain.com; lift tickets adult/youth 13-18 & senior/child under 13 $72/48/free; ⊙8:30am-4pm; 🏂) Winter fun concentrates in this area, which is smaller and less crowded than nearby Mammoth Mountain and perfect for beginner and intermediate skiers. Some 35 trails crisscross 500 acres of terrain served by seven lifts, including two high-speed quads. Boarders can get their adrenaline flowing at three terrain parks with a kick-ass superpipe.

Frontier Pack Train   HORSEBACK RIDING
(☑760-648-7701; www.frontierpacktrain.com; Silver Lake; 1hr/half-day/full-day rides $40/75/120; ⊙Jun-Sep) Area and backcountry horseback rides.

🛌 Sleeping

USFS Campgrounds   CAMPGROUND $
(☑800-444-7275; www.recreation.gov; tent & RV sites $22; ⊙mid-Apr–Oct; 🐕) Of June Lake, Oh! Ridge, Silver Lake, Gull Lake and Reversed Creek, the first three accept reservations.

Silver Lake

June Lake Motel   MOTEL $$
(☑760-648-7547; www.junelakemotel.com; 2716 Hwy 158; r with kitchen/kitchenette $115/95; ❄@🛜🐕) Enormous rooms – most with full kitchens – catch delicious mountain breezes and sport attractive light-wood furniture. There's a fish-cleaning sink and barbecues.

Double Eagle Resort & Spa   RESORT $$$
(☑760-648-7004; www.doubleeaglc.com; 5587 Hwy 158; r $249, cabins $369; 🛜🏊🐕) A swanky spot for these parts. The sleek two-bedroom log cabins and balconied hotel rooms lack no comfort, while worries disappear at the elegant spa. Its **restaurant** (mains $15-30; ⊙7:30am-9pm) exudes rustic elegance, with cozy booths, a high ceiling and a huge fireplace.

🍴 Eating & Drinking

Ohanas 395   HAWAIIAN $
(www.ohanas395.com; 131 S Crawford Ave; mains $8-12; ⊙11:30am-6:30pm Wed-Sat & Mon, noon-5pm Sun) Seek out this food truck, parked at June Lake Brewing, serving wait-worthy 'Hawaiian soul food' with a dash of Mexican fusion. Try a classic plate lunch, the Kalua pig tacos or quesadillas.

DAVID TOUSSAINT / GETTY IMAGES ©

Tiger Bar   AMERICAN $$
(www.thetigerbarcafe.com; 2620 Hwy 158; mains $9-20; ⊙8am-10pm) After a day on slopes or trails, people gather at the long bar or around the pool table of this no-nonsense, no-attitude place. The kitchen feeds all appetites, with burgers, salads, tacos and other tasty grub, including homemade fries.

★ **June Lake Brewing**   MICROBREWERY
(www.junelakebrewing.com; 131 S Crawford Ave, June Lake; ⊙11am-8pm Wed-Mon, to 9pm Fri & Sat; 🅱) A top new regional draw, June Lake Brewing's open tasting room serves ten drafts, including a 'SmoKin' Porter, Deer Beer Brown Ale and some awesome IPAs. They swear the June Lake water makes all the difference. Flights $4 to $6.

Mammoth Lakes

This small mountain resort town is endowed with larger-than-life scenery – active outdoorsy folks worship at the base of its dizzying 11,053ft **Mammoth Mountain**. For most of the year powder clings to these slopes, and when the snow does disappear the area becomes an outdoor wonderland of mountain-bike trails, fishing, alpine hiking and hidden spots for hot-spring soaking. The Eastern Sierra's commercial hub and a four-season resort, outdoorsy Mammoth is backed by a ridgeline of jutting peaks, ringed by clusters of crystalline alpine lakes and enshrouded by the dense Inyo National Forest.

◉ Sights

★ **Earthquake Fault**   NATURAL FEATURE
On Minaret Rd, about 1 mile west of the Mammoth Scenic Loop, detour to gape at Earthquake Fault, a sinuous fissure half a mile long gouging a crevice up to 20ft deep into the earth. Ice and snow often linger at the bottom until late summer, and Native Americans and early settlers used it to store perishable food.

Mammoth Museum   MUSEUM
(☑760-934-6918; www.mammothmuseum.org; 5489 Sherwin Creek Rd; suggested donation $3; ⊙10am-6pm mid-May–Sep; 🅱) For a walk down memory lane, stop by this little museum inside the historic Hayden log cabin.

🏃 Activities

The excellent website of the Mammoth Lakes Trail System (www.mammothtrails.

org) contains a comprehensive guide to local hiking, biking and cross-country ski trails, with maps and information on services available.

Skiing & Snowboarding

Main Lodge and Canyon Lodge have ski schools and state-of-the-art equipment rental.

Mammoth Mountain   SKIING, SNOWBOARDING
(☑760-934-2571, 800-626-6684, 24hr snow report 888-766-9778; www.mammothmountain.com; lift tickets adult/senior/youth 13-18yr/child 7-12yr $105/89/82/35) A skiers' and snowboarders' dream resort, where sunny skies, a reliably long season (usually November to June) and over 3500 acres of fantastic tree-line and open-bowl skiing are a potent cocktail. At the top you'll be dealing with some gnarly, nearly vertical chutes. The other stats are just as impressive: 3100 vertical feet, 150 trails, 28 lifts (including 11 quads).

Cross-Country Skiing

There's free cross-country skiing along the more than 300 miles of nongroomed trails in town and in the Inyo National Forest. Pick up a free map at the Mammoth Lakes Welcome Center.

**Tamarack Cross-Country
Ski Center**   SKIING
(☑760-934-2442; 163 Twin Lakes Rd; all-day trail pass incl equipment adult/child/senior $28/23/28; ⊙8:30am-5pm) Let the town shuttle take you to the Tamarack Lodge, which has almost 20 miles of meticulously groomed track around Twin Lakes and the Lakes Basin. The terrain is also great for snowshoeing. Rentals and lessons are available.

Biking

Stop at the welcome center for a free map with route descriptions and updated trail conditions.

**Mammoth Mountain
Bike Park**   MOUNTAIN BIKING
(☑800-626-6684; www.mammothmountain.com; day pass adult/child 7-12 $50/25; ⊙9am-4:30pm Jun-Sep) Come summer, Mammoth Mountain morphs into the massive Mammoth Mountain Bike Park, with more than 80 miles of well-kept single-track trails. Several other trails traverse the surrounding forest. In general, Mammoth-style riding translates into plenty of hills and soft, sandy shoulders, which are best navigated with big knobby tires.

Mammoth Mountain ski resort

Lakes Basin Path
CYCLING

One of Mammoth's fantastic new multi-use paths, the 5.3-mile Lakes Basin Path begins at the southwest corner of Lake Mary and Minaret Rds and heads uphill (1000ft, at a 5% to 10% grade) to Horseshoe Lake, skirting lovely lakes and accessing open views of the Sherwin Range. For a one-way ride, use the free Lakes Basin Trolley, which tows a 12-bicycle trailer.

Hiking

Mammoth Lakes rubs up against the Ansel Adams Wilderness and John Muir Wilderness, both laced with fabulous trails leading to shimmering lakes, rugged peaks and hidden canyons. Major trailheads leave from the Mammoth Lakes Basin, Reds Meadow and Agnew Meadows; the last two are accessible only by shuttle. Shadow Lake is a stunning 7-mile day hike from Agnew Meadows that can also be part of a backcountry trip to the base of the Ritter Range.

Fishing & Boating

From the last Saturday in April (known as 'Fishmas'), the dozens of lakes that give the town its name lure in fly and trout fishers from near and far. California fishing licenses are available at sporting goods stores throughout town. For equipment and advice, head to **Troutfitter** (760-934-2517; cnr Main St & Old Mammoth Rd; 8am-4pm) or **Rick's Sports Center** (760-934-3416; cnr Main & Center Sts; 6am-8pm).

The **Pokonobe Store & Marina** (760-934-2437; www.pokonoberesort.com), on the north end of Lake Mary, rents motor boats ($20 per hour), pedal boats ($10), canoes ($20) and kayaks ($20 to $25). **Caldera Kayaks** (760-935-1691; www.calderakayak.com) has single ($30 for a half-day) and double kayaks ($50) for use on Crowley Lake.

🛏 Sleeping

Mammoth B&Bs and inns rarely sell out midweek, when rates tend to be lower. During ski season, reservations are a good idea on weekends and essential during holidays. Many properties offer ski-and-stay packages. Condo rentals often work out cheaper for groups.

Davison Street Guest House
HOSTEL $

(760-924-2188; www.mammoth-guest.com; 19 Davison St; dm $35-45, d $75-125;) A cute, five-room A-frame chalet hostel on a quiet

HOT SPRINGS HEAVEN

If you live to soak, the Eastern Sierra will fulfill your every hot-spring fantasy. Thanks to its volcanic past and wealth of underground mountain-fed springs, the stretch of Hwy 395 from just north of Bridgeport south to Lone Pine is sprinkled with secluded spots for simmering. Over the years, first shepherds, then locals, have crafted actual drainable tubs, with rubber hosing used to divert the springs. Many are well known and thus can get crowded on weekends, so if you're after seclusion, it's best to spring-hop in midweek or off-season.

Nestled between the White Mountains and the Sierra Range near Mammoth is a tantalizing slew of natural pools with snowcapped panoramic views. When the high-altitude summer nights turn chilly and you can hear the coyotes cry, you'll never want to dry off. About 9 miles south of town, Benton Crossing Rd juts east off of Hwy 395, accessing a trove of hot springs. Locals call this 'Green Church Rd,' because of the road's unmistakable marker.

For a soaking to-do list with detailed directions and maps, pick up the bible – Matt Bischoff's excellent *Touring California & Nevada Hot Springs*. And keep in mind these three golden rules: no glass, no additives to the water and, if you can, no bathing suit.

residential street, this place has a stocked kitchen, plus mountain views from the living room with fireplace or sun deck. There's self-registration when the manager isn't around. Fills with long-distance backpackers in June and July.

Holiday Haus   HOSTEL, MOTEL **$$**
(☑760-934-2414; www.holidayhausmotelandhostel.com; 3905 Main St; dm $45, d with shared bath $75, d $124-130, 2br apt $180-239; ▣⬤) Mammoth's newest hostel is a gleaming addition to this upgraded motel, with a modern dishwasher-equipped kitchen and colorful contemporary rooms with personal lockers and reading lights. In a separate building, comfortable motel rooms all have kitchenettes, and the nicest include gas fireplaces. There's a Jacuzzi too.

Mammoth Creek Inn   INN **$$**
(☑760-934-6162, 800-466-7000; www.mammothcreekinn.com; 663 Old Mammoth Rd; r $139-149, with kitchen $199-209; @⬤▣) It's amenities galore at this pretty inn at the end of a commercial strip, with down comforters and fluffy terry robes, as well as a sauna, a hot tub and a fun pool table loft. The best rooms overlook the majestic Sherwin Mountains, and some have full kitchens and can sleep up to six.

Tamarack Lodge   LODGE, CABIN **$$$**
(☑760-934-2442, 800-626-6684; www.tamaracklodge.com; 163 Twin Lakes Rd; r with/without bath $219/169, cabins from $299; @⬤) ❂ In business since 1924, this charming year-round resort on Lower Twin Lake has a cozy fireplace lodge, a bar and excellent restaurant,

11 rustic-style rooms and 35 cabins. The cabins range from very simple to simply deluxe, and come with full kitchen, private bathroom, porch and wood-burning stove. Some can sleep up to 10 people. Daily resort fee $20.

Campgrounds

About 15 USFS campgrounds are scattered in and around Mammoth Lakes, and all are pet-friendly, with flush toilets but no showers. Many sites are available on a first-come, first-served basis, and some are reservable. Note that nights get chilly at these elevations, even in July. All close in winter and charge about $22. Stop by the Mammoth Lakes Welcome Center (p151) or check its website for a full list of campgrounds and public shower locations.

Some of the nicest campgrounds are in the lakes basin around Twin Lakes, Lake Mary and Lake George, with well-spaced sites in a pine forest and along crackling creeks. Less picturesque but close to town, New Shady Rest and Old Shady Rest are two sprawling options right behind the Mammoth Lakes Welcome Center.

✖ Eating

Stellar Brew   CAFE **$**
(www.stellarbrewnaturalcafe.com; 3280b Main St; salads & sandwiches $5.50-10; ☉5:30am-7pm mid-Jun–Aug, to 5pm Sep–mid-Jun; ⬤▣▣) ❂ Proudly locavore and mostly organic, settle into a comfy sofa here for your daily dose of locally roasted coffee, homemade granola, breakfast burritos and scrumptious vegan (and some gluten-free) pastries.

Good Life Café CALIFORNIAN, MEXICAN $
(www.mammothgoodlifecafe.com; 126 Old Mammoth Rd; mains $8-13; ⊙6:30am-8pm or 9pm; ☑) Healthy food, generously filled veggie wraps and big bowls of salad make this a perennially popular place. The front patio is blissful for a long brunch on a warm day.

Sierra Sundance Whole Foods HEALTH FOOD $
(26 Old Mammoth Rd; ⊙ 9am-7pm Mon-Sat, to 5pm Sun; ☑) Stock up on organic produce, free range meats and healthy bulk foods at this large store and deli.

Mammoth Tavern GASTROPUB $$
(www.mammothtavern.com; 587 Old Mammoth Rd; mains $12-35; ⊙3:30-11pm Tue-Sun) Warmly lighted wood-paneled walls rise to a circular ceiling, and the big-screen TVs are an unnecessary distraction from the drop-dead views of the snow-capped Sherwin Range. A newcomer to the local dining scene, Mammoth Tavern hits the spot with comfort food like shepherd's pie, oysters, gorgeous salads and fondue garlic turkey meatballs. Worthy libations include tasty house cocktails, local drafts, interesting whiskeys and over two dozen wines by the glass.

★**Lakefront Restaurant** NEW AMERICAN $$$
(☑760-934-2442; www.lakefrontmammoth.com; 163 Twin Lakes Rd; mains $24-45; ⊙5-9:30pm year-round, plus 11am-2pm summer, closed Tue & Wed in fall & spring) The most atmospheric and romantic restaurant in Mammoth, this intimate dining room at Tamarack Lodge overlooks lovely Twin Lakes. A new chef crafts specialties like pork belly, oxtail risotto and braised beef short ribs, and the staff are superbly friendly. Reservations recommended.

Drinking

Clocktower Cellar PUB
(www.clocktowercellar.com; 6080 Minaret Rd; ⊙4-11pm) In the winter especially, locals throng this half-hidden basement of the Alpenhof Lodge. The ceiling is tiled with a swirl of bottle caps, and the bar stocks 150 whiskies, about 30 beers on tap and about 50 bottled varieties.

Mammoth Brewing Company Tasting Room BREWERY
(www.mammothbrewingco.com; 18 Lake Mary Rd; ⊙10am-9:30pm Sun-Thu, to 10:30pm Fri & Sat) In a large and central location, try some of the dozen brews on tap (flights $5 to $7) – including special seasonal varieties not found

elsewhere – then pick up some IPA 395 or Double Nut Brown to go. Tasty bar food available.

Shopping

Footloose OUTDOOR EQUIPMENT
(☑760-934-2400; www.footloosesports.com; cnr Main St & Old Mammoth Rd; ⊙8am-8pm) Full range of footwear and seasonal equipment; local biking info and rentals.

Mammoth Mountaineering Supply OUTDOOR EQUIPMENT
(☑760-934-4191; www.mammothgear.com; 3189 Main St; ⊙8am-8pm) Offers friendly advice, topo maps and all-season equipment rentals.

Information

The **Mammoth Lakes Welcome Center** (☑760-924-5500, 888-466-2666; www.visitmammoth.com; ⊙8am-5pm) and the **Mammoth Lakes Ranger Station** (☑760-924-5500; www.fs.usda.gov/inyo; ⊙8am-5pm) share a building on the north side of Hwy 203. This one-stop information center issues wilderness permits, rents bear canisters, helps find accommodations and campgrounds, and provides road and trail condition updates. From May through October, when trail quotas are in effect, walk-in wilderness permits are released at 11am the day before, though numbers are given out starting at 8am so you don't have to wait in line; permits are self-issue the rest of the year.

Two weekly newspapers, the *Mammoth Times* (www.mammothtimes.com) and the free *Sheet* (www.thesheetnews.com), carry local news and events listings.
Mammoth Hospital (☑760-934-3311; 85 Sierra Park Rd; ⊙24hr) Emergency room.

Getting There & Around

Just south of town, the **Mammoth Yosemite airport** (MMH; www.visitmammoth.com/airport; 1300 Airport Rd) has nonstop service to San Francisco and Denver, operating winter through to spring on **United** (www.united.com). **Alaska Airlines** (☑800-252-7522; www.alaskaair.com) runs year-round service to Los Angeles, and ski-season service to San Diego. Other winter destinations vary year to year.

Taxis meet incoming flights, and some lodgings provide free transfers. **Mammoth Taxi** (☑760-934-8294; www.mammoth-taxi.com) does airport runs as well as hiker shuttles throughout the Sierra.

Mammoth is a snap to navigate by public transportation year-round. In the summertime, **YARTS** (☑877-989-2787; www.yarts.com) runs buses to and from Yosemite Valley, and

AROUND YOSEMITE NATIONAL PARK MAMMOTH LAKES

DEVILS POSTPILE

The most fascinating attraction in Reds Meadow is the surreal volcanic formation of **Devils Postpile National Monument** (☑760-934-2289; www.nps.gov/depo; shuttle day pass adult/child $7/4; ⊗late-May–Oct). The 60ft curtains of near-vertical, six-sided basalt columns formed when rivers of molten lava slowed, cooled and cracked with perplexing symmetry. This honeycomb design is best appreciated from atop the columns, reached by a short trail. The columns are an easy, half-mile hike from the **Devils Postpile Ranger Station** (☑760-934-2289; www.nps.gov/depo; ⊗9am-5pm summer).

From the monument, a 2.5-mile hike passing through fire-scarred forest leads to the spectacular **Rainbow Falls**, where the San Joaquin River gushes over a 101ft basalt cliff. Chances of actually seeing a rainbow forming in the billowing mist are greatest at noon. The falls can also be reached via an easy 1.5-mile walk from the Reds Meadow area, which also has a cafe, store, the **Reds Meadow campground** and a pack station.

the **Eastern Sierra Transit Authority** (☑800-922-1930; www.estransit.com) has year-round service along Hwy 395, north to Reno and south to Lone Pine.

Within Mammoth, a year-round system of free and frequent **bus shuttles** connects the whole town with the Mammoth Mountain lodges; in summer, routes with bicycle trailers service the Lakes Basin and Mammoth Mountain Bike Park.

Around Mammoth Lakes

Reds Meadow

West of the Mammoth Mountain resort, Reds Meadow Valley is one of the most beautiful and varied landscapes in the region. Drive about 1 mile up from the ski area on Hwy 203 to **Minaret Vista** (9265ft) for eye-popping views of the Ritter Range, the serrated Minarets and the remote reaches of Yosemite National Park. At dusk, the lacy granite spires of the Minarets seem to come alive in the rosy alpenglow.

A handful of nice first-come, first-served campgrounds are sprinkled about the valley road. Some, like Minaret Falls, are right on the Middle Fork of the San Joaquin River, and are very popular with anglers. The kiosk at the road entrance lists which campgrounds are full.

The road to Reds Meadow and Devils Postpile is generally open (free of snow) from June until September. When open, between 7am and 7pm you can only get there by hiking or biking or aboard a **mandatory shuttle** (adult/child 3–15 years $7/4). The shuttle leaves from a lot in front of the Adventure Center at the base of Mammoth Mountain's gondola approximately every 30 minutes between 7:30am and 7pm (last bus

out leaves Reds Meadow at 7:45pm). There are also three direct departures from the Village (on Canyon Blvd, under the gondola) before 9am.

You can drive in if you are camping in one of the six valley campgrounds, have reservations at the Reds Meadow Resort, or are a person with a disability (all incur a $10 vehicle fee).

McGee Creek

Around 8 miles south of Mammoth Lakes, off Hwy 395, McGee Creek Rd rises into the mountains and dead-ends in a dramatic aspen-lined canyon, a particularly beautiful spot for autumn foliage. From here, the McGee Pass Trail enters the John Muir Wilderness, with day hikes to **Steelhead Lake** (10 miles round-trip) via an easy walk to subtle **Horsetail Falls** (four miles round-trip).

On the drive up, spacious **McGee Creek campground** (www.recreation.gov; McGee Creek Rd; tent & RV sites $20; ⊗late-Apr–Oct; 🐾) has 28 reservable sites at 7600ft, with sun-shaded picnic tables along the creek and stunning mountain vistas.

At the intersection after you leave the highway, don't miss the coffee and home-baked goodies at the cute **East Side Bake Shop** (☑760-914-2696; www.facebook.com/EastSideBakeShop; 1561 Crowley Lake Dr; mains $8-15; ⊗6:30am-3pm Wed, Thu & Sun, to 9pm Fri & Sat, shorter winter hrs); check its calendar for fun local music on the weekends.

Rock Creek

South off Hwy 395 and roughly equidistant from Mammoth Lakes and Bishop, Rock Creek Rd travels 11 miles into some of the dreamiest landscapes in the Sierra. At roads' end, the Mosquito Flat trailhead into the Little Lakes Valley (part of the John Muir Wilderness) clocks in at a whopping 10,300ft of elevation. Mountaintops seem to be everywhere, with the 13,000ft peaks of Bear Creek Spire, Mt Dade, Mt Abbot and Mt Mills bursting out along the southwestern horizon and lush canyon meadows popping with scores of clear blue lakes. Ecstatic hikers and climbers fan out to explore, though most anglers and hikers just go as far as the first few lakes. An excellent dayhike destination is the second of the Gem Lakes (7 miles round-trip), a lovely aquamarine bowl and five-star lunch spot.

At the Rock Creek Lakes Resort, 9 miles from the highway, don't put off a visit to tiny Pie in the Sky Cafe (☑760-935-4311; www. rockcreeklakesresort.com; pie slice $7-8; ☉7am-3pm late-May–mid-Oct, shorter hrs early & late season). Its confections, baked from scratch, go on sale at 10:30am and usually sell out by 2pm. The slices of chocolate mud pie are gargantuan.

A dozen popular USFS campgrounds (☑877-444-6777; www.recreation.gov; tent & RV sites $22; ☉late May-Sep; 🛉) line Rock Creek Rd; most are along Rock Creek and a few are reservable.

Bishop

The second-largest town in the Eastern Sierra, Bishop is about two hours from Yosemite's east gate. A major recreation hub, Bishop offers access to excellent fishing in nearby lakes, climbing in the Buttermilks just west of town, and hiking in the John Muir Wilderness via Bishop Creek Canyon and the Rock Creek drainage. The area is especially lovely in fall when dropping temperatures cloak aspen, willow and cottonwood in myriad glowing shades.

The earliest inhabitants of the Owens Valley were Paiute and Shoshone Native Americans, who today live on four reservations; the largest is the Bishop Indian Reservation. White settlers came on the scene in the 1860s and began raising cattle to sell to nearby mining settlements.

◉ Sights

★ **Laws Railroad Museum**   MUSEUM
(☑760-873-5950; www.lawsmuseum.org; Silver Canyon Rd, off Hwy 6; donation $5; ☉10am-4pm early Sep-late May, 9:30am-4pm late May-early Sep; 🛉) Railroad and Old West aficionados should make the 6-mile detour north on Hwy 6 to this museum. It re-creates the village of Laws, an important stop on the route of the Slim Princess, a narrow-gauge train that hauled freight and passengers across the Owens Valley for nearly 80 years. You'll see the original 1883 train depot, a post office, a schoolhouse and other rickety old buildings. Many contain funky and eclectic displays (dolls, fire equipment, antique stoves etc) from the pioneer days.

Mountain Light Gallery   GALLERY
(☑760-873-7700; www.mountainlight.com; 106 S Main St; ☉10am-5pm Mon-Sat, 11am-4pm Sun) **FREE** To see the Sierra on display in all its majesty, pop into this gallery, which features the stunning outdoor images of the late Galen Rowell. His work bursts with color, and the High Sierra photographs are some of the best in existence.

Owens Valley Paiute Shoshone Cultural Center   CULTURAL CENTER, MUSEUM
(☑760-873-8844; www.bishoppaiutetribe.com/ cultural-center.html; 2300 W Line St; ☉10am-5pm Tue-Sat) **FREE** A mile west of Hwy 395, this underutilized tribal cultural center includes exhibits on local basketry and the use of medical herbs; behind the building is an interpretive native plant walk.

🏃 Activities

Bishop is prime territory for bouldering and rock climbing, with terrain to match any level of fitness, experience and climbing style. The main areas are the granite Buttermilk Country west of town on Buttermilk Rd, and the stark Volcanic Tablelands and Owens River Valley to the north. For details, consult with the staff at Wilson's Eastside Sports (☑760-873-7520; www.eastsidesports.com; 224 N Main St; ☉9am-9pm), which rents equipment and sells maps and guidebooks. Another excellent resource is Mammoth Mountaineering Supply (☑760-873-4300; www.mammoth gear.com; 298 N Main St; ☉9am-7pm), which also sells used gear. Keep a look out for Native American petroglyphs in the tablelands too.

For hiking, head to the high country by following Line St (Hwy 168) west along Bishop Creek Canyon past Buttermilk Country and on to several lakes, including Lake Sabrina and South Lake. Trailheads lead into the John Muir Wilderness and on into Kings Canyon National Park. Check with the White Mountain Ranger Station (p154) for suggestions, maps and wilderness permits for overnight stays. Fishing is good in all lakes, but North Lake is the least crowded.

Keough's Hot Springs
SWIMMING

(☑760-872-4670; www.keoughshotsprings.com; 800 Keough Hot Springs Rd; adult/child 3-12/child under 3 $10/6/4; ⊙11am-7pm Wed-Fri & Mon, 9am-8pm Sat & Sun, longer hours Jun-Aug; ♠) About 8 miles south of Bishop, this historic institutional-green outdoor pool (dating from 1919) is filled with bath-warm water from local mineral springs and doused with spray at one end. A smaller and sheltered 104°F (40°C) soaking pool sits beside it. Camping and tent cabins are also available.

🛏 Sleeping

USFS Campgrounds
CAMPGROUND $

(www.recreation.gov; tent & RV sites $23; ⊙May-Sep; 🖩) For a scenic night, stretch out your sleeping bag beneath the stars. The closest USFS campgrounds, all but one first-come, first-served, are between 9 miles and 15 miles west of town on Bishop Creek along Hwy 168, at elevations between 7500ft and 9000ft.

Hostel California
HOSTEL $

(☑760-399-6316; www.hostelbishop.com; 213 Academy Ave; dm $28.50, d $80, 6-person r $170; ❋🛜) A historic Victorian house located right in the center of town, this hostel packs in dusty long-distance backpackers during June and July, with a more varied mix of hikers, anglers and climbers and international travelers the rest of the year. Visitors love the full kitchen, laundry-time loaner clothes, and bicycles, as well as the social outdoors-loving atmosphere. Adults only.

Bishop Creekside Inn
MOTEL $$

(☑760-872-3044; www.bishopcreeksideinn.com; 725 N Main St; r $130-209, ste $140-230; ❋@🛜🖩) Request a creekside room and watch ducks paddle by at this independent motel with an enviable central location alongside Bishop Creek. Woodsy art decorates rooms which come with marble bathrooms (with walk-in glass showers), roomy armchairs, Keurig coffee makers and thick duvet bedding.

Joseph House Inn Bed & Breakfast
B&B $$

(☑760-872-3389; www.josephhouseinn.com; 376 W Yaney St; r $143-188; ❋🛜🖩) A beautifully restored ranch-style home with a patio overlooking a tranquil 3-acre garden, and six nicely furnished rooms, some with fireplaces, all with TV. Guests enjoy a complimentary gourmet breakfast and afternoon wine.

🍴 Eating

Great Basin Bakery
BAKERY, CAFE $

(www.greatbasinbakerybishop.com; 275D S Main St, entrance on Lagoon St; salads & sandwiches $5-8; ⊙6am-4pm Mon-Sat, 6:30am-4pm Sun; 🖉) 🍴 On a side street in the southern part of town, this excellent bakery serves locally roasted coffee, breakfast sandwiches on freshly baked bagels with local eggs, homemade soups and lots of delectable baked goods (with vegan and gluten-free options).

Erick Schat's Bakkerÿ
BAKERY $

(☑760-873-7156; www.erickschatsbakery.com; 763 N Main St; sandwiches $6-9; ⊙6am-6pm Sun-Thu, to 7pm Fri) A much-hyped tourist mecca filled to the rafters with racks of fresh bread, it has been making its signature shepherd bread and other baked goodies since 1938. The bakery also features a popular sandwich bar.

Jack's Restaurant & Bakery
AMERICAN $

(437 N Main St; mains $8-19; ⊙6:30am-9pm) In business since 1946, Jack's stocks a full menu of filling, inexpensive comfort food like meatloaf and chicken fried steak, as well as hearty breakfasts. Its bread and pies are baked on-site. Guess which of the mounted fish are real.

ℹ Information

There's free municipal wi-fi along the central part of Main St.

Bishop Area Visitors Bureau (☑760-873-8405; www.bishopvisitor.com; 690 N Main St; ⊙10am-5pm Mon-Fri, to 4pm Sat & Sun)

Inyo County Free Library (☑760-873-5115; 210 Academy Ave; ⊙noon-8pm Tue & Thu, 10am-6pm Wed & Fri, 10am-4pm Sat; 🖥) Free internet access.

White Mountain Ranger Station (☑760-873-2500; www.fs.usda.gov/inyo; 798 N Main St; ⊙8am-5pm daily May-Oct, Mon-Fri Nov-Apr) Wilderness permits, trail and campground information for the entire area.

Ancient Bristlecone Pine Forest

For encounters with some of the earth's oldest living things, plan at least a half-day trip to the **Ancient Bristlecone Pine Forest** (☑760-873-2500; www.fs.usda.gov/inyo; ⊙usually mid-May–Nov). These gnarled, otherworldly trees thrive above 10,000ft on the slopes of the seemingly inhospitable White Mountains, a parched and stark range that once stood even higher than the Sierra. The oldest tree – called Methuselah – is estimated to be over 4700 years, beating even the Great Sphinx of Giza by about two centuries.

To reach the groves, take Hwy 168 east 12 miles from Big Pine, just south of Bishop, to White Mountain Rd, then turn left (north) and climb the curvy road 10 miles to **Schulman Grove**, named for the scientist who first discovered the trees' biblical age in the 1950s. The entire trip takes about one hour. There's access to self-guided trails, and a new solar-powered **visitors center** (⏱760-873-2500; www.fs.usda.gov/inyo; per person/car $3/6; ⏲10am-4pm Fri-Mon late May-early Nov). White Mountain Rd is usually closed from November to April. It's nicest in August when wildflowers sneak out through the rough soil.

A second grove, the **Patriarch Grove**, is dramatically set within an open bowl and reached via a 12-mile graded dirt road. Four miles further on you'll find a locked gate, which is the departure point for day hikes to **White Mountain Peak** – at 14,246ft it's the third-highest mountain in California. The round-trip is about 14 miles via an abandoned road, soon passing through the **Barcroft High Altitude Research Station**; some ride the route on mountain bikes. The easiest 14er in California, the nontechnical and marmot-laden route winds above the tree line, though naturally, high elevation makes the going tough. Allow plenty of time and bring at least two quarts of water per person. For maps and details, stop at the White Mountain Ranger Station (p154) in Bishop.

For altitude adjustment or some good star-gazing, spend a night at the **Grandview Campground** (donation $5; ▣) at 8600ft. About halfway up to the visitor center, it has awesome views, tables and vault toilets, but no water.

Independence

About 16 miles north of Lone Pine, this sleepy highway town is home to the **Eastern California Museum** (www.inyocounty.us/ecmuseum; 155 N Grant St; donation requested; ⏲10am-5pm). It contains one of the most complete collections of Paiute and Shoshone baskets in the country, as well as artifacts from the Manzanar relocation camp, and historic photographs of primitively equipped local rock climbers scaling Sierra peaks, including Mt Whitney.

About 15 miles west of town via Onion Valley Rd (Market St in town), pretty Onion Valley (elevation 9600ft) harbors the trailhead for **Kearsarge Pass** (9.5 miles roundtrip), an old Paiute trade route. This is the quickest eastside access to the John Muir and Pacific Crest Trails, and Kings Canyon National Park. There are three **USFS campgrounds** (⏱877-444-6777; www.recreation.gov; tent & RV sites $18; ⏲approx May-Sep; ▣) alongside Independence Creek, including one at the Kearsarge Pass trailhead.

A low-key hiker favorite, the cute cabins of the **Mt Williamson Motel & Base Camp** (⏱760-878-2121; www.mtwilliamsonmotel.com; 515 S Edwards St; r $85-95, ste $125; ▣▣▣▣) bask among fruit trees and feature flat-screen TVs, calico bedspreads, tea kettles and arresting prints of Sierra Nevada bighorn sheep. Ask about their hiker packages that include trailhead transportation.

Next to the courthouse, **Jenny's Cafe** (246 N Edwards St; mains $9-11; ⏲7am-2pm Thu-Tue) serves rib-sticking burgers, sandwiches and steaks in a country kitchen with rooster-print curtains. Upscale and unexpected in such a flyspeck town, bright, artistic **Still Life Cafe** (⏱760-878-2555; 135 S Edward St; lunch $9-16, dinner $16-24; ⏲11am-3pm & 6-9:30pm Wed-Mon) prepares escargot, steak *au poivre* and other French bistro faves.

Manzanar National Historic Site

A stark wooden guard tower alerts drivers to one of the darkest chapters in US history, which unfolded on a barren and windy sweep of land some 5 miles south of Independence. Little remains of the infamous war concentration camp, a dusty square mile where more than 10,000 people of Japanese ancestry were corralled during WWII following the attack on Pearl Harbor. The camp's lone remaining building, the former high-school auditorium, houses a superb **interpretive center** (⏱760-878-2194; www.nps.gov/manz; ⏲9am-4:30pm Nov-Mar, to 5:30pm Apr-Oct; ▣) **FREE**. A visit here is one of the historical highlights of the state and should not be missed.

Watch the 20-minute documentary, then explore the thought-provoking exhibits chronicling the stories of the families that languished here but were still able to build a vibrant community. Afterwards, take a self-guided 3.2-mile driving tour around the grounds, which includes a re-created mess hall and barracks, vestiges of buildings and gardens, as well as the haunting camp cemetery.

Lone Pine

A tiny town, Lone Pine is the gateway to big things, most notably Mt Whitney, the loftiest peak in the contiguous USA, and Hollywood. In the 1920s cinematographers discovered that nearby Alabama Hills were a picture-perfect movie set for Westerns, and in the decades that followed stars from Gary Cooper to Gregory Peck could often be spotted swaggering about town.

⊙ Sights

★**Alabama Hills**　　　　NATURAL FEATURE
The warm colors and rounded contours of the Alabama Hills, located on Whitney Portal Rd, stand in contrast to the jagged snowy Sierras just behind. The setting for countless ride-'em-out movies, the popular *Lone Ranger* TV series, and more recently, parts of Quentin Tarantino's *Django Unchained*, the stunning orange rock formations are a beautiful place to experience sunrise or sunset.

You can drive, walk or mountain-bike along dirt roads rambling through the boulders, and along Tuttle and Lone Pine creeks. A number of graceful rock arches are within easy hiking distance of the roads. Head west on Whitney Portal Rd and either turn left at Tuttle Creek Rd, after a half-mile, or north on Movie Rd, after about 3 miles. The websites of the Lone Pine Chamber of Commerce (p157) and the Museum of Western Film History (p156) have excellent movie location maps.

Museum of Western Film History　　MUSEUM
(📞760-876-9909;　www.museumofwesternfilm-history.org; 701 S Main St; adult/child $5/free; ⊙10am-5pm Mon-Sat, to 4pm Sun, longer summer hrs) Hundreds of movies have been shot in the area, and this museum contains exhibits of paraphernalia from locally set films. It hosts screenings in its theater twice a month.

🛏 Sleeping

Tuttle Creek　　　　　CAMPGROUND $
(www.blm.gov/ca/st/en/fo/bishop/camping/tuttle.html; Horseshoe Meadows Rd; tent & RV sites $5; 🐾) Off Whitney Portal Rd, this first-come, first-served USFS campground has 83 primitive

sites with panoramic 'pinch-me!' views of the Sierras, White Mountains and the rosy Alabama Hills. There's not much shade, though.

Lone Pine Campground　　CAMPGROUND $
(📞877-444-6777;　www.recreation.gov;　Whitney Portal Rd; tent & RV sites $19; ⊙mid-Apr–Oct; 🐾) About midway between Lone Pine and Whitney Portal, this popular creekside USFS campground (elevation 6000ft) offers vault toilets and potable water.

**Whitney Portal Hostel
& Hotel**　　　　　HOSTEL, MOTEL $
(📞760-876-0030; www.whitneyportalstore.com; 238 S Main St; dm/d $25/85; 🌐🛜🐾) A popular launching pad for Whitney trips and for post-hike wash-ups (public showers available), its hostel rooms are the cheapest beds in town – reserve them months ahead for July and August. There's no common space, just carpeted single-sex bunk-bed rooms, though amenities include towels, TVs, in-room kitchenettes and stocked coffeemakers.

The majority of the establishment consists of plush and modern motel rooms, and many look out towards Whitney and its neighbors.

Dow Hotel & Dow Villa Motel　　HOTEL, MOTEL $$
(📞760-876-5521,　800-824-9317;　www.dowvilla-motel.com; 310 S Main St; hotel r with/without bath $87/69, motel r $115-173; 🌐@🛜🐾🐾) John Wayne and Errol Flynn are among the stars who have stayed at this venerable hotel. Built in 1922, the place has been restored but retains much of its rustic charm. The rooms in the newer motel section have air-con and are more comfortable and bright, but also more generic.

🍴 Eating

Alabama Hills Cafe　　　　DINER $
(111 W Post St; mains $8-14; ⊙7am-2pm; 🍴) Everyone's favorite breakfast joint, the portions here are big, the bread fresh-baked, and the hearty soups and fruit pies make lunch an attractive option too.

Seasons　　　　　NEW AMERICAN $$
(📞760-876-8927; 206 N Main St; mains $17-30; ⊙5-9pm daily Apr-Oct, Tue-Sun Nov-Mar) Seasons has everything you fantasized about the last time you choked down freeze-dried rations. Sautéed trout, roasted duck, filet mignon and plates of carb-replenishing pasta will revitalize your appetite, and nice and naughty desserts will leave you purring. Reservations recommended.

🛍 Shopping

Elevation   OUTDOOR EQUIPMENT
(📋 760-876-4560; www.sierraelevation.com; 150 S Main St, cnr Whitney Portal Rd; ⊙ call for hrs) Rents bear canisters and crampons, and sells hiking, backpacking and climbing gear.

ℹ Information

There's free municipal wi-fi along Main St.

Eastern Sierra Interagency Visitor Center (📋 760-876-6222; www.fs.fed.us/r5/inyo; cnr Hwys 395 & 136; ⊙ 8am-5pm) USFS information central for the Sierra, Death Valley and Mt Whitney; about 1.5 miles south of town.

Inyo County Library (www.inyocounty.us/ library; cnr Bush & Washington Sts; ⊙ 12:30-7pm Wed, 10am-noon & 1-5pm Tue & Thu-Sat; 📶) Free public internet access.

Lone Pine Chamber of Commerce (📋 760-876-4444; www.lonepinechamber.org; 120 S Main St; ⊙ 8:30am-4:30pm Mon-Fri)

Mt Whitney

The mystique of Mt Whitney (14,505ft) captures the imagination, and conquering its hulking bulk becomes a sort of obsession for many. The main **Mt Whitney Trail** (the easiest and busiest one) leaves from Whitney Portal, about 13 miles west of Lone Pine via the Whitney Portal Rd (closed in winter), and climbs about 6000ft over 11 miles. It's a super-strenuous, really, *really* long walk that'll wear out even experienced mountaineers, but doesn't require technical skills if attempted in summer or early fall. Earlier or later in the season, you'll likely need an ice axe and crampons, and overnight.

Many people in good physical condition make it to the top, although only superbly conditioned, previously acclimatized hikers should attempt this as a day hike. Breathing becomes difficult at these elevations and altitude sickness is a common problem. Rangers recommend spending a night camping at the trailhead and another at one of the two camps along the route: **Outpost Camp** at 3.5 miles or **Trail Camp** at 6 miles up the trail.

When you pick up your permit and packout kits (hikers must pack out their poop) at the Eastern Sierra Interagency Visitor Center (p157) in Lone Pine, get the latest info on weather and trail conditions. Near the trailhead, the Whitney Portal Store sells groceries and snacks. It also has public showers ($5) and a cafe with enormous burgers and

Mt Whitney at sunrise

pancakes. The online forums at the website of the Whitney Portal Store (www.whitneyportalstore.com) and Whitney Zone (www.whitneyzone.com) are good resources for up-to-date info and tips for first-timers.

The biggest obstacle in getting to the peak may be to obtain a **wilderness permit**, which is required for all overnight trips and for day hikes past Lone Pine Lake (about 2.8 miles from the trailhead). A quota system limits daily access to 60 overnight and 100 day hikers from May through October. Because of the huge demand, permits are distributed via the online **Mt Whitney lottery** (www.fs.usda.gov/inyo; per group $6, plus per person $15), with applications accepted from February through mid-March.

Want to avoid the hassle of getting a permit for the main Mt Whitney Trail? Consider ascending this popular pinnacle from the west, using the backdoor route from Sequoia and Kings Canyon National Parks. It takes about six days from Crescent Meadow via the High Sierra Trail to the John Muir Trail – with no Whitney Zone permit required – and wilderness permits are much easier to secure.

ED FREEMAN / GETTY IMAGES ©

AROUND YOSEMITE NATIONAL PARK MT WHITNEY

Sequoia & Kings Canyon National Parks

Best Hikes

➡ General Sherman Tree to Moro Rock (p164)

➡ Tokopah Falls (p164)

➡ Lakes Trail (p172)

➡ Zumwalt Meadow Loop (p167)

➡ Mist Falls (p168)

➡ Rae Lakes Loop (p169)

Best Places to Sleep

➡ Lodgepole Campground (p185)

➡ Sheep Creek Campground (p190)

➡ Hume Lake Campground (p189)

➡ John Muir Lodge (p190)

Why Go?

Claiming a cleft deeper than the Grand Canyon and forests harboring the world's largest trees, Sequoia and Kings Canyon National Parks dazzle visitors with superlatives. Throw in opportunities for spelunking, splashing in swimming holes, horseback riding and backcountry hiking through granite-carved Sierra Nevada landscapes, and you have all the ingredients for a peak national-park experience.

Although larger than Yosemite, Sequoia and Kings Canyon National Parks receive less than half as many annual visitors as their more iconic neighbor to the north. Luckily, that makes solitude easy to find in these southern Sierra Nevada parks, even with five-star geological highlights, towering giant sequoias and Technicolor wildflower meadows all within reach. The two parks are administered together as one unit, with a section of the Giant Sequoia National Monument in the Sequoia National Forest looking like a bite out of a cookie.

Road Distances (miles)

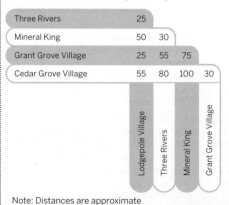

	Lodgepole Village	Three Rivers	Mineral King	Grant Grove Village
Three Rivers	25			
Mineral King	50	30		
Grant Grove Village	25	55	75	
Cedar Grove Village	55	80	100	30

Note: Distances are approximate

Entrances

Both national parks are only accessible by car from the west, and no roads cross the Sierra Nevada mountain range, only trails. Furthest south, Sequoia National Park's main entrance is at Ash Mountain in the foothills. Furthest north, Big Stump is Kings Canyon National Park's only entrance.

All park entrances are open 24 hours a day year-round. Some roads – including Mineral King Rd beyond Three Rivers in Sequoia National Park, Hwy 180 past the Hume Lake turn-off in Kings Canyon National Park, and Big Meadows Rd in the Sequoia National Forest off the Generals Hwy – are closed during winter. Exact opening and closing dates vary by area of the park and depend on the weather from year to year. The most remote and hazardous roads may be inaccessible from autumn's first snowfall until the snow melts in late spring or early summer.

DON'T MISS

Although there's a lot to see just inside both national parks, the neighboring Sequoia National Forest also has amazingly scenic spots, from ancient sequoia groves to alpine lakes. In fact, to drive between the national parks on the Generals Hwy, or from Grant Grove to Cedar Grove via the Kings Canyon Scenic Byway, you'll pass right through the Sequoia National Forest and its Giant Sequoia National Monument, making it easy to stop off and see the sights, score a campsite or hike less-trammeled trails into the wilderness.

When You Arrive

➡ Although administered as a single unit by the National Park Service (NPS), Sequoia and Kings Canyon National Parks are actually two national parks.

➡ The two parks together are commonly referred to as 'SEKI.' The phrase 'Kings Canyon' may refer to the national park or may just mean the canyon itself.

➡ The 7-day entrance fee (per vehicle $20) covers both national parks and the nearby Hume Lake District of the Sequoia National Forest.

➡ If you arrive at night when park entrance stations are unstaffed, pay the entrance fee the next morning at the closest entrance station or upon exiting the park.

➡ The national parks' free seasonal newspaper, *The Visitor Guide*, is loaded with information on activities, campgrounds, lodging, shuttles, visitor services, safety tips and more.

PLANNING TIPS

For 24-hour recorded info, including road conditions and construction updates, call ☏ 559-565-3341. The park website (www.nps.gov/seki) offers free downloads of the seasonal newspaper and trip-planning tips.

Fast Facts

➡ Total area: 1353 sq miles (865,964 acres)

➡ Foothills (Sequoia) elevation: 1720ft

➡ Grant Grove (Kings Canyon) elevation: 6589ft

Reservations

➡ **DNC Parks & Resorts** (☏ 801-559-4930, 866-807-3598; www.visitsequoia.com) Lodging in Sequoia and Kings Canyon National Parks.

➡ **NPS & USFS Campgrounds** (☏ 877-444-6777, 518-885-3639; www.recreation.gov)

➡ **Sequoia-Kings Canyon Park Services Company** (☏ 877-828-1440, 559-565-3388; www.sequoia-kingscanyon.com) Some Sequoia National Forest lodgings.

Resources

➡ **NPS** (www.nps.gov/seki/planyourvisit/lodgingoutsideparks.htm) More area accommodations.

➡ **Sequoia National Forest** (www.fs.usda.gov/sequoia) All about the Giant Sequoia National Monument.

Sequoia & Kings Canyon National Parks

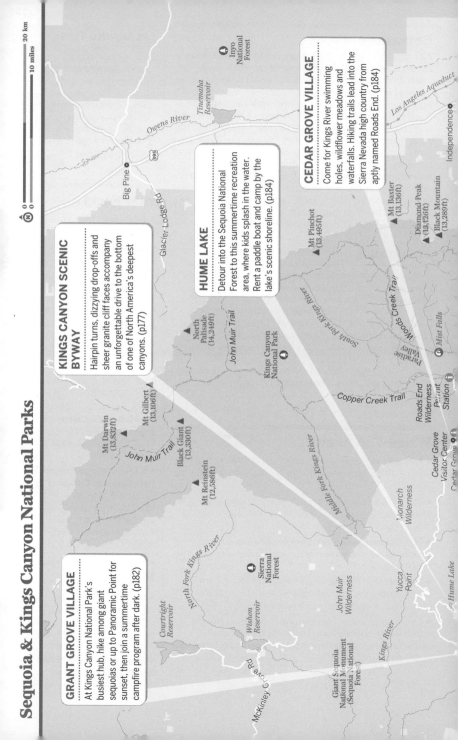

GRANT GROVE VILLAGE

At Kings Canyon National Park's busiest hub, hike among giant sequoias or up to Panoramic Point for sunset, then join a summertime campfire program after dark. (p182)

KINGS CANYON SCENIC BYWAY

Hairpin turns, dizzying drop-offs and sheer granite cliff faces accompany an unforgettable drive to the bottom of one of North America's deepest canyons. (p177)

HUME LAKE

Detour into the Sequoia National Forest to this summertime recreation area, where kids splash in the water. Rent a paddle boat and camp by the lake's scenic shoreline. (p184)

CEDAR GROVE VILLAGE

Come for Kings River swimming holes, wildflower meadows and waterfalls. Hiking trails lead into the Sierra Nevada high country from aptly named Roads End. (p184)

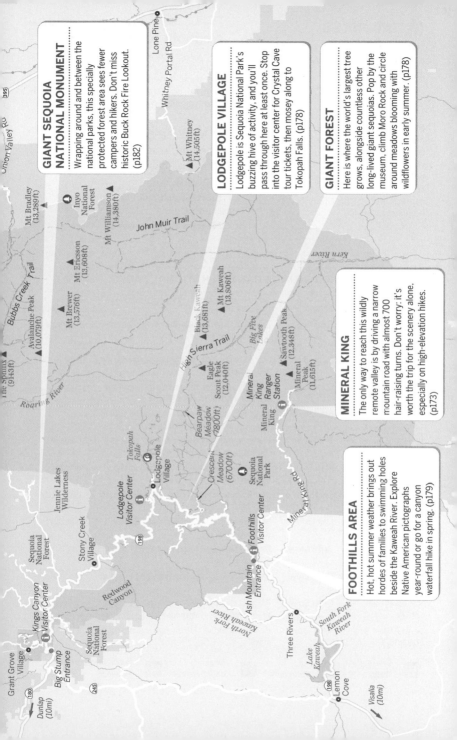

GIANT SEQUOIA NATIONAL MONUMENT

Wrapping around and between the national parks, this specially protected forest area sees fewer campers and hikers. Don't miss historic Buck Rock Fire Lookout. (p182)

LODGEPOLE VILLAGE

Lodgepole is Sequoia National Park's buzzing hive of activity, and you'll pass through here at least once. Stop into the visitor center for Crystal Cave tour tickets, then mosey along to Tokopah Falls. (p178)

GIANT FOREST

Here is where the world's largest tree grows, alongside countless other long-lived giant sequoias. Pop by the museum, climb Moro Rock and circle around meadows blooming with wildflowers in early summer. (p178)

MINERAL KING

The only way to reach this wildly remote valley is by driving a narrow mountain road with almost 700 hair-raising turns. Don't worry: it's worth the trip for the scenery alone, especially on high-elevation hikes. (p173)

FOOTHILLS AREA

Hot, hot summer weather brings out hordes of families to swimming holes beside the Kaweah River. Explore Native American pictographs year-round or go for a canyon waterfall hike in spring. (p179)

🏃 DAY HIKES

Leave your car behind to ramble around wildflower meadows and serene groves of giant sequoias, or hoof it to rushing waterfalls and up polished granite domes for epic views of Sierra Nevada peaks.

The nonprofit **Sequoia Natural History Association** (www.sequoiahistory.org) publishes an excellent series of fold-out trail map brochures covering the Cedar Grove, Grant Grove, Giant Forest, Lodgepole and Mineral King areas (each $3.50). Hiking maps and books are sold at visitor centers and at the Giant Forest Museum bookstore.

Sequoia National Park

The Giant Forest area has the biggest network of hiking routes, with a few wheelchair-accessible paved trails. The high-elevation Mineral King Valley steps you immediately into the Sierra Nevada backcountry.

🏃 Moro Rock

Duration 40 minutes

Distance 0.5 miles

Difficulty Easy

Start/Finish Moro Rock parking lot/shuttle stop

Nearest Town Lodgepole Village

HIKING IN SEQUIOA & KINGS CANYON NATIONAL PARKS

NAME	REGION	DESCRIPTION	DIFFICULTY
Marble Falls (p166)	Foothills	Lower-elevation hike parallels a river canyon to a tumbling cascade	moderate
Moro Rock (p162)	Giant Forest	Steep granite dome stairway to panoramic peak and canyon views	easy
Big Trees Trail (p163)	Giant Forest	Paved, kid-friendly interpretive trail circling a sequoia-bordered forest meadow	easy
Crescent Meadow Loop (p164)	Giant Forest	Beautiful subalpine meadow ringed by giant sequoias and summer wildflowers	easy
General Sherman Tree to Moro Rock (p164)	Giant Forest	Huge sequoias, peaceful meadows, great rock climbing and the top of Moro Rock	moderate
Lakes Trail (p172)	Giant Forest	Epic day hike or overnight backpack to high-elevation lakes	difficult
Tokopah Falls (p164)	Lodgepole	One of Sequoia's most easily accessed scenic waterfalls	easy
Monarch Lakes (p166)	Mineral King	High-country hike to an alpine lake beneath Sawtooth Peak	difficult
Zumwalt Meadow Loop (p167)	Cedar Grove	Meadow boardwalk loop by the Kings River and high canyon walls	easy
Mist Falls (p168)	Cedar Grove	Partly shaded forest and granite hike to a gushing waterfall	moderate
Rae Lakes Loop (p169)	Cedar Grove	Passes a chain of jewel-like lakes and peaks in the Sierra Nevada high country	difficult
General Grant Tree Trail (p167)	Grant Grove	Paved interpretive loop through a giant sequoia grove	easy

 Drinking Water

 Restrooms

 Ranger Station Nearby

 Public Transportation to Trailhead

Transportation Shuttle, car

Summary After a quick ascent to the tippy-top of this granite dome, panoramic views are worth every ounce of effort. On clear days, open your eyes wide for skyscraping peaks and the foothills ever-so-far below.

Built by the Civilian Conservation Corps (CCC) in the 1930s, this trail features almost 400 steps, which shoot up over a quarter-mile to a railed-in viewpoint corridor atop Sequoia's iconic granite dome. Warning – you do *not* want to be anywhere on this trail during a lightning storm. From the summit, you can stare down at the Kaweah River's Middle Fork, across to Sawtooth Peak south in the Mineral King region, and toward the peaks of the Great Western Divide to the east, including the spike of Black Kaweah. Near dusk, the monolith-like crags of Castle Rocks cast dramatic shadows over the dizzyingly deep river canyon.

Beware that on hazy days (most common in summer), air pollution obscures the views.

🚶 Big Trees Trail

Duration 45 minutes
Distance 1.2 miles
Difficulty Easy
Start/Finish Giant Forest Museum
Nearest Town Lodgepole Village
Transportation Shuttle, car

SEQUOIA & KINGS CANYON NATIONAL PARKS SEQUOIA NATIONAL PARK

DURATION	ROUND-TRIP DISTANCE	ELEVATION CHANGE	FEATURES	FACILITIES
3–4hr	7.8 miles	+1600ft	View, Families, Waterfalls	Trash, Shuttle
40min	0.5 miles	+300ft	View, Families	Restroom, Shuttle
45min	1.2 miles	+100ft	Wildlife Watching, Families	Trash, Restroom, Drinking Water, Shuttle
1hr	1.6 miles	+150ft	Wildlife Watching, Families	Trash, Restroom, Drinking Water, Shuttle
3–4hr	6 miles (one way)	+1600ft	View, Wildlife Watching	Trash, Restroom, Drinking Water, Shuttle
2 days	12.5 miles	+2300ft	View, Wildlife Watching	Restroom, Families, Shuttle, Backcountry Campsite
2hr	3.6 miles	+600ft	View, Wildlife Watching, Families, Waterfalls	Trash, Restroom, Drinking Water, Shuttle
4–6hr	8.4 miles	+2600ft	View, Wildlife Watching	Trash, Restroom, Backcountry Campsite
1hr	1.5 miles	+100ft	View, Wildlife Watching, Families	Restroom
3–5hr	9.2 miles	+800ft	View, Waterfalls	Trash, Restroom, Drinking Water, Ranger Station
5 days	40 miles	+7000ft	View, Wildlife Watching, Waterfalls	Trash, Restroom, Drinking Water, Ranger Station, Backcountry Campsite
30min	0.5 miles	+100ft	View, Families	Trash, Restroom, Shuttle

🔭 View   🦌 Wildlife Watching   ▲ Backcountry Campsite   👪 Great for Families   〰 Waterfalls

Summary On a paved trail circling a petite meadow embraced by giant sequoias, this family-friendly nature walk shows off some of the park's signature flora, all growing within one small area.

Starting from the 'Trail Center' outside the Giant Forest Museum, follow a well-marked path beside the Generals Hwy to join with a paved and wooden-boardwalk loop around pretty Round Meadow. Giant sequoias edge the lush meadow, while interpretive panels give the lowdown on sequoia ecology, explaining how the western Sierra Nevada ecosystem supports these ginormous trees' growth. Wildflowers peak in early summer for kaleidoscopic bursts of color.

A wheelchair-accessible route starts from a specially designated parking lot (disabled-parking placard required) off the Generals Hwy, which shortens the total distance to 0.7 miles. The initial section is packed dirt and has a slight incline.

🥾 Crescent Meadow Loop

Duration 1 hour

Distance 1.6 miles

Difficulty Easy

Start/Finish Crescent Meadow parking lot/shuttle stop

Nearest Town Lodgepole Village

Transportation Shuttle, car

Summary At this beautiful and easily reached subalpine meadow, ringed by a canopy of firs and sequoias, early summer wildflowers turn up the color, and black bears often forage nearby.

From the trailhead, stroll either clockwise or counter-clockwise around the peaceful, shady meadow loop. Downed logs make handy steps for peering over the high grass, but don't let your footfalls crunch and compact the fragile meadow itself. If you're quiet and stealthy, you may spy black bears ripping apart logs as they look for tasty insects crawling around underneath the bark. Around the meadow's northeast corner, poke your head inside and look up the hollow fire-scarred Chimney Tree. It's a 0.3-mile detour east toward Log Meadow to inspect Tharp's Log, a fallen giant sequoia that a 19th-century settler converted into a rustic cabin.

🥾 Tokopah Falls

Duration 2 hours

Distance 3.6 miles

Difficulty Easy

Start/Finish Lodgepole Campground

Nearest Town Lodgepole Village

Transportation Shuttle, car

Summary Gradually rising over 500ft in elevation, this riverside stroll reaches one of the parks' most scenic waterfalls, tumbling down a boulder-lined canyon. Starting from the campground, it's a popular hike for families with children.

From the trailhead parking area next to the shuttle-bus stop inside Lodgepole Campground, walk east along the access road. Cross the bridge to the north side of the Kaweah River's Marble Fork, where you'll spot a trailhead sign. The entire hike runs through a sun-dappled forest alongside the river, with exceptional views of the glacier-carved canyon and opportunities to watch mule deer, black bears and tiny pika.

As you near the falls, the severe 1800ft granite face of the Watchtower looms to the south. Now fully exposed to the sun, the rocky trail ascends through granite boulders and slabs before arriving at a viewing area. At 1200ft high, Tokopah Falls doesn't free fall but rather bounces off the granite canyon cliffs with all the noise it can muster, especially when snowmelt gushes in late spring and possibly early summer. When you're ready, return along the same route.

🥾 General Sherman Tree to Moro Rock

Duration 3–4 hours

Distance 6 miles one way

Difficulty Moderate

Start Wolverton Rd parking lot/shuttle stop

Finish Moro Rock parking lot/shuttle stop

Nearest Town Lodgepole Village

Transportation Shuttle, car

Summary A deviation from the popular Congress Trail loop, this rolling one-way hike takes in huge sequoias, green meadows and the pinnacle of Moro Rock.

Sequoia National Park Day Hikes

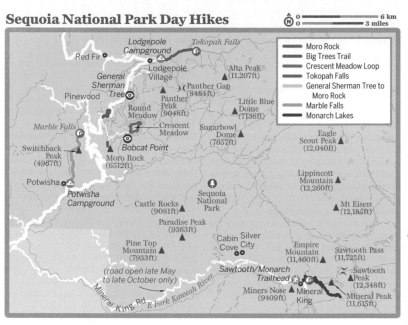

Expect stretches of blissful solitude and potential black bear sightings.

Keep in mind that hiking this route in one direction is possible only when the free seasonal park shuttle buses are running, usually from late May until late September.

From the General Sherman parking lot and shuttle stop off Wolverton Rd, just east of the Generals Hwy, a paved trail quickly descends through towering sequoias. At an overlook on the way down, you'll get the best view of the **General Sherman Tree**. After walking up to the giant's trunk, turn around and walk downhill on the western branch of the Congress Trail loop. (If you end up on the eastern branch by mistake, jog right then left at two minor trail junctions that appear about 0.5 miles south of the General Sherman Tree.)

At a five-way junction by the **McKinley Tree**, continue straight ahead south on the dirt trail towards **Cattle Cabin**. Pass the hollow-bottom **Room Tree** and the pretty cluster of the **Founders Group** as you walk through tufts of ferns and corn lilies. Approaching the bright green strip of 'C'-shaped **Circle Meadow**, there are no more crowds, and all you can hear is the breeze and birdsong. Trace the eastern edge of the

meadow toward another well-named tree group, the **Pillars of Hercules**. Stand between them and look up for a heroic view.

The trail then passes the huge charred maw of the **Black Arch** tree. Continue south, veering slightly right and then left at the next two trail junctions. At a three-way intersection, lush Crescent Meadow finally comes into view. Go straight at this junction and the next one to continue, or make a 0.6-mile round-trip detour to the **Squatters Cabin** by going right on the trail marked 'Huckleberry Meadow.' On the north side of Crescent Meadow stands the hollow-bodied **Chimney Tree**. Continue east past **Tharp's Log**, which once was a pioneer cabin, then turn right (south) on a paved trail along the east side of **Log Meadow**.

Before reaching the Crescent Meadow parking lot, head left then right onto the signed High Sierra Trail, heading west for more marvelous ridge views. Stop at **Bobcat Point** overlook to take in the Great Western Divide and Kaweah Canyon. In 0.2 miles, cross Crescent Creek on a log to join the Sugar Pine Trail. Go left (west) and follow it for 0.9 miles to **Moro Rock**. Climb the granite dome for some of the park's best views, then return to your starting point via shuttle buses.

🕺 Marble Falls

Duration 3–4 hours

Distance 7.8 miles

Difficulty Moderate

Start/Finish Potwisha Campground

Nearest Town Three Rivers

Transportation Shuttle, car

Summary Climb over 1500ft as you follow the curves of chaparral-blanketed hills and parallel a river canyon to reach a tumbling cascade. Prime time is spring, when wildflowers bloom and it's not too hot.

Because of the extreme heat in the low-elevation Foothills, get an early morning start. Turn right near campsite number 14 and follow the dirt road uphill, parking off to the side of the metal-chain gate. Start walking on the dirt road, heading uphill and across a concrete ditch. Look for a sign for the trail, which starts steeply to the right.

Make a quick, yet challenging ascent via steep switchbacks. Watch out for rattlesnakes, ticks and poison oak. Past the switchbacks, shady tree cover gives way to scrubby chaparral. The trail continues north alongside a deep canyon, with views of the Kaweah River's Marble Fork. It crosses several streams and ducks into the woods, then veers towards the river and the booming falls, dead-ending in a heap of granite boulders.

Retrace your steps to return.

🕺 Monarch Lakes

Duration 4–6 hours

Distance 8.4 miles

Difficulty Difficult

Start/Finish Sawtooth/Monarch trailhead parking area

Nearest Town Silver City

Transportation Car

Summary A marmot-lover's paradise! This exceptionally scenic out-and-back high-country route reaches two alpine lakes below jagged Sawtooth Peak. Although it's not very long, the trail can be breathtakingly steep.

A steep climb kicks off this higher-altitude trek. At the Timber Gap Trail junction just over 0.5 miles in, you can see Mineral King Rd back below and snow-brushed peaks looking south. Turn right, following the signs for Sawtooth Pass. Corn lilies and paintbrush speckle **Groundhog Meadow**, named for the whistling marmots that scramble around the granite rocks seemingly everywhere you look during this hike.

Leaving the meadow, rock-hop across burbling Monarch Creek. On its far bank, a shady wooded spot is the perfect place for a picnic lunch. From there, begin ascending a stretch of loose and lazy switchbacks with goose-bump views. It's a slow, steady climb through red fir and pine forest that won't leave you too winded, though you'll feel the altitude the higher you climb. Blue grouse may be spotted on the hillsides.

At about 2.5 miles there's a signed junction for the Crystal Lake Trail, which takes a hard and steep right. Bear left and continue straight up toward Sawtooth Pass instead. After flipping to the opposite side of the ridgeline, the trail rounds **Chihuahua Bowl**, an avalanche-prone granite basin named after a Mexican mining region. The tree line wavers and fades away, opening up gorgeous views of Monarch Creek canyon, Timber Gap and the peaks of the Great Western Divide.

The distinctive pitch of Sawtooth Peak (12,348ft) is visible ahead. A walk through a large talus field and some stream crossings bring you to **Lower Monarch Lake** (10,400ft), where round-topped Mineral Peak (11,615ft) points up directly south. The maintained trail stops here, but **Upper Monarch Lake** (10,640ft) can be reached by a steep use trail heading up the hillside. Established backpacker campsites are by the lower lake; for overnight camping, a wilderness permit is required.

When you're ready, retrace your steps to return. If you're looking for extremely challenging cross-country treks with some steep drop-offs and rock scrambling required, detour up scree-covered **Sawtooth Pass** (11,725ft) or make an alternate return route via **Crystal Lake** (10,900ft). But ask for route advice and safety tips at the Mineral King ranger station first.

Kings Canyon National Park

Towering stands of giant sequoias await in Grant Grove. Deep inside Kings Canyon, a meditative meadow walk and a day hike to a waterfall start near Roads End.

Kings Canyon National Park Day Hikes

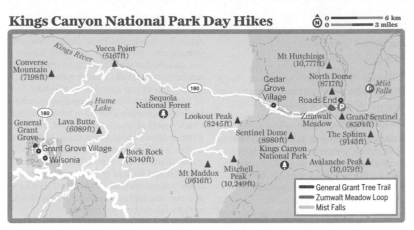

🚶General Grant Tree Trail

Duration 30 minutes

Distance 0.5 miles

Difficulty Easy

Start/Finish General Grant Grove parking lot

Nearest Town Grant Grove Village

Transportation Shuttle, car

Summary On a short, paved, self-guided interpretive loop through one of the parks' most extraordinary giant sequoia groves, meet the General Grant Tree, the second-largest living tree in the world. The trail is wheelchair-accessible.

At the east end of the parking lot, you can see the cheerfully named tree cluster **The Happy Family**. Starting from the fenced main trailhead just west, bear right and begin a counter-clockwise loop. Most of the monster sequoias in **General Grant Grove** are named for US states, and the first you come across is the **Pennsylvania Tree**. Beyond stands the **Robert E Lee Tree**, which, like the grove itself, is another Civil War namesake. What looks like submerged logs in front are actually its exposed roots – the accumulated damage from more than a century of visitors' footsteps. Though it may be tempting not to, always stick to the trail (and make sure kids do, too).

Further along is the **Fallen Monarch**, a toppled log so big that its hollow core has been used as a cabin, a hotel and saloon, and then as horse stables by the US Cavalry. Walk

through a mix of young sequoias and other conifers, including sugar pine and white fir, until you reach the impressive **General Grant Tree**, measuring over 268ft high and more than 100ft around at its sturdy base.

Next is the one-room **Gamlin Cabin**, built from sugar pine in 1872 by the first European settlers in the Grant Grove area; it later served as the park's first ranger station. For another good view of the General Grant Tree, detour right here from the main loop and bear up and around to the left. The path leads to a peaceful overlook called **North Grant View** and, unlike the rest of the trail, there's rarely anyone here to share the scenery.

Continuing along the main trail you'll see the **California Tree**, struck by lightning in 1967. The tree's top was incinerated and fire burned inside until rangers grew concerned that burning branches would hurt visitors. A nimble park employee strung a rope between two adjacent trees and extinguished the blaze with a hose.

Amble onward back to the parking lot.

🚶Zumwalt Meadow Loop

Duration 1 hour

Distance 1.5 miles

Difficulty Easy

Start/Finish Zumwalt Meadow parking lot

Nearest Town Cedar Grove Village

Transportation Car

Summary Beside the Kings River, this extremely scenic, mostly flat loop around a gorgeous meadow is a fun nature walk with kids. The trail flaunts knockout canyon views and excellent chances to spot wildlife.

A mile west of Roads End is **Zumwalt Meadow**, best in the early morning, when mist floats above the meadow and birdsong echoes off the canyon's soaring granite walls. Buy the self-guided nature trail brochure ($1.50) at the visitor center in Cedar Grove Village before driving out to the trailhead, where the honor-system brochure box is often empty.

From the parking lot, walk parallel to the river then across a suspension footbridge spanning the Kings River's South Fork. Behind you to the north is a view of **North Dome**, with a sheer cliff drop of over 3600ft, higher than Yosemite's El Capitan. At the next junction, go left along the River Trail, then keep straight ahead to begin a counter-clockwise loop through a forest of cottonwood, willow, black oak, white fir and ponderosa pine trees. Early mornings hikers will be serenaded by birdsong.

Looking ahead, the granite cliffs of the **Grand Sentinel** cast shadows from more than a half mile above the canyon floor. The trail ascends and continues over a talus slope with great views of canyon cliffs and the lush meadow. At the next signed junction, turn left and follow the Kings River bank through ferns and a carpet of soft pine needles, then traipse across boardwalks that afford panoramic meadow views (do you spy any black bears?) to close the loop. Turn right and retrace your steps across the footbridge to the parking lot.

🏃 Mist Falls

Duration 3–5 hours

Distance 9.2 miles

Difficulty Moderate

Start/Finish Roads End

Nearest Town Cedar Grove Village

Transportation Car

Summary A satisfying long walk along the riverside and up a natural granite staircase highlights the beauty of Kings Canyon. The waterfall is thunderous in late spring and possibly into early summer, depending on the previous winter's snowpack.

Bring plenty of water and sunscreen on this hike, which gains 600ft in elevation before reaching the falls. Get an early morning start, because the return trip can be brutally hot on summer afternoons, and also so you can beat the crowds of big families.

The trail begins just past the **Roads End** wilderness permit station, crossing a small footbridge over **Copper Creek**. Walk along a sandy trail through sparse cedar and pine forest, where boulders rolled by avalanches are scattered on the canyon floor. Keep an eye out for black bears. Eventually the trail enters cooler, shady and low-lying areas of ferns and reeds before reaching a well-marked three-way junction with the Woods Creek Trail, just shy of 2 miles from Roads End.

Turn left (north) toward Paradise Valley and begin a gradual climb that runs parallel to powerful cataracts in the boulder-saturated Kings River. Stone-framed stairs lead to a granite knob overlook, with wide southern views of **Avalanche Peak** and the oddly pointed **Sphinx**, another mountain peak, behind you. Follow cairns up the rock face and continue briefly through shady forest to reach **Mist Falls**, one of the parks' largest waterfalls. Warning: don't wade above the waterfall or swim below it, due to the danger of rockfall and swiftwater currents, especially during snowmelt runoff. In late summer, the river downstream from the falls may be tame enough for a dip – use your own best judgment, however.

Retrace your steps just over 2.5 miles downhill to the three-way trail junction. Instead of returning directly to Roads End, bear left and cross the bridge over the Kings River, briefly joining the Bubbs Creek Trail. After less than a quarter-mile, turn right onto the untrammeled Kanawyer Loop Trail, which is mostly flat. After crossing Avalanche Creek on a makeshift log bridge, the tree canopy opens up to show off sprawling talus slopes along the Kings Canyon's southern walls.

Muir Rock (Map p180) and its late-summer swimming hole come into view across the river before you make a short climb to the River Trail junction. Turn right and walk across the red footbridge, below which is another favorite late-summer swimming hole. Follow the path back to the paved highway, turning right to walk back to the Roads End parking lot.

🏃 OVERNIGHT HIKES

Over 850 miles of maintained trails await your footsteps in both national parks. From sun-bleached granite peaks soaring above alpine lakes, to wildflower-strewn meadows and gushing waterfalls, it's backpacking heaven. Mineral King, Lodgepole and Cedar Grove offer the best backcountry trail access, while the Jennie Lakes Wilderness in the Sequoia National Forest boasts pristine meadows and lakes at lower elevations.

Park-approved bear-proof food canisters, which are always recommended, are mandatory in some places (eg Rae Lakes Loop). Rent bear canisters at park visitor centers and trailhead ranger stations (from $5 per trip) or at the Lodgepole, Grant Grove and Cedar Grove Village markets (price varies, but they typically cost more here). To prevent wildfires, campfires are only allowed in existing campfire rings in some backcountry areas.

Sequoia Natural History Association (SNHA; www.sequoiahistory.org) sells topographic maps at park visitor centers and wilderness permit-issuing stations. Highly recommended are SNHA's *Rae Lakes Loop Trail Map* ($8.95) and the Tom Harrison Maps series, all printed on waterproof, tear-resistant paper.

Permits & Fees

Wilderness permits, which are required for all overnight trips in the national parks, are issued at trailhead ranger stations or the nearest visitor center. Overnight trips in the national forest require only campfire permits (free), available at the Kings Canyon Visitor Center (p194) in Grant Grove Village and the USFS Hume Lake District Office (p194) outside the parks.

For national park trips, there's a $15 permit fee during the quota season (late May through late September). About 25% of all available permits are first-come, first-served, made available to walk-up visitors starting at 1pm *the day before* your trip. Permit reservations are held until 9am on the day of your trip, after which no-show vacancies can be claimed by walk-up visitors. Outside the quota period, self-issuing permits are free.

To reserve your wilderness permit ahead of time (essential for popular trails during the quota season), requests must be received two weeks in advance of your trip date, beginning on March 1 of that year. It's not unusual for permits for popular trails to sell out immediately for all summer weekend departures. Permit applications can be downloaded from the parks' website (www.nps.gov/seki), which also offers a comprehensive wilderness trip planner.

Sequoia National Park

Shoulder your backpack and head for alpine lakes and meadows. The park's busiest trailheads are around Lodgepole and the Giant Forest. Protect your vehicle from hungry marmots if you're starting from the remote Mineral King Valley (see the boxed text, p182), where sculpted granite peaks and glacial cirques await.

Kings Canyon National Park

Myriad backcountry routes to granite peaks, alpine lakes and high-country meadows depart from Roads End, deep inside Kings Canyon, east of Cedar Grove Village.

🏃 Rae Lakes Loop

Duration 5 days

Distance 40 miles

Difficulty Difficult

Start/Finish Roads End

Nearest Town Cedar Grove Village

Transportation Car

Summary The best backpacking loop in Kings Canyon tours sun-blessed forests and meadows, crosses one mind-bending pass and skirts a chain of jewel-like lakes beneath the Sierra crest, joining the famous John Muir Trail partway along.

DAY 1: ROADS END TO MIDDLE PARADISE VALLEY
4–6 HOURS / 7 MILES

The Rae Lakes Loop kicks off with a 4.5-mile hike along the Woods Creek Trail from **Roads End** (5045ft) to **Mist Falls**. Beyond the waterfall, a set of rocky switchbacks leads you up into the shadier forest above the river. The trail levels out as it enters **Paradise Valley**, less than 2 miles north of the falls. The Kings River's South Fork flows through forested meadows, inviting you to linger at the backpacker campsites in **Lower Paradise Valley** (6600ft). Continue up the

Rae Lakes Loop

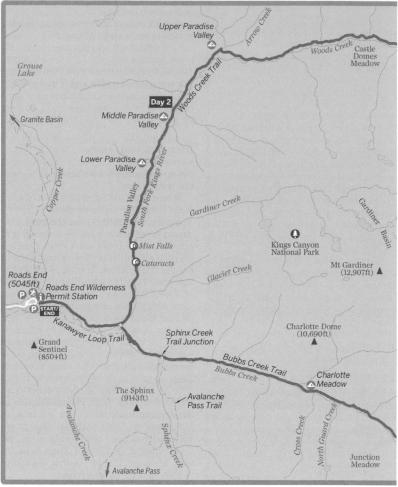

beautiful river valley through mixed-coni-fer forest just over a mile further to **Middle Paradise Valley** (6700ft), with more open views and less crowded campsites.

DAY 2: MIDDLE PARADISE VALLEY TO WOODS CREEK

4–6 HOURS / 7 MILES

Among ponderosa pines, the trail gradually ascends alongside a grassy meadow before dropping back to the river in **Upper Paradise Valley** (6800ft). Forested campsites appear before the confluence of the Kings River's South Fork and Woods Creek, about 1.5 miles from Middle Paradise Valley.

After crossing a footbridge, the trail steadily ascends sun-dappled switchbacks through a forested valley above Woods Creek. Less than 4 miles from the river crossing, the trail rolls into **Castle Domes Meadow** (8200ft), sitting beneath spectacu-lar, polished granite domes.

The trail meanders across the meadow and re-enters pine forest. At the signposted **John Muir Trail (JMT) junction** (8500ft), turn right and cross Woods Creek on the wooden planks of a steel-cable suspension bridge. Backpacker campsites sprawl just south of the bridge.

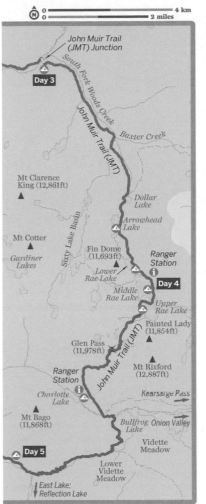

of **Fin Dome** (11,693ft) above Dollar Lake (camping strictly prohibited) sets the theme of mountain splendor.

Skirting Dollar Lake's west shore, the JMT continues up to arrive at larger **Arrowhead Lake** (10,300ft). It ascends more gradually to enchanting **Lower Rae Lake** (10,535ft). The gently rolling trail crosses several small side streams and passes a spur trail to a seasonal ranger station. Continue to the signed turnoff for campsites above the eastern shore of **Middle Rae Lake** (10,540ft).

DAY 4: MIDDLE RAE LAKE TO JUNCTION MEADOW
5–7 HOURS / 9 MILES

Get up early and eat a big breakfast, because this is game day.

Return to the JMT and turn right (south). Walk along the northern shore of **Upper Rae Lake** (10,545ft). Cross the connector stream between the lakes. At a signed trail junction, where a faint trail to Sixty Lake Basin peels off northwest, keep straight ahead on the JMT, which continues south up well-graded switchbacks above the west side of Upper Rae Lake. Heading higher, even more switchbacks take you up a talus slope to a tarn-filled basin, from where Glen Pass is visible ahead on the dark, rocky ridgeline.

The trail passes several small mountain lakes, which glisten in the barren cirque to the west. Then it rises on a series of switchbacks up talus to the very narrow saddle of **Glen Pass** (11,978ft), almost 3 miles from Middle Rae Lake. From the pass, visible in the distance to the southwest are massive Mt Brewer (13,576ft), with its often snowy northeast face, and other peaks along the Great Western Divide and Kings-Kern Divide. Mt Bago (11,868ft) is that distinctive reddish peak in the foreground.

Gravelly but well-graded switchbacks take you down from Glen Pass over a steep scree slope toward a pothole tarn at the tree line. Stop to filter water here – the next reliable water is not until the Bullfrog Lake outlet a few miles ahead. Then head down the narrow canyon, passing above a snow-fed, talus-lined pool until the trail swings south, then contours high above Charlotte Lake. A connector trail to Kearsarge Pass appears about 2.5 miles from Glen Pass, after which you'll soon reach a four-way junction with the main Charlotte Lake (northwest) and Kearsarge Pass (northeast) trails. Continue straight (south).

DAY 3: WOODS CREEK TO MIDDLE RAE LAKE
4–6 HOURS / 6.5 MILES

Heading south, the JMT rolls easily on open slopes along the west side of Woods Creek's South Fork, with good views of the granite high country. Crossing a small stream, the trail continues upvalley, rising over rocky terrain to reach a small meadow. At the next crossing, a bigger stream cascades over a cleft in the rock. Foxtail pines dot the dry slope above the trail as it continues up to **Dollar Lake** (10,220ft), about 3.5 miles from the Woods Creek crossing. The striking view

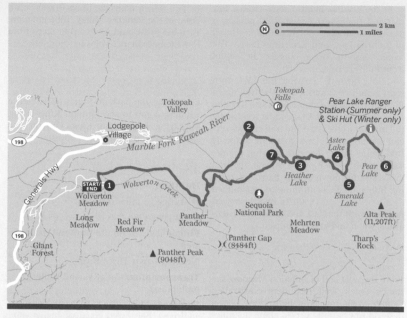

Overnight Hike
Lakes Trail

START/END WOLVERTON MEADOW
PARKING LOT/SHUTTLE STOP
LENGTH 12.5 MILES; TWO DAYS

Ascending steeply from Wolverton Meadow, this popular overnight backpacking trip – or challenging day hike – winds upward more than 2000ft to a string of gorgeous alpine lakes, giving you a tantalizing taste of the Sierra Nevada high country.

At the north side of ❶ **Wolverton Meadow** (Map p180; 7200ft), the trail commences by climbing through pine and red-fir forest, making an undulating traverse along a ridge to reach the Alta Peak Trail junction in less than 2 miles. At the next major junction, the Lakes Trail forks. Keep to the left and forge straight ahead on the Watchtower route (open seasonally when there's no ice and snow, which may last into early summer), then switchback up through sun-dappled forest.

Where the trail emerges high above the canyon of the Kaweah River's Marble Fork, the sheer granite face of the ❷ **Watchtower** stands sentinel. Peer down at tumbling Tokopah Falls far below. Mind your feet as the narrowing trail edges along a sheer cliff

face with dizzying drop-offs. After rejoining the shorter Hump route, the trail soon arrives on the shores of petite ❸ **Heather Lake** (9280ft), surrounded by woods (no camping allowed). A few hikers picnic, fish or even take a swim here, just over 4 miles from the trailhead.

After a short rise during which Alta Peak (11,207ft) comes into view, the trail rolls slowly downhill. Leveling out, it threads between ❹ **Aster Lake** (9100ft), a small tarn to the north, and beautiful ❺ **Emerald Lake** (9230ft), where the first backpacker campsites and a solar-powered outhouse appear. The last mile of the trail climbs out of the glacier-carved basin via steep and rocky switchbacks to ❻ **Pear Lake** (9550ft), sitting in a perfect glacial cirque. A seasonal ranger station, which doubles as a winter ski hut, is located down a spur trail that peels off east before reaching the lake, where more backpacker campsites await.

On the return trip, you can shave off about 0.4 miles by taking the steeper, shadier ❼ **Hump** route – soak up panoramic mountain views of the Tablelands from its crest – instead of going via the vertiginous Watchtower again.

At the head of Bubbs Creek, cross a low rise and then start descending, passing a junction with the trail heading northeast to Bullfrog Lake and Kearsarge Lakes. The scenic descent twice crosses the outlet from Bullfrog Lake to reach **Lower Vidette Meadow** (9480ft). Leaving the JMT, turn right (southwest) and follow the trail down Bubbs Creek past campsites at the forested edge of the meadow. Descending west along the tumbling creekside, the trail crosses several streams and a large rockslide to finally find some shade. Beneath soaring granite walls on either side of the canyon, the trail drops steadily down to now narrower, rushing Bubbs Creek, continuing to aspen-filled **Junction Meadow** (8500ft). Past the signed junction with the East and Reflection Lakes Trails, you'll find grassy campsites.

DAY 5: JUNCTION MEADOW TO ROADS END

5–7 HOURS / 10.5 MILES

From the west end of Junction Meadow, the Bubbs Creek Trail meanders downvalley. Granite walls tower on both sides as you descend to Charlotte Creek, about 3.5 miles from Junction Meadow. After crossing the creek, the trail continues creekside downhill for three more miles to the **Sphinx Creek Trail junction** (6240ft).

Continuing straight ahead, the Bubbs Creek Trail descends steeply on hot, open switchbacks, providing sweeping views into **Kings Canyon** and of the granite pinnacle of the **Sphinx** (9143ft) towering above you. At last reaching the canyon floor, the trail crosses braided Bubbs Creek over wooden footbridges. Just beyond the steel **Bailey Bridge**, which spans the Kings River's South Fork, is the Paradise Valley Trail junction. Turn left (west) and retrace your steps from Day 1 for less than 2 miles to **Roads End**.

🚗 DRIVING

Experience the park on four wheels with a winding climb to the Mineral King Valley, a dizzying descent into Kings Canyon or a short loop around the Giant Forest.

🚗 Mineral King Road

Duration 1½–2 hours

Distance 25 miles (one way)

Start Hwy 198

Finish Eagle/Mosquito trailhead parking area

Nearest Town Three Rivers

Transportation Car (RVs and trailers prohibited)

Summary Steel your nerves and take your time, because this twisting road will test your mettle. Skirting the canyon of the Kaweah River's East Fork, the road makes almost 700 sharp turns while ascending to 7500ft.

Usually only open from the Friday of Memorial Day weekend through late October, this is a twisting 25-mile road that you will not soon forget. Some sections are hair-raisingly narrow and unpaved, but the grade is never too difficult – just remember that uphill vehicles have the right of way.

SEQUOIA & KINGS CANYON NATIONAL PARKS DRIVING

Mineral King Road

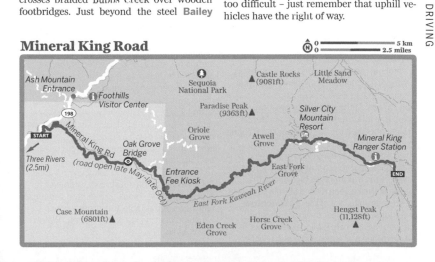

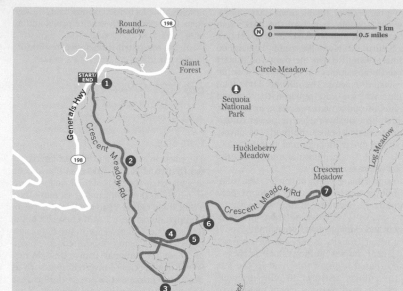

Driving Tour
Moro Rock–Crescent Meadow Road

START/END GIANT FOREST MUSEUM
PARKING AREA/SHUTTLE STOP
LENGTH 6 MILES; ONE HOUR

A narrow, winding and pockmarked road links some of the Giant Forest's popular roadside attractions, with giant sequoias lining the way. This road is closed to private vehicles on summer weekends and holidays. But why fight traffic anyway? Instead, take the free seasonal park shuttle! Shuttle buses usually run between late May and late September. In winter the road closes to all traffic, but you can still cross-country ski or snowshoe along it.

From the **1 Giant Forest Museum**, Moro Rock–Crescent Meadow Rd swoops into the southwestern section of the Giant Forest. Less than a mile in is the **2 Auto Log**, a hefty sequoia that fell in 1917. For early park visitors, a flat section was carved onto its top and the tree was actually used as part of the road. You can't drive on it anymore, but you can walk on it and imagine.

After more than another half-mile, turn into the super-small parking area (we told you to take the shuttle!) to gawk at the pale dome of **3 Moro Rock**. Continuing on a half-mile further, the mesmerizing flamelike roots of the 2300-year-old collapsed **4 Buttress Tree** face the road. On the opposite side of the road just a bit further along is the **5 Parker Group**, named for the eight-person family of US Cavalry Captain James Parker, who served as the park's superintendent during the 1890s.

In days gone by, the renown of Yosemite's Wawona Tunnel Tree prompted many visitors to inquire about Sequoia's drive-through tree, but the park didn't have one. So when a 275ft sequoia bit the dust and went splat across the road in 1937, the park took advantage of this gift and promptly cut a passageway for cars. This **6 Tunnel Log** has an 8ft-high, 17ft-wide opening, which larger vehicles can skirt using an adjacent bypass. From there, it's another mile to the road's end at verdant **7 Crescent Meadow**.

Return as you arrived, bypassing the side trip to Moro Rock.

Outside Three Rivers town (last chance for gas!), 2 miles south of the park's Ash Mountain Entrance, take a deep breath and turn off Hwy 198 onto well-signed Mineral King Rd. On the right you'll start to see long sections of **water flume** cutting a sharp line across the hillside. The metal flume you see now replaced the original sequoia-wood structure dating from 1899, which brought hydroelectric power to this remote region before the road was paved. To get a closer look, stop at the 1923 **Oak Grove Bridge**, around 6.5 miles from the start of the road.

Approximately 10.5 miles in, less than a mile after crossing the national park boundary, you'll reach the self-pay **entrance fee kiosk**, where there are pullovers and canyon views. Occasionally you'll see water troughs to the side of the road, built for horses pulling stagecoaches – the original users of this road in the late 19th century. Just over 16 miles from its start, the road passes a shady picnic area beside giant sequoias.

A little more than 5 miles further up the road is **Silver City Mountain Resort**, a stop for fresh-baked pie and hot coffee. Your final destination, just over a mile past the **Mineral King ranger station**, is where the valley unfolds all of its hidden beauty, and the high country beckons with granite peaks and alpine lakes.

On the return trip, remember to shift into lower gear to save your vehicle's brakes.

OTHER ACTIVITIES

Caving

The caves in Sequoia and Kings Canyon are so extensive that the parks could have been designated on the basis of their cave systems alone. Of all the California caves more than a mile long, half of them are found here, including Lilburn Cave – at 17 surveyed miles, it's the longest known cave in the state. New caves are still being discovered, for example, Sequoia National Park's Ursa Minor. So are new species of invertebrates, such as troglobites (animals that live in dark caves). Those recently identified in Sequoia's **Crystal Cave** (Map p180) include translucent, eyeless insects and a tiny pseudoscorpion. Crystal Cave and Boyden Cavern (p184) are the only caves open for public tours.

SEQUOIA & KINGS CANYON NATIONAL PARKS OTHER ACTIVITIES

DON'T MISS

CRYSTAL CAVE

Accidentally discovered in 1918 by two parks employees who were going fishing, this unique marble cave was carved by an underground river, and has formations estimated to be 10,000 years old. Stalactites hang like daggers from the ceiling, and milky white marble formations take the shape of ethereal curtains, domes, columns and shields. The cave is also a unique biodiverse habitat for spiders, bats and tiny aquatic insects that are found nowhere else on earth.

Beyond the historic Spider Gate at the entrance, underground passageways wind for over 3 miles. To get inside the **cave** (☑ 559-565-3759; www.explorecrystalcave.com; Crystal Cave Rd, off Generals Hwy; tours adult/child/youth from $16/5/8; ⊗ May–Nov;), you must buy a ticket for a 50-minute introductory guided tour. Teens and adults can take a more in-depth, 90-minute 'Discovery Tour' ($18) or sign up in advance for a full-day spelunking adventure ($135).

Tour tickets are *only* sold at the Lodgepole and Foothills visitor centers, *not* at the cave itself. Tours fill up quickly, especially on weekends, so buy them early in the day or a day in advance. Wheelchairs, baby backpacks, purses, strollers, tripods and walking sticks are prohibited inside the cave. Bring a light jacket, as chilly cave temperatures average only 50°F (10°C). No drinking water is available at the cave, which may close during rainy weather (refunds available).

From the Lodgepole or Foothills areas, allow at least 90 minutes to get to the cave, which is a half-mile walk from the parking lot at the end of a twisty 6.5-mile-long paved road. Look for the signed turnoff for Crystal Cave Rd about 2 miles south of the Giant Forest Museum.

Swimming, Canoeing, Kayaking & Boating

Swimming holes abound along the Middle Fork of the Kaweah River in the **Foothills** area of Sequoia National Park, especially on the opposite side of the Generals Hwy from Potwisha Campground and the Hospital Rock picnic area. Families also take dips in pools along the Marble Fork of the Kaweah River inside **Lodgepole Campground** near the Tokopah Falls trailhead. In Kings Canyon, Muir Rock (p185) and the **Red Bridge** by Roads End are favorite swimming holes. In the Sequoia National Forest, Hume Lake (p184) is dreamy on a hot summer day, and you can rent canoes, kayaks and boats by the beach at Hume Lake Christian Camps.

Horseback Riding & Pack Trips

Cedar Grove Pack Station   HORSEBACK RIDING
(☑ 559-565-3464; Hwy 180, Cedar Grove; ☻ late May–mid-Oct) Trail rides along the river deep in Kings Canyon ($40 to $70) and overnight pack trips (reservations required) to mountain lakes, both from Cedar Grove.

Grant Grove Stables   HORSEBACK RIDING
(Map p180; ☑ 559-335-9292; Hwy 180; ☻ mid-Jun–early Sep) Just north of General Grant Grove in Kings Canyon, this pint-sized operation offers one- and two-hour trail rides for $40 to $70.

Horse Corral Pack Station   HORSEBACK RIDING
(Map p180; ☑ 559-565-3404; Big Meadows Rd; ☻ late May–Sep) Inside the Giant Sequoia National Monument, this rustic outfit offers short trail rides and overnight backcountry pack trips (by reservation only).

Rock Climbing

Both parks have tons of rock-climbing spots, though it's not nearly as popular here as in Yosemite and many of the best places require a long backcountry hike before you even *start* climbing. The most spectacular climb is an 1800ft granite wall in the remote Valhalla Cirque called **Angel Wings**, nicknamed 'an alpine El Capitan' by renowned climber and photographer Galen Rowell.

In Kings Canyon, the backcountry Bubbs Creek Trail leads to multipitch climbs at **Charlito and Charlotte Domes** just before crossing Charlotte Creek, an 8-mile trek from Roads End, east of Cedar Grove Village. More accessible locations in Sequoia National Park include **Moro Rock** (closed during peregrine nesting season, usually April through mid-August) and **Little Baldy**, both off the Generals Hwy. In the Sequoia National Forest, west of the Generals Hwy via dirt road FR-14S29, **Chimney Rocks** has dozens of routes (all closed during peregrine nesting season).

Fishing

Rivers, lakes and creeks will delight amateur trout anglers. Tackle is sold at most park markets. In Kings Canyon near Cedar Grove, **Lewis Creek**, **Bubbs Creek** and **Motor Nature Trail** (River Rd) are popular places to fish. So is **Hume Lake**, where the US Forest Service (USFS) stocks trout. A fishing license, which can be obtained at Hume Lake and possibly some park markets, is required for anyone aged 16 and older. Visitor centers can provide a copy of park-specific regulations (eg lures, daily limits, mandatory catch-and-release of protected species).

Snow Sports

Winter is a memorable time to visit Sequoia and Kings Canyon. A thick blanket of snow drapes giant sequoia trees and meadows, the pace of activity slows and a hush falls over the roads and trails.

Dozens of miles of ungroomed trails for **snowshoeing** and **cross-country skiing** criss-cross the Grant Grove and Giant Forest areas (trail maps sold at park visitor centers). There are more tree-marked trails in the Giant Sequoia National Monument. Winter road closures also make for excellent cross-country skiing or snowshoeing on Sequoia's Moro Rock–Crescent Meadow Rd,

❶ WARNING!

Drownings in the Kings and Kaweah Rivers are the leading cause of death in the parks. Swift currents can be deadly, especially when rivers are swollen with snowmelt runoff in late spring and early summer. Never go in if you see any white water. When in doubt, stay out! Get smart advice about current swimming conditions at park visitor centers and ranger stations.

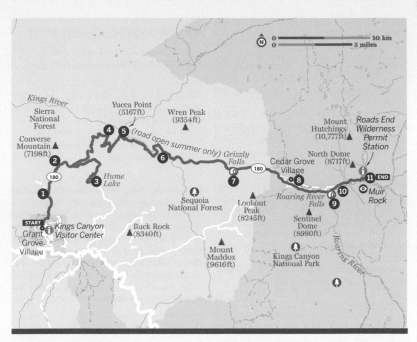

Driving Tour
Kings Canyon Scenic Byway

START GRANT GROVE VILLAGE
END ROADS END
LENGTH 35 MILES (ONE WAY); 1½–TWO HOURS

John Muir called Kings Canyon 'a rival of the Yosemite.' This jaw-dropping scenic drive enters one of North America's deepest canyons, traversing the forested Giant Sequoia National Monument and shadowing the Kings River all the way to Roads End.

Fewer than 3 miles from Grant Grove, pull over to drink in the mountain panorama at **1 McGee Vista Point**. Then keep winding downhill through the Sequoia National Forest past the turn-off to **2 Converse Basin Grove**, a lonely testament to the 19th-century logging of giant sequoias, which turned out to be as economically unprofitable as it was environmentally unwise.

About 6 miles from Grant Grove is the turn-off to **3 Hume Lake**, which offers sandy beaches and coves for summer swims. Keep heading downhill, ever deeper into the canyon. The road snakes past chiseled rock walls, some tinged by green moss and red iron minerals, others laced by waterfalls. Roadside turnouts provide superb views, notably at **4 Junction View**, about 10.5 miles from Grant Grove, and beyond **5 Yucca Point**, another 3.5 miles further along.

After countless ear-popping curves, the road bottoms out and runs parallel to the Kings River, its roar ricocheting off granite cliffs soaring thousands of feet high above. Over 5 miles past Yucca Point, marbled **6 Boyden Cavern** offers guided tours that will delight kids. It's more than another 5 miles to the picnic area by **7 Grizzly Falls**, often a torrent in late spring.

The scenic byway re-enters the national park just over 2.5 miles further along, quickly passing the Lewis Creek bridge and a riverside beach. It's less than 2 miles to **8 Cedar Grove Village**, where you can stop at the visitor center and market before pushing on. Over the next 6 miles, don't miss short walks to **9 Roaring River Falls** and pretty **10 Zumwalt Meadow**. More hiking trails and swimming holes await at honestly named **11 Roads End** – the only way to keep going across the Sierra Nevada is on foot!

Kings Canyon's Panoramic Point Rd and Big Meadows Rd in the Sequoia National Forest.

You'll find **snow-play areas** at Wolverton Meadow in Sequoia's Giant Forest; **Big Stump** and **Columbine** in Kings Canyon's Grant Grove; and **Big Meadows**, **Quail Flat** and **Cherry Gap** in the Sequoia National Forest.

Cross-country ski and snowshoe rentals are available at Grant Grove Village and Wuksachi Lodge, which sell limited winter clothing and snow-play gear. In winter, park rangers lead two-hour **snowshoe walks** (free snowshoe use included) starting from Wuksachi Lodge. These walks fill up fast, so reserve a spot in advance, in person at park visitor centers or by calling the Giant Forest Museum (p179).

Montecito Sequoia Lodge   SNOW SPORTS
(Map p180; ☎ 559-565-3388, 800-227-9900; www.montecitosequoia.com; 63410 Generals Hwy; day-use fee $25, equipment rental $25; 🖼) During winter in the Sequoia National Forest, families come here for cross-country skiing and snowboarding lessons, more than 30 miles of groomed terrain, and sledding and tubing hills. Rent snow-sports equipment for children and adults at Mountain Top ski shop.

Pear Lake Ski Hut   SKIING, SNOWSHOEING
(Map p180; ☎ 559-565-3759; www.sequoiahistory.org; ☉ usually mid-Dec–mid-Apr) Backcountry experts who aren't intimidated by a steep 6-mile cross-country ski or snowshoe trek can enter the lottery (held in early November) to bunk down overnight ($40) at this rustic backcountry hut. Consult the Sequoia Natural History Association website for full details, including important safety tips and a lottery application.

⊙ SIGHTS

Giant sequoia groves, underground marble caves, sculpted granite domes, jagged high-altitude peaks and wildflower meadows where mule deer and black bears graze are just a small taste of what you'll see in both the national parks and nearby national forest lands. When the weather spoils your outdoor plans, the Giant Forest Museum and the educational exhibits and short nature films at park visitor centers are welcome indoor diversions.

⊙ Sequoia National Park

Lodgepole & Wuksachi Villages

Lodgepole Village is the park's main hub. The market, deli, snack bar, ATM, pay showers and coin-op laundromat are usually open from April through October. Two miles further north along the Generals Hwy, Wuksachi Village boasts the park's highest-end hotel, restaurant and bar, all open year-round.

Lodgepole Visitor Center (p194) has exhibits on park history, covering buffalo soldiers, competing land uses from Native American dominion until the present, and contemporary environmental challenges such as air pollution and wildfires. Entertaining and educational, the short movie *Bears of the Sierra* is screened upon request, or check out the video booth at the back to learn about black bears and the human history of the Giant Forest.

Giant Forest

During his travels in the Sierra Nevada, conservationist John Muir wandered into this cathedral-like grove of giant sequoias in 1875, baptizing it the 'Giant Forest.' Having escaped being logged in the late 19th century, today the Giant Forest encompasses an amazing concentration of ancient sequoias, where the happy shouts of kids and trilling birdsong echo through the misty groves.

By the late 20th century, over 300 buildings, including campgrounds and a lodge, that had been built in the Giant Forest encroached upon the giant sequoias' delicate root systems, as did traffic jams. Tourist development had also made it necessary to suppress all wildfires, without which giant sequoias can't reproduce naturally.

Recognizing these adverse impacts, in 1997 the park began to remove structures, reposition parking lots and relocate visitor services further north. A convenient, free, seasonal shuttle-bus system has significantly cut traffic congestion and reduced the potential harm to these majestic trees.

★ **General Sherman Tree**   NATURAL FEATURE
(Map p180; off Generals Hwy; 🖼) By volume the largest living tree on earth, the massive General Sherman Tree rockets into the sky and *waaay* out of the camera frame. Pay your

respects to this giant, which measures more than 100ft around at it base, via a paved, wheelchair-accessible 0.5-mile descent from the upper parking lot off Wolverton Rd. Then join the **Congress Trail**, a 2-mile paved loop that takes in General Sherman and other notable named trees, including the see-through Telescope Tree.

Hint: if the steep walk back up from the grove doesn't thrill you, catch the shuttle from the lower parking lot (disabled-placard parking only) near the General Sherman Tree and ride it back to the main parking area, about 1.5 miles north of Lodgepole Village.

★ **Giant Forest Museum**   MUSEUM
(Map p180; 559-565-4480; Generals Hwy, at Crescent Meadow Rd; 9am-4:30pm;) FREE
For a primer on the intriguing ecology and history of giant sequoias, this pint-sized modern museum will entertain both kids and adults. Hands-on exhibits teach about the life stages of these big trees, which can live for over 3000 years, and the fire cycle that releases their seeds and allows them to sprout on bare soil. The museum itself is housed in a 1920s historic building designed by Gilbert Stanley Underwood, famed architect of Yosemite's Ahwahnee Hotel.

★ **Moro Rock**   NATURAL FEATURE
(Map p180; off Moro Rock–Crescent Meadow Rd) Although not nearly as mammoth as Yosemite's Half Dome, Sequoia's iconic granite dome is nonetheless impressive. A quarter-mile staircase climbs over 300ft to the top for mind-boggling views of the Great Western Divide, running north–south through the middle of the park, and splitting the watersheds of the Kaweah River to the west from the Kern River to the east. Due to pollution drifting up from the Central Valley, this spectacular vantage point is sometimes obscured by thick haze, especially during summer.

Historical photos at the trailhead show the rock's original rickety wooden staircase, erected in 1917. You'll be grateful that the current staircase, built in 1931 by the CCC, has nearly 400 steps solidly carved into the granite, plus sturdy handrails for gripping.

From the Giant Forest Museum, the trailhead is 2 miles up narrow, twisty Moro Rock–Crescent Meadow Rd. The free seasonal shuttle bus stops at the small parking lot, which is often full.

Crescent Meadow   NATURAL FEATURE
(Map p180; end of Moro Rock–Crescent Meadow Rd;) A lush meadow buffered by a forest of fir and giant sequoia trees, it was allegedly once described by John Muir as the 'gem of the Sierra.' High grass and summer wildflowers are good excuses for a leisurely loop hike (see p164), as is watching black bears snack on berries and rip apart logs to feast on insects.

The meadow environment is fragile, so always stay on established trails and don't go tramping willy-nilly across it.

Several short hikes surround the meadow, including spur trails to **Tharp's Log**, where the area's first white settler, Hale Tharp, spent summers in a fallen sequoia, and next to Huckleberry Meadow, the **Squatters Cabin**, an 1880s log cabin that's a ghostly remnant of the failed utopian-socialist Kaweah Colony (see the boxed text, p196).

The meadow is almost 3 miles down Moro Rock–Crescent Meadow Rd, best accessed by the free seasonal shuttle bus. The road closes to all traffic after the first snowfall and doesn't reopen until spring, but you can still snowshoe or cross-country ski along it.

Foothills

From the Ash Mountain Entrance outside the town of Three Rivers, the Generals Hwy ascends steeply through the southwestern section of Sequoia National Park. At an elevation of less than 3500ft, the Foothills area is much drier and warmer than the rest of the park. Hiking here is best in spring, when the air is still cool and wildflowers peak early for a colorful show. Scorching-hot summers are buggy and muggy, but still popular for swimming in the Kaweah River (when waters are calm enough). Fall brings more moderate temperatures and colorful foliage.

The Foothills Visitor Center (p194) is open year-round. A mile north of the Ash Mountain Entrance, it has educational exhibits on the park's human history and ecology, focusing on Sierra Nevada wildlife across different life zones, as well as Native American heritage and 19th-century pioneers and conservationists.

Tunnel Rock   LANDMARK
(Map p180; off Generals Hwy) In the 1930s, no one anticipated the development of monster SUVs. About 1.5 miles north of the Foothills Visitor Center, a flat granite boulder on the west side of the Generals Hwy caps a

SEQUOIA & KINGS CANYON NATIONAL PARKS SIGHTS

Sequoia & Kings Canyon National Parks Region

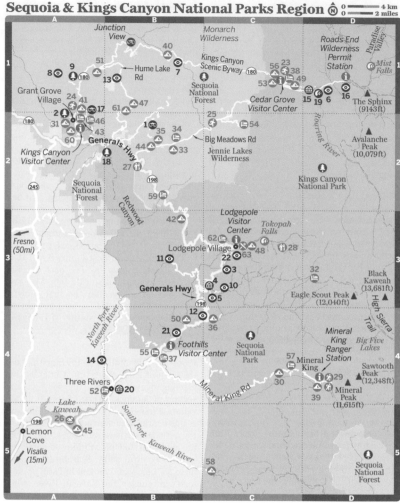

tunnel dug by the CCC. Until the highway was finally widened in 1997, this narrow passageway was the only route through. It's closed to modern-day vehicles, which would have a tough time squeezing through side by side, but pedestrians can still stroll underneath it.

Hospital Rock   HISTORIC SITE
(Map p180; off Generals Hwy) The Potwisha people, a band of Monache (also known as Western Mono), originally lived here. When the first white settler, Hale Tharp, arrived in 1858, this site was home to about 500 villagers and had been inhabited for five centuries. Pictographs (rock paintings) and grinding holes used by tribeswomen to make acorn meal can still be seen at the picnic area, about 5 miles northeast of the visitor center.

In the 1860s, diseases introduced by white settlers from Three Rivers quickly killed many of the Native Americans, and within a decade the village had been abandoned.

In 1873 pioneer Alfred Everton injured his leg by getting it caught in his own bear trap. He lay down here to recuperate from his injury, hence the rock's name.

Sequoia & Kings Canyon National Parks Region

Mineral King

Perched at 7500ft, this giant, gorgeous and glacially sculpted valley ringed by massive mountains, including jagged Sawtooth Peak, is a supremely good place to find solitude. The **Mineral King Preservation Society** (www.mineralking.org) has all kinds of historical information about the area.

For two decades starting in the 1870s, Mineral King witnessed heavy silver mining and lumber activity. There are still remnants of old shafts and stamp mills around, though it takes some exploring to find them. After mining turned out to be a bust, Mineral King became a cool mountain retreat for families escaping the Central Valley's summer heat. A contentious proposal by the Walt Disney Company to develop the area into a ski resort was thwarted by a Sierra Club–led campaign. The issue was forever put to rest when Congress annexed Mineral King to Sequoia National Park in 1978.

Hiking anywhere from here involves a steep climb out of the valley along strenuous trails. Be aware of the high altitude, even on short hikes. Beautiful day hikes or overnight backpacking trips head up to Monarch, Crystal, Eagle, Mosquito, Franklin, Little Five and Big Five Lakes. If you're not up for the tough stuff, take a serene mile-long ramble along the **nature trail** from Cold Springs Campground to the Eagle/Mosquito trailhead parking area.

The valley is reached via narrow, twisting 25-mile Mineral King Rd, which heads east from Hwy 198 south of the park's Ash Mountain Entrance. The road is usually open only from late May through late October. Scattered along the last 6 miles of road are two first-come, first-served park campgrounds, a ranger station and the private Silver City Mountain Resort, offering lodging, a restaurant and a tiny market.

Generals Highway

As it winds for almost 11 miles through the Sequoia National Forest, the Generals Hwy bridges the gap between Sequoia and Kings Canyon National Parks. A few campgrounds, lodging and tourist services are right off the highway, while paved Big Meadows Rd (Forest Service road 14S11) burrows east into the Giant Sequoia National Monument near the Jennie Lakes Wilderness, a popular backpacking area.

A seasonal outpost, **Stony Creek** has a gas station (pumps available 24 hours with credit cards), ATM, pay phones, wi-fi, coin-op laundry and pay showers, a lodge, small market and restaurant, and nearby campgrounds. Everything closes from mid-October until mid-May, including the gas station.

Four miles further north, **Montecito Sequoia Lodge** is primarily a summer family camp set around a small private lake, offering groomed cross-country ski trails and other snow sports in winter.

⭐**Buck Rock Fire Lookout**   VIEWPOINT
(Map p180; www.buckrock.org; FR-13S04, off Big Meadows Rd; ☺ usually 9:30am-6pm Jun-Oct) Built in 1923, this active fire lookout is one of the finest restored watchtowers you could ever hope to visit. Staffed during the wildfire season, 172 stairs lead to a dollhouse-sized wooden cab on a dramatic 8500ft granite rise.

From the Generals Hwy, turn east onto Big Meadows Rd (FR-14S11). At approximately 2.5 miles, turn north on the signed dirt road (FR-13S04) then drive another 3 miles to the lookout parking area.

Opening hours vary, so check the website or the seasonal park newspaper, or ask at a visitor center beforehand. The lookout closes during lightning storms and fire emergencies.

⊙ Kings Canyon National Park

Grant Grove Village

About 3 miles northeast of the park's Big Stump Entrance, Grant Grove Village is the park's main tourist hub year-round, with lodge and cabin accommodations, a restaurant, decent-sized market and free wi-fi. ATMs are located inside the lodge lobby and at the market. The closest gas is at Hume Lake or Stony Creek.

ⓘ MARMOT ALERT!

You've locked the doors and rolled up the windows. All food and scented stuff has been removed to deter bear break-ins. So why is your car still at risk? Mineral King is swarming with hungry yellow-bellied marmots, and what's under your hood might be what's for dinner.

In late spring through midsummer, Mineral King's curious marmots come out of hibernation and anxiously await parked cars at trailheads. Besides such epicurean items as sweaty boots, backpack straps and hiking pole grips, these rodents also love to feast on the radiator hoses, belts and wiring of vehicles to get the salt they crave. They can chew through brake lines and completely disable your car. Toxic antifreeze tastes sweet, like dessert, to them.

Marmot-proofing one's vehicle has become a local art form. A few folks swear by wrapping the engine block in chicken wire, but most people swaddle the entire undercarriage with an enormous tarp and secure it with rope. You'll see how it's done just by looking at other cars parked at the trailheads. Vehicle tarps and rope can usually be bought (though not cheaply) before driving up to Mineral King at **Three Rivers Mercantile** (p227) in the town of Three Rivers.

Always check under the hood before you drive off. Some marmots have ended up hitching as far as Southern California before they were finally discovered, still munching away.

PANORAMIC POINT

For a breathtaking view of Kings Canyon, head 2.3 miles up narrow, steep and winding Panoramic Point Rd (trailers and RVs aren't recommended). Follow a short paved trail uphill from the parking lot to the **viewpoint** (Map p180), where precipitous canyons and the snowcapped peaks of the Great Western Divide unfold below you. Snow closes the road to vehicles during winter, when it becomes a cross-country ski and snowshoe route.

From the visitor center in Grant Grove Village off Hwy 180, follow the paved side road east, turning left after 0.1 miles, then right at the John Muir Lodge.

Grant Grove's busy visitor center (p194) has interesting exhibits on nature conservation, wildlife habitats and environmental issues, and screens an introductory movie about Kings Canyon – all titled in both English and Spanish. Families head toward the 'Discovery Room' at the back, which has independent nature-themed activities for younger kids.

★ **General Grant Grove**   FOREST
(Map p180; off Generals Hwy; 🚻) This sequoia grove is nothing short of astounding. The paved half-mile **General Grant Tree Trail** (p167) is an interpretive walk that visits a number of mature sequoias, including the 27-story **General Grant Tree**. This giant holds triple honors as the world's second-largest living tree, a memorial to US soldiers killed in war, and the nation's official Christmas tree since 1926. The nearby **Fallen Monarch**, a massive, fire-hollowed trunk you can walk through, has been a cabin, hotel, saloon and horse stables.

To escape the bustling crowds, follow the more secluded 1.5-mile **North Grove Loop**, which passes wildflower patches and bubbling creeks as it gently winds underneath a canopy of stately sequoias, evergreen pines and aromatic incense cedars.

The magnificence of this ancient sequoia grove was nationally recognized in 1890 when Congress first designated it General Grant National Park. It took another half century for this tiny parcel to be absorbed into much larger Kings Canyon National Park, established in 1940 to prevent damming of the Kings River.

Redwood Canyon   FOREST
(Map p180; off Generals Hwy) Over 15,000 sequoias cluster in Redwood Canyon, making it one of the world's largest groves of these giant trees. In an almost-forgotten corner of the park, this secluded forest lets you revel in the grandeur of the trees away from the

crowds while hiking mostly moderate trails. What you won't find here, however, are any of California's coast redwood trees – that's what early pioneers mistook these giant sequoias for, hence the erroneous name.

The trailheads are at the end of a 2-mile bumpy dirt road (closed in winter) that starts across from the Hume Lake/Quail Flat signed intersection on the Generals Hwy, just over 5 miles southeast of Grant Grove Village.

Kings Canyon Scenic Byway

The park's two main visitor areas, Grant Grove and Cedar Grove, are linked by narrow, twisting Hwy 180, which makes a dramatic descent into Kings Canyon, carved by glaciers and the mighty Kings River. The canyon itself, plunging over 8000ft when measured from the tip of Spanish Peak, is one of North America's deepest.

Expect spectacular views along this outstandingly scenic drive (p177), where rugged peaks, sheer granite cliffs and a roaring river jostle for your attention. Hwy 180 all the way down to Cedar Grove is closed during winter (usually from mid-November until late April), but the stretch from Grant Grove to Hume Lake Rd is open year-round.

Converse Basin Grove   FOREST
(Map p180; off Hwy 180) Tragically, Converse Basin once contained the world's largest grove of mature sequoias, but it's now an unsettling cemetery for tree stumps. In the late 19th and early 20th centuries, the entire privately owned grove was felled by lumber companies. A financial boondoggle, in part because of high transportation costs, the trees ravaged in this grove were not even suitable for lumber, and many shattered when they hit the ground. Most of the salvageable wood ended up as fence posts and matches.

The only survivor left is a colossus called the **Boole Tree**. The sixth-largest known

SEQUOIA & KINGS CANYON NATIONAL PARKS SIGHTS

giant sequoia, it's ironically named for the lumber mill's foreman, and for reasons unknown it was left to live. A 2.5-mile loop hike reaches it from the dirt access road to the trailhead; bring plenty of water and insect repellant. On the way in, stop at **Stump Meadow** to see the oversized remains of 19th-century logging.

Off another dirt road further south, the 20ft-high **Chicago Stump** (Map p180) is all that's left of the once-mighty 3200-year-old General Noble tree. The 285ft giant was cut into sections and transported to the 1893 World's Columbian Exposition in Chicago to demonstrate the unbelievable scale of the newly discovered giant sequoia trees. Dubious viewers soon nicknamed it the 'California hoax'!

The roads to the Boole Tree and the Chicago Stump are unpaved, and the turnoff signs are hard to spot. The Chicago Stump turnoff is next to a stone marker at a four-way intersection off Hwy 180, about 3 miles north of Grant Grove Village; from there, it's another 2 miles to the trailhead, then an easy 0.5-mile loop walk. The last quarter-mile of road is somewhat steep; consider parking in the turnout just before the descent if it's muddy or you don't have 4WD. The turnoff for the Boole Tree road is 1.2 miles further north along Hwy 180; the trailhead is another 2.5 miles in, with the last half-mile often in rough, slippery and sandy condition that may require 4WD.

A 2015 wildfire roared through this area of the Sequoia National Forest; for updates, check at the visitor center in Grant Grove.

Hume Lake Recreation Area   LAKE
(Map p180; ☑559-338-2251; www.fs.fed.us/r5/sequoia; Hume Lake Rd) When it was originally dammed in 1908, this 87-acre artificial lake powered a huge log flume that whisked sequoias harvested in Converse Basin Grove to a mill more than 70 miles away. Today, a popular USFS campground and sandy coves and beaches line the lakeshore. Privately operated Hume Lake Christian Camps runs a snack bar for burgers and milkshakes, a small market for groceries and camping sundries, gas pumps (available 24 hours with credit cards) and beachside canoe and boat rentals.

Boyden Cavern   CAVE
(Map p180; ☑888-956-8243; www.caverntours.com/BoydenRt.htm; Hwy 180; tours adult/child from $14.50/8.75; ⊙late Apr–Sep; 🚻) While the rooms are smaller and the interiors less eye-popping than Crystal Cave in Sequoia

National Park, touring the beautiful and fantastical formations here requires no advance tickets. Just show up for the basic 45-minute tour, which departs hourly from 10am to 5pm during peak summer season. Reaching the cave entrance requires a short walk up a steep, paved grade.

Cedar Grove

At the bottom of Kings Canyon, the commercial area of **Cedar Grove Village** consists of a market, ATM, restaurant, lodge, pay showers and coin-op laundry. Across the road next to Sentinel Campground is a small, seasonal visitor center (p194). Tourist services here are available from mid-May until mid-October. Hwy 180 beyond Hume Lake to Cedar Grove closes completely during winter, usually from mid-November through late April.

Six miles east of the village, **Roads End** is just that. A seasonal ranger station (p194) issues wilderness permits, sells maps and hiking guides, and rents bear canisters. Hikes starting here head out into the wilderness; it's the closest park trailhead to both the Pacific Crest National Scenic Trail (PCT) and the John Muir Trail (JMT).

Knapp's Cabin   HISTORIC BUILDING
(Map p180; off Hwy 180) During the 1920s, wealthy Santa Barbara businessman George Knapp built this simple wood-shingled cabin to store gear during his extravagant fishing and camping excursions into Kings Canyon. From a signed roadside pullout, about 2 miles east of the village, a short trail leads to this hidden building, the oldest in Cedar Grove. Come around dusk, when the views of the glacier-carved canyon are glorious.

Roaring River Falls   WATERFALL
(Map p180; off Hwy 180) One of the park's most accessible waterfalls, a five-minute walk on a paved trail leads to a 40ft chute that gushes into a granite bowl. In late spring and maybe early summer, the strength of this cascade won't disappoint. Look for the parking lot and trailhead on the south side of the road, about 3 miles east of the village, slightly closer to Roads End.

★ Zumwalt Meadow   NATURAL FEATURE
(Map p180; off Hwy 180) This verdant meadow bordered by the Kings River and soaring granite canyon walls offers phenomenal views. In the early morning, the air hums

with birdsong, the sun's rays light up the canyon walls, and mule deer and black bears can often be spotted foraging among the long grasses, wildflowers and berry bushes in the meadow. Following the partly shaded nature trail gives you a quick snapshot of the canyon's beauty.

Muir Rock   NATURAL FEATURE
(Map p180) On excursions to Kings Canyon, John Muir would allegedly give talks on this large flat river boulder, a short walk from the Roads End parking lot and less than a mile past Zumwalt Meadow. A sandy river beach here is taken over by gleeful swimmers in midsummer. Don't jump in when raging waters, swollen with snowmelt, are dangerous. Ask at the Roads End ranger station if conditions are calm enough for a dip.

🛏 SLEEPING

🛏 Sequoia National Park

Camping

Lodgepole, Potwisha and Buckeye Flat Campgrounds in the national park and both Stony Creek campgrounds in the national forest offer reservations (essential in summer); all other campgrounds are first-come, first-served.

Campfires are allowed only in existing fire rings. When the risk of wildfires is high, all campfires may be prohibited, especially in the lower-elevation Foothills area.

LODGEPOLE & WUKSACHI VILLAGES

★**Lodgepole Campground**   CAMPGROUND $
(Map p180; ☑ reservations 877-444-6777, 518-885-3639; www.recreation.gov; Generals Hwy; tent & RV sites $22; ⊙ late Mar–mid-Oct) Closest to the Giant Forest area with over 200 closely packed sites, this place quickly fills because of its proximity to Kaweah River swimming holes and Lodgepole Village amenities. A dozen or so walk-in sites are more private. Reservations available (and strongly recommended) from late May through September.

Dorst Creek Campground   CAMPGROUND $
(Map p180; Generals Hwy; tent & RV sites $22; ⊙ mid-Jun–early Sep; 🐾) Big and busy campground with more than 200 sites. The quieter back sites are for tents only, while the front loops can fill with RVs. It's about 7

miles northwest of Wuksachi Village. At the time of research, reservations were not accepted here.

FOOTHILLS

Lower-elevation campgrounds are very hot and dry, especially in summer. Potwisha and Buckeye Flat are often packed with groups and rowdy.

Potwisha Campground   CAMPGROUND $
(Map p180; ☑ reservations 877-444-6777, 518-885-3639; www.recreation.gov; Generals Hwy; tent & RV sites $22; ⊙ year-round; 🐾) Popular campground with decent shade near swimming spots on the Kaweah River. It's 3 miles northeast of the Ash Mountain entrance, with 42 sites. Reservations (highly recommended) taken May through September.

Buckeye Flat Campground   CAMPGROUND $
(Map p180; ☑ reservations 877-444-6777, 518-885-3639; www.recreation.gov; off Generals Hwy; tent sites $22; ⊙ late Mar–late Sep; 🐾) This tent-only campground is in an open stand of oaks, about 6 miles northeast of the Ash Mountain Entrance, down a winding road that's off-limits to RVs and trailers. Reservations accepted (and strongly advised) between late May and late September.

South Fork Campground   CAMPGROUND $
(Map p180; end of South Fork Rd, off Hwy 198; tent sites $12, mid-Oct–late May free; ⊙ year-round) Remote, little-used tent-only campground on the river, 13 miles from Three Rivers down a partly unpaved, rough and narrow road. No water from mid-October until late May.

MINERAL KING

Two small campgrounds sit near the end of remote Mineral King Rd (no trailers or RVs allowed). Water taps are turned off in mid-October.

Cold Springs Campground   CAMPGROUND $
(Map p180; Mineral King Rd; tent sites $12; ⊙ late May–late Oct; 🐾) A short walk from the ranger station, this campground has a peaceful creekside location with ridge views and a gorgeous forest setting of conifers and aspen. If you spend the night here at 7500ft, you'll be well on your way to acclimatizing for high-altitude hikes. It often fills up on summer weekends, including its secluded walk-in sites.

Atwell Mill Campground   CAMPGROUND $
(Map p180; Mineral King Rd; tent sites $12; ☺late May–late Oct; 🐻) Smaller and quieter than elsewhere, Atwell Mill has damp sites scattered under sky-obscuring forest canopy on the Kaweah River, inside a sequoia grove that was partly logged for timber. Getting a site here is rarely a problem.

GENERALS HIGHWAY

Developed USFS campgrounds off the Generals Hwy in the Sequoia National Forest are open seasonally. Primitive campsites and dispersed camping off Big Meadows Rd may open earlier and shut down later in the year, depending on when snow closes the forest service roads.

Habituated bears are active here. Pick up required campfire permits (free) at the Kings Canyon Visitor Center (p194) in Grant Grove Village or the USFS Hume Lake District Office (p194) outside the parks.

Stony Creek Campground   CAMPGROUND $
(Map p180; ☑ reservations 877-444-6777, 518-885-3639; www.recreation.gov; Generals Hwy; tent & RV sites $24; ☺ mid-May–late Sep; 🐻) A mile north of the national park boundary near Stony

SEQUOIA NATIONAL PARK CAMPGROUNDS

CAMP-GROUND	LOCATION	DESCRIPTION	NO OF SITES	ELEVATION
Buckeye Flat (p185)	Foothills	Hot, exposed and sometimes noisy; tent only	28	2800ft
Potwisha (p185)	Foothills	Hot in summer, often noisy; near the Kaweah River	42	2100ft
South Fork (p185)	Foothills	Remote oak-shaded river sites (no water mid-Oct–late May); tent only	10	3600ft
Big Meadows (p187)	Generals Hwy	Spacious but primitive forest campsites	45	7600ft
Buck Rock (p187)	Generals Hwy	Remote primitive campsites near a fire lookout	11	7600ft
Horse Camp (p188)	Generals Hwy	Primitive wooded campsites; metal horse corral	5	7600ft
Stony Creek (p186)	Generals Hwy	Woodsy campsites, including some creekside	49	6400ft
Upper Stony Creek (p187)	Generals Hwy	Primitive, mostly quiet sites near Stony Creek Lodge	18	6400ft
Dorst Creek (p185)	Lodgepole & Wuksachi Villages	Sprawling forest campground; quieter tent-only sites in back	210	6800ft
Lodgepole (p185)	Lodgepole & Wuksachi Villages	Busy family campground; some sites and features available summer only	205	6700ft
Atwell Mill (p186)	Mineral King	Shady, often damp sites under forest canopy; tent only	21	6650ft
Cold Springs (p185)	Mineral King	Pretty creekside setting in high-elevation valley; tent only (some walk-in sites)	40	7500ft

All of the above campgrounds have bear-proof boxes, picnic tables, fire pits and trash cans.

 Drinking Water   *Rest-rooms*   *Ranger Station Nearby*   *Great for Families*   *Pay-phone*   *RV Dump Station*

SEQUOIA & KINGS CANYON NATIONAL PARKS SLEEPING

Creek Lodge, this forest campground fills with families in summer. Its nearly 50 sites are spacious and shady.

Upper Stony Creek Campground
CAMPGROUND $

(Map p180; ☑ reservations 877-444-6777, 518-885-3639; www.recreation.gov; off Generals Hwy; tent & RV sites $20-22; ⊙ late May–late Sep) With fewer than 20 sites, this primitive campground, accessed via unpaved roads, feels like a less crowded option. It's under a mile from Stony Creek Lodge.

Big Meadows Campground
CAMPGROUND $

(Map p180; Big Meadows Rd (FR-13S11); tent & RV sites free; ⊙ usually Jun–Oct) Over 40 primitive campsites that are spacious, shady and often peaceful. Though there's no potable water, a creek is nearby. The campground is less than 5 miles east of the Generals Hwy.

Buck Rock Campground
CAMPGROUND $

(Map p180; FR-13S04, off Big Meadows Rd; tent sites free; ⊙ usually Jun–Oct) Less than a dozen primitive campsites (no water) are hidden near a fire lookout, deep in the forest.

OPEN (APPROX)	RESERVATION AVAILABLE?	DAILY FEE	FACILITIES/FEATURES
late Mar–late Sep	yes (late May–late Sep)	$22	
year-round	yes (May–Sep)	$22	
year-round	no	$12 (free mid-Oct–late May)	
Jun–Oct	no	free	
Jun–Oct	no	free	
Jun–Oct	no	free	
mid-May–late Sep	yes	$24	
mid-May–late Sep	yes	$20–22	
mid-Jun–early Sep	maybe	$22	
late Mar–mid-Oct	yes (late May–Sep)	$22	
late May–late Oct	no	$12	
late May–late Oct	no	$12	

SEQUOIA & KINGS CANYON NATIONAL PARKS SLEEPING

| Dogs Allowed (On Leash) | Grocery Store Nearby | Restaurant Nearby | Wheelchair Accessible | Summertime Campfire Program |

TONDA / GETTY IMAGES ©

General Grant Tree (p167) in Grant Grove

SEQUOIA & KINGS CANYON NATIONAL PARKS SLEEPING

Horse Camp CAMPGROUND $
(Map p180; Big Meadows Rd (FR-13S11); tent & RV sites free; ☉ usually Jun–Oct) Primitive forest campground (no water) with a horse corral for overnight stock use.

Lodging

LODGEPOLE & WUKSACHI VILLAGES

Wuksachi Lodge LODGE $$
(Map p180; ☑ 559-565-4070, 866-807-3598; www.visitsequoia.com; 64740 Wuksachi Way, off Generals Hwy; r $185-290; 🛜) Built in 1999, Wuksachi Lodge is the park's most upscale lodging and dining option. But don't get too excited – the wood-paneled atrium lobby has an inviting stone fireplace and forest views, but charmless motel-style rooms with coffee makers, mini fridges, oak furniture and thin walls have an institutional feel. The lodge's location nearby Lodgepole Village, however, can't be beat.

Bearpaw High Sierra Camp CABIN $$$
(Map p180; ☑ reservations 866-807-3598, 801-559-4930; www.visitsequoia.com; d/tr tent cabin without bath incl breakfast & dinner $350/400; ☉ usually mid-Jun–mid-Sep) An 11.3-mile hike east of Crescent Meadow on the High Sierra Trail, this canvas-tent village is ideal for exploring the backcountry without lugging your own camping gear. Rates include showers, dinner and breakfast, as well as bedding and towels. Bookings start at 7am PST every January 2 and sell out almost immediately, though you can always check for last-minute cancellations.

MINERAL KING

⭐ **Silver City Mountain Resort** CABIN $$
(☑ 559-561-3223; www.silvercityresort.com; Mineral King Rd; cabins with/without bath from $195/120, chalets from $250; ☉ late May–late Oct; 🛜) The only food and lodging option anywhere near these parts, this rustic, old-fashioned place rents everything from cute and cozy 1950s-era cabins to modern chalets that sleep up to eight. Bring your own sheets and towels (otherwise, rentals cost $45 per cabin). There's a ping-pong table, outdoor playground and a small pond. It's 3.5 miles west of the ranger station. Most cabins don't have electricity, and the property's generator usually shuts off around 10pm.

GENERALS HIGHWAY

Big Meadows Guard Station CABIN $$
(Map p180; ☑ reservations 877-444-6677, 518-885-3639; www.recreation.gov; Big Meadows Rd (FR-13S11); cabin $125; ☉ usually mid-Jun–mid-Oct) For a rustic overnight stay, this restored 1930s USFS patrol station built by the CCC sleeps six people. Just over 4 miles east of the Generals Hwy between the parks, the one-bedroom cabin sits at an elevation of 7600ft. Although you'll need to bring bedding and towels, it's equipped with hot water, electricity and a full kitchen.

Stony Creek Lodge LODGE $$
(Map p180; ☑ reservations 877-828-1440, 559-565-3388; www.sequoia-kingscanyon.com; 65569 Generals Hwy; r $179-199; ☉ mid-May–early Oct; 🛜) About halfway between Grant Grove Village and Giant Forest, this wood-and-stone lodge has a big river-rock fireplace in its lobby and almost a dozen aging motel rooms with telephones and TVs.

⭐ **Sequoia High Sierra Camp** CABIN $$$
(Map p180; ☑ 866-654-2877; www.sequoiahighsierracamp.com; tent cabin without bath incl all meals per adult/child $250/150; ☉ mid-Jun–mid-Sep) A mile's hike deep into the Sequoia National Forest, this off-the-grid, all-inclusive resort is nirvana for those who don't think luxury

camping is an oxymoron. Canvas bungalows are spiffed up with pillow-top mattresses, feather pillows and cozy wool rugs. Restrooms and a shower house are shared. Reservations required, and there's usually a two-night minimum stay.

🛏 Kings Canyon National Park

Camping

All park campgrounds are first-come, first-served. In the Sequoia National Forest, Hume Lake, Princess and Landslide campgrounds accept reservations (highly recommended in summer).

Campfires are allowed only in existing fire rings. When the risk of wildfires is high, all campfires may be prohibited.

GRANT GROVE

Sunset Campground CAMPGROUND $
(Map p180; Generals Hwy; tent & RV sites $18; ⊘ mid-May–early Sep; 🐾) Grant Grove's biggest campground has more than 150 shady sites set among evergreen trees. With ranger campfire programs in summer, it's a five-minute walk from the village.

Azalea Campground CAMPGROUND $
(Map p180; off Generals Hwy; tent & RV sites $18; ⊘ year-round; 🐾) Among stands of evergreens, the nicest of the 110 sites at this busy campground border a green meadow. It's a short walk downhill to the General Grant Grove.

Crystal Springs Campground CAMPGROUND $
(Map p180; off Generals Hwy; tent & RV sites $18; ⊘ mid-May–Sep; 🐾) At the smallest campground in the Grant Grove area, a few dozen wooded, well-spaced sites are generally very quiet.

KINGS CANYON SCENIC BYWAY

Developed USFS campgrounds in the Sequoia National Forest off Hwy 180 (Kings Canyon Scenic Byway) and Hume Lake Rd are open seasonally.

⭐**Hume Lake Campground** CAMPGROUND $
(Map p180; 🖉 reservations 877-444-6777, 518-885-3639; www.recreation.gov; Hume Lake Rd; tent & RV sites $24-26; ⊘ mid-May–mid-Sep; 🐾) Almost always full yet still managing a laid-back atmosphere, this campground offers almost 75 relatively uncrowded, shady campsites, a handful with lake views. It's on the lake's northern shore. Reservations highly recommended.

Princess Campground CAMPGROUND $
(Map p180; 🖉 reservations 877-444-6777, 518-885-3639; www.recreation.gov; Hwy 180; tent & RV sites $24-26; ⊘ late May-late Sep; 🐾) Just off the scenic byway and only a few miles from Hume Lake, here almost 90 reservable sites border a pretty meadow, with sequoia stumps at the registration area. It's especially popular with RVs. Reservations essential.

Landslide Campground CAMPGROUND $
(Map p180; 🖉 reservations 877-444-6777, 518-885-3639; www.recreation.gov; Hume Lake Rd; campsites $20, before mid-May or after late Sep free; ⊘ usually May-Nov) Primitive but spacious and woodsy sites are a few miles uphill from Hume Lake. Reservations recommended between mid-May and late September.

Tenmile Campground CAMPGROUND $
(Map p180; 🖉 reservations 877-444-6777, 518-885-3639; www.recreation.gov; Hume Lake Rd; campsites $20; ⊘ usually May-Nov) Bigger, forested campground another 1.5 miles uphill from Landslide Campground, with a seasonal camp host on-site. No water. Reservations may be available in peak summer season.

Convict Flat Campground CAMPGROUND $
(Map p180; Hwy 180; campsites free; ⊘ late Apr-mid-Nov) Five secluded, primitive sites near Yucca Point with tree-sheltered views of cliffs deep inside Kings Canyon. It's remote, so personal safety can be an issue. No water.

> ### ℹ PROTECTING WILDLIFE IN THE PARKS
>
> ➜ It probably won't come as a surprise that the parks don't let visitors climb giant sequoias. You also shouldn't walk too closely to them and trample their roots, which damages the trees.
>
> ➜ Never feed any wild animals, no matter how cute or tame that bird or squirrel seems – it's illegal, and food handouts teach wild animals to act aggressively towards humans. Wildlife also carry diseases, such as plague, that can infect humans.
>
> ➜ Use bear-proof storage lockers in developed areas. In day-use areas where they aren't provided, all food and scented items (eg trash, empty recyclables, toiletries, coolers) must be stored inside your vehicle's trunk.

CEDAR GROVE

Open seasonally, these campgrounds are spread out alongside the Kings River.

★**Sheep Creek Campground** CAMPGROUND $
(Map p180; Hwy 180; tent & RV sites $18; ☺mid-May–mid-Oct) Just a short walk west of the visitor center and village, Cedar Grove's second-biggest campground has shady waterfront loops that are especially popular with RVers. Don't expect much quiet at night, though.

Sentinel Campground CAMPGROUND $
(Map p180; Hwy 180; tent & RV sites $18; ☺late Apr–early Nov) It's Cedar Grove's busiest and most centrally located campground, near the visitor center and campfire ranger programs in summer. Premier riverside sites at the beginning of the first loop fill fastest.

Moraine Campground CAMPGROUND $
(Map p180; Hwy 180; tent & RV sites $18; ☺late May & early Jul–early Sep) About 120 well-spaced, but often sunny and exposed, sites open intermittently as overflow space is needed (eg summer weekends and holidays). Because it's further east of the village, you can often find a last-minute site here.

Lodging

GRANT GROVE

★**John Muir Lodge** LODGE $$
(Map p180; ☎559-335-5500, 866-807-3598; www.visitsequoia.com; off Hwy 180, Grant Grove

KINGS CANYON NATIONAL PARK CAMPGROUNDS

CAMPGROUND	LOCATION	DESCRIPTION	NO OF SITES	ELEVATION
Moraine (p190)	Cedar Grove	Large, well-spaced but only partly shaded; used as overflow	120	4600ft
Sentinel (p190)	Cedar Grove	Centrally located at Cedar Grove Village; fills up fast	83	4600ft
Sheep Creek (p190)	Cedar Grove	Pretty riverside loops; almost as crowded as Sentinel	111	4600ft
Azalea (p189)	Grant Grove	Shady forest sites near giant sequoia trees	110	6500ft
Crystal Springs (p189)	Grant Grove	Quieter campsites are wooded and well-spaced	36	6500ft
Sunset (p189)	Grant Grove	Huge evergreen-shaded forest campground near the village	157	6500ft
Hume Lake (p189)	Hume Lake	Lakeside campsites popular with families and anglers	74	5200ft
Landslide (p189)	Hume Lake	Primitive forested sites are fairly spacious	9	5800ft
Princess (p189)	Hume Lake	Meadow-edged sites off scenic byway, convenient for RVs	88	5900ft
Tenmile (p189)	Hume Lake	Bigger but still primitive woodsy campground	13	5800ft
Convict Flat (p189)	Kings Canyon Scenic Byway	Secluded primitive sites with tree-sheltered canyon views	5	3000ft

All of the above campgrounds have bear-proof boxes, picnic tables, fire pits and trash cans.

 Drinking Water

 Flush Toilets

Ranger Station Nearby

 Great for Families

Pay-phone

 RV Dump Station

Village; r from $170; 🕿) An atmospheric wooden building hung with historical black-and-white photographs, this year-round hotel is a place to lay your head and still feel like you're in the forest. Wide porches have wooden rocking chairs, and homespun rooms contain rough-hewn wood furniture and patchwork bedspreads. Cozy up to the big stone fireplace on chilly nights with a board game.

Grant Grove Cabins CABIN $$
(Map p180; 🖉 866-807-3598, 559-335-5500; www.visitsequoia.com; off Hwy 180, Grant Grove Village; cabins $70-145; ⊙ some cabins Apr-Oct only) Set amid towering sugar pines, cabins range from aging tent-top shacks to rustic camp cabins with electricity and outdoor wood-burning stoves to heated duplexes (a few are wheelchair-accessible) with private bathrooms and double beds. Number 9 is the lone hard-sided, free-standing 'Honeymoon Cabin' with a queen bed, and it books up fast.

CEDAR GROVE

Cedar Grove Lodge LODGE $$
(Map p180; 🖉 559-565-3096, 866-807-3598; www.visitsequoia.com; Hwy 180, Cedar Grove Village; r from $130; ⊙ early May–mid-Oct; ❋ 🛜) The only indoor sleeping option in the canyon, this riverside lodge offers 21 unexciting motel-style rooms. A recent remodel has banished some of the frumpy decor. Three ground-floor rooms with shady furnished patios have spiffy river views and kitchenettes. All rooms have phones and TVs.

OPEN (APPROX)	RESERVATION AVAILABLE?	DAILY FEE	FACILITIES/FEATURES
late May & early Jul– early Sep	no	$18	🚽 🚻 🧒 🐕 🏬 🍴 ♿
late Apr–early Nov	no	$18	🚽 🚻 🧒 👨‍👩‍👧 📞 🐕 🏬 🍴 ♿ 🔥
mid-May–mid-Oct	no	$18	🚽 🚻 🧒 🐕 🏬 🍴
year-round	no	$18	🚽 🚻 🧒 👨‍👩‍👧 📞 🐕 🏬 🍴 ♿
mid-May–Sep	no	$18	🚽 🚻 🧒 🐕 🏬 🍴
mid-May–early Sep	no	$18	🚽 🚻 🧒 👨‍👩‍👧 🐕 🏬 🍴 🔥
mid-May–mid-Sep	yes	$24–26	🚽 🚻 📞 🐕 🏬 🍴
May–Nov	yes (mid-May– late Sep)	$20	🚽 🐕
late May–late Sep	yes	$24–26	🚽 🏪 🐕
May–Nov	maybe	$20	🐕
late Apr–mid-Nov	no	free	🐕

🐕 Dogs Allowed (On Leash)   🏬 Grocery Store Nearby   🍴 Restaurant Nearby   ♿ Wheelchair Access   🔥 Summertime Campfire Program

✕ EATING & DRINKING

✕ Sequoia National Park

Lodgepole & Wuksachi Villages

Lodgepole Market Center　　MARKET, DELI $
(Map p180; ☑559-565-3301; www.visitsequoia.
com; Lodgepole Village; mains $5-10; ☺market
8am-9pm early May–mid-Sep, 9am-6pm mid-Apr–
early May & mid-Sep–mid-Oct, grill & deli hours vary
early May–mid-Sep) Inside is the park's biggest
general store, selling groceries, camping
supplies and snacks; a fast-food grill sling-
ing pizza, burgers and breakfast burritos;
and a tad healthier deli, making focaccia
sandwiches, wraps and salads.

Wolverton BBQ　　BUFFET $$
(Map p180; ☑559-565-4070; Wolverton Rd, off Gen-
erals Hwy; dinner adult/child $25/12.50; ☺from
5pm nightly late May–early Sep, weather permit-
ting; ☻) Buy tickets before 2pm at Wuksachi
Lodge, Lodgepole Market or Grant Grove
Market for this popular all-you-can-eat out-
door BBQ with all the fixin's, including ribs,
cornbread and homemade desserts. Tickets
include an evening living-history program
designed for families.

Peaks Restaurant　　AMERICAN $$
(Map p180; ☑559-565-4070; www.visitsequoia.
com; Wuksachi Lodge, 64740 Wuksachi Way, off
Generals Hwy; mains lunch $8-15, dinner $12-34;
☺dining room 7-10am, 11:30am-3pm & 5-9pm,
lounge 4-10pm, all shorter off-season hours; ☏☻)
The lodge's dining room has a breakfast buffet and soup-and-salad lunch fare, but dinners aim somewhat successfully to be more
gourmet, with mains like pan-seared trout
and seared venison. In the lounge, nosh on
appetizers like grilled flatbreads and swill
cocktails, beer and wine.

Mineral King

**Silver City Mountain Resort
Restaurant**　　AMERICAN $$
(Map p180; ☑559-561-3223; www.silvercityresort.
com; mains $10-20; ☺usually 8am-8pm Thu-Mon,
9am-5pm Tue-Wed late May–early Sep, shorter hours
early Sep–late Oct) This little country store
serves simple fare on wooden picnic tables.
On Tuesday and Wednesday, only thick slabs
of homemade pie ($5) and French press cof-
fee are served. It's 3.5 miles west of the ranger
station.

Generals Highway

Stony Creek Lodge Market　　MARKET $
(Map p180; ☑559-565-3909; www.sequoia-kings-
canyon.com; 65569 Generals Hwy; ☺8am-8pm
Sun-Thu, to 9pm Fri & Sat mid-May–early Oct) A
small market selling groceries and limited
camping supplies.

Stony Creek Lodge Restaurant　　AMERICAN $
(Map p180; ☑559-565-3909; www.sequoia-kings-
canyon.com; 65569 Generals Hwy; pizzas & mains
$8-20; ☺11am-7:30pm Sun-Thu, to 8:30pm Fri &
Sat mid-May–early Oct; ☻) The lodge's basic
restaurant serves decent pizzas and salads.

✕ Kings Canyon National Park

Grant Grove

Grant Grove Market　　MARKET $
(Map p180; Grant Grove Village, off Generals Hwy;
☺8am-9pm late May–early Sep, shorter hours
Apr–late May & early Sep–Oct) On the village's
north end, this good-size grocery store has
firewood, camping supplies and packaged
food, with a small selection of fruits and
veggies.

Grant Grove Restaurant　　AMERICAN $$
(Map p180; Grant Grove Village, off Generals Hwy;
mains $8-24; ☺7-10am, 11:30am-4pm & 5-9pm
late May-early Sep, shorter hours Apr–late May &
early Sep–Oct ; ☏☻) At the only place to
chow down in Grant Grove Village, the so-so
menu highlights seasonal dishes and locally grown ingredients, but doesn't leave out
comfort foods like freshly baked pie.

In summer, sip just-OK espresso from the
coffee cart outside.

Cedar Grove

Cedar Grove Market　　MARKET $
(Map p180; Cedar Grove Village, Hwy 180; ☺8am-
7pm mid-May–mid-Jun & mid-Sep–mid-Oct, 7am-
8pm mid-Jun–mid-Sep) This small market is the
hub of the village complex, hawking packaged
food and all the camping supplies you forgot
to pack.

Cedar Grove Snack Bar　　AMERICAN $
(Map p180; mains $6-15; ☺7:30-10:30am, 11:30am-
2:30pm & 5-8pm late May–mid-Oct; ☏☻) Adjacent to the market, a basic counter-service
grill dishes up hot meals and cold deli sand-

The Rae Lakes area (p169)

wiches. Dine outside on the riverside deck. In summer, BBQ gets smoked all afternoon long through dinnertime.

ⓘ Orientation

Most of the star attractions are off the Generals Hwy, the main road that starts in the Foothills area and continues north to Grant Grove, traversing both parks and parts of the Giant Sequoia National Monument in the Sequoia National Forest.

Visitor activity concentrates around the Giant Forest area and Lodgepole Village, which has the most tourist facilities. Just outside the gateway town of Three Rivers, south of Sequoia's Ash Mountain Entrance, the switchbacking road to remote Mineral King Valley veers east of Hwy 198.

Hwy 180 passes the Big Stump Entrance before reaching Grant Grove Village, which has tourist amenities. Continuing northeast, the Kings Canyon Scenic Byway winds through a section of the Giant Sequoia National Monument, then descends to Cedar Grove, where it dead ends at aptly named Roads End.

ⓘ Information

For 24-hour recorded information, including winter road conditions and closures, call ☏ 559-565-3341; the comprehensive park website is www.nps.gov/seki.

BOOKS & MAPS

Books and topographic recreational maps are sold at the Giant Forest Museum (p179) and all park visitor centers (Lodgepole has the biggest selection).

INTERNET ACCESS

No internet-access terminals are currently available. Look for free wi-fi in the lobby of Wuksachi Lodge (p188), near the lodging check-in desk in Grant Grove Village and at Stony Creek Lodge (p188) in the Sequoia National Forest.

LAUNDRY

Coin-op laundries are available seasonally at Lodgepole Village, Grant Grove Village and Stony Creek.

MONEY

Find ATMs at Lodgepole Village, Grant Grove Village, Cedar Grove Village and Stony Creek.

No foreign-currency exchange is available in the parks.

POST

Grant Grove Post Office (⊘ usually 9am-4pm Mon-Fri) Next to the village market.

SHOWERS

Pay showers are available seasonally at Lodgepole Village, Grant Grove Village, Cedar Grove

Village, Stony Creek Lodge and Silver City Mountain Resort.

TELEPHONE

Cell-phone coverage is practically nonexistent, except for limited reception at Grant Grove.

Pay phones are found in all village areas and at all visitor centers and some campgrounds; many accept only credit cards or prepaid phonecards.

TOURIST INFORMATION

Cedar Grove Visitor Center (☑ 559-565-3793; Hwy 180, Cedar Grove Village; ☺ 9am-5pm late May–late Sep) Small, seasonal visitor center in Cedar Grove Village selling books and maps.

Foothills Visitor Center (☑ 559-565-4212; 47050 Generals Hwy; ☺ 8am-4:30pm) One mile north of the Ash Mountain Entrance, this busy visitor center has a well-stocked bookstore that also sells maps. Buy Crystal Cave tour tickets here or at Lodgepole's larger visitor center.

Kings Canyon Visitor Center (☑ 559-565-4307; Hwy 180, Grant Grove Village; ☺ 8am-noon & 1-5pm late May–early Sep, shorter off-season hours) Just over 3 miles north of the Big Stump Entrance in Grant Grove Village, this busy visitor center has a very good selection of books and maps. Staff issue wilderness permits (usually until 30 minutes before closing).

Lodgepole Visitor Center (☑ 559-565-4436; off Generals Hwy, Lodgepole Village; ☺ 8am-5pm early May–early Oct, 7am-7pm peak season) Often less than helpful or informative, non-NPS staff sell books, maps and tickets for Crystal Cave tours. Rangers issue wilderness permits here.

Mineral King Ranger Station (☑ 559-565-3768; Mineral King Rd; ☺ 8am-4pm late May–late Sep) Almost 24 miles east of Three Rivers, this small, seasonal ranger station issues wilderness permits, rents bear canisters and sells a few books and maps.

Roads End Wilderness Permit Station (end of Hwy 180; ☺ usually 7am-3:45pm late May–late Sep) Dispenses wilderness permits, rents bear canisters and sells a few trail guides and maps. It's 6 miles east of Cedar Grove Village.

USFS Hume Lake District Office (☑ 559-338-2251; www.fs.fed.us/r5/sequoia; 35860 E Kings Canyon Rd (Hwy 180), Dunlap; ☺ 8am-4:30pm Mon-Fri) Before visiting the parks, stop here for recreation information, maps and campfire and wilderness permits for the Sequoia National Forest. The office is over 20 miles west of the Big Stump Entrance.

❶ Getting There & Around

Hitchhiking is legally allowed in the parks, as long as it's done safely. See p240 for more information.

BUS

During peak summer season, **Sequoia Shuttle** (☑ 877-287-4453; www.sequoiashuttle.com; round-trip incl park entry $15; ☺ late May–late Sep) run buses five times daily between Visalia, Three Rivers and the Giant Forest Museum in Sequoia National Park (two hours); advance reservations required. Also in summer, five daily buses with **Big Trees Transit** (☑ 800-325-7433; www.bigtreestransit.com; round-trip incl park entry fee $15; ☺ late May–early Sep) connect Fresno with Grant Grove in Kings Canyon National Park (2½ hours); reservations strongly advised. All shuttles are wheelchair-accessible and equipped with bicycle racks.

Inside Sequoia National Park, free, fast and convenient shuttle buses typically operate from late May until early September. Routes include:

Gray Route Giant Forest Museum to Moro Rock and Crescent Meadow; every 15 minutes.

Green Route General Sherman Tree parking areas and Lodgepole Village; every 15 minutes.

Orange Route General Sherman Tree parking areas and Wolverton Rd picnic area and trailhead; every 30 minutes.

Purple Route Lodgepole, Wuksachi Lodge and Dorst Campground; every 20 minutes.

Red Route Giant Forest Museum and Potwisha Campground in the Foothills area (a 45-minute ride); every two hours.

In Kings Canyon National Park, free shuttle buses make a loop around Grant Grove Village, stopping at the visitor center, campgrounds and General Grant Grove every 45 minutes. Shuttles usually operate from late May until early September.

Note there is no shuttle bus service to Cedar Grove in Kings Canyon or to Crystal Cave or Mineral King in Sequoia National Park.

CAR & MOTORCYCLE

For current road conditions, call ☑ 559-565-3341. Expect road delays and closures along the Generals Hwy during and after snowstorms. In winter, tire chains may be required at any time. The Kings Canyon Scenic Byway (Hwy 180) past Hume Lake to Cedar Grove is usually closed from mid-November through late April, while Sequoia's Mineral King Rd typically closes from late October through late May.

Gas is not available in either park, but is sold on USFS land year-round at Hume Lake and seasonally at Stony Creek from mid-May through mid-October.

Around Sequoia & Kings Canyon National Parks

Best Places to Sleep

➜ Spalding House (p196)

➜ Buckeye Tree Lodge (p198)

➜ Sequoia Village Inn (p198)

Best Places to Eat

➜ Char-Cu-Te-Rie (p196)

➜ Brewbaker's Brewing Company (p196)

Why Go?

Entering the parks from the south, Hwy 198 passes through the small city of Visalia and the tiny gateway town of Three Rivers, which borders Sequoia National Park. Visalia is the last sizable city on your drive up to the park's Foothills area, while Three Rivers, named for the nearby convergence of three forks of the Kaweah River, is a friendly small town populated mostly by long-term locals, retirees and a few artsy newcomers.

To the north, Hwy 180 accesses Kings Canyon, but no sizable towns are located along the way from Fresno, the Central Valley's biggest city.

Road Distances (miles)

	Lodgepole Village	Three Rivers	Mineral King	Grant Grove Village
Three Rivers	25			
Mineral King	50	30		
Grant Grove Village	25	55	75	
Visalia	55	30	60	55

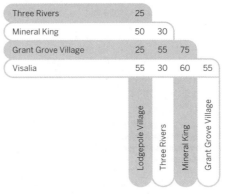

Note: Distances are approximate

Visalia

In the middle of the hotter-than-hell Central Valley and with a population of 130,000, Visalia is the main southern gateway to the parks. Its old-fashioned downtown is walkable, although blistering summer heat will have you scouting for shade. Hwy 198 runs just south of the middle of town; Main St is the major east–west commercial strip.

🛏 Sleeping

Budget and midrange motels and hotels line Hwy 198 and are scattered around downtown.

Lamp Liter Motel MOTEL $

(☑ 800-662-6692, 559-732-4511; http://lamp liter.net; 3300 W Mineral King Ave; r $75-125; ✳@☎☀⚠) It could be a run-of-the-mill two-story courtyard motel, but this family-owned establishment surprises with its spotlessly clean, if dated, rooms and country cottages facing an outdoor pool. The Sequoia Shuttle stops here.

Spalding House B&B $

(☑ 559-739-7877; www.thespaldinghouse.com; 631 N Encina St; s/d incl breakfast $85/95; ✳☎) Built by a lumber baron, this atmospheric 1901 Colonial Revival–style home offers three cozy guest suites with private sitting areas and gorgeous details such as mosaic-tiled bathrooms, a stained-glass ceiling or a sleigh bed.

🍴 Eating & Drinking

Downtown is chockablock with cafes, restaurants, bars, taquerias and take-out shops.

Char-Cu-Te-Rie CAFE $

(☑ 559-733-7902; http://char-cu-te-rie.com; 211 W Main St; mains $6-9; ⊙7am-4pm Mon-Fri, from 9am Sat & Sun) Truffled eggs on brioche French toast, sourdough sandwiches spread with goat cheese and sweet figs, maple-bacon popcorn, date and Nutella ice-cream shakes and artisan coffee are just a few of the treats at this downtown storefront. Kitchen closes at 3:30pm.

Brewbaker's Brewing Company AMERICAN $

(☑ 559-627-2739; http://brewbakersbrewingco. com; 219 E Main St; mains $8-18; ⊙11:30am-10pm; ☎) Always jam-packed, Brewbakers beckons thirsty hikers with house-made sodas and craft beers like Sequoia Red. A huge menu of burgers, pizzas, pastas and salads promises more than it delivers. Expect to wait, and then wait some more.

Visalia Farmers Market – Downtown MARKET $

(www.visaliafarmersmarket.com; cnr E Main & N Church Sts; ⊙5-8pm Thu mid-Mar–Sep; ⚠) Fresh fruits and veggies sold downtown.

Visalia Farmers Market – Sequoia Mall MARKET $

(www.visaliafarmersmarket.com; cnr S Mooney Blvd & W Caldwell Ave; ⊙8am-11:30am Sat; ⚠) Year-

---

UTOPIAN DREAMS: THE KAWEAH CO-OPERATIVE COMMONWEALTH

A few years before Sequoia National Park was created, an idealistic organization of union workers, skilled craftspeople and social progressives settled in the foothills around Three Rivers. The radical group planned a utopian community based on cooperative assets and collective land ownership. In 1886 they applied for inexpensive land grants and got to work setting up a logging business in the Giant Forest.

As the socialist colony toiled to build a logging road, local citizens grew concerned about their unusually large claims. At the time, it wasn't uncommon for railroads and other corporations to fraudulently purchase huge tracts of land, quietly expanding their monopolies. George Stewart, the editor of the Visalia *Delta* newspaper led a campaign for Congress to protect the giant sequoias, and spurred an inquiry into colonists' land claims. Ironically, the Kaweah Colony was suspected of the very capitalist motives it abhorred.

By the summer of 1890, the colony finished a rough road to the edge of the mature sequoia groves and logging began. But within months, Sequoia National Park was created, shielding the sequoias from being cut down, which became the colony's undoing. Their settlement sat squarely inside the national park, so their claims and sweat equity became worthless.

A few relics remain from the colony's heyday, including the Kaweah Post Office, north of Three Rivers town. In Sequoia National Park, the Squatters Cabin at Crescent Meadow is another legacy of the former community.

round market, rain or shine, held in the Sears parking lot.

Sequoia Brewing Company   MICROBREWERY
([☑]559-627-2537; http://sequoiabrewing.com; 124 W Main St; ⊙11am-10pm Mon-Thu, to 11pm Fri & Sat, to 9pm Sun) Downtown's sports-themed brewpub names its beers in honor of local landmarks: down a cold pint of General Sherman IPA or General Grant ESB.

☆ Entertainment

Visalia Fox Theatre   CINEMA, LIVE MUSIC
([☑]559-625-1369; www.foxvisalia.org; 300 W Main St; tickets $13-100) A 1930s 'talkie' movie palace, the Fox has a stunning East Indian temple–themed interior and occasionally hosts film screenings, live music concerts, stand-up comedy and special events.

🛍 Shopping

Big 5 Sporting Goods   OUTDOOR EQUIPMENT
([☑]559-625-5934; www.big5sportinggoods.com; 1430 S Mooney Blvd; ⊙10am-9pm Mon-Fri, 9am-9pm Sat, 9:30am-8pm Sun) Stock up on camping, fishing and outdoor-sports equipment here, less than a mile south of Hwy 198.

ℹ Information

Kaweah Delta Medical Center ([☑]559-624-2000; www.kaweahdelta.org; 400 W Mineral King Ave; ⊙24hr) 24-hour emergency room.

Tulare County Library (www.tularecounty library.org; 200 W Oak Ave; ⊙9am-8pm Tue-Thu, noon-6pm Fri, 9am-5pm Sat) Free public internet access.

Visalia Convention & Visitor's Bureau ([☑]800-524-0303, 559-334-0141; www. visitvisalia.org; 303 E Acequia Ave; ⊙8am-5pm Mon-Fri) Maps and brochures for touring Visalia and the Central Valley.

ℹ Getting There & Away

Amtrak ([☑]800-872-7245; www.amtrak.com) For Amtrak passengers, connecting Thruway buses run between Visalia's Transit Center and Hanford's train station (30 to 40 minutes away) by reservation only. From Hanford, Amtrak routes connecting to destinations state-wide include the *San Joaquin*, which travels north to Sacramento ($32, four hours) via Fresno ($5, 35 minutes) and Merced (($17, 1½ hours), for bus connections to Yosemite Valley.

Sequoia Shuttle ([☑]877-287-4453; www. sequoiashuttle.com; round-trip incl park entry free $15; ⊙late May-late Sep) Five daily wheelchair-accessible buses equipped with bicycle racks make the two-hour run between Visalia's

Transit Center, Three Rivers town and the Giant Forest Museum in Sequoia National Park. Advance reservations required; pick-ups available from some motels and hotels.

Visalia Transit Center (www.ci.visalia.ca.us; 425 E Oak Ave) Local buses (regular fare $1.50), downtown's Towne Trolley (25¢) and the Sequoia Shuttle all stop here.

Three Rivers

Just southwest of Sequoia National Park, tiny Three Rivers has a population of only 2182. Its main drag, Sierra Dr (Hwy 198), is sparsely lined with motels, eateries and shops.

◉ Sights & Activities

Kaweah Post Office   LANDMARK
(43795 North Fork Dr; ⊙1-2pm Mon-Fri) Founded by the utopian Kaweah Co-operative Colony (see the boxed text opposite), it's one of the USA's smallest and oldest still-operating post offices, now staffed by volunteers. Look for the rustic wooden building about 2.7 miles north of Hwy 198.

Three Rivers Historical Museum   MUSEUM
(Map p180; [☑]559-561-2707; www.3rmuseum.org; 42268 Sierra Dr; ⊙9am-3pm Oct-Mar, to 5pm Apr-Sep) FREE Holds a small collection of local ranching, mining and domestic artifacts, as well as an archive of historical photographs and newspaper clippings.

Lake Kaweah   SWIMMING, FISHING
(Map p180; [☑]559-597-2526; http://kaweah marina.com; 34467 Sierra Dr, Lemon Cove) Want to slough off the heat in summertime? Just west of Three Rivers, Slick Rock Recreation Area has pools amid big boulders that make for cool swimming spots. When water levels are high enough, rent boats (from $20) and paddle boards (from $15) at the marina, which also sells fishing tackle and has a snack bar.

🛏 Sleeping

Lodgings in Three Rivers are modest and may not have phones or TVs; a two-night minimum stay is often required on summer weekends. In-town RV parks may let you pitch a tent, sometimes right on the river.

Horse Creek Campground   CAMPGROUND $
(Map p180; [☑]info 559-597-2301, reservations 518-885-3639, reservations 877-444-6777; www. reserveamerica.com; Hwy 198, Lemon Cove; tent &

RV sites $20-25) At Lake Kaweah, about 3 miles east of the dam, this developed family campground has all the amenities, including hot showers, flush toilets and an RV dump station. In late spring and early summer, flooding may close all or some of the campsites.

Buckeye Tree Lodge   MOTEL $$
(Map p180; 559-561-5900; www.buckeyetreelodge.com; 46000 Sierra Dr; d incl breakfast $119-159; ❋ ❐ ❄ ❄) ✔ Sit out on your grassy back patio or perch on the balcony and watch the river ease through a maze of boulders. Cheerful motel rooms, one with a kitchenette, feel airy and bright. The outdoor picnic area has BBQ grills.

Sequoia Village Inn   CABIN, COTTAGE $$
(Map p180; 559-561-3652; www.sequoiavillageinn.com; 45971 Sierra Dr; d $109-319; ❋ ❐ ❄ ❄) These 10 cottages, cabins and chalets (most with kitchens and the rest with kitchenettes) border the park and are great for families or groups. Most have outdoor woodsy decks and BBQs; the largest can sleep 12 people.

Rio Sierra Riverhouse   INN $$
(Map p180; 559-561-4720; www.rio-sierra.com; 41997 Sierra Dr; d $170-275; ❄ Feb-Dec; ❋ ❄) Right on the river beach in the middle of town, this cottage-style inn rents four suites, each with a TV/DVD player, telephone, minifridge and microwave. For more privacy, rent the tree-shaded RV out back with a BBQ grill and a campfire ring.

🍴 Eating & Drinking

Sierra Subs & Salads   SANDWICHES $
(559-561-4810; www.sierrasubsandsalads.com; 41717 Sierra Dr; mains $6-9; ❄ 10:30am-6pm Tue-Sat, to 5pm Sun) Friendly roadside sandwich shop with a riverside back deck giving you a choice of fresh breads along with healthy wraps, salads, fruit smoothies and cheesy quesadillas.

Ol' Buckaroo   AMERICAN $
(559-799-3665; http://theolbuckaroo.com; 41695 Sierra Dr; mains $8-15; ❄ brunch 8:30am-2:30pm Sat & Sun, dinner 5-9pm Mon, Thu & Sun, to 10pm Fri & Sat) Line up outside this food truck early on weekends for cheddar waffles with fried chicken, or stop by after dark, when strings of lights cast a glow over riverside picnic tables, for burgers, sliders and grilled cheese with crispy sweet-potato fries.

Antoinette's Coffee & Goodies   CAFE $
(559-561-2253; www.antoinettescoffeeandgoodies.com; 41727 Sierra Dr; items $2-6; ❄ 5:30am-1pm Mon & Wed-Fri, 7am-3pm Sat & Sun; ❄) Relax on the garden deck, sip coffee made from locally roasted beans, hot chai tea or fresh-squeezed juices, and bite into baked goods and bagel sandwiches.

Three Rivers Village Market   SUPERMARKET $
(40869 Sierra Dr; ❄ 10:30am-6pm Tue-Sat, 10:30am-5pm Sun) Small supermarket selling campfire food supplies, snacks, drinks and take-out deli picnic salads, sandwiches and BBQ.

River View Restaurant & Lounge   BAR
(559-561-2211; 42323 Sierra Dr; ❄ 11am-9pm, to 10pm Fri & Sat, bar until midnight or later) Riverview honky-tonk that has live music some nights. The food is mediocre and overpriced, but the raucous bar stays busy.

🛍 Shopping

Three Rivers Mercantile   OUTDOOR EQUIPMENT
(559-565-2378; 41152 Sierra Dr; ❄ 8am-5pm Mon-Fri) Local hardware store near the fire station carrying limited camping and outdoor gear. It sells vehicle tarps and rope, which are essential for marmot-proofing your car in Sequoia National Park's Mineral King Valley (see the boxed text, p182).

ℹ Information

Pick up a copy of the Kaweah Commonwealth (www.kaweahcommonwealth.com) weekly newspaper for local information and area history. It prides itself as 'a journal for those who labor and who think.'

Sierra Foothills Chamber of Commerce (559-561-3300, 877-530-3300; www.threerivers.com; 42268 Sierra Dr; ❄ 9am-5pm May-Sep, off-season hours vary; ❄) Shares space with the town museum, and has tourist maps and information.

Tulare County Library (www.tularecountylibrary.org; 42052 Eggers Dr, off Hwy 198; ❄ noon-5pm & 6-8pm Tue & Thu, 10am-1pm & 2-6pm Wed & Fri, 10am-1pm & 2-5pm Sat) Free public internet access.

ℹ Getting There & Away

Sequoia Shuttle (p237) runs five daily round-trip buses between Visalia and the Giant Forest Museum in Sequoia National Park, stopping at Three Rivers' historical museum and the Comfort Inn motel; advance reservations required.

Understand Yosemite, Sequoia & Kings Canyon National Parks

The Parks Today

California's extended drought has stressed natural resources and altered the rhythm of the seasons in an unprecedented way. Without a robust snowpack, the Sierra Nevada has experienced extraordinary conditions that have left forests vulnerable to fire, and caused wildlife to alter their habitat. Yosemite has made progress on plans to restore its river corridors and forests, kicking off major projects to preserve Mariposa Grove and the Merced and Tuolumne river areas.

Best in Print

Off the Wall: Death in Yosemite (Michael Ghiglieri and Butch Farabee; 2007) A cautionary compendium of fatalities and daring search and rescue operations.

The Wild Muir: Twenty-Two of John Muir's Greatest Adventures (2013) An essential collection of Muir's writings on Yosemite and the Sierra.

An Uncertain Path: A Search for the Future of National Parks (Bill Tweed; 2010) A retired Sequoia park planner hikes and ponders park management in an era of climate change.

A Way Across the Mountain: Joseph Walker's 1833 Trans-Sierran Passage and the Myth of Yosemite's Discovery (Scott Stine; 2015) A reevaluation of how white explorers first encountered Yosemite.

Best on Film

Valley Uprising (2014) Fast-paced documentary on Yosemite's Camp 4 rock-climbing revolution.

The National Parks: America's Best Idea (2009) Documentary series on US park history.

Star Trek V: The Final Frontier (1989) Captain Kirk does El Capitan.

Yosemite (2015) Meditative coming-of-age film with park scenes, starring James Franco.

Parched Parks

The 2013 Rim Fire scorched 402 sq miles of the Stanislaus National Forest and the northwestern periphery of Yosemite. The largest recorded wildfire in the Sierra Nevada (and the third largest in California history), many viewed its rapid acceleration as an unsettling portent. If severe climate change became the new normal for California, would drought convert its forests to kindling stockpiles?

Other shifts reinforce these concerns. Small, upper-elevation mammals such as the beloved little pika (a tiny relative of the rabbit) have moved to higher, previously uninhabitable elevations and abandoned their lower stomping grounds. Remaining glaciers such as the Lyell Glacier are rapidly receding as temperatures rise. In 2013 scientists determined that it had thinned to the extent that it had become stagnant, a clear indicator of climate change.

Visitors are more likely to notice something's amiss when ski resorts are grassy in mid-winter and waterfalls turn off the taps in early spring. In 2015 Yosemite's April snowpack was measured to be a mere 7% of its historical average and the Mariposa Grove road hadn't closed in winter for four years.

Rivers & Resources

The parks continue to dance the tricky footwork of facilitating preservation while accommodating high levels of tourism. After considerable public comment – and an equal amount of litigation – Yosemite has begun to carry out comprehensive management plans along the Tuolumne and Merced River corridors. Tuolumne Meadows will see the curtailment of its development footprint, with the closure of the gas station and stables, as well as a reconfiguration of parking areas and the restoration of native riparian habitat and vegetation. In the Valley, which teeters on the edge of being loved to pieces, the comprehensive Merced plan will spearhead riverbank restoration coupled with improved traffic patterns and additional campsite capacity.

A two-year restoration project to remove development in Mariposa Grove kicked off in 2015, revitalizing the long-term health of the stately trees and the awesome experience of visiting them. With a pared down parking area and the introduction of new shuttle system from the South Entrance, visitors will be shepherded to the grove via public transportation and new trails. Yosemite also trialed free shuttle services along Glacier Point Rd and between the Valley and Tuolumne Meadows during summer 2015, and many hope that these traffic-thwarting routes will continue when the new park concessionaire takes over in 2016.

Responsible Use

A pressing issue is the perpetual conversation about the parks' duty to warn visitors about dangers in the natural world and the responsibility that people must take for their actions. Near drownings and slip-and-fall injuries are commonplace along waterways in both parks. There have been so many injuries from hikers rock hopping or scrambling off-trail at Yosemite Falls that the park posted a warning sign illustrated by an x-ray of broken bones. And with the popularity of personal locator beacons, an increasing number of people are counting on search and rescue teams to extricate them in the case of emergency – or sometimes mere inconvenience. Connectivity is no substitute for knowing one's abilities and using good judgment.

Backcountry use continues to rise steadily throughout the Sierra Nevada, highlighting the importance of minimizing human impact and practicing Leave No Trace principles. There are time-tested reasons for all the regulations. Campfire and stove restrictions prevent accidental blazes. Wilderness permits regulate overuse of popular trails and campsites. Bear canisters protect bears from habituating and being destroyed. And no one wants to accidentally discover what someone else saw fit to leave behind: pack out your trash and toilet paper and keep the wilderness pristine for generations to come.

Looking Ahead

The year 2016 marks the centennial of the National Parks Service (NPS), a time of reflection, assessment and celebration for the nation's 400-plus national parks and monuments. As clichéd as it sounds, the future of the parks lies in public hands – the more time you spend up here, the more obvious that becomes.

AREA: **YOSEMITE 1169 SQ M, SEQUOIA & KINGS CANYON 1353 SQ M**

MILES OF TRAILS: **YOSEMITE 800, SEQUOIA & KINGS CANYON 826**

ANNUAL VISITATION (2014): **YOSEMITE 3.9 MILLION, SEQUOIA & KINGS CANYON 1.5 MILLION**

if 100 people visited Yosemite, where they would enter

33 South Entrance
27 Arch Rock
24 Big Oak Flat
15 Tioga Pass
1 Hetch Hetchy

seasonal visitation – Yosemite
(% of annual visitors)

46 summer
24 fall
20 spring
10 winter

visitors per sq m

YOSEMITE   SEQUOIA   KINGS CANYON

≈ 695 people

History

History unfolds here at varying rates of speed: the timelessness of the physical land-scape; the presence of its first people, Native American tribes who still call the Sierra Nevada home; the decomposing ghost towns left behind by California's early settlers and miners; and the record-setting feats of modern rock climbers and mountaineers have all left their mark. The names you'll encounter as you explore – Tenaya, Ahwahnee, Whitney, Olmsted, Degnan, Muir, Adams – tell the story of the parks' human past.

Native Americans

Archeologists believe indigenous peoples were living in the Sierra Nevada – and Yosemite Valley, with its abundance of natural resources – for several thousand years before Spanish explorers and, later, American pioneers first arrived.

Most Sierra Nevada tribes migrated with the seasons, and though they established warm-weather hunting sites in the High Sierra, they generally kept to lower elevations. Heavy snow cover on the range's western slopes discouraged year-round habitation above 5000ft, but the oak forests of the lower western foothills and piñon-juniper forests on the eastern escarpments were hospitable year-round.

Both sides of the mountain range were occupied by distinct linguistic groups. The western slopes of today's Yosemite region were home to the Sierra Miwok. To the south, the Western Mono (or Monache) and the

THE AHWAHNEECHEE

The Sierra Miwok referred to Yosemite Valley as Ahwahnee (or Awahni), meaning 'place of the gaping mouth,' describing its shape. Tribespeople who lived in the valley were thus known as the Ahwahneechee. Before the arrival of foreigners, a fatal illness decimated their numbers, and the survivors dispersed to join other tribes. By the mid-19th century, Chief Tenaya, an Ahwahneechee chief born and raised with the Mono Lake Paiute in the Eastern Sierra, had gathered together other Ahwahneechee descendants and reestablished his people's ancestral home in Yosemite Valley.

TIMELINE	AD 1400	1848	1851
	The Ahwahneechee ('people of the gaping mouth'), a subtribe of the Sierra Miwok, settle in Yosemite Valley and become its first known permanent residents.	Mexico cedes California to the US under the Treaty of Guadalupe Hidalgo; gold is discovered at Sutter's Mill, starting California's epic gold rush.	Members of the Mariposa Battalion, led by James Savage in paramilitary pursuit of Native Americans, become the first white men to enter Yosemite Valley.

BUFFALO SOLDIERS
....

Beginning in 1899, US Army infantry and cavalry troops drawn from well-respected, though segregated, African American regiments of 'Buffalo Soldiers' were sent to patrol the Sierra Nevada's new national parks. In Sequoia National Park and what was then General Grant National Park, the troops built roads, created a trail system and set a high precedent as stewards of the land. These first park rangers were commanded by Captain (later Colonel) Charles Young, who at the time was the army's only African American captain. In 1903 he became the first African American acting superintendent of a US national park.

Tubatulabal inhabited the western slopes of what is now Sequoia and Kings Canyon National Parks, with the Yokut residing in the lowest-elevation foothills and across the Central Valley. Meanwhile, the Eastern Sierra was home to the Paiute.

While most tribal groups traveled only when hunting and gathering or migrating, trading and warring parties regularly crossed the Sierra on foot to exchange goods and fight battles. Obsidian and pine nuts from the Eastern Sierra were in great demand by western slope and coastal peoples, who traded them for acorns and seashells. Early Euro-American explorers making their way over the Sierra often followed these ancient trade routes – as do hikers and backpackers today.

Early Explorers

As early as the 18th century, Spanish explorers described a great *sierra nevada* – a snow-covered mountain range – glimpsed from the San Joaquin Valley. In 1805 a Spanish military expedition stumbled across a great canyon in the southern Sierra and named the river El Río de los Santos Reyes, having discovered it on the Christian Feast of Epiphany.

Even before California became a US state in 1850, American trappers and explorers started arriving from the east. Trailblazer Jedediah Smith become the first European to cross the Sierra Nevada in 1827. In 1833 frontiersman Joseph Walker led the first party of American emigrants across the range. Even if he was indeed the first nonindigenous person to gaze down into Yosemite Valley, he was probably too exhausted to appreciate the extraordinary sight.

Over the next decade, rumors of rich farmlands in Alta California (a province of Mexico) reached migrants on the Oregon Trail. Several immigrant groups made the difficult trans-Sierra trek, which inevitably ended at the region's only pioneer settlement: Sutter's Fort, a nascent utopian community on the Sacramento River founded by Swiss immigrant John Sutter.

Historical Sights
....

Yosemite Museum & Indian Village of the Ahwahnee, Yosemite Valley
....

Pioneer Yosemite History Center, Wawona
....

Mineral King, Sequoia National Park
....

Bodie State Historic Park

1853	1858	1864	1868
Chief Tenaya, the last chief of the Ahwahneechee, is killed under still-mysterious circumstances, and the last of his people disperse from Yosemite Valley.	Homesteader Hale Tharp becomes the first white man to enter the grove of giant sequoias that would later be named the Giant Forest in Sequoia National Park.	President Lincoln signs the Yosemite Grant, establishing the Yosemite Valley and Mariposa Grove as a state park, the first such park in the world.	Hired to watch over a flock of sheep and its wayward herder, naturalist John Muir makes his first visit to the Sierra Nevada mountains and Yosemite Valley.

Gold Rush & the Mariposa Battalion

In February 1848, during construction of John Sutter's sawmill in the Sierra Nevada foothills, foreman James Marshall found flecks of gold in the water. News of Marshall's discovery immediately spread around the world. As many as 200,000 people poured into the Sierra Nevada over the next decade alone. The newly minted state of California sanctioned the creation of militias to settle any conflicts the new arrivals had with indigenous inhabitants.

During the gold rush, prospector James Savage began mining on the Merced River. After clashes with local tribes culminated in the burning of his trading post, Savage sought revenge by forming a militia called the Mariposa Battalion. When Savage learned that the raiding tribespeople might belong to a holdout group of Sierra Miwok from a valley upriver, the militia hastily marched to root them out.

On March 27, 1851, after a brief encounter with Ahwahneechee Chief Tenaya, the battalion entered Yosemite Valley. Determined to drive out the valley's indigenous inhabitants, it burned Native American camps and provisions, but failed to find many tribespeople on their first expedition. (A young recruit named Lafayette Bunnell gave the valley the name Yosemite, a corruption of the Miwok word Oo-soo'-ma-te, meaning 'grizzly bear.')

The cruel Mariposa Battalion made several forays into the Yosemite region that spring, forcing Tenaya and most of his people from their Yosemite Valley home to a reservation near Fresno. The following winter, the chief and some of his people were allowed to return to Yosemite. But hostilities continued and in circumstances that are still debated, Chief Tenaya was killed in Yosemite Valley, allegedly by Mono Lake Paiute tribespeople angered by the theft of some horses.

> Written while exploring with Josiah Whitney and the California Geological Survey between 1860 and 1864, botanist William Brewer's entertaining journal *Up and Down California* makes scaling a mountain sound like a Sunday picnic.

The Secret Is Out!

Tales of cascading waterfalls and towering stone columns followed the Mariposa Battalion out of Yosemite and soon raised public awareness. In 1855 an entrepreneurial Englishman named James Hutchings led the first tourist party into Yosemite Valley. Another visitor that same summer was Galen Clark, who returned the following year to establish a homestead near the Mariposa Grove of giant sequoias, where he lived for several decades. Clark took on the role of Yosemite guardian, a title that became official when the park became public land in 1864.

As word got around, entrepreneurs and homesteaders began arriving to divvy up the real estate of Yosemite Valley, creating ramshackle residences and roads, cutting down forests and planting the meadows with gardens and orchards. They brought in livestock, and started running sheep into high mountain meadows where trampling hooves destroyed wildflowers and delicate grasses.

> Pick up the historical novel *Gloryland* by Yosemite ranger Shelton Johnson, a well-known historian of the African American 'Buffalo Soldiers' who served as the Sierra Nevada's first national park rangers.

1890	1892	1899	1900
In late September, President Harrison authorizes the creation of Sequoia National Park; one week later, Congress passes the Yosemite Act, establishing Yosemite National Park.	The Sierra Club is founded with 182 charter members, and John Muir is elected its first president; its first task is to defeat proposed reductions in Yosemite's boundaries.	David and Jennie Curry establish Camp Curry, offering home-cooked meals and board in military-style canvas tents for just $2 – half of Yosemite Valley's going hotel rate.	The first automobile sputters into Yosemite Valley, but a ban on cars inside the park is immediately established by park rangers, citing vehicular disturbance to livestock and tourists.

Despite a flurry of silver-mining claims that were filed in the optimistically named Mineral King Valley of present-day Sequoia National Park, the area failed to turn up much of value. Instead, it was ranching that brought the first homesteader, Hale Tharp, to the southern Sierra. In 1858, led by a Native American guide, Tharp became the first nonindigenous man to enter the Giant Forest, where he famously fashioned a cabin inside a fallen giant sequoia tree.

On the Road to Protection

In 1860 Thomas Starr King, a Unitarian minister, orator and respected nature writer, helped rescue Yosemite from runaway commercialism. King wrote a series of widely read letters to the *Boston Evening Transcript* describing his trip. Shortly after the publication of King's letters, an exhibition opened in New York featuring photographs of Yosemite by Carleton E Watkins. The exhibition was a critical success, and Watkins' work caught the attention of California Senator John Conness.

Meanwhile, Frederick Law Olmsted, the landscape architect who designed New York's Central Park, brought his ideals to bear on Yosemite. He believed government should play a role in preserving natural spaces that nourished the human spirit. Olmsted met with San Francisco businessman Israel Ward Raymond, who had become concerned about the fate of Yosemite's giant sequoias.

In 1864 Raymond wrote a letter to Senator Conness, proposing a bill that would grant Yosemite Valley and the Mariposa Grove to the state of California. Conness presented the bill to Congress, and on June 30, 1864, in the midst of the Civil War, President Abraham Lincoln signed the Yosemite Grant into law. This marked the first time the US federal government had ever mandated the preservation and protection of a natural area for public use, making Yosemite the first state park.

Josiah Whitney & John Muir

As the gold rush waned, in 1860 the newly appointed California State geologist, Josiah Whitney, assembled a crew of scientists, surveyors and cartographers to map out the state's natural resources. Officially the California Geological Survey, Whitney's team explored Yosemite in 1863, and the Kings Canyon and Mt Whitney regions the following year. During their expeditions, they surveyed and named lakes, passes and peaks, including after themselves – Mt Dana in Yosemite National Park and Mt Whitney in Sequoia National Park, for example.

As Whitney's survey cobbled together its theories on Yosemite's formation, a naturalist named John Muir, who first visited Yosemite Valley in 1869, began to put forth his own ideas. Muir attributed the Valley's formation to glaciers, a theory Whitney himself vehemently shot down, but that would later prove correct. Meanwhile, the Scottish-born Muir,

The Sierra Club's online John Muir Exhibit (http://vault.sierraclub.org/john_muir_exhibit) is a storehouse of everything Muir, featuring the author's complete books, as well as historical photos, essays and documentaries.

To immerse yourself in the yesteryear world of the Sierra Nevada, you can do no better than to dive into John Muir's many books and collections of essays, including *My First Summer in the Sierra* (1911) and *The Yosemite* (1912).

1903	1916	1923	1927
Led by Colonel Charles Young, a regiment of 'Buffalo Soldiers,' the African American cavalry and infantry regiments of the US Army, arrive for duty in Sequoia National Park.	Congress authorizes establishment of the National Park Service (NPS), and Stephen T Mather becomes its first director; Tioga Rd and John Muir Trail under construction.	Construction of O'Shaughnessy Dam finished, costing $100 million and 68 lives, damming the Tuolumne River and flooding Hetch Hetchy Valley, which John Muir likened to a holy temple.	Yosemite's luxurious Ahwahnee Hotel, which was dreamed up to promote tourism by NPS director Stephen Mather, opens on the site of a former Native American tribal village.

a prolific writer and indefatigable advocate for conservation, would become Yosemite's most adamant and successful defender.

Campaigning for National Parks

Thousands of pages of digital books fill the Yosemite Online Library (www.yosemite.ca.us/library), including century-old newspaper articles and the complete text of books by John Muir, Galen Clark and others.

In 1889 John Muir took Robert Underwood Johnson, publisher of the national magazine *Century*, on a camping trip to Tuolumne Meadows. Under the stars, the two men hammered out a plan to save the area from 'hoofed locusts' (what Muir infamously called sheep) and commercial interests. Their plan drew upon the precedent set by Yellowstone, established as the country's first national park in 1872. Muir agreed to write some articles promoting the concept, which were published in *Century* the following summer, while Johnson exercised his considerable political influence in Washington DC.

Around the same time, the giant sequoia groves south of Yosemite were falling at an alarming rate beneath the saws of lumber companies acquiring enormous tracts of old-growth forest through government loopholes. Visionary Visalia newspaper editor George Stewart began pushing for federal protection of a sequoia grove that Muir had baptized the Giant Forest. Muir, Johnson and others quickly joined Stewart's fight.

On September 25, 1890, President Benjamin Harrison signed a bill into law that protected the Giant Forest, thus creating Sequoia National Park, California's first national park. A week later, Congress passed the Yosemite Act, creating Yosemite National Park (although Yosemite Valley and Mariposa Grove remained under state control) *and* General Grant National Park, which encompassed Grant Grove and would later be incorporated into Kings Canyon National Park. In 1906, after lobbying by John Muir and the Sierra Club that he had co-founded, California finally ceded Yosemite Valley and the Mariposa Grove to Yosemite National Park.

Growing Pains & Pleasures

Part history and part adventure tale, Clarence King's *Mountaineering in the Sierra Nevada* (1872) is a dramatic account of his exploits in the Sierra Nevada and a gripping read to boot.

Hotels came and went in Yosemite Valley's early years. Hastily erected of wood and canvas to house the ever-increasing hordes of tourists, many of the early hotels burned down when sparks escaped from stoves or lanterns got too close to curtains. Tourism started off more slowly in Sequoia National Park, where in 1898 a horse-and-mule packing service started bringing visitors to Giant Forest, housing them in a simple tent hotel.

In 1899, when a night in Yosemite's popular Sentinel Hotel cost $4, David and Jennie Curry established a tourist camp at the base of Glacier Point in Yosemite Valley. At Camp Curry, campers were provided with a bed in a large canvas tent, shared bath facilities and home-cooked meals for a mere $2 a day. What's more, Camp Curry offered an evening program of music, stunts, nature talks and views of the nightly 'firefall.'

The first automobile sputtered into Yosemite Valley in the summer of 1900, but cars were quickly prohibited from the park on the grounds that

1935	1940	1978	1984
After years of work, the Generals Hwy is extended from the Giant Forest to General Grant National Park; it's immediately declared one of the nation's most scenic roads.	Congress creates Kings Canyon National Park, encompassing General Grant National Park and including a large part of the namesake canyon John Muir once called 'a rival to the Yosemite.'	Mineral King Valley, a glacially formed canyon of vast natural beauty, is added to Sequoia National Park, preventing the Walt Disney Company from building a ski resort there.	Unesco declares Yosemite National Park a World Heritage site; Congress passes the sweeping California Wilderness Act, designating almost 90% of Yosemite as specially protected wilderness.

they spooked livestock and ruined tourists' experience (those were the days!). A few years after the ban was lifted in 1913, a serviceable dirt road opened through Tioga Pass. By 1922 annual visitation surpassed 100,000.

In Sequoia National Park, the first automobile arrived in 1904. The Generals Hwy opened in 1926 between the park's foothills and the Giant Forest. It took almost another decade to push the highway through to Grant Grove, in what would later become Kings Canyon National Park. Though the Generals Hwy was one of the country's most scenic (and expensive) roads, the park still received less than a quarter of the visitors that Yosemite did.

The automobile increased visitation to all three parks, but it was the enthusiastic – and sometimes extreme – policies of Stephen T Mather, the first director of the National Park Service (NPS) established in 1916, that sent the numbers climbing. During his tenure (1917–29), Mather oversaw the development of Yosemite's Wawona Golf Course, Ahwahnee Hotel, Yosemite Museum and Camp Curry ice rink, and he initiated nature walks and educational programs at all three parks.

First published in 1965, Francis P Farquhar's *History of the Sierra Nevada* is still one of the region's definitive books on the subject. It's an enjoyable read for armchair travelers.

War, a Riot & New Plans

In 1940, just before the US entered WWII, Congress passed a law creating Kings Canyon National Park, which absorbed General Grant National Park into its much larger boundaries. As the national war effort gobbled up federal funds, Sequoia and Kings Canyon National Parks were merged into a single administrative body in 1943.

In Yosemite, the Ahwahnee Hotel became a wartime naval hospital and the US Army set up camps at Wawona and Badger Pass. The California National Guard was stationed at Hetch Hetchy to protect the public water supply, while 90,000 troops occupied Yosemite Valley. At the height of the war, public visitation plummeted to just 116,000 people.

After WWII, families taking vacations started visiting in record numbers. Tensions over crowding came to a head on July 4, 1970, during the Stoneman Meadow Riot, when park rangers on horseback forcefully removed partying youth who were illegally camped out. Rangers were pulled from their horses and beaten, dozens of revelers suffered injuries, and by morning, 135 people had been arrested and the National Guard called in.

In 1980 Yosemite adopted its first General Management Plan, calling for restrictions on private cars, increases in public transportation, changes to Merced River campgrounds and relocation of many commercial services outside the park. Mired in political and public opposition, the plan foundered until a major flood in 1997 forced it into its final revision. New management plans for Yosemite's Mariposa Grove and the Tuolumne River share the same goal: restoring health to the park's natural environment while minimizing the impacts of human visitation.

1996	1997	2006	2016
Annual visitation to Yosemite National Park peaks at over 4 million people, then abruptly declines over the next decade before beginning to bounce back.	Massive New Year's flooding on the Merced River washes out sections of Hwy 140 and damages campgrounds, trails, bridges and more; Yosemite National Park closes for several months.	In August, four amateur cave researchers discover Ursa Minor cave in Sequoia National Park, one of the most significant cave discoveries in recent history.	The NPS celebrates the centennial of its founding, urging all Americans to get out and explore with the motto 'Find Your Park.'

Geology

Poetically nicknamed the 'Range of Light' by conservationist John Muir, the 400-mile-long Sierra Nevada mountain range gives California much of its astonishing geological diversity. With peaks over 14,000ft, it creates a towering wall that captures clouds and douses western slopes in water, while shutting off the supply of rain to eastern slopes into the Great Basin desert beyond. Stretching ever skyward, the Sierra Nevada provides living, earth-shaking evidence of the irresistible geological forces still shaping the landscape today.

The Lay of the Land

Geologists call the Sierra Nevada a tilted fault-block range – and it's a particularly impressive example at that, spreading over 40 to 60 miles wide, with hundreds of peaks over 10,000ft. Picture a tilted fault block as an iceberg listing to one side while floating in the earth's crust. In the Sierra Nevada, that imaginary 'iceberg' is actually an immense body of granite known as a batholith that formed deep within the earth's crust, then 'floated' up and became exposed on the surface over millions of years. Today park visitors can see the tip of this batholith, though it's obscured in places where older rocks (mostly metamorphic) still cling, like pieces of a torn cloak, or where newer rocks (mostly volcanic) have been added on top, like icing.

Drifting on Ancient Seas

Around 225 million years ago, the area that is now the Sierra Nevada was actually a shallow sea lying off the coast of a young North American continent. Material from island volcanoes exploding offshore, plus tons of debris that were eroding from the continental landmass, gradually began filling in this sea with weighty layers of sediment.

At the same time, the continental North American Plate started drifting westward and riding over the leading edge of the oceanic Pacific Plate. With almost unimaginable force, this movement drove the edge of the Pacific Plate down to depths where it melted into magma, later cooling to form the Sierra Nevada batholith (a term derived from the Greek words for 'deep rock').

Today's Sierra Nevada and Cascade mountain chains mark the edge of this submerged, melting plate. The force of the continental and oceanic plates colliding and crushing together also generated such enormous heat and pressure that old sedimentary and volcanic rocks turned into the metamorphic rocks now found throughout the Sierra Nevada range.

Building Mountains: Batholiths & Plutons

As it made its huge, continual push over the Pacific Plate, the North American Plate buckled so strongly that it formed a proto-Sierra Nevada mountain range of folded rock that may have reached as high as 15,000ft. This initial phase of building the Sierra Nevada ceased about 130 million years ago, when the older mountains began a long erosional phase that

California claims both the highest point in contiguous US (Mt Whitney, 14,505ft) and the lowest elevation in North America (Badwater, Death Valley, 282ft below sea level) – and they're only 90 miles apart, as the condor flies.

reduced them to gently rolling uplands by 50 million years ago, leaving the batholith exposed on the earth's surface.

Between 80 and 210 million years ago, the Sierra Nevada batholith began as magma deep in the earth's crust, cooling to form giant blocks of rock over 100 different times. Each magma event formed a discrete body of granitic rock known as a pluton (from Pluto, the Roman god of the underworld), each with a characteristic composition and appearance. Hikers today can trace the layout of these well-mapped plutons by examining the mix of minerals and the size of the crystals within rocks alongside park trails.

Pushing Up, Sliding Down

About 10 million years ago, the Sierra Nevada's granite batholith began to lift and bulge upward between parallel sets of faults (that is, cracks in the earth's crust). Regions of much older rocks were uplifted on the newly forming crest of the Sierra Nevada. Remnants of old rocks perched on top of granite ridges are today called roof pendants, of which Yosemite's Mt Dana is an outstanding example.

The Sierra Nevada batholith has continued to lift, reaching its current height an estimated two million years ago. Since then, the counterbalancing forces of uplift and erosion have created an equilibrium that keeps the Sierra Nevada at more or less the same size, although the range continues to grow at a miniscule, yet measurable, rate.

From two million years ago until about 10,000 years ago, Ice Age glaciers covered portions of the Sierra Nevada with snow and ice. The largest ice field was a giant cap of ice that covered an area 275 miles long and 40 miles wide between Lake Tahoe and Yosemite. From high-elevation ice fields, rivers of ice (glaciers) flowed down and scoured out rugged river canyons, simply enlarging some or beautifully sculpting others, like Yosemite Valley, Mineral King Valley in Sequoia National Park, and the upper portions of Kings Canyon.

After the Ice Age came a warm period when there were no glaciers in the Sierra, but during the last thousand years or so, about 99 glaciers and 398 glacierets (small glaciers or pockets of ice) reformed during the Little Ice Age. The largest remaining glaciers are on Mt Lyell and Mt Maclure in the Yosemite region, and on the Palisades in the John Muir Wilderness in the Eastern Sierra further south. However, due to global warming, these glaciers are all melting rapidly and are in danger of disappearing entirely within decades. Maclure Glacier is only half the size that it was when John Muir visited it in the mid-19th century, and Lyell Glacier is so thin that it has completely stopped moving downhill.

The vast wilderness of the High Sierra (lying mostly above 9000ft) presents an astounding landscape of glaciers, sculpted granite peaks and remote canyons, beautiful to look at but difficult to access on foot or horseback – presenting one of the greatest challenges for 19th-century settlers attempting to reach California.

GEOLOGY THE LAY OF THE LAND

THE EASTERN SIERRA'S SHAKY GROUND

Uplift of the Sierra's batholith continues to occur along its eastern face, where a zone of geologic activity keeps life exciting for folks living along Hwy 395 between Mammoth Lakes and Lone Pine.

In 1872 the Eastern Sierra jerked upward 13ft in a single earthquake, while over the past two decades Mammoth has endured a nerve-wracking series of minor earthquakes and tremors. The Sierra crest is estimated to lift as much as 1.5in per century and, as a result of this skewed tilting, the eastern face of the Sierra is now an abrupt wall rising up to 11,000ft high while the western face is a long gentle incline.

Due to uplift along the eastern face, rivers flowing down the range's western slopes have picked up speed and cut progressively deeper canyons into the formerly flat, rolling landscape. Today, over a dozen major river canyons mark the western slope, and the rock that formerly filled those canyons now buries the Central Valley under 9.5 miles of sediment. Talk about rolling stones!

The Forces at Work

The dramatic tale of how the Sierra Nevada range first formed is only the beginning of the geologic story – as soon as its rocks were exposed on the earth's surface, a host of new forces shaped them into the impressively varied landscape you see today. Hugely powerful glaciers have played a dramatic role, but erosion and weathering have also done their part, as have volcanic lava and ash eruptions.

The highest single-tier waterfall in North America is not Yosemite Falls – it's Ribbon Fall, which plummets 1612ft from a precipice west of El Capitan. With three distinct falls, Yosemite Falls gets disqualified, despite measuring an astonishing 2425ft from top to bottom.

Glaciers

Most of the Sierra Nevada's landscape has been substantially shaped by glaciers. In fact, of all the forces that have contributed to the landscape, none have had greater impact than the relentless grinding caused by millions of tons of ice over a period of two million years. Evidence of this dramatic grinding process is often right at your feet in areas of the Sierra Nevada, where glaciers have worn granite surfaces down to a smooth, shiny finish. Along the road at Tenaya Lake, for example, flat granite shelves are so polished they glisten in the early morning light. In contrast, hikers to high-alpine nunataks (peaks and plateaus that were too high to be glaciated) such as Mt Conness will find rough-textured, sharp-edged and jagged granite formations. For a living geology lesson, hike the gentle, half-mile Nunatak Nature Trail in the Inyo National Forest, off Hwy 120 just east of Tioga Lake and Yosemite's Tioga Pass Entrance.

Glaciers arise where snowfields fail to melt completely by summer's end. Over time, delicate snow crystals dissolve into tiny spheres that connect and fuse into solid ice. True glacial ice forms after hundreds of years, with the original snowflakes becoming nine times heavier and 500 times stronger in the process. These ice fields develop in high mountain valleys where snowdrifts readily accumulate, and from there they flow downhill at the rate of inches or yards per day. The longest known glacier in the Sierra Nevada was a 60-mile tongue that flowed down the Tuolumne River canyon about 20,000 years ago.

In some Sierra Nevada valleys, the ice field once measured 500ft to 4000ft thick. Hundreds of thousands of cubic feet of ice thus created an unbelievable amount of pressure and shearing strength that completely altered the landscape. Massive boulders were plucked up and dragged along like giant rasping teeth on a file's edge. Smaller rocks and sand carried along the glacier's bottom acted like sandpaper that polished underlying bedrock. Every rock that was loose or could be pried loose was caught up and transported for miles.

Glaciers have the funny effect of rounding out landscape features that lie below the ice while sharpening features that rise above the ice. The same grinding force that smooths out valleys also quarries rocks from the base of peaks, resulting in undercutting that forms towering spikes. In Tuolumne Meadows this effect is particularly dramatic – compare the smooth domes on the valley floor, like Lembert Dome and Pothole Dome, with the sheer spires of Cathedral and Unicorn Peaks visible nearby.

Take a virtual field trip into the Sierra Nevada, courtesy of the myriad links put together by the California Geological Survey online (www.consrv.ca.gov/cgs/geotour).

Rocks: Cracking, Fracturing, Weathering & Falling

The distinctive granite of the Sierra Nevada owes its appearance not only to the tremendous sculpting power of glaciers but also to something far more subtle – the internal properties of the rock itself, and how it behaves in its natural environment. The first rule of thumb is that granite tends to crack and separate along regular planes, often parallel to the surface of the rocks. Everywhere you travel in the High Sierra, you'll easily be able to see evidence of this ongoing cracking.

At Olmsted Point along the Tioga Pass Rd, visitors can see a surrealistic view of vast granite walls peeling off like onion layers below Clouds

SIERRA NEVADA ROCKS: A PRIMER

The Sierra Nevada is one of the world's premier granite landscapes, yet these mountains include much more than just granite!

Metamorphic rocks Older volcanic and sedimentary rocks whose structure has been dramatically altered by intense heat and pressure deep within the earth's crust. These rocks predate the Sierra Nevada batholith, and their reddish, purplish or greenish hues are a distinctive change from the speckled grays of granite. In Sequoia and Kings Canyon National Parks, vast cave systems have been formed by limestone metamorphosed into marble.

Granite Describes a broad category of rocks formed when molten magma cools within the earth's crust (called lava when it erupts or flows onto the earth's surface). Sierra Nevada granite is actually composed of five separate minerals occurring in complex combinations that produce a characteristic salt-and-pepper appearance.

Volcanic rocks In the Sierra Nevada, these rocks have mostly weathered away except for high, uplifted pockets. Chemically identical to rocks that form deep within the earth's crust, volcanic rocks change as they erupt on the surface as lava. Gases injected into the liquid rock give it a pockmarked or bubbled appearance. Rocks that cool deep underground do so very slowly, forming large, visible crystals; liquid rock exposed to air cools so quickly that crystals can't form.

Rest. This exfoliation is the result of massive rock formations expanding and cracking in shell-like layers as the pressure of overlying materials erodes away. Over time, sharp angles and corners give way to increasingly rounded curves that leave us with distinctive landmarks like Yosemite Valley's Half Dome, Moro Rock in Sequoia National Park and Charlotte Dome in the backcountry of Kings Canyon National Park.

Weathering breaks granite down through a process different from glacial erosion or internal cracking, yet its effects are equally profound. Joints in the granite allow water to seep into deep cracks where the liquid expands during winter's freezing temperatures. This pushes open cracks with pressures up to 1000lb per sq inch and eventually forces square-angled blocks to break off from the parent formation.

Granite rock edges and corners are further weathered over time to create rounded boulders. Rain and exposure to the elements wear down granite's weaker minerals, leaving an unstable matrix of hard, pale minerals (quartz and feldspar) that crumble into fine-grained rubble called grus. Hikers walking on granite slabs might experience the unnerving sensation of slipping on tiny pebbles of grus that roll underfoot like ball bearings. In the presence of water, grus eventually break down into crumbly soil.

On the western slopes of the Sierra Nevada, granites are mostly fine-grained, with joints spaced fairly widely. As a result, rock formations tend to be massive structures shaped by exfoliation, like Yosemite's Half Dome. Further east, granites are more likely to be coarse-grained and to have closely spaced joints. There the process of water seeping into cracks and pushing rocks apart results in characteristically jagged, sawtooth ridges such as those in the Cathedral Range of Yosemite's high country and aptly named Sawtooth Peak looming above Mineral King Valley in Sequoia National Park.

So what causes those dramatic rockfalls? Once a chunk of the granite is primed to break off and fall, a final precipitating factor could be a tree whose roots pry the rock apart, extreme temperature changes or perhaps water that seeps into the rock and freezes, then thaws. Earthquakes can also trigger rockfall. Sometimes the reason for a rockfall is a mystery,

Can't see yourself backpacking for days into the Sierra Nevada to glimpse a glacier, or hanging around for weeks in Yosemite Valley to witness a rockfall? Download the free video podcast series 'Yosemite Nature Notes,' available on iTunes and from www.nps.gov/yose/photosmultimedia/ynn.htm.

which makes future events more difficult for the parks to predict and prevent. Around 1000 rockfalls have happened in Yosemite Valley alone since the mid-19th-century, as is clearly evidenced by the jumble of talus sitting at the base of the valley's tall weathered cliffs.

Roadside Geology

Glacier Point, Yosemite National Park

Tunnel View, Yosemite Valley

Olmsted Point, Yosemite National Park

Moro Rock, Sequoia National Park

Junction View, Kings Canyon Scenic Byway

Volcanoes

Between five and 20 million years ago, a series of lava and mud flows covered about 12,000 sq miles of the Sierra Nevada region north of Yosemite, with some volcanic activity extending south to the area now enclosed by the national park. While much of this violent geological history has since eroded away, caps of old volcanic material still exist along Hwy 108 at Sonora Pass, an otherworldly landscape of eroding debris.

About three million years ago, the zone of volcanic activity shifted from the region north of Yosemite to the slopes east of the Sierra Nevada crest. Massive eruptions between Mammoth Lakes and Mono Lake created a series of calderas and volcanic mountains, including Mammoth Mountain itself. Mono Lake gained two islands and a small chain of hills on its southern side during this period of activity, which is still ongoing. Over time, the volcanic landscape at Mono Lake has undergone dramatic changes, with the last eruption at the lake's Paoha Island taking place fewer than 700 years ago.

The most familiar and popular landmark formed in the current (geologically speaking) era of volcanic activity is Devils Postpile, a national monument located west of Mammoth Lakes. About 80,000 to 100,000 years ago, a violent volcanic vent filled a river canyon and a natural lake with lava 400ft deep. The lava cooled so quickly that it formed one of the world's most spectacular examples of columnar basalt, today reaching up to 60ft high. These multisided columns are virtually perfect in their symmetry, and the iconic formation can be viewed by taking just a short hike.

The rawness and relative newness of all of these volcanic formations reminds us how active and ongoing the Sierra Nevada's evolution is. For example, just consider how the Ice Age glaciers retreated a mere 10,000 years ago, not even enough time for soil to develop in most places! This is a remarkably young range, still jagged and sharp, still rising – and yes, still shaking.

Wildlife

Sierra Nevada wildlife – like lumbering bears, whistling marmots, soaring birds, skittering lizards and fleeting butterflies – are scattered across vast and untamed terrain. Only in a few places do animals congregate in conspicuous numbers. But if you remain patient and alert in the parks, you'll be rewarded with lifelong memories of wildlife spotting. An especially good time to visit is during late spring or early summer, when the foothills and mountains are abloom with wildflowers.

Mammals

Black Bears

Arguably the animal that visitors would most like to see is the black bear. Weighing in on average around 300lb, these bears can be formidable fighters, but they generally shy away from human contact.

Whether climbing trees, poking under logs and rocks or crossing rivers, bears are basically big noses in search of food – they'll eat almost anything. Bears may spend a considerable amount of time grazing like cows on meadow plants. Later in summer, they switch over to berries and acorns, with insects (including ants, beetles, termites and wasps) making up about 10% of their diet.

California's mountain forests are home to an estimated 25,000 to 35,000 black bears, whose fur actually ranges in color from black to dark brown, cinnamon or even blond.

Mule Deer

The most common large mammals in the Sierra Nevada, mule deer dwell in all forest habitats below the timberline. In parks, they have become remarkably unconcerned about human observers and tend to frequent meadows. White-spotted fawns first appear in July, while tannish adults with big floppy ears become numerous in early winter, when deep snows push them out of the high country to forage at lower elevations. Deer favor leaves and young twigs as a source of food; in late fall, they feed heavily on acorns.

Mountain Lions & Bobcats

You'll rarely glimpse a mountain lion bounding into the woods. Reaching up to 8ft from nose to tail tip and weighing as much as 150lb, this solitary and highly elusive creature is a formidable predator. In the Sierra Nevada, mountain lions roam all forested habitats below the timberline in search of mule deer and, occasionally, endangered bighorn sheep. Humans are rarely more than a curiosity or nuisance to be avoided, although a few attacks have occurred.

Hikers are more likely to see the handsome bobcat, looking like a scaled-up version of the domestic tabby, with a brown-spotted, yellowish-tan coat and a cropped tail.

You'll be amazed by the 2800 hand-drawn watercolor illustrations and easy-to-understand descriptions of more than 1700 species found in *The Laws Field Guide to the Sierra Nevada,* by John Muir Laws.

Coyotes & Foxes

The ubiquitous coyote and its much smaller cousin, the gray fox, share the same grayish-brown coat. Both have adapted to human habitats, becoming altogether too comfortable around roads, campgrounds and any food left unguarded. You stand a good chance of seeing a coyote

MOUNTAIN KINGS: MARMOTS & BIGHORN SHEEP

••

Among the most curious mammals in the Sierra high country, the yellow-bellied marmot inhabits rock outcrops and boulder fields at or above 7500ft. Sprawled lazily on sun-warmed rocks, marmots scarcely bear notice until closely approached, when they jolt upright and send out shrieks of alarm to the entire marmot neighborhood. Marmots have a great appetite – they spend four to five months putting on weight (incredibly, up to 50% of their body weight can be fat) before starting a long, deep hibernation through winter until the following spring.

Another high-elevation dweller, but one that's rarely seen, is the endangered Sierra Nevada bighorn sheep. Although they once numbered in the thousands, their wild population declined to just 125 animals by the year 2000 due to hunting and exposure to diseases from domesticated livestock. Thanks to interagency conservation efforts, that number has rebounded to 400 and is still rising. Your best chance of spotting bighorns is during summer as they scale granite slopes and peaks above 10,000ft in the Eastern Sierra to graze on alpine plants and escape predators.

during the daytime, especially in meadows, where they hunt rodents. Foxes mainly come out at night, when you might spy one crossing a road.

Rodents

That odd little 'bleating' call coming from jumbles of rocks and boulders is likely a pika. A careful search will reveal the hamster-like vocalist peering from under a rock with small beady eyes. Pikas typically live on talus slopes above 8000ft, especially in the alpine realm of mountain hemlock, whitebark pine and heather plants.

The golden-mantled ground squirrel is often mistaken for a chubby chipmunk. However, ground squirrels have no stripes on their heads and shoulders, while chipmunks are striped all the way to the tip of their noses. Ground squirrels spend the winter hibernating, so in late summer they start gaining an extreme amount of weight.

A large cousin of the chipmunk, the western gray squirrel, with its long, fluffy tail trailing behind, tends to live at low to mid-elevations in the Western Sierra. The smaller Douglas squirrel, recognized by its slender tail and rusty tone, inhabits conifer forests up to the timberline.

Birds

Whether you enjoy the aerial acrobatics of swifts and falcons over Yosemite Valley's waterfalls, the flash of brilliant warblers in oak woodlands, or the bright, inviting lives of more than 250 other bird species found in the Sierra Nevada, it goes without question that birding is a highlight here.

The Yosemite Conservancy (www.yosemite conservancy.org) is a nonprofit group that publishes books and teaches a wide variety of natural history classes about the Sierra Nevada, including family-friendly outings, day hikes, wilderness backpacking trips and art workshops.

No other bird commands attention quite like the ubiquitous Steller's jay, found in virtually every forested habitat and around campgrounds. Flashing a shimmering cloak of blue feathers and an equally jaunty attitude, these noisy birds wander fearlessly among picnic tables and parked cars in pursuit of overlooked crumbs.

Another conspicuous bird, the small mountain chickadee, with its distinctive black cap, is a perennial favorite with children because its merry song sounds like 'cheese-bur-ger.' You'll hear this song often in forested areas at middle elevations.

Hikers at higher elevations are greeted by the raucous and inquisitive Clark's nutcracker, a hardy resident of subalpine forests recognized by its black wings and white tail. A flock of nutcrackers will survive the winter by gathering and storing up to four million pinenuts each fall, burying the nuts in thousands of small caches.

John Muir favored the American dipper (also known as a water ouzel) for its ceaseless energy and good cheer even in the depths of winter. This 'singularly joyous and lovable little fellow' rarely leaves the cascading torrents of cold, clear mountain streams, where it dives to capture underwater insects and larvae.

Amphibians

Among the region's several unique amphibians is the Yosemite toad. This endemic, high-elevation toad used to abound, but in recent years it has mysteriously disappeared from many of its former haunts. At lower elevations, the western toad is still quite common and often observed moving along trails or through campgrounds at night. To identify a toad, look for a slow, plodding walk and dry, warty skin, which easily distinguishes them from smooth-skinned, quickly hopping frogs.

Another unusual amphibian of the High Sierra is the scarce mountain yellow-legged frog, whose numbers have declined sharply around alpine lakes stocked with trout. The abundant Pacific tree frog, by contrast, is extremely widespread and diverse in habitat preferences. Tree frogs have the familiar 'ri-bet' call that nearly everyone associates with singing frogs.

Oddest among amphibians is the rare Mt Lyell salamander, first discovered in Yosemite in 1915 when accidentally captured in a trap. This brownish-grey salamander resides on domed rocks and talus slopes from 4000ft to over 11,000ft, where it uses its webbed toes and strong tail to climb sheer cliffs and boulders in search of food.

Reptiles

The most abundant and widespread reptile is the western fence lizard, a 6in-long creature you're likely to see perched on rocks and logs or scampering across the forest floor. During breeding season, you'll notice males bob energetically (doing 'push ups') as they conspicuously display their iridescent-blue throats and bellies.

Found in forest-floor debris, southern alligator lizards wiggle off noisily like clumsy snakes when disturbed. These 10in-long yellow-tan lizards with crossbars on their backs reside from the lower foothills up into the mixed conifer zone.

The region has over a dozen snake species, including garter snakes, which live in the widest diversity of habitats and are the snakes you're most likely to see. Two kinds of garter snake sport mainly black skin, with yellow or orange stripes running the length of their bodies.

No other snake elicits as much fear as the western rattlesnake. Even if they're not rattling, you can quickly recognize rattlers by their bluntly

Wildlife Spotting

Yosemite Valley, Yosemite National Park

Tuolumne Meadows, Yosemite National Park

Giant Forest, Sequoia National Park

Kings River, Kings Canyon National Park

Mono Lake, Eastern Sierra

WILDLIFE AMPHIBIANS

YOSEMITE'S BIRDS OF PREY

While almost a dozen species of owls in the Yosemite region, no other evokes the mystery of the nocturnal realm quite like that rare phantom, the great gray owl. Easily the most famous and sought-after bird in Yosemite, this distinctive owl stands 2ft tall with a wingspan of 5ft. A small population (less than 200 individuals) of these birds survive in the park. These majestic owls have been spotted at Crane Flat, where they hunt around large meadows in the early morning and late afternoon.

You'll also be fortunate if you see the peregrine falcon, a species that has climbed back from the brink of extinction and is now present in healthy numbers. This streamlined, fierce hunter with long, pointed wings and a black 'moustache' mark on its cheek nests in cliffs in the Yosemite Valley, where seasonal rock-climbing route closures protect chicks until they've fledged, usually by late summer.

triangular heads perched on remarkably slender necks. Rocky or brushy areas below 8000ft are the preferred haunts of this venomous though generally docile snake.

Often confused with deadly coral snakes (which don't live in California), the mountain king snake – with bright orange, black and white-colored bands around its body – is harmless to humans, and lives throughout the Sierra Nevada.

Fish

The most widely distributed fish in the Western Sierra is the rainbow trout. Formerly limited to the lower reaches of streams below insurmountable barriers (eg waterfalls), rainbow trout have been introduced into countless alpine and eastern creeks and lakes for sportfishing. Now threatened with extinction, the California golden trout – the state's official fish – inhabits the Kern River drainage of Sequoia and Kings Canyon National Parks.

Further complicating the natural order of things, non-native species such as brook trout, lake trout, brown trout and kokanee salmon have been successfully introduced throughout the Sierra Nevada. Introduced fish have had a devastating impact on aquatic ecosystems, especially in formerly fishless alpine areas, where fragile nutrient cycles and invertebrate populations have changed dramatically as a result.

Insects

Most visitors won't notice the amazing variety of insects in the Sierra Nevada, except for a handful of conspicuous butterflies and other charismatic creatures. Foremost among the large, showy butterflies are the five swallowtail species. The Western tiger swallowtail, yellow in color with bold black bars and beautiful blue and orange spots near its 'tail,' follows stream banks from the lower foothills up to subalpine forest. The stunning, iridescent-blue pipevine swallowtail flits in large numbers along foothill canyons and slopes almost year-round.

Plants

The Sierra Nevada boasts one of the most varied selections of plants found anywhere in North America. Yosemite National Park alone is home to over 20% of California's 7000 plant species, even though it encompasses less than 1% of the state's total land.

Wildflowers

You can see flowering plants from early March until late August, and taking time to find them will enrich your park experience.

At low elevations in early spring, when wildflowers carpet low-elevation hillsides, you can't miss the brilliant orange, native California poppy, each with four floppy, silken petals. At night and on cloudy days, poppy petals fold up and become inconspicuous.

At least a dozen species of Indian paintbrush of varying colors and shapes can be found in the region. Most are red or orange in color and appear somewhat hairy. Surprisingly, the flowers themselves are hidden and accessible only to hummingbirds (the plants' pollinators), while a set of specialized colored leaves take on the appearance of petals. Paintbrushes are semiparasitic, often tapping into the roots of their neighbors to draw nourishment. So are snow plants, which feed on fungi in the soil and shoot up fleshy stems with brilliant red flowers that bloom early and often at the edges of melting snow banks.

Mountaineers climb into a rarified realm rich in unique flowers, and if you need a single target flower to hunt for, one that's rare and mysterious like a distant peak, you couldn't make a better choice than the Sierra

Located in the stunning southern Sierra, the Sequoia Natural History Association (www.sequoiahistory.org) has one of the best outdoor classrooms in the region, offering guided hikes, underground cave tours, campfire programs, stargazing and other family fun.

Top The great gray owl (p215) stands 2ft tall.

Bottom The most popular animal with visitors is the elusive black bear (p213) which shies away from human contact.

BJORN BAKSTAD / GETTY IMAGES ©

Giant sequoia trees in Sequoia National Park

primrose. Confined to a handful of high subalpine slopes and peaks, this brilliant magenta beauty is a real find for the lucky hiker. Arising from clumps of toothed, succulent leaves, primroses sometimes grow in large patches sprawling across rocky slopes.

Highest and showiest of all is the aptly named sky pilot. Usually found only above 11,000ft, this plant erupts into flagrant displays of violet-blue flowers arranged in dense, ball-like clusters. After a long and grueling ascent, hikers to the highest peaks will better understand its name, a slang term for a military chaplain or priest said to lead others to heaven.

Wildflower Blooms

Tuolumne Meadows, Yosemite National Park

McGurk Meadow, Yosemite National Park

Wawona Meadow, Yosemite National Park

Crescent Meadow, Sequoia National Park

Zumwalt Meadow, Kings Canyon National Park

Trees

While flowers rise and fade with ephemeral beauty, trees hold their majesty for centuries. Given a few simple tips, you can easily learn to identify many of the region's prominent species and appreciate the full sweep of trees cloaking the parks' landscape.

Pines are conifers whose needles appear in tight clusters, with two, three or five needles per cluster. Named for its straight, slender trunk, the abundant lodgepole pine has two-needled clusters and globular cones that are less than 2in long. Lodgepoles are the most common tree around mountain meadows because this species has adapted to survive in waterlogged soils or in basins where cold air sits at night (so-called frost pockets).

The ponderosa pine, with some examples of the Jeffrey pine mixed in, covers vast tracts of low to mid-elevation Sierra Nevada slopes. Three-needled clusters characterize both trees. Virtually identical in appearance, the two species do have distinct cones; on ponderosa cones the barbs protrude outward, and on Jeffrey pines they curve inward. If you're unsure of the identification, simply hold a cone in your hand and remember the adage: 'Gentle Jeffrey, prickly ponderosa.'

THE SMALL KINGDOM OF GIANT SEQUOIAS

The Sierra Nevada's most famous tree, the giant sequoia, is also the source of much legend and ballyhoo. Even information as basic as the trees' maximum height and width remains uncertain because loggers and claim-seekers who cut down many of the original giants found it beneficial to exaggerate records. Today, the General Sherman tree of Sequoia National Park, which measures 274.9ft tall and 102.6ft in circumference, is recognized as the largest known living specimen (and it's still growing!).

Giant sequoias cluster in fairly discrete groves on the western slopes of the Sierra Nevada. You can recognize them by their spongy, cinnamon-red bark and juniper-like needles. Despite claims that these are the world's oldest trees, it's now thought that the longest they can live is just over 3000 years, far short of the age reached by ancient bristlecone pines.

Between five and 25 million years ago, the giant sequoias' arboreal ancestors covered a vast area between the Sierra Nevada and the Rocky Mountains. Migrating westward, possibly through low mountain passes, these trees got a foothold on the west slope of the Sierra Nevada just as the range began to reach its current height. The formation of the Sierra Nevada isolated those sequoias on the west slope while at the same time creating a rain shadow that killed off the main population of sequoias to the east.

Giant sequoias survive today in 67 scattered groves. In Yosemite National Park, the Tuolumne Grove and Merced Grove along Hwy 120 and the Mariposa Grove along Hwy 41 are relatively small groves, while the more than 20 groves in Sequoia and Kings Canyon National Parks are generally more extensive, because the soil is deeper and better developed in areas that weren't covered by glaciers.

The wide variety of deciduous trees in the region includes the quaking aspen, with its smooth, white bark and oval leaves. Every brief gust sets these leaves quivering on their flattened stems. Aspens consist of genetically identical trunks arising from a single root system that may grow to be more than 100 acres in size. By sprouting repeatedly from this root system, aspens have what has been called 'theoretical immortality,' and some aspens are thought to be over 80,000 years old.

Magnificent black oaks grow up to 80ft high at mountain elevations between 2000ft and 7000ft, where their immense crops of acorns are a food source for many animals, including bears, deer and woodpeckers.

Want to learn more about the local ecosystem? For an explanation of just about everything, check out *Sierra Nevada Natural History* (University of California Press), by Tracey Storer, Robert Usinger and David Lukas.

Shrubs

No other shrub may be as worthy of note as poison oak, which can trigger an inflammatory skin reaction in people who come into contact with it. The shrub is distinguished by shiny, oak-like leaves that occur in groups of three; clusters of white berries appear by late summer. If you'll be exploring the western slopes of the Sierra Nevada, learn how to identify this common trailside plant.

At higher elevations, huckleberry oak and greenleaf manzanita form a dense, nearly impenetrable habitat, known as montane chaparral, that carpets the high country around granite boulders and outcrops. There bears, deer, rabbits and many other animals find food and shelter not provided by nearby forests.

At lower elevations, you'll find foothill chaparral characterized by whiteleaf manzanita. Greenleaf and whiteleaf manzanita feature the same smooth, reddish bark and small, red, apple-like berries (*manzanita* is Spanish for 'little apple'), but they differ in the color of their leaves. During late summer, the scat of animals like black bears, coyotes and foxes is chock-full of partly digested manzanita berries.

Conservation

Since the discovery of gold in 1848, the Sierra Nevada's natural world has been forever altered. The 19th-century human stampede to find gold and profit at any cost had a devastating impact on Native Americans and the landscape. Today, California is the most populous US state with the nation's highest projected growth rate, which strains the region's precious natural resources. Tourism also impacts, with over five million people visiting these national parks each year, as does California's persistent drought.

Water Diversion, Dams & Drought

Known as the little organization that triumphed over Los Angeles, the Mono Lake Committee (www.monolake.org) has matured into a successful environmental powerhouse in the Eastern Sierra, offering field seminars and naturalist-guided walks, talks and kayak tours.

Without doubt, the greatest benefit that the Sierra Nevada provides to the state of California is a (recently dwindling) supply of fresh, clean water. Ironically, the greatest harm to the Sierra Nevada has come from using, managing and collecting this essential resource.

During the mid-19th century, rivers were diverted, rocks moved and entire hillsides washed away to reveal gold deposits north of Yosemite. More than 1.5 billion tons of debris and uncalculated amounts of poisonous mercury flowed downstream, with harsh consequences for aquatic ecosystems and watershed health, which are still felt today in both the Sierra Nevada and Central Valley.

Early-20th-century construction of a dam in Yosemite's Hetch Hetchy Valley to provide the city of San Francisco with water apparently broke conservationist John Muir's heart. In the Eastern Sierra, the diversion of water for the city of Los Angeles contributed to the destruction of Owens Lake and its fertile wetlands, and the degradation of Mono Lake.

Throughout the 20th century, dams drawn across the Sierra Nevada severely altered aquatic habitats and eliminated spawning habitat for fish such as salmon. Native fish populations and aquatic ecosystems have been further decimated by the introduction of dozens of non-native fish species, mostly through sportfishing.

But there's good news, too. In 2004, the removal of the Cascades Diversion Dam west of Yosemite Valley has helped to restore the wild and scenic Merced River. In the Eastern Sierra, the ongoing restoration of Mono Lake is another water-conservation success story: lake levels rose over 10ft after reaching their lowest point in 1982.

However, there's no longer enough water to go around. California's ongoing, multiyear drought has seen Sierra Nevada lakes and rivers dramatically shrink, waterfalls dry up to just a trickle earlier in summer, bigger wildfire blazes, and forests gouged by more than 10 million dead, dying and falling-down trees. In 2015 the Sierra Nevada snowpack measured only 5 percent of its annual average, alarmingly setting a new record low.

Air Quality & Pollution

After drought, perhaps the most pernicious environmental issue in the parks today is air pollution. In 2004 Yosemite joined a growing list of national parks that violate federal smog standards, and the situation

JOHN MUIR: A MAN OF THE MOUNTAINS
••

Arriving in San Francisco in the spring of 1868, John Muir started out to walk across California's Central Valley to the then scarcely known landmark of Yosemite Valley, where his wanderings and writings later earned him lasting worldwide fame.

This Scotsman's many treks led him into the highest realms of Yosemite's backcountry, where he took little more than a wool overcoat, dry crusts of bread and a bit of tea on his wanderings. Though not a trained scientist, Muir looked at the natural world with a keen curiosity, investigating glaciers, trees, earthquakes, bees and even the most plain-coated of Sierra Nevada birds, recording them in great detail.

Muir's prolific and poetic writings spanned the gap between literature and science. His popular magazine articles and lobbying efforts became the foundation of the campaign that established Yosemite as a national park in 1890. Despite that success and his other accomplishments with the Sierra Club, Muir was unable to save Hetch Hetchy Valley, which he said rivaled Yosemite Valley in beauty and grandeur. Muir lost that final battle in 1913, when Hetch Hetchy was sacrificed to the water and power needs of a growing San Francisco.

Today, you can visit the farm where Muir once lived with his family, and view the writing desk where he penned those famous words, at **John Muir National Historic Site** (☎925-228-8860; www.nps.gov/jomu; 4202 Alhambra Ave, Martinez; ☉10am-5pm) FREE in the San Francisco Bay Area. Or virtually learn more about the man, his writings and his politics at the Sierra Club's online John Muir Exhibit (http://vault.sierraclub.org/john_muir_exhibit).

in Sequoia and Kings Canyon is much worse. Monitoring stations in Sequoia's Foothills area detect high ozone levels over 50 times per year, and it's not uncommon for higher-elevation park views to be obscured by haze all summer long. Tighter regulations are slowly making California's air cleaner, but plenty of pollution still drifts up from the Central Valley.

Tourism also has a detrimental effect on air quality, as every visitor arriving by car or bus contributes to the overall impact of vehicle emissions and worsens traffic jams. You can help the parks' air quality by leaving your car parked and riding shuttle buses or renting or bringing bicycles. Always turn the car engine off rather than letting it idle at roadside viewpoints.

Livestock & Logging

Following the mid-19th-century gold rush, ranchers began driving millions of sheep into the Sierra Nevada's mountain meadows, where they wreaked havoc. Sheep turned meadows into choking dustbowls by devouring fragile plants before they could flower and produce seeds. Even now, over a hundred years later, the pattern of vegetation in the high mountains largely reflects this grazing history, with many hillsides still dry, barren or choked with species that the 'hoofed locusts' didn't like.

Fortunately, the Sierra Nevada's mountain environments can be so extreme that few weed species ever took hold. The opposite is true of its foothill slopes, where weed species introduced by humans and their livestock now utterly dominate and choke out native plants. Global climate change has further imperiled native plants across the Sierra Nevada.

John Muir's concern over destructive logging practices, especially those that felled giant sequoia trees, played an important role in establishing Yosemite National Park, but Muir didn't live long enough to see the worst of what could happen. Industrial-scale logging took

Co-founded by John Muir in 1892, the Sierra Club (www.sierraclub.org) was the USA's first conservation group and it remains the nation's most active, offering educational programs, group hikes, organized trips and volunteer vacations.

A forest fire at Half Dome, in Yosemite National Park (p44), in 2014.

off after WWII, when gasoline-powered chainsaws, logging trucks and heavy equipment were brought into national forests surrounding the parks, causing lasting soil and watershed damage and devastating forest fires.

Since the 1960s, national forest management directives have begun to reverse course, aiming to better balance conservation and public recreation with big-business tree 'harvesting.' Toward the end of the 20th century, both national forests and parks also changed their minds about wildfire management. Wildfires that were once suppressed have been shown to be part of the healthy life cycle of forests. Today, they may be allowed to burn naturally if they don't endanger park visitors or infrastructure.

Survival Guide

Clothing & Equipment

Much of what you should bring to the parks depends on when you're visiting and what activities you plan to do. If you're going backpacking, you'll be shouldering everything for a few days, so a comfortable pack weight is crucial. Pare down to the essentials, and make sure that what you bring isn't unnecessarily bulky; having a clean shirt every morning is not as important as how your back feels at day's end. Use a checklist to ensure all the important stuff gets remembered.

Clothing

Layering

For comfortable hiking, wear several layers of light clothing, which you can easily take off or put on as you warm up or cool down. Most hikers use three main layers: a base layer next to the skin, an insulating layer and an outer, shell layer for protection from wind, rain and snow.

➡ For the upper body, the base layer is typically a shirt of synthetic material for wicking moisture away from the body.

➡ The insulating layer retains heat next to your body, and is often a synthetic fleece or down jacket.

➡ The outer shell should be a waterproof jacket that protects against cold winds.

➡ For the lower body, the layers generally consist of either shorts or loose-fitting pants; Capilene 'long-john' underwear; and waterproof rain pants.

Waterproof Shells

The ideal specifications are:

➡ breathable, waterproof fabric (Gore-Tex is popular)

➡ a hood that's roomy enough to cover headwear but still allow peripheral vision

➡ a capacious map pocket

➡ a heavy-gauge zipper protected by a storm flap If heavy rain is unlikely, a poncho is a lightweight option.

Footwear, Socks & Gaiters

Trail-running shoes are fine over easy terrain, but for more difficult trails and across rocks and scree, the ankle support offered by boots is invaluable.

➡ Hiking boots should have a flexible midsole and an insole that supports the arch and heel. Nonslip soles (such as Vibram) provide the best grip.

➡ Buy boots in warm conditions or go for a walk before trying them on, so that your feet can expand slightly as they would on a walk.

➡ Many hikers carry a pair of river sandals to wear at night, at rest stops and/or when fording waterways.

➡ For longer hikes, synthetics wick away moisture better than cotton and wool. Also consider wearing lightweight liner socks for comfort and to avoid blisters.

➡ If you'll be hiking through snow, deep mud or scratchy vegetation, gaiters will protect your legs and help keep your socks dry. Choose gaiters made of strong fabric, with a robust zip protected by a flap, that secure snugly around your hiking boots.

Navigation

Maps & Compass

Carry a good map of the area you are hiking, and know how to read it.

➡ Before setting off, ensure that you understand the contours and map symbols, plus the main ridge and river systems in the area.

➡ Familiarize yourself with the true north–south directions and the general direction in which you are heading.

➡ On the trail, try to identify major landforms (eg mountain peaks) and locate them on your map. This will give you a better grasp of the region's geography.

➡ Buy a compass and learn how to use it. The attraction of magnetic north varies in different parts of the world, so compasses need to be balanced accordingly.

Make sure your compass is balanced for your destination zone. There are also 'universal' compasses on the market that can be used anywhere in the world.

How to Use a Compass

This is a very basic introduction to using a compass and will only be of assistance if you are proficient in map reading. For simplicity, it doesn't take magnetic variation into account. Before using a compass we recommend you obtain further instruction.

READING A COMPASS

Hold the compass flat in the palm of your hand. Rotate the bezel so the red end of the needle points to the N on the bezel. The bearing is read from the dash under the bezel.

ORIENTING THE MAP

To orient the map so that it aligns with the ground, place the compass flat on the map. Rotate the map until the needle is parallel with the map's north–south grid lines and the red end is pointing to north on the map. You can now identify features around you by aligning them with labeled features on the map.

TAKING A BEARING FROM THE MAP

Draw a line on the map between your start and end points. Place the edge of the compass on this line with the direction of travel arrow pointing towards your destination. Rotate the bezel until the meridian lines are parallel with the north–south grid lines on the map and the N points to north on the map. Read the bearing from the dash.

FOLLOWING A BEARING

Rotate the bezel so that the intended bearing is in line with the dash. Place the compass flat in the palm of your hand and rotate the base plate until the red end points to N on the bezel. The

---

ROUTE FINDING

While accurate, our maps are not perfect. Inaccuracies in altitudes are commonly caused by air-temperature anomalies. Natural features such as river confluences and mountain peaks are in their true position, but sometimes the location of a trail is not always so. This may be because the size of the map does not allow for the detail of the trail's twists and turns. However, by using several basic route-finding techniques, you should have few problems following our hike maps and descriptions:

➡ Be aware of whether the trail should be climbing or descending.

➡ Check the north-point arrow on the map and determine the general direction of the trail.

➡ Time your progress over a known distance and calculate the speed at which you travel in the given terrain. From then on, you can determine with reasonable accuracy how far you have traveled.

➡ Watch the path – look for boot prints, broken branches, cut logs, cairns and other signs of previous passage.

---

direction-of-travel arrow will now point in the direction you need to walk.

DETERMINING YOUR BEARING

Rotate the bezel so the red end points to the N. Place the compass flat in the palm of your hand and rotate the base plate until the direction-of-travel arrow points in the direction in which you have been walking. Read your bearing from the dash.

GPS

GPS receivers are small, computer-driven devices that can give users an extremely accurate reading of their location – to within 15m, anywhere on the planet, any time, in almost any weather.

➡ The cheapest hand-held GPS receivers now cost less than $100 (although these may not have a built-in averaging system that minimizes signal errors). Other important factors to consider when buying a GPS receiver are its weight and battery life.

➡ Remember that a GPS receiver is of little use to hikers unless used with an accurate topographical map. The receiver simply gives your position, which you must then locate on the map.

➡ GPS receivers will only work properly in the open. The signals from a crucial satellite may be blocked (or bounce off rock or water) directly below high cliffs, near large bodies of water or in dense tree cover, giving inaccurate readings.

➡ GPS receivers are more vulnerable to breakdowns (including dead batteries) than a magnetic compass – a low-technology device that has served navigators faithfully for centuries – so don't rely on them entirely for your navigational needs.

Altimeter

Altimeters determine altitude by measuring air pressure. Because pressure is affected by temperature, altimeters are calibrated to take lower temperatures at higher altitudes into account. However, discrepancies can still occur, especially in unsettled weather, so it's wise to take a few precautions:

➡ Reset your altimeter regularly at known elevations

such as spot heights and passes. Do not take spot heights from villages where there may be a large difference in elevation from one end of the settlement to another.

→ Use your altimeter in conjunction with other navigation techniques to fix your position. For instance, taking a back bearing to a known peak or river confluence, determining the general direction of the track and obtaining your elevation will usually give you a pretty good fix on your position.

→ Altimeters are also barometers and are useful for indicating changing weather conditions. If the altimeter shows increasing elevation while you are not climbing, it means the air pressure is dropping and a low-pressure weather system may be approaching.

Equipment

Backpacks & Daypacks

→ For day hikes, a daypack (1800 to 2450 cu inches, or 30L to 40L) usually suffices. Those with built-in hydration systems are convenient.

→ For multiday hikes you will need a backpack of between 2750 and 5500 cu inches (45L and 90L) capacity.

→ A good backpack should be made of strong fabric, have a lightweight internal or external frame and an adjustable, well-padded harness that evenly distributes weight (internal frames distribute weight better than external).

→ Look for backpacks with robust, easily adjustable waist-belts that can support the entire load; shoulder straps should serve only to steady the pack.

→ Even if the manufacturer claims your pack is waterproof, use heavy-duty liners or a pack cover.

Tents

→ A three-season tent will usually suffice, except during winter, when you'll need a sturdy four-season tent to combat windy, wet and freezing conditions, especially in the backcountry.

→ Regardless of the season, the tent's floor and outer shell, or fly, should have taped or sealed seams and covered zips to stop leaks.

→ Dome- and tunnel-shaped tents handle windy conditions better than flat-sided tents.

→ Ultralight backpackers can ditch the tent and opt for using the fly and ground tarp during warm, dry weather.

Sleeping Bag & Mat

→ Mummy bags are the best shape for weight and warmth.

→ Down fillings are warmer than synthetic for the same weight and bulk, but unlike synthetic fillings they do not retain warmth when wet.

→ The given figure (eg 10°F/-12°C) is the coldest temperature at which a person should feel comfortable in the bag (but ratings are notoriously unreliable).

→ An inner liner helps keep your sleeping bag clean, as well as adding an insulating layer. Silk liners are lightest, but they're also made with less expensive synthetics.

→ Self-inflating sleeping mats work like a thin air cushion between you and the ground and insulate you from the cold. Foam mats are a low-cost, but less comfortable, alternative.

Stoves & Fuel

Fuel stoves fall roughly into four categories: propane, multifuel, methylated spirits (eg denatured alcohol) and butane gas.

→ Bulky car-camping stoves run on propane canisters. This fuel is inexpensive

and available everywhere, including many gas stations.

→ Multifuel stoves are small, efficient and ideal for places where a reliable fuel supply is difficult to find. However, they tend to be sooty and require frequent maintenance.

→ Stoves running on methylated spirits are slower and less efficient, but are safe, clean and easy to use.

→ Butane gas stoves are clean and reliable, but may be slow. The gas canisters can be awkward to carry and a potential hazardous-waste problem.

→ Propane and butane stove performance decreases in below-freezing temps.

Bear Canisters

Most backcountry hikes require a bear-resistant container for storing all scented items (eg food, toiletries).

→ If you have your own canister, confirm that your model is approved for the Sierra Nevada, where black bears have learned how to open some models.

→ All-black Garcia canisters can be rented cheaply in the parks and at US Forest Service (USFS) ranger stations.

→ Buying canisters costs anywhere from $70 for a heavier Garcia to $255 for an ultralight Wild Ideas 'Bearikade' model.

Buying & Renting Locally

Renting equipment is a good way to go if you've never tried an activity. Why sink money into equipment that might live in a closet forever after? That said, rentals aren't cheap if you plan to use something for more than a weekend.

Yosemite National Park

→ **Curry Village Mountain Shop** (Map p100; ☎209-372-

8396; ⊗8am-8pm summer, shorter hours rest of year) Sells clothing, maps, books and climbing, hiking, backpacking and camping gear.

➡ **Yosemite Village Sport Shop** (Map p100; ⊗9am-6pm, reduced hours in winter) Sells clothing, shoes, daypacks and car-camping gear and supplies.

Around Yosemite

➡ **Mammoth Mountaineering Supply** (☑760-934-4191; www.mammothgear.com; 3189 Main St, Mammoth Lakes; ⊗8am-8pm) Hiking, backpacking and snow-sports gear rentals and sales, plus topo maps and shoes. Also has a **Bishop store** (☑760-873-4300; www.mammothgear.com; 298 N Main St; ⊗9am-7pm), selling used clothing and gear too.

➡ **REI** (☑559-261-4168; www.rei.com; River Park Shopping Center, 7810 N Blackstone Ave, Fresno; ⊗10am-9pm Mon-Sat, 11am-6pm Sun) Rents bear canisters and camping and backpacking equipment; sells clothing, maps, books and four-seasons outdoor gear.

➡ **Wilson's Eastside Sports** (☑760-873-7520; www.eastsidesports.com; 224 N Main St, Bishop; ⊗9am-9pm) Rents camping, climbing, backpacking and winter-trekking gear and sells shoes, clothing and backpacks.

➡ **Elevation** (☑760-876-4560; www.sierraelevation.com; 150 S Main St, cnr Whitney Portal Rd, Lone Pine; ⊗call for hrs) Rents bear canisters and crampons and sells hiking, backpacking and climbing gear.

➡ **Lone Pine Sporting Goods** (☑760-876-5365; 220 S Main St, Lone Pine; ⊗call for hrs) Sells camping gear, clothing, fishing licenses and maps.

➡ **Bell's Sporting Goods** (☑760-647-6406; Hwy 395, Lee Vining; ⊗usually 7am-8pm May-Oct) One-stop shop for everything fishers need.

EQUIPMENT CHECKLIST

Your list will depend on the kind of hiking you do, whether you're car camping or backpacking, and the weather.

Clothing

➡ broad-brimmed sun hat

➡ hiking boots, socks, gaiters and spare laces

➡ jacket (waterproof) and rain pants

➡ shorts and lightweight trousers

➡ sweater or fleece jacket

➡ thermal underwear

➡ T-shirt and collared long-sleeved shirt

➡ warm hat and gloves

Equipment

➡ backpack with waterproof liner or cover

➡ first-aid kit (see the Medical Checklist on p242)

➡ insect repellent

➡ map and compass

➡ pocketknife

➡ sunglasses, sunscreen and lip balm

➡ survival blanket or bivvy bag

➡ toilet paper and trowel

➡ flashlight or headlamp, spare batteries and bulb

➡ watch

➡ water containers

➡ whistle

Overnight Hikes

➡ bear canister

➡ cooking, eating and drinking utensils

➡ sleeping bag and liner

➡ sleeping mat (and if inflatable, patch kit)

➡ spare cord, duct tape and sewing/repair kit

➡ stove, fuel and lighter/matches

➡ tent, pegs, poles and guylines

➡ towel

➡ water-purification filter or tablets

Optional Items

➡ camera and spare batteries

➡ cell phone (see also p233)

➡ emergency distress beacon

➡ GPS receiver and spare batteries

➡ groundsheet

➡ mosquito net

➡ swimsuit

➡ walking/hiking/trekking poles

Sequoia & Kings Canyon National Parks

➡ **REI** (☑559-261-4168; www.rei.com; River Park Shopping Center, 7810 N Blackstone Ave, Fresno; ⊗10am-9pm Mon-Sat, 11am-6pm Sun) Rents bear canisters and camping and backpacking equipment; sells clothing, maps, books and four-seasons outdoor gear.

➡ **Big 5 Sporting Goods** (☑559-625-5934; www.big5sportinggoods.com; 1430 S Mooney Blvd, Visalia; ⊗10am-9pm Mon-Fri, 9am-9pm Sat, 9:30am-8pm Sun) Basic camping, fishing and outdoor-sports equipment.

➡ **Three Rivers Mercantile** (☑559-565-2378; 41152 Sierra Dr, Three Rivers; ⊗8am-5pm Mon-Fri) Limited camping, fishing and outdoor-sports equipment sales.

Directory A–Z

Accommodations

Accommodations options in both Yosemite and Sequoia and Kings Canyon National Parks run the gamut from basic to bourgeois. You can shack up in rustic tent cabins in both parks, sleep in comfort at one of the lodges within or around the parks or go totally overboard staying somewhere like Yosemite's famous Ahwahnee Hotel. And, of course, you can camp under the night sky.

Seasons

➡ Most campgrounds, many lodges and some B&Bs close during the winter season (generally October through March, April or May), but you'll find something open in and around both national parks year-round.

➡ If an accommodations option or campground is open only part of the year, we include its opening hours following the symbol ☺.

Reservations

➡ If you want to stay within either park, make a reservation no matter what time of the year you plan to visit. Anyone hoping to sleep in Yosemite during the peak months of May through September should reserve *far* in advance.

➡ If you don't have a reservation, don't write off your trip – you might get lucky, especially if you're camping in May, early June or September and you turn up before noon.

B&Bs

There are no B&Bs per se in the national parks. But they are easily found in towns along the gateway routes into the parks. B&Bs generally average around $150 to $200 and offer intimate accommodations, usually in an old house or small historical building. Service is always personal (often by the owners themselves), and breakfasts are generally wholesome and filling.

Campgrounds

TYPES OF CAMPGROUNDS

➡ Most of the parks' sites are designated for car camping, meaning you pull up, unload your car and pitch your tent or park your RV.

➡ Some sites are walk-in campgrounds, meaning you have to park your vehicle in a designated lot and carry your camping equipment and supplies to the campsite. The advantage of walk-in sites is the lack of cars and RVs, which makes for a more 'natural' experience.

➡ Yosemite has four backpacker campgrounds to accommodate people heading into or out of the backcountry. You must have a wilderness permit to stay in these. There are no backpacker campgrounds in Sequoia and Kings Canyon National Parks.

INSIDE THE PARKS

Camping inside the parks offers the distinct advantage of putting you closest to what you came to see. You likely won't have to drive to the trailhead nor (and this pertains primarily to Yosemite) deal with the day-parking nightmare that day-trippers face. On the other hand, park campgrounds generally fill up the fastest.

OUTSIDE THE PARKS

➡ The advantage of staying outside the park is that

SLEEPING PRICE RANGES

The following price ranges refer to double occupancy in high season (generally May to September), and don't include taxes, which can add 10% to 15%. When booking, ask for the rate including taxes.

$ less than US$100

$$ $100–250

$$$ more than $250

reservations are often easier to make closer to the date you wish to camp. You'll likely pay a little less as well, but it's almost negligible.

➡ Though some are privately owned, most campgrounds outside the national parks are operated by the US Forest Service (USFS). A few are run by other local or federal government entities.

➡ Campgrounds at lower elevations are open year-round, while upper-elevation campgrounds usually open only seasonally.

➡ There are also many free car-accessible campgrounds within the national forests surrounding the parks, though they generally lie at the end of long dirt roads and don't offer access to the parks or potable water.

RESERVATIONS

All reservable park and USFS campgrounds are bookable through **Recreation.gov** (☎877-444-6777, international 518-885-3639; www.recreation. gov). It's always worth checking for last-minute cancellations.

FIRST-COME, FIRST-SERVED

Some campgrounds, both within and around the parks, operate on a first-come, first-served basis. For folks without reservations (especially those heading to Yosemite), these generally offer the only hope. The key to scoring a first-come, first-served campsite is arriving between 8am and noon. Arrive too early and the previous night's guests haven't yet left; too late and sites are full with new campers.

In Yosemite, seven campgrounds operate on a first-come, first-served basis. In Sequoia and Kings Canyon most of the 14 campgrounds are first-come, first served.

Even in the heat of summer, getting a first-come, first-served campsite isn't that difficult if you arrive

BOOK YOUR STAY ONLINE

For more accommodation reviews by Lonely Planet authors, check out http://lonelyplanet.com/hotels/. You'll find independent reviews, as well as recommendations on the best places to stay. Best of all, you can book online.

early enough. Yosemite recommends mid-morning, but on weekdays you'll probably be fine before noon. Drive or walk around the campground loops until you see an unoccupied site – that means no tents, equipment or hired bodyguards there to hold it, and no receipt hanging from the site's little signpost. If it's free, take it, because if you're too picky it might be gone the next time you drive by. Remember that check-out time is not until noon at most campgrounds, so late risers may not clear out until close

to lunchtime. Take a look at the check-out date printed on the campsite receipt for some guidance. And be patient.

Once you have claimed a site, head back to the campground entrance and follow instructions listed there for paying and properly displaying your receipt. If you extend your stay, just pay again in the morning before check-out time.

WILDERNESS CAMPING

Also called 'backcountry camping' or 'dispersed camping,' wilderness camping

DIRECTORY A–Z ACCOMMODATIONS

Climate

Yosemite Village

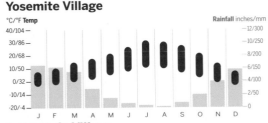

Lodgepole Village

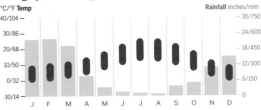

Mammoth Lakes

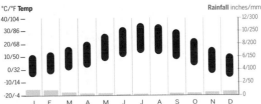

INTERNATIONAL VISITORS

Electricity

➡ US domestic electrical current is 120V, 60Hz (same as Canada).

Money

➡ If you're arriving from abroad and need to change money, do so at the airport or at an exchange bureau or bank in a major city. It is nearly impossible to exchange money in most small towns throughout the Sierra.

➡ Major credit cards (Visa, MasterCard, Amex) are widely accepted throughout the region and are almost always required as deposits when renting a car or reserving a hotel room.

Post

➡ Nearly every town around the national parks has a post office. Yosemite National Park has four and there is one at Grant Grove in Kings Canyon.

Telephone

➡ Cell phones will need a multiband GSM phone to make calls in the USA. Popping in a US prepaid SIM card is usually cheaper than using your network. Cards are sold at electronics and telecommunications stores, which also sell inexpensive prepaid phones. Verizon and AT&T have the best cell phone coverage area in the Sierra Nevada region.

Time

➡ California is on Pacific Standard Time (UTC minus eight hours).

➡ Clocks are set forward one hour during Daylight Saving Time, from the second Sunday in March to the first Sunday in November.

Weights & Measures

➡ The USA uses the imperial system of weights and measures; road signs are in miles.

---

is just what it sounds like: camping in the wilderness. Provided you meet certain requirements, you can camp wherever you want. Along popular trails there are often established wilderness campsites; in heavily visited areas (such as Little Yosemite Valley) pit toilets minimize camper impact. Although sleeping in an established campsite might not seem your idea of wilderness camping, doing so helps minimize impact on other areas.

Hostels

There are a handful of hostels in the area. In addition to the hostel-cum-lodge of Yosemite Bug Rustic Mountain Resort, on Hwy 140 just outside of Yosemite National Park, there are options in the Eastern Sierra towns of Mammoth Lakes, Bishop and Lone Pine.

Hotels & Motels

Most hotels and motels options are found outside the parks – you'll pay a premium for in-park lodging. Rooms are often priced by size, view, and the number of beds, rather than the number of guests. There may be a small surcharge for a third or fourth occupant, though children under a certain age may be free. Many non-park lodgings offer free continental breakfast, but quality is highly variable.

At the upper end of the midrange category, you can expect good beds, hot water and private bathrooms as a bare minimum. For a top-end joint you can generally expect solid service, comfier beds, spacious accommodations and extra amenities like telephone, room service and (mostly outside the parks) cable TV.

Lodges

The word 'lodge' usually connotes a stately structure with stone fireplaces, beamed ceilings and rustic but well-kept rooms. Lodges in and around the parks often fit the stereotype, and most offer choices of rooms in the main lodge (which sometimes have shared bathrooms) or cabins (with private bathrooms). Rates can start as low as $80 off-season and climb as high as $500 for a cabin in July and August. The latter may seem high, but when you consider that some cabins can hold up to several families, the price is more manageable.

Tent Cabins

Tent cabins are a sort of in-between option: not quite camping, not quite a hotel. Generally, these consist of cement walls with canvas roofs, and amenities mean a light bulb, an electrical outlet and cots. Bedding usually costs extra, so you're better off (and more comfortable) bringing your own. All parks have tent cabins. Sleeping up to four (sometimes more) and costing anywhere from $80 off-season to $120 in summer, they're an affordable alternative to lodges. If you're staying in a tent cabin in spring or winter, remember that the ones that lack heating can get very cold.

Courses

Both parks and surrounding areas offer a wide range of learning opportunities, from fun family-style nature walks to photography excursions and college-credit courses.

Yosemite

Art Yosemite Art Center runs inexpensive, informal art classes.

Astronomy and stargazing There are programs at Glacier Point and throughout the park.

Outdoor education and hikes The park's main support organization, **Yosemite Conservancy** (209-379-2317; www.yosemiteconservancy.org) presents a huge range of classes and guided hikes. **NatureBridge** (20 9-379-9511; www.naturebridge.org) runs outdoor environmental education programs for youth.

Park ranger and naturalist-led walks Check the *Yosemite Guide* or stop by a visitor center for a schedule.

Photography Free photography walks are offered through the park service and the Ansel Adams Gallery.

Around Yosemite

Mono Lake Committee (760-647-6595; www.monolake.org/visit/canoe; tours $25; 8am, 9:30am & 11am Sat & Sun late Jun-early Sep) Affordable and highly respected programs and seminars with the goal of educating people about the unique lake and its surroundings.

Eastern Sierra Interpretive Association (ESIA; www.esiaonline.com/) Interpretive calendar with activity listings throughout the Eastern Sierra.

SNARL (Sierra Nevada Aquatic Research Laboratory; http://vesr.nrs.ucsb.edu/public/lecture-series) Free public lectures by area research scientists; in early summer near Mammoth Lakes.

Sequoia & Kings Canyon

Sequoia Natural History Association (559-565-3759; www.sequoiahistory.org) Natural history hikes and stargazing programs.

Discount Cards

➡ All National Park Service (NPS) passes cover the cardholder and up to three adult occupants of their vehicle and can be purchased at park entrances. An annual pass for Yosemite costs $60; for Sequoia and Kings Canyon it's $30.

➡ An Interagency Annual Pass costs $80 and grants the holder (and everyone in his or her vehicle) entrance to any national park or federal recreation area for one year.

➡ Two 'America the Beautiful' passes are valid for life and available to US citizens and permanent residents: the $10 Senior Pass (62 years or over) and the free Access Pass for people with permanent disabilities. These passes cover free entry to all US national parks and federal recreation areas, plus deep discounts on some campgrounds and services.

➡ The parks offer no student or youth discount cards. Children under 16 years enter the parks free of charge with a paying adult.

Electricity

120V/60Hz

120V/60Hz

Food

Self-Catering

➡ Grocery stores inside both parks stock items such as packaged foods, ice, beer, s'more fixings and other staples as well as junk food, but they charge top dollar, so it's best to buy food en route

EATING PRICE RANGES

The following price ranges refer to a main course. Tax (5% to 10%) and tip (generally 15% to 20%) is not included in price listings unless otherwise indicated.

$ less than $15

$$ $15–25

$$$ more than $25

to the parks. The Yosemite Village Store has the largest selection.

➡ Most campsites have fire pits (you can grill your food if you bring a grill), and most have picnic tables.

Bear-Proof Lockers

➡ All campsites, most trailheads and many parking lots have bear-proof metal storage boxes. You are required by law to store *all* your food (including canned goods, beverages and coolers) and all scented products (toothpaste, shampoo, sunscreen etc) in these boxes at all times.

➡ Never leave food unattended in your car, especially in Yosemite, whether you're taking a multiday backpacking trip or just spending a few hours meandering through the museum. It may seem like a hassle to put your picnic lunch in a locker, but having a bear break your window, ransack your car and tear up your upholstery is even more hassle. What's more, you can be fined for leaving anything in your car (or in your bike's panniers).

➡ Proper storage helps keep bears from becoming 'problems,' which can mean a bad end for the bear.

➡ Backcountry hikers must use bear-proof canisters, which can be rented inexpensively when you pick up your wilderness permit or bought at stores in and nearby the parks.

Insurance

If you're traveling very far to get here (and especially if you're flying), it's a good idea to get some travel insurance to cover baggage theft, trip cancellation and, most importantly, medical emergency. When choosing a policy, read the fine print; some policies will not cover 'extreme' activities, which could include anything from river rafting to rock climbing. Domestic rental and homeowners' insurance policies often cover theft while you're on the road.

Worldwide travel insurance is available at www.lonelyplanet.com/travel-insurance. You can buy, extend and claim online anytime – even if you're already on the road.

Internet Access

Most lodgings in and outside the parks offer free wi-fi for their guests. Free internet access can be found in most public libraries (including two in Yosemite).

Maps

For multiday hikes, purchase an appropriately detailed topographical map. GPS navigation can be helpful, but isn't 100% reliable for drivers in remote areas.

Recommended maps:

National Geographic (www.nationalgeographic.com) One Sequoia/Kings Canyon and five hiking maps for Yosemite in its Trails Illustrated series.

Tom Harrison (www.tomharrisonmaps.com) Waterproof topo maps of the Sierra Nevada; the John Muir Trail map pack is the gold standard.

DeLorme California Atlas and Gazetteer (www.delorme.com) Excellent driving atlas.

Eastern Sierra: Bridgeport to Lone Pine Produced and sold locally by Sierra Maps (www.sierramaps.com); detailed recreation information.

Opening Hours

Businesses and services maintain opening hours based on a wide range of factors: some close for the winter, and 'winter' can begin and end on different dates each year. Others stay open year-round, but maintain shorter hours in winter and their longest hours in summer.

Note that even when opening hours are listed, they're still subject to change based on weather, demand and budgetary constraints.

➡ Cafes and restaurants generally serve breakfast from 7am to 10:30am, lunch from 11am to 2:30pm and dinner from about 5pm to 9pm.

➡ Bars in the parks are usually open from approximately 5pm to 10pm. Outside the parks they may close as late as 2am.

➡ Shops and services are open from about 9:30am to 5:30pm.

Public Holidays

The parks (and the areas surrounding the parks) are at their absolute busiest during the summertime school-holiday period, which runs roughly from mid-June through August. During this period, *everything* is packed, and reservations are a must. The greatest numbers of visitors also hit the parks during the following public holidays.

New Year's Day January 1

Martin Luther King Jr Day Third Monday in January

Presidents' Day Third Monday in February

Easter A Friday through Sunday in March or April

Memorial Day Last Monday in May

Independence Day July 4

Labor Day First Monday in September

Columbus Day Second Monday in October

Veterans' Day November 11

Thanksgiving Day Fourth Thursday in November

Christmas December 25

Solo Travelers

➡ Group hikes and other park programs are good options for meeting other travelers.

➡ It is common (and considered safe) for both men and women to backpack alone in the Sierra Nevada.

Telephone

➡ In the parks, you'll find pay phones at almost every developed location. Cell phone reception is patchy through the Sierra region, depending on your carrier (forget about T-Mobile). In Yosemite, the Valley, Tuolumne Meadows, Crane Flat and Wawona generally have good to fair reception. In Sequoia and Kings Canyon, Grant Grove is the only option.

➡ When breaking out that cell phone, consider the reality of noise pollution. Hearing someone's cell phone ring in a neighboring campsite or at a scenic lookout is annoying at best, while being subjected to a loud and lengthy phone conversation is grounds for a pine-coning.

Tourist Information

Tourist information offices (known as visitor centers) are found throughout Yosemite and Sequoia and Kings Canyon, and in nearly every town in the Sierra.

Yosemite National Park (www. nps.gov/yose) Official Yosemite National Park Service website with the most comprehensive and current information. News and road closures/openings are often posted first on its Facebook page (www.facebook.com/YosemiteNPS).

Sequoia & Kings Canyon National Parks (www.nps.gov/seki) Official website.

Visit California (www.visitcalifornia.com) The official state tourism website.

Mammoth Lakes Welcome Center The largest Eastern Sierra visitor center, with excellent regional information, maps and brochures.

Useful sources for areas around the national parks:

Inyo National Forest (www.fs.usda.gov/inyo)

Sierra National Forest (www.fs.usda.gov/sierra)

Stanislaus National Forest (www.fs.usda.gov/stanislaus)

Yosemite Sierra Visitors Bureau (☑559-683-4636; www.yosemitethisyear.com)

Tours

In Yosemite, the park-affiliated Yosemite Conservancy nonprofit offers multiday courses and seminars that are great alternatives to tours.

Discover Yosemite Tours (☑800-585-0565, 559-642-4400; www.discoveryosemite.com) Operates bus tours year-round from Oakhurst, Fish Camp and Bass Lake.

Yosemite Hospitality/Aramark (☑209-372-4386, 209-372-1240) The park's main concessionaire runs bus and tram tours throughout the park, including a very popular wheelchair-accessible two-hour Valley Floor Tour and day trips from the Valley to either Glacier Point or Tuolumne Meadows. However, this new park operator had not yet taken the reins at press time, so check the *Yosemite Guide* for updated information and pricing.

Green Tortoise (☑800-867-8647, 415-956-7500; www.greentortoise.com) Runs backpacker-friendly two-day (about $186) and three-day (about $295) trips to Yosemite from San Francisco where travelers sleep in the converted bus or in campgrounds, cook collectively and choose among activities like hiking, swimming or just hanging out (and there's always some great hanging out). Prices (which change annually) include most meals and the park entry fee.

PRACTICALITIES

➡ **Newspapers** Major US newspapers are available from coin-operated newspaper boxes in Yosemite and Sequoia and Kings Canyon National Parks.

➡ **Weather Services** National Weather Service forecasts are available at www.forecast.weather.gov.

➡ **Radio** Local FM and AM radio stations can be picked up within Yosemite Valley. In the Eastern Sierra, 92.5 FM broadcasts news and regional information.

➡ **Smoking** Prohibited in restaurants and bars throughout California. Most accommodations are completely nonsmoking and will charge a hefty cleaning fee if you smoke indoors.

Incredible Adventures (☐415-642-7378, 800-777-8464; www.incadventures.com) This outfit uses biodiesel vans for its San Francisco–based tours to Yosemite, from one-day sightseeing tours ($159) to three-day camping tours ($369). Park entry fees and most meals are included, and it provides all cooking and camping gear except sleeping bags.

Sierra Club (www.sierraclub.org/outings) The national environmental nonprofit has both paid trips and free activity outings sponsored by local chapters.

Travelers with Disabilities

➡ Both national parks publish an accessibility brochure (Yosemite www.nps.gov/yose/planyourvisit/accessibility.htm; Sequoia and Kings Canyon www.nps.gov/seki/planyourvisit/accessibility.htm) and have an accessibility coordinator. Both are excellent sources of information on everything from hotels and campgrounds to visitor sites and ranger-led activities. If you need to make arrangements in advance, call any park visitor center or contact the coordinator prior to your arrival.

➡ Most sights and campgrounds within the parks are wheelchair accessible; for a complete and detailed list, download the accessibility brochures. As of 2015, all Yosemite campgrounds had accessible sites except for Camp 4, Bridalveil Creek and Hodgdon Meadow.

➡ All lodging options within Yosemite have wheelchair-accessible rooms.

➡ Shuttle buses in Yosemite all have wheelchair lifts and tie-downs, and the drivers can assist disabled passengers on and off. The Yosemite Lodge Bike Stand and the Curry Village Rental Stand both have wheelchairs for rent; call ☐20 9-372-8319 for reservations. In Sequoia and Kings Canyon, free wheelchairs can be borrowed from the Kings Canyon Visitor Center, Lodgepole Visitor Center and the Giant Forest Museum.

➡ For hearing-impaired visitors, a ranger may be available during summer months for American Sign Language (ASL) interpretation during park-led walks and talks. For information, contact one of the visitor centers or call ☐209-372-4726 (TTY). For paid tours, ASL interpretation can be arranged through the **Yosemite Lodge tour desk** (☐209-372-1240).

➡ Based in Mammoth Lakes, the nonprofit organization **Disabled Sports Eastern Sierra** (☐760-934-0791; www.disabledsportseasternsierra.org) offers a variety of educational opportunities for disabled travelers, including skiing and climbing courses.

➡ Discount passes (p231) to the parks and national forests are available for people with disabilities.

Volunteering

Besides helping the national parks, volunteering is a great way to see a side of Yosemite and Sequoia & Kings Canyon that most tourists never do. It's also a great way to meet locals and fellow volunteers – contacts that can last a lifetime. As a volunteer you can do everything from weeding and sweeping to working on restoration projects, monitoring bears and leading educational walks. Most volunteer positions require advanced application and background checks.

➡ The extensive **Yosemite Volunteer Program** (☐20 9-379-1850; www.nps.gov/yose/getinvolved/volunteer.htm) has a number of sought-after long-term positions (some include housing), as well as shorter projects for individuals and groups, and a weekly drop-in program that does hands-in-the-dirt activities like removing invasive plants in some of the most scenic areas of the park.

➡ The **Volunteer.gov** website maintains a comprehensive database on positions available at all national parks and federal recreation areas, allowing you to browse openings by category (eg backcountry, fish and wildlife, historical preservation).

➡ The **Yosemite Conservancy** (☐20 9-379-2317; www.yosemiteconservancy.org) runs an established volunteer program for its members that includes restoration and revegetation projects as well as staffing information stations. Long-term volunteers receive free camping and bookstore discounts.

➡ Earth Day (April 22) celebrations in Yosemite feature chances to help out the park and includes cleanup projects and tree planting as well as kids' educational events, a

---

LOST & FOUND

➡ **Yosemite** For anything left or recovered in restaurants, hotels, gift shops or on buses, call the **park concessionaire** (☐209-372-1390). For items astray elsewhere, call the **NPS** (☐209-379-1001). In the Valley, you can also go to the information desk at the Yosemite Valley Visitor Center, where rangers keep a stash of things found.

➡ **Sequoia & Kings Canyon** Each visitor center maintains its own lost and found.

vendors' fair, and live music and poetry.

➡ The **Sierra Club's LeConte Memorial Lodge** (Map p100; ☏209-372-4542; www.sierraclub.org/education/leconte) in Yosemite puts Sierra Club members to work as volunteers assisting in the operation of the lodge for one-week stints between May 1 and mid-September.

➡ The huge week-long Yosemite Facelift (p23) event picks up tons of trash throughout the park, with free campsites for volunteers and fun evening activities. Check its Facebook page for info.

Work

➡ Most workers inside the parks are employed either by the NPS or by park concessionaires. Most employment opportunities within the parks are seasonal – roughly Memorial Day (the last Monday in May) through Labor Day (the first Monday in September). Applications are almost always due at least six months in advance.

TIPS FOR TEACHERS

Educational and scientific groups who want to study in Yosemite can get their entrance fees waived if they apply in advance and provide the proper documentation. The trip must be for educational purposes, not simply recreation. For details, contact the **Yosemite Fees Office** (☏209-372-0207) or check the Yosemite website at www.nps.gov/yose/planyourvisit/waivers.htm. Sequoia and Kings Canyon also has academic fee waiver applications available on its website; call ☏559-565-3136 for more information.

Both Yosemite and Sequoia and Kings Canyon National Parks run field-trip programs specifically for teachers who wish to bring their students to study in the parks. Teachers can contact **Yosemite's education office** (☏209-375-9503) or the **Sequoia and Kings Canyon education program** (☏559-565-4211). Also check under 'Education' in the Yosemite and Sequoia and Kings Canyon park websites.

➡ Yosemite's new concessionaire, Yosemite Hospitality/Aramark, runs nearly all of the park's businesses and transportation and is your best bet – about 1800 employees are needed per summer. If you're already in the Valley and are struck by the need to stay and work, drop by the Human Resources department in the administration offices in Yosemite Village.

➡ **DNC** (☏604 559-565-4070; www.visitsequoia.com) is the park concessionaire for Sequoia and Kings Canyon.

➡ Seasonal and year-round positions with the NPS are posted at www.usajobs.gov. Only US citizens are eligible for NPS employment.

Transportation

Getting to the parks by car or public transportation is easy. Flights, cars and tours can be booked online at lonelyplanet.com/bookings.

GETTING THERE & AWAY

Air

➡ A number of airports have good public transportation connections to the parks; YARTS buses run directly from the Fresno airport.

➡ Backpackers should look over TSA guidelines for flying with equipment at http://blog.tsa.gov/2014/05/tsa-travel-tips-travel-tips-for.html. Camp stoves and empty fuel containers are OK; fuel fumes are not.

Airports

Major international airports three to five hours' driving time from Yosemite and Sequoia and Kings Canyon:

Los Angeles International (LAX; www.lawa.org/lax) California's largest and busiest airport.

McCarran International (LAS; www.mccarran.com) In Las Vegas.

Mineta San José International (www.flysanjose.com) Around 45 miles south of San Francisco, near Silicon Valley.

Oakland International (OAK; www.oaklandairport.com) In San Francisco's East Bay.

Reno-Tahoe International (RNO; www.renoairport.com)

Sacramento International (SMF; www.sacramento.aero/smf) Midway between the San Francisco Bay Area and Lake Tahoe.

San Francisco International (SFO; www.flysfo.com) Northern California's major hub.

Two smaller, closer airports are:

Fresno Yosemite International Airport (FAT; www.flyfresno.com) Approximately 70 miles southwest of Yosemite and 60 miles west of Sequoia and Kings Canyon.

Mammoth Yosemite Airport (MMH; www.visitmammoth.com/airport) Closest airport to the east side of Yosemite (it's 2½ hours' drive from Yosemite Valley).

Land

Bicycle

Cycling is a great way to get to the national parks, but roads are narrow, grades are steep and summer temperatures can climb well over 90°F (32°C).

➡ Long-distance cyclists can overnight in Yosemite's backpacker campgrounds.

CLIMATE CHANGE & TRAVEL

Every form of transport that relies on carbon-based fuel generates CO_2, the main cause of human-induced climate change. Modern travel is dependent on airplanes, which might use less fuel per mile per person than most cars but travel much greater distances. The altitude at which aircraft emit gases (including CO_2) and particles also contributes to their climate change impact. Many websites offer 'carbon calculators' that allow people to estimate the carbon emissions generated by their journey and, for those who wish to do so, to offset the impact of the greenhouse gases emitted with contributions to portfolios of climate-friendly initiatives throughout the world. Lonely Planet offsets the carbon footprint of all staff and author travel.

➡ Better World Club
(☑866-238-1137; www.betterworldclub.com) offers emergency roadside assistance for cyclists for an annual membership fee of about $40.

➡ If you need a lift, YARTS buses can stash bikes in their storage areas if there's enough space, and Eastern Sierra Transit Hwy 395 buses have bike racks.

Bus

Greyhound (☑800-231-2222, international customer service 214-849-8100; www.greyhound.com) runs to the parks' hub cities – Merced for Yosemite, Visalia for Sequoia and Kings Canyon, and Fresno for all.

TO/FROM YOSEMITE

Buses with **Yosemite Area Regional Transportation System** (YARTS; ☑877-989-2787; www.yarts.com) accept cash or credit cards, and fares include park entry. Bicycles can be transported along with all your gear. There are discounts for seniors (62 or over), and with each adult ticket, one child rides free. Reservations are not required, but it's best to obtain Hwy 140 bus tickets before boarding. You can purchase them from area motels and the visitor center in Mariposa.

Routes

Hwy 140 Merced to Yosemite Valley (3¼ hours) year-round. Buses originate from the Merced Transpo Center & Greyhound Terminal and stop at Merced's Amtrak station before heading to Yosemite.

Hwy 41 Fresno to Yosemite Valley (4¼ hours) via Wawona year-round.

Hwy 120/395 Mammoth Lakes to Yosemite Valley (3½ hours) once daily in July and August; Saturday and Sunday only during June and September.

ROUTES INTO THE PARKS

Yosemite National Park

Yosemite operates three entrance stations on the west side of the Sierra Nevada: the South Entrance on Hwy 41 (Wawona Rd) north of Fresno – convenient from southern California; the Arch Rock Entrance on Hwy 140 (El Portal Rd) east of Merced – convenient from northern California; and the Big Oak Flat Entrance on Hwy 120 W (Big Oak Flat Rd) east of Manteca – the quickest route from the Bay Area. Roads are generally kept open all year, though in winter (usually November to April), drivers may be required to carry tire chains.

The Tioga Pass Entrance, along Hwy 120 E (Tioga Rd) on the east side of the park, is open from about June to October, depending on when the snow is cleared. From Tioga Pass, drivers connect with Hwy 395 and points such as Reno and Death Valley National Park.

Sequoia & Kings Canyon National Parks

The two routes into Sequoia and Kings Canyon approach from the west, departing Hwy 99 from Fresno or Visalia. From Visalia, Hwy 198 leads 46 miles east into Sequoia National Park. From Fresno, Hwy 180 east leads 57 miles east to Kings Canyon. The two roads are connected by the Generals Hwy, inside Sequoia. There is no access to either park from the east, and no internal roads between the parks.

Hwy 120 From Sonora to Yosemite Valley between mid-May and mid-September, with stops in Groveland and Buck Meadows.

TO/FROM SEQUOIA & KINGS CANYON

Sequoia National Park Sequoia Shuttle (☑877-287-4453; www.sequoiashuttle.com; ☺late May–late Sep) runs from the San Joaquin Valley town of Visalia to Giant Forest Museum (two hours) during summer, via Three Rivers and other towns en route. Advance reservations required.

Kings Canyon National Park Big Trees Transit (☑800-325-7433; www.bigtreestransit.com; round-trip incl park entry fee $15; ☺late May–early Sep) has summer service from Fresno to Grant Grove (2½ hours). Reservations recommended.

Car & Motorcycle

Driving is by far the most popular way to get to and around the national parks. In Yosemite, this means traffic, smog and sometimes frustrating battles for parking spaces during peak summer months.

AUTOMOBILE ASSOCIATIONS

American Automobile Association (AAA; ☑877-428-2277, emergency roadside assistance 800-222-4357; www.aaa.com; annual membership from $52) Has free maps and discounts on accommodations, theme parks and other services.

Better World Club (☑866-238-1137; www.betterworldclub.com) Similar services to AAA and donates 1% of its revenue to environmental clean-up and advocacy.

DRIVING DISTANCES & TIMES

FROM	DISTANCE / TIME TO YOSEMITE VALLEY	DISTANCE / TIME TO SEQUOIA
San Francisco	210 miles / 4hr	280 miles / 5½hr
Los Angeles	276 miles / 6hr	225 miles / 4hr
Las Vegas	400-475 miles / 8-8½hr	400 miles / 6½hr

DRIVER'S LICENSE

➡ Non-US residents can legally drive in the US for up to a year with only their home driver's license and passport, but proffering an international driver's license if you get pulled over can make things easier on everyone.

➡ Most car-rental companies don't require an international driver's license, but claim that having one makes the rental process easier.

INSURANCE

➡ California requires liability insurance for all vehicles; proof must be carried in the car at all times.

➡ Credit cards or your own auto insurance policy (be sure to check both) often cover insurance for rentals; if not, you can purchase optional liability insurance that adds between $10 and $20 per day to the rental rate.

➡ If you're driving a friend's car, you'll be insured under their policy (assuming they have one).

RENTAL

Most rental companies require that you be at least 25 years old, have a valid driver's license and a major credit card, not a check or debit card. Rentals are available at all airports and major cities. Most agencies rent kids car seats with advance notice.

CAR

Alamo (☎877-222-9075; www.alamo.com)

Avis (☎800-633-3469; www.avis.com)

Budget (☎800-218-7992; www.budget.com)

Dollar (☎800-800-3665; www.dollar.com)

Enterprise (☎800-261-7331; www.enterprise.com)

Fox (☎800-225-4369; www.foxrentacar.com)

Hertz (☎800-654-3131; www.hertz.com)

National (☎877-222-9058; www.nationalcar.com)

Rent-a-Wreck (☎877-877-0700; www.rentawreck.com) Minimum rental age and under-25 driver surcharges vary at a dozen locations, mostly around LA and the San Francisco Bay Area.

Super Cheap! Car Rental (www.supercheapcar.com) Locations in LAX, Orange County and San Francisco Bay Area. No surcharge for drivers aged 21 to 24 years; nominal daily fee for drivers under age 21 with full-coverage insurance.

Thrifty (☎800-847-4389; www.thrifty.com)

RECREATIONAL VEHICLES (RVS)

Most campgrounds in the Sierra Nevada don't have electricity or water hookups for RVs. RVs are cumbersome to drive and they burn fuel at an alarming rate. That said, they do solve transportation, accommodation and cooking needs in one fell swoop. Even so, there are many places in parks and in the mountains that RVs can't go.

Book RV rentals as far in advance as possible. Rental costs vary by size and model, but you can expect to pay over $100 per day. Rates often don't include mileage,

taxes, vehicle prep fees and bedding or kitchen kits. If pets are even allowed, a surcharge may apply.

Cruise America (☎480-464-7300, 800-671-8042; www.cruiseamerica.com) Nationwide RV rental company with almost two dozen locations statewide.

El Monte (☎562-483-4956, 888-337-2214; www.elmonterv.com) With 15 locations across California, this national RV rental agency offers AAA discounts.

Escape Campervans (☎877-270-8267, 310-672-9909; www.escapecampervans.com) Awesomely painted campervans at economical rates in LA, Las Vegas and San Francisco. No extra charge for 21-plus or multiple renters.

Happy Travel Campers (☎310-929-5666, 855-754-6555; www.camperusa.com) Campervan rentals in the San Francisco Bay Area, LA and Las Vegas.

Jucy Rentals (☎800-650-4180; www.jucyrentals.com) Campervan rentals in San Francisco, LA and Las Vegas.

ROAD RULES

➡ Cars drive on the right-hand side of the road.

➡ Unless signed otherwise, it's legal to make a right turn on a red light after coming to a complete stop.

➡ Distances and speed limits are shown in miles.

➡ On a two-lane highway, you can pass cars on the left-hand side if the center line is broken (not solid yellow).

➡ Talking on a hand-held cell phone or texting while driving is illegal.

Train

No trains serve the parks directly, but **Amtrak** (☑800-872-7245; www.amtrak.com) offers daily service to the transport hubs of Merced and Fresno for Yosemite, and Fresno and Visalia (via Hanford) for Sequoia and Kings Canyon, where bus service is available into the parks. From most major airports, the first leg of Amtrak service is often by bus to the nearest train station. The earlier you book your Amtrak ticket, the cheaper the fare.

TO YOSEMITE

From San Francisco, you can book an Amtrak ticket all the way to Yosemite Valley (6½ hours) or Tuolumne Meadows. Quick Amtrak Thruway buses connect San Francisco to Emeryville, where San Joaquin trains run to Merced. At Merced station, transfer directly to the YARTS bus.

Connections to Tuolumne Meadows can be difficult to book without calling. The park entry is included in the fare, and you're guaranteed a seat on the YARTS bus.

TO SEQUOIA & KINGS CANYON

Take a San Joaquin train to Hanford (20 miles west of Visalia), where an Amtrak bus picks you up and takes you to Visalia. From there, transfer to the Sequoia Shuttle (summer only).

TO EASTERN SIERRA

From Los Angeles' Union Station, frequent **Metrolink** (☑800-371-5465; www.metrolinktrains.com) trains service Lancaster (two hours), which has ESTA bus service to Mammoth Lakes. From Mammoth, onward bus connections run to Yosemite when Tioga Pass is open.

GETTING AROUND

Bicycle

➡ The easiest way to get around Yosemite Valley is by bike. Cycling other areas of the park, like Tioga Rd or Glacier Point Rd, is for experienced cyclists.

➡ All trails within the national parks are off-limits to mountain bikes – head to Mammoth Lakes instead.

Bus

➡ Yosemite has an excellent free shuttle system, making it easy to get around Yosemite Valley and other areas.

➡ Sequoia National Park has five free shuttle routes within the park; Kings Canyon has no shuttles.

RVS & TRAILERS

For the most part, all three parks are RV- and trailer-friendly. Consider the following if you're visiting **Yosemite National Park**:

➡ There are no electrical hookups.

➡ Generators can only be used in campgrounds during certain hours.

➡ In Yosemite Valley, maximum length for RVs is 40ft, for trailers it's 35ft.

➡ No vehicles over 25ft on Mariposa Grove Rd; trailers aren't permitted.

➡ No vehicles over 25ft on Hetch Hetchy Rd; maximum width 8ft mirror-to-mirror.

➡ No trailers or vehicles over 30ft on Glacier Point Rd past the Sentinel Dome/Taft Point trailheads.

➡ RVs over 24ft are not recommended for Yosemite Creek and Tamarack Flat campgrounds or for Porcupine Flat or White Wolf.

➡ Yosemite's only year-round dump station is in Yosemite Valley near the Upper Pines Campground. Wawona and Tuolumne Meadows stations open in summer.

➡ For more information see www.nps.gov/yose/planyourvisit/rv.htm.

The following applies to **Sequoia and Kings Canyon National Parks**:

➡ Generator hours vary, but they exist.

➡ No RVs or trailers permitted on Mineral King Rd.

➡ Vehicles over 22ft are not recommended on Crystal Cave Rd or at Panoramic Point.

➡ Vehicles over 24ft are not recommended on the Moro Rock–Crescent Meadow road between Potwisha and the Giant Forest Museum.

➡ RV dump stations are available at Potwisha, Dorst Creek and Lodgepole (seasonal).

➡ There is no direct public transportation *between* any of the parks. However, you can use Fresno to connect between Yosemite (via YARTS) and Grant Grove in Kings Canyon (with Big Trees Transit).

➡ For information on YARTS buses over Tioga Rd as far as Mammoth Lakes, see p237.

Car & Motorcycle

The vast majority of visitors get around the parks by a combination of car and free shuttle bus. To reach some parts of Sequoia and Kings Canyon – or to go between the two – you have to drive. Also, some of the greater Yosemite area (especially Hetch Hetchy and Tioga Rd) is best to explore with your own wheels. During peak summer season, however, the traffic can be extremely frustrating in Yosemite Valley. In Yosemite Valley and Sequoia, park in a day parking lot and take the excellent free shuttles instead of adding to the problem.

Fuel

➡ Fuel becomes more expensive the closer you are to the parks, with gas stations just outside the parks' borders charging almost comical rates. In the Eastern Sierra, Bishop is your best bet and Bridgeport may be the worst.

➡ The nearest place to Yosemite Valley for fuel is El Portal, about 14 miles west of Yosemite Village on Hwy 140.

➡ Diesel fuel is available at Yosemite's Wawona and Crane Flat stations.

➡ There are no gas stations in Sequoia and Kings Canyon; the nearest ones are at Stony Creek Lodge (open mid-May to mid-October only) and Hume Lake, and both carry diesel.

➡ There are two electrical charging stations in Yosemite Valley: the Yosemite Garage in the Valley, and the Ahwahnee parking lot, which has two chargers (one for Teslas). There is no fee.

Road Conditions

The parks are accessible year-round, and almost all roads are paved. In Yosemite, there are a few unpaved roads unsuitable for long trailers or large RVs.

Outside the parks lies an endless network of fire and forest-service roads, many leading to remote campgrounds and lakes. While many of these roads are drivable with a standard-clearance vehicle, potential explorers would be better off with above-average clearance and 4WD.

Snow closes Yosemite's Tioga Rd (Hwy 120 east of Crane Flat) all winter long. In Sequoia and Kings Canyon, the Kings Canyon Scenic Byway and the Generals Hwy both close periodically in winter. Mineral King Rd, in Sequoia, closes November 1 to late May.

California Department of Transportation (CalTrans; ☏800-427-7623; www.dot. ca.gov) Current road conditions for highways throughout California.

Yosemite Road Information ☏209-372-0200

Sequoia and Kings Canyon Road Information ☏559-565-3341

Road Hazards

Speeding Speeding motorists represent one of the parks' principal road hazards. Not only does speeding put humans in danger, it also endangers park wildlife. Many animals, including bears, deer and coyotes, are hit by motorists every year. The roadside 'red bear–dead bear' signs you see in Yosemite mark where cars have hit bears. Slow down!

Winter weather Snow and ice present hazards and road closures. During snowy months motorists will encounter 'chain controls' on many mountain roads; continuing past these without snow tires or four- or all-wheel drive is illegal. Unless you're properly equipped, your only option is to buy or rent chains or turn back. If you plan to drive to the parks when there's any chance of snow, the easiest solution is to bring your own chains, as renting or purchasing at or near chain controls is expensive. Permitted workers along the roadside will fit the chains for about $20, and save your knuckles in the process. If you plan to put your chains on yourself, bring gloves.

Winter emergencies A smart precaution in winter is to pack emergency food and water and a sleeping bag for each person in the car. If you're on a remote road and get stuck or lose control and slide off the road, assistance could be hours or days away. Provisions and warmth in the car can literally save your life.

Hitchhiking

Hitchhiking is never entirely safe anywhere in the world, and we don't necessarily recommend it. Travelers who hitch should understand that they are taking a small but potentially serious risk. That said, hitching is quite common in Yosemite and the Eastern Sierra and is sometimes necessary to get to or from a trailhead. While hitchers are generally viewed with suspicion in the US, Sierra backpackers will often get a break.

➡ If you're trying to get home from Yosemite, check the bulletin board at Camp 4 for rides offered and needed, or just stick out your thumb at the parking lot entrance.

➡ To get a ride to the parks, check out the rideshare forums on Craigslist (www. craigslist.org).

➡ For Eastern Sierra trailheads, try the 'Transportation To & From' board of High Sierra Topix (www.highsierratopix.com/ community).

Health & Safety

Keeping safe while visiting the parks depends on your predeparture preparations, daily routines and how you handle any dangerous situations that develop. While the potential problems can seem quite frightening, in reality few park visitors experience anything worse than mosquito bites or a skinned knee.

BEFORE YOU GO

If you're planning on doing any hiking, start getting regular physical exercise a few weeks prior to your trip. When possible, visitors from lower elevations should allow at least a day or two to acclimatize before undertaking any strenuous activity.

Insurance

Review the terms of your health insurance policy before your trip; some policies won't cover injuries or emergency evacuation sustained as a result of 'dangerous' activities like backpacking, rock climbing or mountaineering. Some policies require you to get pre-authorization for medical treatment from a call center before seeking help. Be sure to keep all receipts and documentation.

For travel insurance, see p232.

Websites

Yosemite National Park – Safety (www.nps.gov/yose/planyourvisit/yoursafety.htm)

Sequoia & Kings Canyon National Park – Safety (www.nps.gov/seki/planyourvisit/yoursafety.htm)

Wilderness Medicine Institute (www.nols.edu/wmi) Classes, case studies and articles.

Further Reading

Backcountry First Aid and Extended Care (Buck Tilton, Falcon, 2007) Inexpensive pocket-sized wilderness survival manual.

NOLS Wilderness Medicine (Tod Schimelpfenig, Stackpole Books, 2013) Comprehensive wilderness first-aid curriculum.

IN THE PARKS

The parks are not immune from crime – and it's no wonder, considering they see millions of visitors each year. However, the majority of crimes are small-time theft, vandalism and public drunkenness. Though weapons and unpiloted aircraft (eg drones) are strictly prohibited in the parks, beware of visitors who flout the law and use them; better yet, report illegal activity to the nearest park ranger. Car break-ins are more often the work of opportunistic bears than burglars. Carry money and valuables with you at all times – if you leave anything in the car, store it out of sight in the trunk. When possible, avoid parking your vehicle at an isolated trailhead; instead, park in a more heavily used area within walking distance of the trail, or ride park shuttle buses.

Availability of Health Care

For emergencies, call ☏911. Inside the parks, cell phones often won't work. Carrying a satellite phone or personal locator beacon is an option for backcountry trips. Park rangers with medical training can provide basic first aid, free of charge. For serious ailments, drive to the nearest hospital emergency room (ER). Search-and-rescue (SAR) and helicopter evacuations are *only* for life-threatening emergencies; they are very costly for the parks and put employees' lives at risk.

Yosemite National Park & Around

In Yosemite Valley, **Yosemite Medical Clinic** (☏209-372-4637; 9000 Ahwahnee Dr, Yosemite Village; ☉9am-7pm daily late-May–late Sep, 9am-5pm Mon-Fri late-Sep–late-May) is just east of Yosemite Village.

Hospitals near Yosemite include:

Doctors Medical Center (☎209-578-1211; www.dmc-modesto.com; 1441 Florida Ave, Modesto; ☺24hr) The nearest Level II trauma center, in the Central Valley.

John C Fremont Hospital (☎209-966-3631; www.jcf-hospital.com; 5189 Hospital Rd, Mariposa; ☺24hr) A 24-hour emergency room, west of Yosemite.

Mammoth Hospital (☎760-934-3311; 85 Sierra Park Rd; ☺24hr) A 24-hour emergency room in the Eastern Sierra.

Sequoia & Kings Canyon National Parks & Around

First-aid is available at visitor centers and ranger stations. Hospitals nearby include:

Community Regional Medical Center (☎559-459-6000; www.communitymedical.org; 2823 Fresno St, Fresno; ☺24hr) The region's Level I trauma center, west of Kings Canyon.

Kaweah Delta Medical Center (☎559-624-2000; www.kaweahdelta.org; 400 W Mineral King Ave, Visalia; ☺24hr) A 24-hour emergency room near Sequoia's south entrance.

Adventist Medical Center (☎559-638-8155; www.adventisthealth.org; 372 W Cypress Ave, Reedley; ☺24hr) Limited emergency services, closer to Kings Canyon.

Infectious Diseases

Amoebic Dysentery

Serious diarrhea caused by contaminated water is an increasing problem in heavily used backcountry areas. If diarrhea occurs, fluid replacement is key: drink weak black tea with a little sugar or a soft drink allowed to go flat and 50% diluted by water.

With severe diarrhea, a rehydrating solution is necessary to replace minerals and salts. Commercially available oral rehydration salts are useful. Gut-paralyzing drugs such as diphenoxylate or loperamide can be used to bring relief from the symptoms but do not actually cure the problem.

Giardiasis

If you drink snowmelt, stream, lake or groundwater, you risk being infected by waterborne parasites. Giardiasis is an intestinal disease marked by chronic diarrhea, abdominal cramps, bloating, fatigue and weight loss; symptoms can last for weeks. Though not usually dangerous, giardiasis requires treatment with antibiotics. To protect yourself, always boil, filter or chemically treat water before drinking. Do not even brush your teeth or rinse dirty dishes with untreated water.

Hantavirus & Plague

Hantavirus and plague are rare but serious diseases endemic to the Sierra Nevada. Hantavirus is transmitted by infected rodents through droppings, urine, saliva or blood. Plague is most commonly transmitted by the bite of infected fleas who live on plague-carrying rodents. Initial flu-like symptoms usually manifest within a week of exposure to the plague, and up to seven weeks afterward for hantavirus. If you show symptoms or suspect you were exposed, seek medical attention immediately.

Rare cases of both diseases have occurred in the parks, most recently in Yosemite. In 2012, several visitors were infected with hantavirus after staying in tent cabins in Yosemite Valley and the high country. In 2015,

---

MEDICAL CHECKLIST
··

In addition to any prescription or over-the-counter medications you typically take, consider adding these to your first-aid kit:

➡ acetaminophen/paracetamol (eg Tylenol) or aspirin

➡ adhesive or paper tape

➡ antibacterial ointment for cuts and abrasions

➡ antidiarrhea and antinausea drugs

➡ antifungal cream or powder

➡ antihistamines (for hay fever and allergic reactions)

➡ anti-inflammatory drugs (eg ibuprofen)

➡ bandages, gauze pads and rolls

➡ calamine lotion, sting-relief spray or aloe vera

➡ cortisone (steroid) cream for allergic rashes

➡ elasticized support bandage for knees, ankles etc

➡ eye drops

➡ insect repellent

➡ moleskin (for blisters)

➡ nonadhesive dressings

➡ oral rehydration mix

➡ pocketknife

➡ poison-oak skin cleanser

➡ scissors, safety pins, tweezers

➡ sunscreen and lip balm

a child was diagnosed with plague after camping in the Yosemite region. To protect yourself from infection, store all food in animal-proof containers; avoid pitching your tent near rodent habitat (eg woodpiles); use insect repellent with DEET; check for rodent droppings and avoid stirring up dust in park lodgings; and never feed or touch (alive or dead) a wild animal.

Environmental Hazards

Altitude

Most people adjust to altitude within a few hours or days. Occasionally Acute Mountain Sickness (AMS) occurs, usually at elevations greater than 8000ft. Being physically fit offers no protection; the risk increases with faster ascents, higher altitudes and greater exertion. When traveling to high elevations, avoid overexertion, eat light meals and abstain from alcohol.

Initial symptoms of AMS may include headaches, nausea, vomiting, dizziness, weakness, shortness of breath and loss of appetite. The best treatment is descent. If symptoms are severe or don't resolve promptly, seek medical help. AMS can be life-threatening.

Black Bears

Black bears are the only species of bears that live in California. They're active day and night throughout the Sierra Nevada. While wild black bears often flee at the sight, sound or smell of people, many park bears have lost their natural fear of humans.

So what's the big deal if a bear nabs a little human food? Bears that associate people with food become increasingly bold about approaching humans, to the point where they become dangerously aggressive. Once a bear becomes a serial campground bandit, or begins charging visitors, rangers may be obligated to 'haze' or eventually kill it.

Habituated bears regularly break into vehicles and raid campgrounds and backcountry campsites in search of food. You must remove

---

BLACK BEAR ENCOUNTERS: DOS & DON'TS

To many visitors, black bears represent a mix of the fascinating and the frightening. It's not often we get to see such powerful, majestic animals in the wild – at the same time, some visitors would just as soon not see one while in the park. Bears entering developed areas in search of human food should be treated differently to wild bears observed in their natural environment.

Be Loud in the Campground

➡ If you spot a bear, do not drop your food and run. Gather others together and wave your arms to look big and intimidating. Make noise by banging pots and pans, clapping your hands and yelling.

➡ Do not attempt to retrieve food from a bear, and don't corner the bear – give it plenty of room to escape.

➡ Never throw rocks, which can seriously injure or kill a bear.

Be Deferential on the Trail

➡ Do not drop your pack or run, which may trigger the bear's instinct to chase – you can't outrun a bear!

➡ Stay together and keep small children next to you, picking up little ones. Give the bear lots of room (150ft or more). If a bear chuffs (ie huffs and puffs), stamps its feet and paws the ground, you're *way* too close.

➡ Never get between a sow and her cubs. If you spot a lone cub, its mother and siblings are likely nearby.

➡ Stand still and watch the bear (nonflash photos are OK) but don't linger. If a bear starts moving toward you, step far off-trail and let it pass by, making sure not to block its escape routes.

➡ A bear may 'bluff charge' to test your dominance. Stand your ground by making yourself look as big as possible (eg wave your arms above your head) and shouting menacingly.

➡ It's extremely rare for a black bear to attack humans, but if one does, fight back using any means available.

all scented items from your car, including any food, trash (scour the car for empty potato-chip bags, soda cans, recyclables etc) and products such as gum, toothpaste, and sunscreen. Cover up anything in your car that even resembles food or a cooler. Place all food and scented items in bear boxes – large metal storage lockers found in most parking lots and every park campsite.

When camping, think of the bear box as your refrigerator: keep it shut and latched when you are not actively using it. Keep all food within arm's reach at all times. Bears can sneak up and steal food from picnic tables or campsites when your back is turned, even just for a second. Failure to use bear boxes may result in a fine (law-enforcement rangers do regular campground and parking-lot monitoring).

Backpackers without a park-approved bear-resistant food container must usually rent one from a wilderness-permit-issuing station, visitor center or park store. Hanging your food in a tree (the counter-balancing method) no longer works, as too many black bears have figured out that trick.

Bites & Stings

Do not attempt to pet, handle or feed any wild animal, including squirrels and deer, that may bite humans. Any animal bite or scratch should be promptly and thoroughly cleansed with soap and water, followed by application of an antiseptic (eg iodine, alcohol) to prevent infection. Ask local health authorities about the advisability of rabies treatments.

SNAKES

Snakes frequent areas below 5000ft, so keep your eyes on the trail, wear hiking boots and don't stick your hands into any places that you can't see (eg under rocks).

Rattlesnakes usually give warning of their presence.

Backing away (slowly!) from rattlers usually prevents confrontation. Most rattlesnake bites are caused by people intentionally picking up the snake or poking it with a stick. Rattlesnake bites are seldom fatal and adult rattlers don't always inject venom when they bite (younger snakes are more prone to inject more venom).

If bitten, place a light, constricting bandage above the bite, keep the wounded part below the level of the heart and move it as little as possible. Stay calm and get to a medical facility as soon as possible. Bring the dead snake for identification if you can, but don't risk being bitten again.

The use of tourniquets and sucking out the venom have been comprehensively discredited.

INSECTS & SPIDERS

Much of the Sierra Nevada teems with annoying mosquitoes, especially in midsummer. You're more likely to get bitten near standing water or snowmelt. Apply insect repellent and wear long-sleeved shirts and long pants when hiking, especially in late spring and early summer.

Present in brush, forest and grassland, ticks may carry Lyme disease. Early symptoms are similar to the flu (eg chills, high fever, headache, digestive problems, general aches). Also look for an expanding red rash. Check your clothes, hair and skin after hiking, and your sleeping bag if it has been outside. If you find unattached ticks, simply brush them off. Otherwise, carefully grab the tick's head with tweezers, then gently pull upwards – do not twist or force it.

Some spider bites (eg from black widows or brown recluses) contain toxic venom, which children are more vulnerable to. Apply ice or cool water to the affected area, then seek medical help immediately.

Cold
HYPOTHERMIA

Temperatures in the mountains can quickly drop from balmy to below freezing. A sudden downpour and high winds can also rapidly lower your body temperature.

Seek shelter when bad weather is unavoidable. Woolen clothing and synthetics, which retain warmth even when wet, are superior to cottons. Always carry waterproof layers and high-energy, easily digestible snacks like chocolate or dried fruit.

Symptoms of hypothermia include exhaustion, numbness (especially in fingers and toes), shivering, stumbling, slurred speech, disorientation or confusion, dizzy spells, muscle cramps and irrational or even violent behavior.

To treat early stages of hypothermia, get victims out of the wind or rain, remove any wet clothing and replace it with dry, warm clothing. Give victims hot liquids (no alcohol or caffeine) and high-calorie, easily digestible food.

In advanced stages, gently place victims in warm sleeping bags cocooned inside a waterproof outer wrapping. Do not rub a victim's skin.

FROSTBITE

Frostbite refers to the freezing of extremities, including the fingers, toes and nose. Signs and symptoms include a whitish or waxy cast to the skin, as well as itching, numbness and pain.

Warm the affected areas by immersion in warm (not hot) water, only until the skin becomes flushed. Frostbitten body parts should not be rubbed, and blisters should not be broken. Pain and swelling are inevitable. Seek medical attention immediately.

Heat
DEHYDRATION

To prevent dehydration drink plenty of fluids (minimum one gallon per day). Eat enough salty foods – when you sweat, you lose electrolytes, too. Avoid diuretics like caffeine and alcohol.

Because your body can only absorb about a quart (liter) of water per hour, prehydrate before starting a long hike.

HEAT EXHAUSTION

It's easy to forget how much fluid you are losing via perspiration while you are hiking, particularly at cooler, higher elevations or if a strong breeze is drying your skin quickly.

Symptoms of heat exhaustion include feeling weak; headache; irritability; nausea or vomiting; dizziness; muscle cramps; heavy sweating and/or cool, clammy skin; and a fast, weak pulse.

Treatment involves getting out of the heat and/or sun to rest, removing clothing that retains heat (cotton is OK), cooling skin with a wet cloth and fanning continuously, and rehydrating with water. Recovery is usually rapid, though you may feel weak for days afterward.

HEATSTROKE

Heatstroke is a serious, life-threatening condition that occurs when body temperature rises to dangerous levels. Symptoms come on suddenly and include weakness; nausea; hot, flushed and dry skin (sweating stops); elevated body temperature; dizziness; confusion; headaches; hyperventilation; loss of coordination; and, eventually, seizures, collapse and loss of consciousness.

Seek medical help immediately. Meanwhile, rapidly cool the person by getting them into the shade; removing clothes; covering them with a wet cloth or towel; fanning vigorously; and applying ice or cold packs to the neck,

armpits and groin. Give fluids if they're conscious.

SUNBURN

You face a greater risk from sun exposure at high elevations. Sunburn is possible on hazy or cloudy days, and even when it snows. Use sunscreen and lip moisturizer with UV-A and UV-B protection and an SPF of 30 or greater, and reapply throughout the day. Wear a wide-brimmed hat and sunglasses; consider tying a bandanna around your neck for extra protection.

Safe Hiking

Avoid poison oak by paying attention to the shrubbery on low-elevation hikes (see the boxed text, p30).

Waterfalls, Cliffs & Rockfall

Smooth granite beside rivers, streams and waterfalls is often slippery, even when dry. Approach any waterfall with caution and, above all, don't get into the water. If you slip, the current will drag you over the top of the fall, likely killing you. Despite warning signs in several languages and protective railings in many places (eg Yosemite's Mist Trail), people have died after wading above waterfalls.

Use caution when hiking around cliff edges and precarious viewpoints. Some park overlooks have railings, but plenty of others don't.

Always be alert to the danger of rockfall, especially after heavy rains. If you accidentally let loose a rock on a trail, loudly warn other hikers below.

Crossing Streams & Rivers

On some backcountry trails, you may have to ford a river or stream swollen with snow-

melt that is fast-flowing and cold enough to be a potential risk. Before stepping out from the bank, ease one arm out of the shoulder strap of your pack and unclip the belt buckle – should you lose your balance and be swept downstream, it will be easier to slip off your backpack.

If you're linking hands with others, grasp at the wrist or cross arms at the waist, both using tighter grips than a simple handhold. If you're fording alone, plant a stick or your hiking poles upstream to give you greater stability and to help you lean against the current.

Walk side-on to the direction of flow so that your body presents less of an obstacle to rushing water.

Lightning & Storms

Before starting your hike – especially if you're heading up an exposed peak or dome – check the weather forecast first at a visitor center or ranger station. Regardless of the forecast, if you're planning a long hike, you should carry rain gear and be prepared for the worst. Changeable weather is a given in the mountains.

When a storm is brewing, avoid exposed ridges, summits and granite domes (eg Yosemite's Half Dome). Lightning has a penchant for crests, lone trees, small depressions, gullies and cave entrances, as well as wet ground.

If you are caught out in the open during a lightning storm, crouch or squat on dry ground with your feet together; keep a layer of metallic-free insulation (eg sleeping pad) between you and the ground; and place all metal objects (eg metal-frame backpacks and hiking poles) far away from you.

Behind the Scenes

SEND US YOUR FEEDBACK

We love to hear from travelers – your comments keep us on our toes and help make our books better. Our well-traveled team reads every word on what you loved or loathed about this book. Although we cannot reply individually to postal submissions, we always guarantee that your feedback goes straight to the appropriate authors, in time for the next edition. Each person who sends us information is thanked in the next edition – the most useful submissions are rewarded with a selection of digital PDF chapters.

Visit **lonelyplanet.com/contact** to submit your updates and suggestions or to ask for help. Our award-winning website also features inspirational travel stories, news and discussions.

Note: We may edit, reproduce and incorporate your comments in Lonely Planet products such as guidebooks, websites and digital products, so let us know if you don't want your comments reproduced or your name acknowledged. For a copy of our privacy policy visit lonelyplanet.com/privacy.

AUTHOR THANKS

Beth Kohn

My deepest thanks to Sara Benson, who loves this region and is always a dream to work with. Hats off to the awesome Cliff Wilkinson and Alison Lyall in-house. Sincere appreciation to Lara Kaylor at Mammoth Lakes Tourism and Kari Cobb and Scott Gediman at Yosemite National Park. Cohorts June and Woody fearlessly dunked into Harden Lake quicksand, and Zap and Lulú patiently waited for me to write up. Love to Claude. In memory of SKS.

Sara Benson

Hiking trail high-fives to my co-author Beth Kohn, with whom I obsessively talk about the Sierra Nevada, even if we don't get to travel together there often enough. Thanks to all my buddies in Sequoia & Kings Canyon National Parks and to park rangers across the US who I'm proud to call my friends. Jonathan, I owe you big-time for driving, marmot-proofing my car, hiking really fast across talus slopes near 10,000ft in a rainstorm, and fending off those notorious cow-bears.

ACKNOWLEDGMENTS

Climate map data adapted from Peel MC, Finlayson BL & McMahon TA (2007) 'Updated World Map of the Köppen-Geiger Climate Classification', Hydrology and Earth System Sciences, 11, 163344.

Cover photograph: Taft Point, Yosemite National Park; Gary J Weathers/Alamy

THIS BOOK

This 4th edition of Lonely Planet's *Yosemite, Sequoia & Kings Canyon National Parks* guidebook was researched and written by Beth Kohn and Sara Benson. The previous edition was also written by Beth and Sara, while the 2nd edition was written by Beth, Danny Palmerlee and David Lukas. This guidebook was produced by the following:

Destination Editor Clifton Wilkinson **Product Editors** Kate Kiely, Martine Power **Regional Senior Cartographer** Alison Lyall **Book Designer** Michael Buick **Cartographer** Anthony Phelan **Assisting Editors** Judith Bamber, Nigel Chin, Melanie Dankel, Jodie Martire, Kristin Odijk, Ross Taylor **Cover Research** Marika Mercer **Thanks to** Cam Ashley, Ryan Evans, Andi Jones, Denis LeBlanc, Katherine Marsh, Kate Mathews, Catherine Naghten, Karyn Noble, Lauren Wellicome, Amanda Williamson, Jane Wise

Index

MARKO MAMULA

LONELY PLANET IN THE WILD

Send your 'Lonely Planet in the Wild' photos to social@lonelyplanet.com
We share the best on our Facebook page every week!

Map Legend

Sights
- Beach
- Bird Sanctuary
- Buddhist
- Castle/Palace
- Christian
- Confucian
- Hindu
- Islamic
- Jain
- Jewish
- Monument
- Museum/Gallery/Historic Building
- Ruin
- Shinto
- Sikh
- Taoist
- Winery/Vineyard
- Zoo/Wildlife Sanctuary
- Other Sight

Activities, Courses & Tours
- Bodysurfing
- Diving
- Canoeing/Kayaking
- Course/Tour
- Sento Hot Baths/Onsen
- Skiing
- Snorkeling
- Surfing
- Swimming/Pool
- Walking
- Windsurfing
- Other Activity

Sleeping
- Sleeping
- Camping

Eating
- Eating

Drinking & Nightlife
- Drinking & Nightlife
- Cafe

Entertainment
- Entertainment

Shopping
- Shopping

Information
- Bank
- Embassy/Consulate
- Hospital/Medical
- Internet
- Police
- Post Office
- Telephone
- Toilet
- Tourist Information
- Other Information

Geographic
- Beach
- Gate
- Hut/Shelter
- Lighthouse
- Lookout
- Mountain/Volcano
- Oasis
- Park
- Pass
- Picnic Area
- Waterfall

Population
- Capital (National)
- Capital (State/Province)
- City/Large Town
- Town/Village

Transport
- Airport
- BART station
- Border crossing
- Boston T station
- Bus
- Cable car/Funicular
- Cycling
- Ferry
- Metro/Muni station
- Monorail
- Parking
- Petrol station
- Subway/SkyTrain station
- Taxi
- Train station/Railway
- Tram
- Underground station
- Other Transport

Note: Not all symbols displayed above appear on the maps in this book

Routes
- Tollway
- Freeway
- Primary
- Secondary
- Tertiary
- Lane
- Unsealed road
- Road under construction
- Plaza/Mall
- Steps
- Tunnel
- Pedestrian overpass
- Walking Tour
- Walking Tour detour
- Path/Walking Trail

Boundaries
- International
- State/Province
- Disputed
- Regional/Suburb
- Marine Park
- Cliff
- Wall

Hydrography
- River, Creek
- Intermittent River
- Canal
- Water
- Dry/Salt/Intermittent Lake
- Reef

Areas
- Airport/Runway
- Cemetery (Christian)
- Cemetery (Other)
- Glacier
- Mudflat
- Park/Forest
- Sight (Building)
- Sportsground
- Swamp/Mangrove

OUR STORY

A beat-up old car, a few dollars in the pocket and a sense of adventure. In 1972 that's all Tony and Maureen Wheeler needed for the trip of a lifetime – across Europe and Asia overland to Australia. It took several months, and at the end – broke but inspired – they sat at their kitchen table writing and stapling together their first travel guide, *Across Asia on the Cheap*. Within a week they'd sold 1500 copies. Lonely Planet was born.

Today, Lonely Planet has offices in Franklin, London, Melbourne, Oakland, Beijing and Delhi, with more than 600 staff and writers. We share Tony's belief that 'a great guidebook should do three things: inform, educate and amuse'.

OUR WRITERS

Beth Kohn

Yosemite National Park, Around Yosemite National Park A lucky long-time resident of San Francisco, Beth lives to play outside or splash in big puddles of water. For this guide, she navigated late season snow on Yosemite's North Rim, tipped her hat to a trailside yearling near North Dome and saw the biggest shooting star of her life while camping in Tuolumne Meadows. When not busy at her laptop, she crosses off sections of the Pacific Crest Trail and explores the never-ending playground of the Eastern Sierra. An author of Lonely Planet's California and Mexico guides, you can see her work at www.bethkohn.com. Beth also wrote the Welcome to Yosemite, Sequoia & Kings Canyon National Parks; Yosemite, Sequoia & Kings Canyon's Top 16; Need to Know; What's New; If You Like; Month by Month; The Parks Today; Transportation and Directory A-Z chapters.

Read more about Beth at:
http://auth.lonelyplanet.com/profiles/bethkohn

Sara Benson

Sequoia & Kings Canyon National Parks, Around Sequoia & Kings Canyon National Parks After graduating from college, Sara jumped on a plane to California with just one suitcase and $100 in her pocket. She has worked seasonally for the National Park Service as a wilderness trailhead ranger in Kings Canyon National Park. For this book, she hiked across tricky talus slopes nearly 10,000ft in elevation during a rainstorm, and sidestepped black bears and wildfires. The author of more than 65 travel and nonfiction books, Sara is the lead writer for Lonely Planet's California guide. Follow her latest adventures online at www.indietraveler.blogspot.com, www.indietraveler.net, @indie_traveler on Twitter and indietraveler on Instagram. Sara also wrote the Yosemite, Sequoia & Kings Canyon's Top 16; Activities; Travel with Children; Travel with Pets; History; Geology; Wildlife; Conservation; Clothing & Equipment; and Health & Safety chapters.

Read more about Sara at:
http://auth.lonelyplanet.com/profiles/Sara_Benson

Published by Lonely Planet Publications Pty Ltd
ABN 36 005 607 983
4th edition – April 2016
ISBN 978 1 74220 744 5
© Lonely Planet 2016   Photographs © as indicated 2016
10 9 8 7 6 5 4 3 2 1
Printed in China

Although the authors and Lonely Planet have taken all reasonable care in preparing this book, we make no warranty about the accuracy or completeness of its content and, to the maximum extent permitted, disclaim all liability arising from its use.

...rved. No part of this publication may be copied, stored in a retrieval system, or transmitted in any form by any means, electronic, ...cording or otherwise, except brief extracts for the purpose of review, and no part of this publication may be sold or hired, without the ...sion of the publisher. Lonely Planet and the Lonely Planet logo are trademarks of Lonely Planet and are registered in the US Patent ...Office and in other countries. Lonely Planet does not allow its name or logo to be appropriated by commercial establishments, such ...taurants or hotels. Please let us know of any misuses: lonelyplanet.com/ip.